The Policing Web

Recent Titles in
STUDIES IN CRIME AND PUBLIC POLICY
Michael Tonry and Norval Morris, General Editors

Saving Children from a Life of Crime
Early Risk Factors and Effective Interventions
David P. Farrington and Brandon C. Welsh

Imprisoning Communities
How Mass Incarceration Makes Disadvantaged Neighborhoods Worse
Todd R. Clear

The Next Frontier
National Development, Political Change, and the Death Penalty in Asia
David T. Johnson and Franklin E. Zimring

The World Heroin Market
Can Supply Be Cut?
Letizia Paoli, Victoria A. Greenfield, and Peter Reuter

The Politics of Imprisonment
How the Democratic Process Shapes the Way America Punishes Offenders
Vanessa Barker

Making Public Places Safer
Surveillance and Crime Prevention
Brandon C. Welsh and David P. Farrington

Banished
The New Social Control in Urban America
Katherine Beckett and Steve Herbert

Policing Problem Places
Crime Hot Spots and Effective Prevention
Anthony A. Braga and David Weisburd

The Policing Web
Jean-Paul Brodeur

The Policing Web

Jean-Paul Brodeur

OXFORD
UNIVERSITY PRESS
2010

OXFORD
UNIVERSITY PRESS

Oxford University Press, Inc., publishes works that further
Oxford University's objective of excellence
in research, scholarship, and education.

Oxford   New York
Auckland   Cape Town   Dar es Salaam   Hong Kong   Karachi
Kuala Lumpur   Madrid   Melbourne   Mexico City   Nairobi
New Delhi   Shanghai   Taipei   Toronto

With offices in
Argentina   Austria   Brazil   Chile   Czech Republic   France   Greece
Guatemala   Hungary   Italy   Japan   Poland   Portugal   Singapore
South Korea   Switzerland   Thailand   Turkey   Ukraine   Vietnam

Library of Congress Cataloging-in-Publication Data
Brodeur, Jean-Paul.
The policing web / Jean-Paul Brodeur.
    p. cm. — (Studies in crime and public policy)
Includes bibliographical references and index.
ISBN 978-0-19-974059-8
1. Police.   I. Title.
HV7921.B693 2010
363.2'3—dc22   2009045850

To Nicole

To the memory of Dominique Monjardet

Acknowledgments

This book could not have been written without the financial support of the Killam fellowships program, which is administered by the Canada Council for the Arts. I was awarded a two-year Killam fellowship in 2002–2004, which allowed me to devote all of my time to conduct the research that led to the writing of this book. The first of these two years was spent at the Institut des hautes études de la sécurité intérieure in Paris. I wish to thank my friend and colleague Anne Wyvekens for having made my stay at the institute fruitful and pleasant. The second year of my Killam fellowship was spent at the Cambridge Institute of Criminology, which was then chaired by Professor Michael Tonry. Professor Tonry was particularly kind to me in inviting me as a fellow of the Cambridge institute and in providing support and friendship during my stay. Mrs. Helen Crudup, a librarian at the Institute, helped me to get access to the many University of Cambridge libraries, particularly to its rare book department. All the Institute's librarians were helpful to me. Mrs. Sarah Harrop, the Institute's secretary, did everything she could to make my stay in Cambridge as pleasant as it was. After 2004, I also received funding from the Social Sciences and Humanities Research Council of Canada and from the Fonds québécois de la recherche sur la société et la culture. I offer my most sincere gratitude to these funding institutions, without which it would be impossible to pursue long-term research projects in Canada and in Québec.

My fellow researchers Benoît Dupont, Maurice Cusson, Dominique Monjardet, Peter K. Manning, and Jonny Steinberg read part of this book and provided me with insightful comments. The late Richard V. Ericson invited me to the Centre of Criminology of the University of Toronto to present some of the ideas underlying the book in a stimulating seminar. Professor Ericson provided much-needed encouragement for completing this project. My colleague

Stéphane Leman-Langlois helped me to solve the problems related to the formatting of the tables and figures presented in the book. Mrs. Gillian Pritchett revised the whole manuscript, making it more readable in English, which is not my native tongue. Without her dedication, the manuscript could not have been finalized in time. As always, my secretary Nicole Pinsonneault played a key role in the realization of this project. My student assistants Madeline Lamboley and Fernanda Prates helped me with the bibliography. I also want to extend my thanks to all the colleagues and students at the International Centre for Comparative Criminology (Université de Montréal) with whom I had many occasions to debate my ideas on policing over the years. They provided constant stimulation in our frequent exchanges.

Throughout my research career, I have had countless meetings in various countries with police persons involved in all aspects of security, including both private and military policing. Those meetings always proved to be as stimulating as they were courteous. I was also granted a considerable access to police files by police chiefs, policing administrators, and various criminal law authorities, all of whom wholeheartedly supported my work. Without their cooperation, I would have achieved very little and I thank them for their generosity.

Finally, I want to express my deepest gratitude to my wife, Nicole, for her unceasing support and fortitude, particularly in the last months of the writing of this book. It took precious time away from her, which should have been entirely devoted to us.

Contents

List of Abbreviations   xi

Introduction   3

1. The Police Assemblage   17

2. History   43

3. Police Images   79

4. Elements of a Theory of Policing   103

5. Police in Uniform   139

6. Police Investigation   185

7. High and Low Policing   223

8. Private Security   255

9. Edges of Policing   309

Conclusion   335

Appendix   351

Bibliography   361

Index   395

Abbreviations

ATF   Bureau of Alcohol, Tobacco, Firearms, and Explosives
CBC   Canadian Broadcasting Corporation
CCC   Canadian Criminal Code
CCTV   closed circuit television
CEPOL   Council of the European Police College
CEW   conducted energy weapon (stun gun)
CID   Criminal Investigation Department
CRS   Compagnies républicaines de sécurité
CSIS   Canadian Security Intelligence Service
DEA   Drug Enforcement Administration
DST   Direction de la surveillance du territoire
DTI   Department of Trade and Industry (United Kingdom)
EU   European Union
FLQ   Front de libération du Québec
GdF   Guardia di Finanza
GN   Gendarmerie nationale
ILP   intelligence-led policing
KGB   Komitet Gossoudarstvennoï Bezopasnosti (Committee for State Security)
MPD   Montreal Police Department
NYPD   New York Police Department
PFLS   Policing for London Survey
PSP   possession of stolen property
PUFP   police-use-of-force paradigm
QPF   Quebec provincial police force
RCMP   Royal Canadian Mounted Police
ROTA   Rondas Ostensivas Tobias de Aguiar (Brazil)

The Policing Web

Introduction

This book, which takes the form of a treatise encompassing the main forms of policing, is based on four guiding ideas and their consequences. Two of these ideas or themes concern the methodological requirements that were followed, while the other two underpin the substance of the theory of policing that is developed in this book.

The first idea guiding this book is that a theory of policing should strive to be descriptively complete, for only then can it aim for explanatory adequacy. In order to be descriptively complete, a theory of policing should enlarge its scope well beyond uniformed police personnel and encompass as many of the components of the policing web as possible. So far, almost all the research devoted to public policing has focussed on uniformed patrols; criminal investigation, perhaps the most glaring omission, is one of the most neglected fields. In much the same way, it is the activities of uniformed guards that have attracted the most attention from researchers on private security. This focus on uniformed policing is misguided in two respects. First, it impedes the development of a sound body of knowledge on policing, since all policing is then viewed through the prism of the work performed by uniformed public police or private security guards. Second, it unduly narrows police innovation. From community policing to evidence-based policing, almost all reforms of policing have attempted to change how uniformed personnel perform their work. In many cases, these reforms have increased the gap between patrol and investigative units. In addition, notorious shortcomings of policing organizations in the collection and analysis of criminal and security intelligence were left unaddressed or not tackled with sufficient determination to remedy them. There are however, signs that this situation is beginning to change.

The first chapter of this book attempts to formulate the conditions that should be met by a theory of policing in order to be relatively complete. The word "theory" is used in two related senses in this book. In its colloquial sense, "theory" first means to give a factual account of the whole range of phenomena that make up its subject matter (in this case, policing). In its epistemological sense, the word refers to a set of hypotheses aiming to identify the distinctive characteristics of their subject and to explain its behavior. As is argued in chapter 1, a descriptive theory of policing should account for the variety of policing models in different countries and provide the historical background that led to the creation of policing organizations. It should also analyze the representations of police work in fiction and in media reporting, since these representations often conflict with the findings of research and are generally at least as influential in policy making as research findings. Finally, such a theory of policing ought to discuss the features of the various components that can be combined to make up the police apparatus of a particular country. In order to facilitate the latter discussion, chapter 1 also provides a chart of the various agencies that are involved in policing.

One of the preliminary findings of the research that led to the writing of this book is that any listing of policing agencies is both tentative and open-ended. Considered in all of its ramifications, a theory of policing is ultimately impelled to provide an answer to a much wider question: what makes a society secure and orderly? The magnitude of this question sets limits on the fulfillment of the requirement that a descriptive theory of policing should be complete. This is why it was said that a descriptive theory of policing should encompass as many of the components of the policing web as it could. Furthermore, the use of such words as the policing *web* or the policing *assemblage* instead of the policing *network* or the policing *system* stresses the fact that the various components of the policing apparatus do not form an integrated whole and generally operate independently from one another, with few coordinating mechanisms.

The book is devoted to fulfilling as much as possible the research agenda that was just outlined. Chapter 2 is devoted to the history of policing in various geographical settings. It describes the birth of organized policing in seventeenth-century France, its reinvention in nineteenth-century England, and its later importation into North America. Chapter 3 addresses the issue of the images of policing and of the police as they are found in fiction and in the press. It argues that the intertwining of images and reality is so pervasive in the case of policing that it generates what is called the "low-definition environment," where fact and fiction become barely distinguishable. With the exception of chapter 4, which will be returned to shortly, the rest of the treatise is devoted to the main components of the policing assemblage: the uniformed constabulary (chapter 5), criminal investigation (chapter 6), the political police and police informants (chapter 7), and private security (chapter 8). The last chapter, entitled "Edges of Policing," deals with militarized policing in continental Europe, paramilitary policing in Latin American, and various criminal organizations that are (or were) in part acting as providers of private protection. With the exception of chapter 9, the chapters devoted to the main components of the policing web are based on a review of the research, and on metaanalyses, and they each comprise various sections providing fresh empirical findings from research that I conducted during recent years.

The second guiding notion of this book is the need for a transnational approach. As was just stressed, the requirement for descriptive completeness implies that a theory of policing should extend beyond the uniformed police and security guards and cover as many of the agencies involved in policing as is possible. In the same way that there are different components of the policing apparatus, there are also many different police forces that are operating in the various countries of the world. The requirement of completeness would then also imply that an international perspective be developed. However, there can be no pretence here to cover all countries, or even to cover a few in detail, unless one intends to produce an encyclopaedia of policing or specifically engage in comparative studies, as David Bayley did in *Patterns of Policing* (1985) or in *Forces of Order* (1991)—also see Bayley 1983b for India. Rob Mawby also compared police systems (Mawby, 1991 and 1992). Nevertheless, the police forces of several countries will be referred to in this book, and the spirit of comparative studies bravely exemplified in David Bayley's work is resuscitated in this book, albeit on a much more modest scale.

The third theme that is developed is a well-known paradox of criminal justice, which also applies to policing. Crime and penal justice mirror each other in several respects. The original illustration of this paradox is the so-called *Lex Talionis* in its timeless (and mythical) formulation: "an eye for an eye, a tooth for a tooth." According to this dictum, the same act—maiming people—has a different moral and legal status depending on the circumstances in which it is performed. He who starts the fight commits a crime; he who ends it successfully and exacts retribution is doing justice. In both cases, however, we are referring to the very same act of physical violence. Furthermore, the criterion that is applied to give the act its moral and legal qualification—whether one started the conflict or responded to it—is notoriously controversial and often depends on who emerges as the winner. It is for reasons such as these that penal justice has been seen as the sullied side of the virtue of justice since at least the time of Plato.

The mirror effect between crime and penal justice can also be found in the case of policing. There is no better illustration of this mirror effect than an article of the Canadian Criminal Code (CCC), which clearly states the principle underlying what has been rightly called the "legal lawlessness" in which the Canadian police at times operate (Webber, 2005).

(2) Principle—It is in the public interest to ensure that public officers may effectively carry out their law enforcement duties in accordance with the rule of law and, to that end, to expressly recognize in law a justification for public officers and other persons acting at their direction to commit acts or omissions that would otherwise constitute offences. [CCC, art. 25.1 (2)]

The significance of "legal lawlessness" is thoroughly discussed in chapter 4, which attempts to provide a new definition of policing and introduces some of the elements of a theory of policing. The fact that the police are the fire with which you fight fire has been repeatedly acknowledged by police scholars. Offending and policing are the opposite terms of a reversible process. There are historically documented cases that show that secret criminal organizations were performing policing tasks and were involved in the provision of private protection. Canadian criminal law explicitly states that a criminal informant "who commits an act that would otherwise constitute an offence is justified in committing it if a public officer directs him or her to commit that act" [Canadian Criminal Code, sect. 25.1 (10)].

The standard definition of the police by their monopoly on the legalized use of force implies that they have the authority to use a means which, with few exceptions, is prohibited as a crime for the rest of society. One of these exceptions is the practice of medical surgery, which is often referred to by police scholars as a counterpart of coercive policing. Through their use of force, the police provide to society the same kind of service that is afforded to a patient by a surgical intervention. This comparison is also often used in relation to war, where there is talk of surgical bombing raids (which generally end up causing numerous civilian casualties). There is one crucial difference between the use of violent means by surgeons and by the police and the military. Medical surgeons perform operations in a hospital environment and under stringently controlled conditions that have nothing in common with the use of firepower to neutralize opponents in the field. There is no substantial difference between how the police and their criminal opponents use their weapons in a firefight.

The definition of the police that will be proposed in this book builds on the notion of legally using means prohibited to others. The major thrust of the proposed definition will be to conceive the police authority to use such prohibited/legalized means to perform their duty as encompassing a greater number of illegal means than just the use of force. The notion of possessing the authority to use means that are otherwise illegal is quite complex and will be focused on in chapter 4 and discussed throughout the book. In the same way that defining the police through their use of force does not imply that they are to be conceived of as an army of brutes, defining them by their use of a wide array of illicit means does not imply that they are to be viewed as a legion of legally empowered delinquents.

The fourth of the main ideas underlying this book is related to the nature of theory. There may be serious discordances between the twin epistemological requirements of descriptive completeness and full theoretical consistency. As the number of pieces of the policing assemblage included in the descriptive theory increases, it becomes progressively more difficult to find a common thread binding them all together. It will be argued that the definition of policing that is provided in chapter 4 applies in substantial degree to all the policing organizations reviewed in the book. However, it will also be found that there are antinomies (discordances) in a theory of policing that cannot be entirely resolved.

These antinomies are of two types. The first type is theoretical. For instance, there are policing organizations, such as public urban departments and private guard companies, that rely on police visibility to produce security and reassurance. For other policing organizations, such as security and intelligence services, stealth plays a necessary and pervasive role in the fulfillment of their mandate. There is no way to completely resolve this policing antinomy between openness and secrecy. It is embedded in the nature of policing, when it is considered in its entire scope. Many other examples of such theoretical antinomies are discussed in chapter 1.

There is also a second kind of antinomy, which is specific to the theory of policing. Values such as legitimacy and security and normative judgments about what is right and what is wrong are incontrovertibly linked to policing. Their conflicting role in policing generates what can be called normative antinomies. Not only do the police use means that are condemned when used by others but they also have to develop a working relationship with active criminals, according to which they trade immunity for covert intelligence. No police organization can afford to sever all links of mutual assistance with criminal elements. Yet, in a perfect world, police work should not be tainted by having to develop a secret interface with criminal activities.

These discordances within a theory of policing are only a reflection of the fundamentally ambivalent character of its subject matter. They impact on the nature of police theory and, ultimately, on all theorizing about penal justice, which has never succeeded in providing a satisfactory justification for punishment. The theory of policing is an unquiet and, at times, equivocal theory. It is affected by conceptual turbulence, unruliness, and pockets of ambiguousness that cannot be reduced to insignificance. The difference between critical and unquiet theory is that the former can aim at a substantial reform of what it is critical of, whereas the latter can only hope for efficient damage control. There is little moral comfort to be found in the (much abused) notion of "the necessary evil."

The four basic ideas on which this book is based provide together a unified perspective to the book. Before reviewing each of them in the light of the type of unity that they bring to the book, something needs to be said about making generalizations about policing. These generalizations are relatively few. For the purposes of illustration, three general points about the police can however be singled out, that are now still largely undisputed: the police are ultimately defined by their authority to use physical force; they spend only part of their time in fighting crime and enforcing the law; and recent police innovation is primarily about increasing police visibility, particularly through the use of foot patrols. The special theoretical feature about these general assertions is that they are only valid when applied to the public police working in uniform. With respect to the first assertion, it finds little application in the work of criminal investigation departments (detectives), as we shall see in chapters 4 and 6, and has to be substantially qualified to apply to private security (see chapter 8). In relation to the second assertion, it cannot be used to describe the work of detectives, which is wholly oriented toward the processing of crime (with various degrees of success). Needless to say, this second assertion is spurious when applied to the work of the security and intelligence apparatus. Finally, as has already been said, police visibility is only one face of the policing coin, the other one being stealth and undercover operations. Police visibility plays almost no part in the all-important fight against organized crime.

The upshot of these remarks is that the difficulty of proposing generalizations applying to the whole spectrum of policing grows in proportion to the breath of the spectrum that is under consideration. So far, only a small part of the spectrum—uniformed public policing—has been considered for the purposes of making general statements about the police. Even then, generalizing about public uniformed policing has not proven to be easy. When the whole spectrum of policing is embraced, as it is tentatively in this book, then making general assertions that are valid in all police configurations becomes a real challenge. This challenge is met in three ways. First, there is an attempt to bring together the various threads of the policing web into an integrated model. This is the approach that is the most consonant with the wealth of the material studied in this book. The model is proposed in two stages: to begin with, high and low public policing are incorporated into a first version of the model at the end of chapter 7; in a second step, private security is integrated with public policing to produce a more complete, albeit nonexhaustive, model (chapter 8). Second, what will become an ongoing argument on the nature of policing is initially formulated in chapter 4. It is based on the definition of policing proposed in this chapter and is developed with varying degrees of emphasis throughout the book. Third, there are several themes that recur in the chapters of the book, where they act as leitmotifs linking the various components of the policing web, which are independently studied. This procedure is considered preferable to stressing throughout the book a single highly diluted point. We start by outlining the themes recurring throughout the book and the general argument that follows from them.

Completeness

The general point that is at the core of the notion of completeness is self-imposing and does not need to be explicitly reiterated in every chapter. This basic point is that the police apparatus is composed of many more parts than public constabularies operating in uniform. Despite its obviousness, this point has been reluctantly acknowledged in research on the police over the last two decades. It first led researchers to focus on policing, as an activity undertaken by a variety of agencies, rather than on the police, which is strongly associated with public constabularies. To stress even more the fact that policing is carried on by several kinds of agents, researchers have coined new expressions such as "plural policing" and "the governance of security"(Johnston and Shearing, 2003; Wood and Dupont, 2006). This theoretical shift toward plural policing and similar concepts was essentially the product of one factor: the growing awareness of the exponential growth in certain Western countries of private security. The role of citizens in self-help initiatives was also instrumental in challenging the monopoly of public police forces in the provision of security.

It is claimed in this book, however, that the composite character of the police apparatus reaches much beyond the mere combination of the public police with private security. This is stressed in three ways. First, the internal diversity of the public police forces has been far from adequately explored. The initial focus on public policing was in itself highly selective, since it almost exclusively encompassed the work of uniformed patrol persons. As previously mentioned, criminal investigation units were seldom studied, and their working relationship with patrol divisions is still almost unknown. The whole field of security intelligence and of the protection of national security against such threats as terrorism—what is referred to in this book as "high policing"—is not even fully acknowledged as a legitimate field of study for police scholars. The various components of the public policing assemblage are explored in depth in the chapters of this book. Second, private security is investigated, as it needs to be. Here, however, the idea of completeness implies that the scope of the investigation be extended beyond the people involved in private policing activities and also include police technology, which is manufactured by private corporations. The potential of technology to transform policing is at least equal to changes in the policing personnel, if not greater, as argued in chapter 8. Third, grey areas of policing such as the use of informants and undercover operatives (chapter 7) and the role of organized crime (chapter 9) are examined. The role of hired police informants grows in proportion to the increasingly stealthy nature of criminal activities (for example, money laundering as opposed to a bank robbery), where information provided by cooperative citizens is wanting.

Finally, the notion of completeness implies, at least in theory, that the relationships between the various parts of the police web under study are also a focus of inquiry. In practice, however, this is a very thorny issue. In treating this issue, we should be guided by one key principle: desirable relationships should not be confused with existing ones. It should not be assumed that networks drawn up on paper are effectively operating in the field. For instance, if the various agencies involved in counterterrorism worked in close coordination, they would be more efficient. There is yet no such coordination for various reasons, however, including the legal constraints imposed by differences among police in their respective level of security clearance. Before repeating policy recommendations that have been made by every report on counterterrorism, the ingrained police resistance to sharing information needs to be accounted for. Eight years after the terrorist attacks of September 2001, the same failure to share intelligence made it possible for Adbul Farouk Abdulmutallab to carry out an attempt to destroy an airplane landing in Detroit on Christmas Day 2009.

International Perspective

Taking an international perspective follows from the requirement of completeness. Taking such an approach may be interpreted in two ways, which are complementary rather than mutually exclusive. Even if limited, an international perspective can be used as an antidote against ethnocentricity and as an instrument of discovery and validation. It can also address the issue of transnational policing and of international cooperation among the police forces operating in different countries. As was said at the beginning of this introduction, this issue of international police cooperation will not be addressed as such, since it would require the addition of an extra chapter to a book that already covers extensive ground. The international perspective is thus used throughout this book as a critical background against which ideas may be tested, emerging trends can be assessed, and new components of the police assemblage can be found, as illustrated below.

First, as we just pointed out, desirable relationships between policing organizations should not be confused with existing ones. The international context proves to be a crucial testing ground for this principle and its underlying ideas. Anglo-American policing is characterized by the relatively high number of public police forces operating in common law countries. If one includes both geographic and nongeographic police forces, there are over sixty different forces operating in the United Kingdom alone. Canada has some two hundred forces. At the other end of the spectrum, the U.S. Bureau of Justice Statistics estimated in 2004 that there were close to eighteen thousand police forces in the United States, most of them municipally based; there are also at least sixteen agencies responsible for the protection of national security. In contrast, there are very few public police organizations in each of the countries of continental Europe. The general rule there is that one national police force is deployed in the cities, and another large policing organization, which is often militarized and accountable to the Department of Defense, is responsible for policing small towns and rural areas. As a rule, there are no more than five public police forces for each country, generally fewer. Yet the Europeans, most notably the French, have coined the expression "the war between the police" to refer to the endemic battles for turf that hinder cooperation and information sharing among their few police forces and among the various departments within one force. Profiling the high number of Anglo-American policing organizations against the European background leads to the conclusion that we cannot be too cautious in evaluating the level of true networking and of effective cooperation between policing agencies. If the French believe that there is an ongoing "war" between their police, even though they have only two main police organizations, how should we assess the U.S. situation in terms of police coordination, when there are some eighteen thousand police forces in operation? Other concepts such as consent may also be tested against an international backdrop.

Second, there is the issue of emerging trends in policing and of estimating how robust they are. As will be shown in chapter 5, the recruitment of women into public police forces is gaining momentum in Canada. Canada is no exception in this regard, as is shown by a review of the research undertaken in both the United Kingdom and in France. However, there is something peculiar about the scholarly treatment of the issue of the feminization of policing. For a profession that is currently defined by its use of force and its masculine culture, the hiring of a large number of women as police staff puts important issues into play. Yet this trend has so far been mainly researched by women such as, for example, Frances Heidensohn in Britain and Geneviève Pruvost in France, and their findings are not integrated into mainstream research on policing. This academic separateness is puzzling and should be remedied. The international spread of other trends also needs to be assessed. This observation is particularly pertinent in the case of private security. It is often asserted that "all developed countries" have more private security personnel than public police on the basis of what is happening in the United States and the United Kingdom. This is incorrect, however, in the case of continental Europe and indeed of many other countries (chapter 8).

Finally, but most important, developing an international perspective allows us to broaden the scope of the police web. Using the military for policing purposes is not a frequent practice in Anglo-Saxon countries. In the United States, the Posse Comitatus Act puts stringent limits on the power of the U.S. federal government to use the military for law enforcement and internal security purposes. Consequently, military policing has attracted little attention in Anglo-Saxon research on policing. The situation is different in almost all other countries, where the military are deeply involved in policing. Their involvement shows a great diversity, ranging from European *gendarmeries* and *maréchaussées*, which are essentially militarized police organizations bound by the requirement to use minimal force, to Latin-American military police divisions and paramilitary units, which are under no such requirement. Within an international perspective, military policing is a movement that may be of equal importance to the growth of private security.

Reversibility

The main thesis of this book is that when the requirements of completeness and of developing an international perspective are duly taken into account, the current definition of the police by its use of force must be replaced by a more encompassing one that is not incompatible with the standard definition. This new definition is formulated in chapter 4. Assertions to the effect that the police are the "fire with which you fight fire," that policing is a "tainted" profession, in addition to references to notions such as the "necessary evil," keep on recurring in policing research and in public discourse. They basically point to a fact that has been acknowledged since the philosophy of Plato: crime and punishment are reversible processes, many crimes being actually committed for punitive purposes. This reversibility became institutionalized with the development of a penal justice system. In the same way that crime and criminal justice often mirror each other, the perpetration of crime and the repression of crime by the police also reflect each other to a significant extent. These considerations, which are elaborated in chapter 4, led to a definition of the police through their capacity to use means that are legally prohibited to the rest of of the population. The use of violence is but one of these means, although it plays a crucial role. Needless to say, recourse by the police to means that would otherwise be deemed criminal is fully legalized and qualifies as being lawful lawlessness. The practical overlap between policing and criminal means does not imply that they exactly coincide. There are criminal ways that have no place in policing and will never be legalized. Conversely, there are sophisticated instruments that are used by the police—for example, the interception of communications—and which, as a rule, will not be used by common delinquents. The reason for this is not that such interceptions are criminalized (as in fact they are), but that performing them successfully is well beyond the capability of the majority of criminals, albeit not all of them.

The definition that we just outlined is tested throughout the book. It must, however, be emphasized that it is tested with various degrees of explicitness. When the validity of the definition is questionable—as it is, for instance, when applied to private security personnel—it is discussed thoroughly (see chapter 8; also see chapters 7 and 9). When there is no need for a thorough demonstration, since it has been repeatedly made by other researchers (as in the case of the authority to use violence by public uniformed police), we do not belabor the point.

Self-Discordant Theory

The notion of reversibility that was discussed above applies to policing itself. The corresponding notions of discordance and antinomy apply to the *theory* of policing. There is one claim about the theory of policing that is repeatedly made throughout this book: there cannot be a one-sided theory of an object that is as ambivalent as policing in most of its aspects. The tensions that are present in policing have a way of imposing themselves and of coming back to haunt one-sided approaches. A great deal of the early work on community policing developed an uplifting perspective on policing, according to which increased police visibility through foot patrols and other enhancements was the panacea to cure most of the shortcomings of public policing. Nearly all the innovations in policing that were proposed from the mid-1970s had a darker side that was not at first acknowledged by the proponents of a particular innovation, but which came to light when the vaunted new approaches were implemented. Taking the most famous example, the "broken windows" approach begat the "bastard child" (George Kelling) of zero tolerance policing. The pressures to meet quantified objectives generated by the CompStat approach (CompStat uses up-to-date computerized crime data, crime analysis, and advanced crime mapping as the basis for regularized, interactive crime strategy meetings which hold managers accountable for specific crime strategies and solutions in their areas; Silverman, 2006) first used in New York and exported to many police departments, resulted in the creation of trigger-happy "intensive policing" units that operated at night and in the rigging of local crime statistics to show that crime was decreasing. The rigging of local crime statistics has been recently confirmed by Silverman, who interviewed retired NYPD precinct commanders (Chen, 2010; Rashbaum, 2010). Several other examples that show that a promising innovation is always in danger of giving birth to a more sinister doppelgänger could be given. In a similar way, the optimism that first characterized pioneer work on private security was dampened when the involvement of certain agencies, such as Blackwater, in the most brutal forms of policing came to light. What is called here self-discordant theory is not a euphemism for unresolved inconsistencies, but a stand against sanitized social sciences and, most of all, a method of research. The theoretical discordances only reflect tensions that are deeply embedded within policing itself. As it will become clear in the various chapters of the book, the research procedure that is followed throughout is to reveal these strains and find out how policing organizations are coping with them.

Self-discordant theory is not a remake of critical theory. One recurrent problem with critical theory is that most of the time it is as dogmatic as what it purports to criticize. Recent work on policing such as Forst and Manning (1999) and Weisburd and Braga (2006), which present the pros and cons of practicing various innovative approaches to policing, are closer to the type of research that is pursued in this book, the main difference being that the pros and cons are not treated in a dichotomous way.

Although this "treatise" is already a long book, it could have been longer. It basically deals with policing organizations, viewed through their history, images, powers, and activities. There are a certain number of distinct key issues that were originally to be discussed, including: policing and the courts, police occupational culture, police deviance, police accountability, policing reform, democratic policing, and transnational policing. It soon became evident that addressing these issues was the subject matter of another volume. In a way, writing a treatise that aims to cover most of the significant aspects of policing is, in the current state of rapidly developing scholarship, a wide-ranging project that cannot be achieved by one researcher alone. A single author cannot go over all the ground that is covered in textbooks and handbooks on policing, as they comprise a collection of outstanding articles written by many different authors. What a single author can do is map out a research agenda and fulfill it as best as one person can. It is hoped that what this book lacks in exhaustiveness will be compensated for by the relative unity of perspective that sole authorship can provide.

The Police Assemblage

The first requirement of a theory of "police"—using the word in quotation marks so as not to prejudge what it refers to—is to identify the object to be accounted for in its principal aspects. As Cain (1973) has shown, this is not an easy task. It is generally resolved by assuming that the proper object of a theory of policing is the most visible part of the police apparatus, that is, the public police in uniform. This position seems to me unduly narrow and uncritical, one that merely accepts the dictum of sensory perception: the police are to be equated with a group of persons outwardly displaying the signs of being police.

This chapter, which attempts to display the wider spectrum of policing, is divided into four parts. First, the various meanings of the word "police" and its derivatives are discussed, and they are presented so as to provide a way to set out the main dimensions of the police, viewed as an object of knowledge. Second, a tentative chart of the diverse formal agencies and informal groups performing public and private policing activities is provided. Third, this chart is extended to the action of various agents engaged in alternative forms of social control. These two sections of this chapter are intended to set the stage for the subsequent chapters of the book. Finally, some of the theoretical principles underpinning my account of policing are considered.

The Word "Police"

A good way to begin discussing the object(s) of a theory of "police" is to examine what the word refers to and what it means in its various usages. The word "police" is both a common noun and a verb, and can also be used as an adjective (for instance, in the expression "police state").

"Police" as a Common Noun

As a common noun, the word "police" has several meanings, each referring to different things. The word became laden with several layers of meaning throughout history, and I will try to follow the historical order in my discussion of its various meanings.

Order and Governance

With the exception of *The Laws* of Plato, which covers the whole field of criminal justice and occasionally mentions policing, the first treatise on the police was published in France between 1722 and 1729 by Nicolas de La Mare, a royal commissioner living in Paris. For him, "police" was synonymous with "order" (*ce bel ordre*), order being considered to be the cornerstone of a happy state (La Mare, 1722, vol. 1, letter to the king). It also meant the process by which this "beautiful" order was generated. This process is made up of three forms of governance: the general government of the body politic; the government of the main constituents of the realm, such as the Church, the military, and civil society; and the government of cities, most notably of Paris (La Mare, 1722, 1:2; also see Napoli, 2003: 8). According to La Mare, the word "police" comes from the Greek word *politia* (actually *politeia*), which clearly derives from *polis*, the Greek word for "city." As we shall argue in more detail in the next chapter, the government of cities was the original meaning of "police." This use of the word was later adopted by various other schools of thought in addition to the French, particularly by the German tradition of the *policey* (later, *polizei*). It should be noticed that in its initial sense, the word "police" encompassed both a process (governance) and its outcome (order). Thus, the gerund "policing" was from the beginning embedded in the meaning of the common noun.

Science

"Police" was also the name of a new science, which was developed in Germany during the period of the Enlightenment by Christian Wolff (1679–1754; see Napoli, 2003: 255) and Von Justi (1717–1771; see Napoli, 2003: 266–271) under the name of *Policeywissenschaft* (police science). It was basically a new science of government administration, as compared to the more politically oriented police studies in France (Napoli, 2003: 255). Its subject coincided with what would now be called the various branches of the welfare state. The British police reformer Patrick Colquhoun also referred to "police" as a new science. In his treatise on the police, "police" means at the same time a new science and its subject matter, defined as "the Prevention and Detection of Crimes, and...those other functions which relate to internal regulations for the well ordering and comfort of civil society" (Colquhoun, 1800: preface, p.1). The focus on crime is new with respect to the German *Policeywissenschaft*, which was composed of eight functions that included security (Napoli, 2003: 259). Unsurprisingly, Colquhoun's works were quickly translated into German (Volkmann, 1801).

A State Institution

In his treatise, La Mare argued that human passions caused a breakdown of the city's order that led to the proclamation of laws, which are divided into public and private laws (La Mare, 1722: 1). He made it clear that the police, as he understood the word, were instituted by public law and were thus a state institution. Today, this restriction does not apply in certain countries, where private police far outnumber their colleagues in the public sector. However, most countries are now trying to fill the legal vacuum in which private security has been operating, and consequently private security organizations are increasingly regulated by public law, even though they are not a state institution.

Police Staff

Finally, the common noun "police" refers to a police staff, that is, men and women who are members of police organizations, whether public, private, or hybrid. The words "police staff" are meant to emphasize that the organizational dimension plays a defining role for the police. In this understanding of the word, police are members of public agencies, of private firms (however small), or have a formal link with a police organization, such as paid police informants whose link to the organization is increasingly formalized by a contract. In the latter case, we would rather speak of recruited policing agents than of police. Particularly in these times of community and problem-oriented policing, there are many private citizens who engage in various forms of policing and of self-help. They should not be viewed as police, even in a loose sense of the word. Considering police as staff members of formal organizations implies that they are professionals with their own standards and specific occupational culture. Most important, they belong to various types of associations, such as formal labor unions or police brotherhoods, which defend their corporate interests.

"Police" as an Adjective

The use of "police" as adjective changes its meaning, depending on which object it describes. For instance, such expressions as "police car," "police professionals," or "police procedures" have no particularly threatening connotations. As we change the level of abstraction, however, moving up from police attitude, perspective, and subculture all the way to the "police state," we seem to be shifting the meaning of the attribute into a more sinister key. When applied to persons who are not professional police, the word "police" generally has pejorative connotations.

This subtle change in the semantics of the adjective "police" reflects a profound ambivalence toward the police, which Egon Bittner, for example, considered to be a tainted occupation (Bittner, 1970/1990: 94).[1] Notwithstanding their unpopularity within certain segments of society, the image of the police is generally positive in English-speaking countries; in opinion polls rating the public confidence in various professions, the police are usually ranked at the top of the scale, with medical doctors. Their ranking is lower in continental Europe and elsewhere. There is also a considerable body of dystopian literature on the police, which can be dated back much earlier than the work of George Orwell or even of Franz Kafka.

The dichotomous valuation of the police image rests largely on four factors.

Who is doing the imaging. As was said before, the police image varies considerably from country to country. In addition, popular representations are often more positive, while literary and academic representations are more critical.

Police penetration. The deeper the police pervade civil society, the more they are viewed as threatening. Even the staunchest supporters of the police within the business community are less supportive when trade practices become the focus of police surveillance. The best police are always the police of others.

Politicization. The closer the police are to the state, the more civil society is critical of them. This can be confirmed even in the context of democracies. In continental Europe, where the police are highly centralized and closer to the political authorities, their image is less positive.

Use of force. This is the most salient reason for the fracture in the police image. Because of their intrinsic link to the use of force, the police belong to an institution that is fundamentally ambivalent, being both sacred and reviled. There is no doubt that when the police are systematically brutal, as they are in nondemocratic countries, they are perceived as an instrument of oppression. Nonetheless, the police can be comparatively more violent in one country than in another and yet still enjoy a high level of support. Comparing the United States with the United Kingdom provides a striking illustration of this divorce between levels of violence and levels of public support.

Police integrity was not included in the factors listed above, because it—or the lack of it—essentially accounts for public condemnation rather than public ambivalence. The idea of corruption being the opposite of the police idea, it is

---

1. Most, if not all, of Bittner's writings on the police are collected in Bittner (1990). I shall refer to this collection, but will also mention the year of the original publication of a paper. Hence, "Bittner, 1970/1990: 94" means that the paper I am referring to was originally published in 1970 and that the page I am referring to (94) to is to be found in the 1990 collected papers.

self-evident that the reputation of a police force will be tarnished if it is known to be in fact corrupted.

When used as an adjective, the word "police" brings out the profound ambiguity of our representations of the police. For instance, in military parlance a "police action" is an operation where the Geneva Conventions on human rights in times of war does not apply. We will address the whole issue of ambiguity and ambivalence in the development of a theory of the police in the final part of this chapter. This issue is of critical significance. Police reality and its ambiguous representations constantly feed back into each other, and they must be jointly considered.

"Police" as a Verb

The activity in which police engage is policing. In recent years, it has been claimed by many researchers that the goal of police studies was to provide a theory of policing rather than a theory of the police. A police-centered theory tends to focus on the public police working in uniform, whereas a policing-centered theory is based on the recognition that policing is a plural enterprise in which many agents can be involved. As suggested earlier, the main impetus of this book is to move from a theory of the police to a theory of policing, as it is undertaken by a large variety of agents. Two consequences follow from such a move. First, the considerable diversity of agencies engaged in policing has to be acknowledged. It is at this point premature to determine how wide the full spectrum of policing agencies is. However, it must be recognized from the start that the scope of policing encompasses, at a minimum, public police forces and private security agencies. The second consequence of focusing on policing rather than the police is that it changes the benchmark for assessing the validity of a definition of the police. The police can be defined by their unique competence—for instance the use of force—without taking into account how much they actually exercise it in their daily activities. However, when we focus on policing as an ongoing activity performed by a diversity of agents, our definition cannot provide only a limited characterization of what the public police are empowered to do as a last resource.

Agents of Policing

In drawing a tentative map of policing, we have to break out of a definitional circle. On the one hand, it would seem that we need to know what policing is, before mapping out which agencies are involved in policing. On the other hand, it is difficult to frame a definition of policing out of context and without examining empirically what police organizations really do. This theoretical circularity can be avoided in actual research practice. We can build on a common preconception of the business of policing: providing a general sense of order and security and offering protection against personal aggression. We can also begin our inquiry by examining policing organizations that are socially recognized as such rather than by developing a fully fledged concept of policing. Assuming that organizations commonly referred to as public or private police potentially share a number of defining features, we can begin to draw our map with the best-known policing agencies—the various public police forces—and use them as signposts to advance into territory that is not as well charted, with each new agency found acting in its turn as a clue on how to proceed further. This procedure is empirical and does not involve any theoretical assumptions on the nature of policing organizations other than that they are involved in providing order and security, either on a public or a private basis.

George Rigakos has developed a typology of policing that "transcends the public-private dichotomy" (Rigakos, 2005: 261). Whatever the merits of this position, it cannot be considered obvious. Rigakos reached this conclusion at the end of his detailed investigation of a private security agency (Rigakos, 2002), which we shall discuss in a later chapter. In this preliminary unpacking of the police assemblage, the distinction between public and private policing will be retained. As we proceed toward the outer edges of policing, our procedure of looking for common features will reveal its limitations: organizations overtly or covertly performing policing functions without sharing the core features of public policing agencies and their private counterparts will be increasingly difficult to spot. If agencies providing protection were to be found operating in a legal vacuum or outside the law, we would have to raise the issue of whether they could still be called policing agencies. A thorough discussion of this issue might lead us to a drastic revision of our assumptions as to the nature of policing.

Notwithstanding these difficulties, we may now draw a tentative map of policing agents. This map will cover public and private territory. It will also make use of the notion of hybrid policing that was proposed by Les Johnston in reference to the interface between public and private police (Johnston, 1992). As it is understood here, hybrid policing has a broader range than initially envisaged by Johnston, blending other key distinctions, such as internal and external security, the police and the military, and legal and extralegal activities.

Public Policing Agencies

This is still the largest part of the map. It is divided between the provinces of internal and external security. Policing focuses on internal security. However, in the current context of globalization, internal security increasingly interfaces with external protection. Transnational terrorism exemplifies this interfacing, as it originates from outside a country but is carried out within its territory, with the consequence that governments do not know whether to treat it as an act of war or as a crime.

Internal policing agencies are diverse in kind and are not always referred to as police forces. The following enumeration of the main categories of such agencies is far from exhaustive. For example, the diagram listing all the agencies that the U.S. Department of Homeland Security is supposed to coordinate comprises some 132 different components.

Public Police Departments

These forces are the main component of the public police apparatus. They comprise a majority of personnel in uniform, a criminal investigation division (various plainclothes details), and support services (operational and administrative personnel). Depending on the country, they are nationally, regionally, or municipally based. The countries of continental Europe, the United Kingdom, and the United States and Canada, respectively, exemplify these three models. In rural jurisdictions, police departments also provide various services, such as fire fighting and ambulance; they also depend upon larger police forces for criminal investigation.

Specialized Policing Agencies

There are several kinds of special public forces. These forces are specialized with respect to their methods or their targets (often with respect to both). Domestic security and intelligence services, which target behavior threatening the state, such as terrorism, are included in this category. Questioning this inclusion potentially implies that counterterrorism lies outside policing.

Some highly militarized forces are specialized in *collective violence* (riots) and more generally in crowd control, such as the Compagnies républicaines de sécurité (CRS) in France and the Bereitschaftspolizei (Bepo) in Germany. Anglo-Saxon policing does not generally field such units.

Countries such as the United States and Germany have created national services specializing in *criminal investigation*, the Federal Bureau of Investigation (FBI) and the Bundeskriminalamt (BKA), respectively.

Security and intelligence services protect the state against *violent domestic threats*, such as homegrown terrorism. Their legal status differs from country to country. In the United States, it is a police organization—the FBI—that mostly handles these threats. Likewise, the French Direction de la surveillance du territoire (DST) is part of the Police nationale. In Canada, the internal Security Service was part of the Royal Canadian Mounted Police (RCMP) before 1984.

A new civilian organization was created in 1984—the Canadian Security Intelligence Service (CSIS); its members do not have powers of arrest, as the police do. In the United Kingdom, the main agency responsible for domestic security answers to the home secretary, although it is designated as "military intelligence" (MI5). Although the apparatus for protecting national security varies considerably in its structure across countries, the police are generally involved in this task in one way or another.

Countries have also created special police organizations to enforce *particular laws and regulations*. Some of these forces play a significant role in policing, such as the Drug Enforcement Administration (DEA) and the Bureau of Alcohol, Tobacco, Firearms, and Explosives (ATF) in the United States, or the Guardia di Finanza (GdF) in Italy, which enforces income tax and other related legislation.

Specialized Administrative Policing Agencies

These agencies could have been classified in the previous category of specialized policing agencies. However, because of their number and importance, they deserve to be listed under their own heading. As was noted by Nalla and Newman (1990), a significant number of government departments have their own administrative policing agencies. The first that comes to mind is the ministry charged with collecting income tax and various other duties. There are many others, such as the departments of welfare, health, education, labor, and protection of the environment and wildlife, to cite just a few examples. The importance of such police agencies has been recently highlighted in the United Kingdom. Between 1997, when it was elected, and 2008, the Labour government has created 3,605 new offences (1,208 were brought in by legislation and 2,367 by secondary legislation such as orders in council and statutory documents). The Department for Environment, Food and Rural Affairs has created 852 new offences; the Department for Business, Enterprise and Regulatory Reform and its predecessor, the Department for Trade and Industry, has introduced 678 offences; and the Home Office is responsible for 455 offences (Irvine, 2008; also see Morris, 2006). These policing agencies enforce various kinds of regulations, and they also issue special permits. They share a feature that sets them apart from most other public policing agencies, that is, they act in two different capacities. They act first as a policing agency and try to detect violations of the regulations that they are tasked to enforce. They are also endowed with the quasi-judicial power to impose penalties (which can be appealed in court). Most of these penalties are fines, which can be very substantial. However, fines are not the only penal sanctions they can impose. Depending on their mandate, some of these agencies have wide powers of seizure, foreclosure, and of freezing assets. When the administrative policing agencies uncover behavior that may be prosecuted as a crime, they generally transfer the case to a criminal law enforcement agency. It should be added that when public police departments enforce traffic regulations and various kinds of bylaws, they also act as both a policing and a penal agency (mostly imposing fines).

Military Policing Agencies

The countries of continental Europe were originally policed by the military. The armed forces progressively gave rise to militarized police forces. Depending upon the degree of their militarization, there are several variants of this kind of internal policing organization. In some democratic countries, such as France, rural and small town policing is carried out by a militarized police force—the Gendarmerie nationale—that used to answer to the Department of Defense rather than a home secretary until 2009. It is now accountable to the French ministry of the Interior. Several other countries of Europe—such as Spain (Guardia Civil) and Italy (Carabinieri)—have similar militarized police organizations, although not all of them are officially part of the national armed forces. In nondemocratic countries, one finds military police forces that barely differ from the army; they operate against internal "enemies" with the same violence as the armed forces would use to wage war against an external foe. The most brutal of these forces are often designated as paramilitary, this word being highly ambiguous, as it is applied indiscriminately to official and nonofficial police forces. Paramilitary units operate in several countries of South America.

Policing the Military

The armed forces of most countries have their own special police. These internal police departments are staffed by military and are exclusively used to police military personnel. These military police are part of the national armed forces and travel with them when they are officially deployed in a foreign country. To this extent, their action transcends borders.

Parapolice

There are several other government units that play a role similar to the police and are endowed with the same powers. The members of such units sometimes wear a distinct uniform. Such is the case in Canada for antipoaching details, which are also involved in the protection of the environment. However, most parapolice units are comprised of civil servants who investigate fraud against a particular government ministry (Revenue, Welfare, Health and Defense; see Nalla and Newman, 1991, for a discussion of these investigative units). For instance, when the Pentagon opened a criminal inquiry of alleged overpricing by Halliburton in the shipment of fuel to U.S. troops in Iraq in 2004, this investigation was conducted by the Defense Criminal Investigative Service (Oppel, 2004).

External security services—the protection of the state against external threats—is carried out by security services involved in foreign intelligence. As these services do not belong to the police as such, only basic information about them will be mentioned here. External security services are of two kinds. The traditional kind, often referred to as espionage services, mainly collects human intelligence (HUMINT), that is, intelligence provided by human sources. Well-known examples are the U.S. Central Intelligence Agency (CIA), the British MI6, and the French Direction générale de la sécurité extérieure (DGSE). The second kind of external intelligence apparatus collects signal intelligence (SIGINT) through various technological sources, such as huge antennae that collect electronic intelligence (ELINT), satellites that capture image intelligence (IMINT), and so forth. The best known of these services is the U.S. National Security Agency (NSA), which operates jointly with corresponding services in Australia, Canada, New Zealand, and the United Kingdom, according to the UKUSA treaty (Bamford, 1982 and 2001). This alliance was accused of running the notorious ECHELON spying program against the countries of continental Western Europe (Keefe, 2006). Foreign intelligence services are thus not limited to playing a defensive role, and they even engage in special operations against foreign countries.

Although these services appear to be far removed from the police, they are called upon to play an increasing role in policing. There is a growing interface between internal and external security in the struggle against organized and economic crime, because they both cut across borders. Counterterrorism also requires a closer cooperation between the police and the security services (Brodeur, 2005a; for an alternative view, see Bayley and Weisburd, 2009). In the months following the terrorist attacks against the World Trade Center and the Pentagon in September 2001 (henceforth, 9/11), Canada enacted enabling legislation for the Community Security Establishment (CSE), which is the much smaller Canadian equivalent of the NSA. The CSE was first created in 1975 by a decree of the executive (Order-in-Council PC 1975–95) and operated without a legislative framework. This new legislation added a new dimension to the CSE's mandate, which was to support police operations if need be. According to recently released Canadian government information, the CSE is effectively engaged in policing.

Hybrid agencies of several kinds also perform at the juncture of internal and external security.

Border Police

The prototype for these agencies is the department of customs. In certain countries, policing agencies performing border patrol duties have an increased burden due to the rise of illegal immigration, contraband, and the infiltration of terrorists. In France, the border patrol (Police aux frontières—PAF) is part of the national police. In most other countries, they are an independent agency.

International Police

Properly speaking, there is not yet any police agency that can operate across national borders without requiring special authorization, like a national police that can operate in the various provinces or states of a country. Organizations now exist that are dedicated to improving the cooperation between different national police forces. The oldest of these organizations is Interpol, which links police forces across continents but does not rest on a convention signed by member states (Anderson, 1989; Deflem, 2002). The organization that has the greatest potential is Europol, since its existence is enshrined in a formal convention signed in 1995 between the member states of the European Union (Bigo, 1996 and 2000). Europol strives to improve the efficiency of its members mainly through the collection and sharing of police information.

There are other police intelligence systems developed in Europe, such as the Schengen Information System and the Visa Information System (Hayes, 2004). Although it is a national agency, the U.S. Drug Enforcement Agency (DEA) is perhaps the closest thing we have to a police organization operating de facto with few constraints in various countries, particularly in Latin America. National power rather than international law is the most likely explanation for the transnational licence apparently possessed by the DEA.

International Peacekeeping Forces

These are only listed here for the purpose of developing a research agenda. They consist of military units that act in a policing capacity under a United Nations mandate in foreign countries. The purpose of these peacekeeping missions is generally to prevent an armed conflict from breaking out in the open. In fact, peacekeeping operations are often impelled by the political interest of the sponsoring states—such as stemming the tide of illegal immigration, or preserving the stability of a region rich in raw materials. Although there were still sixteen UN peacekeeping operations ongoing in 2008 and an additional nineteen peace operations supported or directed by the UN, they do not seem to enjoy as much favor with the international community as they did in the twentieth century.

Private Policing Agencies

Like public policing agencies, there are internal, external, and hybrid private security agencies that will be successively reviewed here.

Internal security in the private sector is structured in a way similar to the public sector, with one notable exception.

Multifunctional Contract Agency
These are the best-known private security firms. They offer a wide spectrum of services to several clients, and most of their staff are uniformed. They are to some extent the private counterpart of the urban public police departments.

Specialized Agencies—Human Resources
Security agencies specialize in two ways. In-house agencies have only one client (the company to which they belong). Strictly speaking, these agencies are the security department of a company rather than an independent enterprise. Private security agencies can also specialize by providing specific services, such as investigation, alarm systems, and the transport of valuables. Their size can be minimal (one person), particularly with respect to private investigation.

Specialized Agencies—Technological Resources
Some of these private firms are able to provide various kinds of surveillance technology, with the staff needed to operate them. Other firms just provide the technology. The largest number of these corporations cannot be labelled as security agencies in the narrow sense of the word. They form a special part of the technological industry and are often embedded in larger corporations that provide various kinds of equipment, particularly weapons. Security technology has been a growth industry for several years. In the post-9/11 context, its rate of development will predictably be exponential. Not only is airport security increasingly relying on body imaging technology, but the threat of weapons of mass destruction (WMD) is creating a huge demand for chemical and biological sensors.

The Knowledge Industry
It is widely known that there is a great number of true "knowledge workers" who are operating in the private sector, many of them retired intelligence officers. It is less well known that private corporations are involved in the development of data banks in relation to various aspects of security. For instance, the Pinkerton agency and the Rand Corporation have built the largest data banks on worldwide terrorist incidents. These two data banks are now in the process

of being merged together for the purposes of the U.S. government (Lafree and Dugan, 2009).

Private security agencies vary greatly in size. Most agencies operate on a local level, but there is also a growing set of large firms that are doing business on the national and international levels. In such an environment, the traditional divide between internal and external security does not make as much sense as it does for the public sector. Still, private enterprise is involved in something corresponding to *external security* in two fields.

First, private corporations founded by exmilitary personnel market their services as mercenaries (Singer, 2003). French mercenaries, for example, have operated in Africa for a long time. However, a great number of soldiers were demobilized at the end of the Cold War and after the collapse of the Soviet Union, and are now available as private military personnel (Davis, 2000). They mainly intervene in developing countries, Africa remaining the continent where most mercenaries are hired either by African governments and political factions or by other states that want to interfere covertly in African conflicts. The use of mercenaries in the context of armed conflicts is not unrelated to policing. For instance, since the war in Iraq, private mercenary contractors such as Blackwater supply a growing number of bodyguards for government officials (Scahill, 2007). In an economic context favorable to outsourcing, exmilitary personnel are also hired as police advisors or supervisors in countries where police forces have to be reconstructed.

Second, private corporations provide security intelligence to various customers. There already exist several newsletters with expensive subscription fees that provide security intelligence. It is not unreasonable to expect that entrepreneurs who once belonged to public foreign intelligence services will progressively create the private equivalent of these services. By definition, the private security knowledge industry straddles both sides of the divide between internal and external security.

In the private sector, there are numerous forms of *hybrid agencies*. As just observed, hybrid agencies may blend elements related to internal and external security, particularly when they operate on the international level, which is relatively blind to the difference between internal and external security. For instance, a government may contract with a private corporation to secure its communications both within its borders and throughout the network of its foreign embassies. It is likely that globalization will benefit the private sector because it has more flexibility than the state security apparatus in integrating internal and external security.

Second, the hybrid character of an agency may result from a general interface between public and private security. At the present time, such an interface does not so much lead to the establishment per se of a novel type of agency as it generates trends that involve both individual operators and organizations. These trends represent movements in opposite directions.

From the private to the public sector. In the fight against organized crime and terrorism, police informants of all sorts are assuming an increased importance. Several of these informants are under contract with police and public security organizations and operate under a legal regime of exception that is similar to the special powers granted to the public police. The career informant typically performs in a no-man's land between policing and offending, between private entrepreneurship and public employment. Bounty hunters are another kind of private operators who live in a twilight zone.

From the public to the private sector. Albert Reiss called attention several years ago to the phenomenon of public police moonlighting (Reiss, 1988). It does not merely consist of having a second job. "Peace officers" actually market their services through their police union and act as public police in private pay to maintain order at boisterous events such as popular music concerts, where private guards are not sufficiently intimidating. This trend has now reached its apex: public police departments are now offering, on a contractual basis, a wide array of special services to communities that can afford them. These services are often offered in partnership with insurance companies and private security firms, as is the case in the city of Montreal.

Hybrid networks. Public police begin their career early and retire young. Many of them undertake a second career in private security, often at the top of in-house security agencies. They maintain their ties with former colleagues still in public police forces. Both parties call upon each other, particularly with respect to the sharing of information. There are also other effects of these trends toward hybrid forms of policing, and these will be reviewed in more detail in later parts of this book.

Agents of Control

Although one might question the inclusion of such agencies as the security and intelligence services in the policing assemblage presented above, the tentative chart so far developed is uncontroversial to the extent that all listed agencies operate legitimately. To them can be added individuals or groups who exercise social control with questionable legitimacy, if not outside the law. Without prejudging the issue of the nature of policing, research on social control has shown the notions of policing and of enforcing various forms of social control to be germane. However, the concept of social control is broader than the concept of policing, and it does not carry the implication that control is performed by agents who are acting under the rule of law (Black, 1976). Indeed, Black (1983) argued that crime could be considered as a form of social control, and even extended this argument to terrorism (Black, 2004). For our map of policing to be accurate in its scope, aspects of policing that are either unregulated or illegal should be covered. The notions of policing and law enforcement being culturally synonymous, it is preferable to use the terminology of social control to discuss aspects of policing that are at the edge of the policing spectrum. The two main sorts of social control that will be briefly discussed are, respectively, unregulated control and deviant enforcement.

Unregulated Control

Unregulated control refers to policing activities that are carried out without a legal framework or within an extremely loose set of rules. Such activities do not violate the law as such; they are simply carried out in a legal or a quasi-legal vacuum. There are actually large fields of public policing that are also loosely regulated by the law, particularly with respect to the use of coercion. Postponing until later a discussion of this public policing issue, we will focus here on various forms of social control that are applied on top of public policing or as an alternative to it.

Special Status Populations

A cluster of difficult issues pertain to the control of populations that enjoy a special legal status. The members of the First Nations of Canada, Native Americans, or Australian Aborigines are but a few of these populations. In Canada, for example, first nations have been demanding self-government for a long time, and they have been granted a fair measure of independence in policing their territory. However, a great deal of the policing taking place in these territories, occurs in a chaotic state: in one notorious instance in 2008, special constables acting on behalf of one faction of the community took all members of the official police department as hostages. Furthermore, influential members of these nations claim that the Canadian legal framework is alien to their culture and that they have not been able to enact an alternative regulatory framework for their communities.

Contrary to common beliefs, policing Aboriginal people is not a problem that only concerns a few "New World" countries. The countries of Scandinavia, to give an example from Europe, have sizable Aboriginal populations living in the north and experience serious difficulties in policing them.

Undercover Policing

A second area of concern is the field of undercover policing. The issues surrounding the management of police informants are particularly pressing. One example should be sufficient to show the extent of the vacuum: until a recent judgment by the Supreme Court of Canada, it was assumed that sting operations in which police sold or bought drugs through informants and other undercover operatives in order to make a bust were legal. In *R. v. Campbell* (1999), the Supreme Court decided that they were not and ruled that the Canadian Criminal Code had to be amended to legalize them. The code was quickly amended and police informants and their handlers are now allowed to break narcotics legislation in order to better enforce it.

In-House Private Security

Private security is the most conspicuous of these added forms of social control. Taken as a whole, the growth of private security is a massive phenomenon, although it is not spread evenly among countries. Because of their visibility and their outward resemblance to the public police forces, it is assumed that private police are just as legally accountable as the public police. Yet there are few countries that have followed the example of Spain by providing an explicit legal framework for the activities of private security agencies (Gimenez-Salinas, 2001). Pieces of legislation not intended to regulate the private security industry, such as the rules for performing a citizen's arrest, are used to fill the vacuum. The general trend is to establish a broad legal framework that allows the industry to regulate itself, which it is in no hurry to do. The unregulated character of private security is particularly obvious in the case of in-house private security, where persons may be coerced to submit to practices that potentially violate their rights, under the threat of losing their job. In Canada, the effort to regulate the private security industry has exclusively borne on contract agencies. There is almost no reliable data on private in-house security.

Fringes of Private Security

In groundbreaking work, Dick Hobbs and his colleagues (2003) have shown that large parts of city centers slip into a policing twilight zone when night falls. These are the areas where bars, nightclubs, and other businesses making up the "nighttime economy" are clustered. These amusement districts, where violent disputes constantly erupt, are controlled by private individuals who trade on the fringe of private security. Doormen, bouncers, and other strong-arm operators are the indispensable associates of the police in maintaining a modicum of order in these no-man's lands. Apart from the occasional requirement for possessing a licence, the regulatory framework of this nighttime control is almost nonexistent and basically consists of varying practical arrangements with the local police. Many individuals involved in the governance of the nighttime economy operate on both sides of the law.

As we proceeded through the various categories of unregulated control, we moved closer to forms of social control that are in breach of the law.

Delinquent Enforcement

Two things are meant by "delinquent enforcement." First, it refers to social control activities that are carried out by known members of delinquent organizations, although these activities may not violate the law and consist at times in nonviolent mediation and conflict solving. The successful carrying out of these activities nonetheless rests on the authority that is derived from the fear inspired by criminal organizations. Second, these words are used to stress that many—indeed even the greater part—of these activities actually break the law, when they imply the use of violence and coercion. The word "enforcement" is used instead of control because control is usually defined as a response to the violation of a rule (Black, 1976: 105). Delinquent enforcement is not only a response to a failure to submit to preestablished rules but it also consists of the imposition of new patterns of behavior—for example, the extortion of money for bogus protection—through intimidation. What is referred to as delinquent enforcement merits discussion because it sheds light on law-abiding social control and even on legal policing, as will be seen in chapter 9. If policing is understood as the provision of protection and of a degree of order, the social territory that is controlled by forces operating outside the law may in many countries be equal to or even greater in scope than the territory under the control of legalized policing organizations.

There are criminal organizations and secret societies, such as the Mafia, Cosa Nostra, triads, and yakuzas, that remain largely out of the reach of legal policing. Despite notable police successes against many of their members, these organizations have proven remarkably resilient over time. Such stability could only be achieved through internal discipline enforced by violence. In this sense, these organizations represent alternative normative orders, a theory first proposed in 1918 by Sicilian lawyer Santi Romano and brilliantly reassessed by Letizia Paoli (2003: 120–130). Not only have these organizations various mechanisms for controlling their own members, but historical research into the organizations operating in the south of Italy has shown that they originally acted as substitutes for the weak Italian state for administrating justice (Paoli, 2003: 162) and for providing private protection (Gambetta, 1993). The important point deriving from this research is that there is no wall separating legal from illegal authority, and that they substantially overlap. Letizia Paoli (2003: 189) cites a variety of reliable sources to the effect that when the Allies occupied Sicily in 1943, they appointed Mafia chieftains as mayors, because the Mafia was the only authority left after the collapse of Italian fascism. This interface between legal policing and delinquent enforcement can be found in countries other than Italy (see Varese, 2001, for the Russian mafiya, and Hill, 2003, for Asian gangs). John Beattie has shown that the "thief-takers" of eighteenth-century England were thieves that were used by the legitimate authorities to catch other thieves (Beattie, 1986 and 2001).

In society, there are many pockets of the population that are either underpoliced or not policed at all by the public forces or by registered private agencies. Some of these pockets correspond to whole communities, which have mainly sprung from immigration. A large part of immigration being illegal, the members of these communities who reside in a country in breach of its immigration laws are unwilling to resort to the police for protection and view them, with justification, as a threat. They become, in this way, prey to various individuals and gangs who take advantage of their misery under the pretext of offering them protection. The migratory fluxes have swelled in the twenty-first century, and they cannot be reduced to population movements from one country to another; the massive influx of country people toward the urban centers is as little controlled as illegal immigration (Davis, 2006). It is to be feared that increasing parts of a country' population living in reservations, refugee camps, and slums will escape official control or be submitted to it only in a minimal sense. These populations are brutally overpoliced at their periphery and underpoliced in their midst. Yet there are improvised forms of social control that are imposed on them by persons or organizations who have neither entitlement to nor aptitude for enforcing regulations. This "wild control" is often completely arbitrary and even predatory. Enforcement tends in these cases to be violent and contrary to the law.

Despite its sketchy character, the map of policing and social control that has been drawn allows us to make conclusions that may act as guidelines for the development of a theory of policing. The first conclusion is obvious: the policing apparatus is far more extensive than its most visible component, the public police forces. A consensus has developed on this conclusion, which now seems trivial since the publication of many research findings on the rise of private security at the beginning of the 1970s. It is still instructive, however, to stress that there is no need to emphasize the importance of private security in order to show that the reduction of policing to the activities of the public forces is untenable. The number and diversity of the *kind* of agencies that belong to the sphere of public policing are sufficient to warrant this conclusion. Put another way, public policing is itself insufficiently explored.

Second, one of the most oft-repeated statements in research on the police is the limited role of law enforcement in their activities. This may be true of uniformed patrolpersons. However, this assertion does not pay enough attention to the fact that large units within police forces are almost exclusively devoted to criminal law enforcement, such as the criminal investigation departments. As a matter of fact, whole police forces, like the FBI in the United States and the BKA in Germany, are in great part devoted to law enforcement. In terms of staff, the number of investigators is much lower than the mass of uniformed personnel. However, their role as the main channel of suspects to the courts enhances the social significance of their activities.

Third, the public and the private sphere of policing are both highly differentiated; they are composed of public agencies with different mandates (such as the DEA and the ATF) and private firms that offer very different services. Consequently, discourse that refers to the public or to the private spheres of policing as a whole necessarily demonstrates a high level of generality. Although they play an unavoidable role in the articulation of paradigms, we ought to be cautious with all-encompassing theoretical generalizations, when they also claim to apply at the police operational level. One must be especially critical of the assumption that public police forces or private security agencies operate as a coordinated network within their own sphere. On the contrary, it is fragmentation rather than integration that seems to be the rule for each policing organization; the vaunted policing partnerships generally exist only on paper.

Finally, it should be realized that restructuring policing involves more than just reconfiguring in novel ways police units that are assumed to operate in an integrated way at their own level (Bayley and Shearing, 2001). For instance, the implementation of community policing has increased the gap between uniformed patrolpersons and investigators in many jurisdictions. Thus, connecting a police department with yet another agency—a private security agency—may further disrupt police coordination if neither of these components was previously acting by itself in a concerted way. The fact that the "nodes" of a potential policing network are in themselves a basket of loosely connected pieces that may not behave in a consistent way should be taken into account in developing a theory of "nodal governance" in the field of security (Johnston and Shearing, 2003). The capacity of the police to coordinate internally should be part of our research agenda before we embark upon a course of multilateralization. However, before addressing the issue of coordination, it must be asked whether the components of the police assemblage share anything in common besides their function of providing order and security.

Concepts for a Theoretical Framework

The chapters that follow will try to answer this question with respect to the main components of the police assemblage. In many of these chapters, new empirical findings will be provided. Whenever this is the case, the methodology that I followed in my research will be briefly described. The theoretical principles that will be discussed in the concluding section of this chapter are thus of a higher level of generality than empirical methodology, although they have implications for empirical research. I will briefly discuss the main rules that have guided my work. For want of a better word, the considerations that follow could be said to belong to epistemology in its most unpretentious sense.

Deceptive Objects

Objects of knowledge do not spontaneously reveal their nature to research. This is true of all objects, even physical ones. However, physical objects do not actually hide from those seeking to know them, as animals may do. We may draw a tentative distinction between passive objects of knowledge and objects that actively oppose resistance to being known, particularly through the use of deception. Although human beings agree in certain circumstances—for example, when they are sick—to submit to an examination, they also resent undue curiosity about their habits and tend to view research on them as an intrusion into their privacy or as a threat, when they have something to hide. Organizations are no different from people in this respect. Business organizations facing competitors and security forces offering protection against external aggression, such as the military and the police, actively try to escape external scrutiny. Preserving secrecy is claimed by security forces to play a crucial role in the success of their operations. The very reasons supporting this claim cannot be fully disclosed to the public. It is justifiably argued that a party engaged in a struggle cannot reveal how it intends to win, and that the element of surprise plays a crucial role in conflict. However, it is also true that all parties in a conflict abide by the slippery principle that the end justifies the means. The extent to which this principle is applied is best kept hidden.

Leaving aside the military that are not, as such, part of this enquiry, confidentiality in the field of policing is maintained in several ways. The first obstacle to external scrutiny is legal. It is the most overwhelming, and it even impedes the sharing of information between the various players within the security establishment: giving access to classified information and allowing it to be made public are legally prohibited and may carry criminal sanctions. The operations of the security and intelligence services—which are referred to in this book as high policing—are screened by the law. In an eye-opening report, the late U.S. Senator Patrick Daniel Moynihan has revealed the astonishing ambit of his country's government practices in classifying information as secret (United States, Congress, 1997). Secrecy is also a matter of institutional policy. The centralized policing organizations of continental Europe are notably closed to academic researchers. A third way to preserve secrecy is to threaten a researcher with reprisals, such as a civil suit, for publishing his findings. Richard V. Ericson was threatened with legal action by the police to keep him from publishing his book on criminal investigations (Ericson, 1981; see Ocqueteau, 2006 for a more recent example).

There is one more way of resisting knowledge that is more conceited. In the same way that journalists were "embedded" in military units during the war in Iraq, public police forces and private security agencies have increasingly allowed researchers to undertake research within the organization. Needless to say, this is a welcome development that is greatly beneficial to police studies. Nevertheless, this openness may be deceptive and imply a trade-off between research and advertisement. The police were never more open to research than when they wanted to publicize initiatives that might win them public acceptance, such as community policing with CompStat. The private security agency that gave Rigakos (2002) access to its operations also used selected quotes from his book for advertising purposes on its Web site (Intelligarde, 2008). The president of Intelligarde published a book whose title—*Parapolice* (McLeod, 2002)—closely paralleled Rigakos' (*The New Parapolice*) and was published in the same year. By contrast, criminal investigation is, as we shall see, the least researched topic in police studies (along with human rights). Criminal investigators have more clout than patrolpersons in police organizations, and they are not keen on being investigated themselves.

A theory of policing should strive to remedy the imbalance between research on uniformed street personnel and plainclothes police. This is easier said than done, particularly when we include high policing practitioners among plainclothes police. Deception is a legitimate and indispensable tool of the trade of investigators and intelligence officers; it has become an ingrained part of an occupational culture that often makes no distinction between legitimate and illegitimate targets of deception: all outsiders are fair game.

The collection of data should systematically rest on various forms of methodological triangulation to overcome this situation. This obvious requirement may not be sufficient. Meta-analyses that examine repeated soundings of the same question are essential. There are also archival and official documentation sources that are used by investigative journalists and seldom exploited by social science researchers. Instead of using access to information acts, police research-ers rely on secondhand newspaper clippings by journalists who went through the frustrating procedure of obtaining access to official documents. Testimonies given under oath by police and intelligence operatives to government commis-sions of inquiry are an invaluable source of knowledge, although tedious to use. From personal experience in government commissions of inquiry, the author can confirm that police officers who think nothing of skirting around the truth in criminal court proceedings are extremely reluctant to commit perjury before an investigating magistrate. The overarching point of these remarks is that field work should, whenever possible, be preceded by thorough archival work. A researcher interviewing a criminal investigator without making it clear to the interviewee that he has done the background research to check, at least in part, the truth of what is said is just asking for a lie.

Antinomies

In a brief paper on the work of playwright George Bernard Shaw, for whom he had the greatest admiration, Husserl expressed in nontechnical language his conception of phenomenology:

> [phenomenology] aims at the renewal of science based on the most radi-cal self-reflection upon its ultimate sources of life, in the "I live" and the "We live in community." In other words, its basis is a radical self-explanation of the life in which science itself arises and arises as a process that serves a genuine life. The task is to develop a science that thoroughly understands and justifies itself by way of the greatest possible advance to freedom from presuppositions, a science that returns to the ultimate con-ceivable limit of disbelief to secure the invaluable. (Husserl, in McCormick and Elliston, 1981: 357)

This conception of science can be exploited in two ways. It first serves as a precautionary principle against uncritical beliefs and presuppositions of all kinds. In a more radical sense, however, freedom from all presuppositions entails being liberated from the generally unquestioned assumption that social science theory can ultimately be rid of paradox and be at rest with itself. In effect, several of the concepts forming the basis of a theory of policing break up, upon analysis, into antinomies (an antinomy is composed of a pair of contra-dictory statements, each of which can be independently demonstrated to be true). As we saw in the introduction, the concept of antinomy is one of the core ideas of this book. All theory of policing must face the core antinomy of violence. Violence is considered at the same time to be the prime expression of evil and the necessary instrument of peace and order when it is used by the police. This paradox is at the heart of political theory and was given a definitive formulation in Hobbes' *Leviathan*: the answer to the wanton violence of all lies in the institutionalized violence of one.

The theory of policing is confronted with several antithetical notions. For instance, Jeremy Bentham prized security over all other values, including freedom, throughout his work (Bentham, 1996). His argument was that one first needs security in order to enjoy freedom. The classic counterargument against this position is that security can be carried to the point that there is no more liberty to enjoy. No single argument can decide the issue, which can be resolved only provisorily through political compromise. These remarks are not meant to allow inconsistencies in thinking about the police. Theoretical inconsistencies should be resolved as much as it is possible. However, building a theory is not an operation of sanitization. What is contradictory, conflicting, and ultimately tragic in reality should not be ironed out to produce a quiescent, self-satisfied theory.

Intensive Quantity

People tend to believe that public policing is a more dangerous profession than most other occupations and that police proportionally lose their lives more often in the course of their work than people in other kinds of jobs. This belief is factually inaccurate. The U.S. Bureau of Labor Statistics periodically issues a list of the most dangerous occupations in terms of the proportional number of fatalities. Policing has never been listed among the top ten, this list being generally topped by loggers, fishermen, and small aircraft pilots. Yet, it seems that no matter how often such statistics are repeated, public opinion will persist in considering policing as a dangerous occupation.

There are numerous examples of this failure of statistics to affect public beliefs. For instance, the number of deaths resulting from the abuse of alcohol is incomparably higher than the fatalities resulting from the abuse of narcotics. Yet substance abuse is viewed by the public as a much bigger threat to society than alcoholism. Also, the number of terrorist casualties in democratic countries is insignificant compared to the victims of traffic accidents, even when exceptional events such as the attacks carried out in the United States on 9/11 are taken into account. Yet no threat other than terrorism ever impelled the U.S. government to declare a state of war against a form of harmful behavior except for the "the war on drugs," which is the other paradigmatic example of an extreme disproportion between risk and response. Momentous government decisions are often made on the basis of single instances, such as the "Megan laws" on the compulsory registration of sex offenders.

Many explanations are offered for the disproportion between limited risks and the scope of the policies that they often trigger, such as the action of lobbies or of crusading parents and relatives of a victim. Yet these movements would not be as successful if they were not spurred by events that resonate far beyond their single occurrence. Events widely differ in their mobilizing power. This observation could be potentially formalized by attempting to devise a procedure by which a coefficient of intensity would be affixed on an event. Such a coefficient would translate as a multiplier of the perceived frequency of an event. The actual multiplication would take place in media space. Thus, to provide a simple illustration, an ordinary burglary would have a null coefficient ($1=1$). By comparison, a homicide would have a much higher coefficient (for instance, $1=100$), which would mean that the single actual event is literally multiplied into at least 100 media clones. Through such a multiplying process, a single event with a high coefficient of intensity would completely offset the social and political impact of events with a much higher first-level statistical frequency. The notion of intensive quantities (or units) might begin to explain, for instance, why the nexus between policing and law enforcement cannot be broken, despite overwhelming statistical data showing that law enforcement accounts for a rather small portion of police activity. Law enforcement events have a much higher coefficient of intensity than false alarms, service occurrences, and the writing of reports. If their number is tabulated on the basis of the amount of reporting stories that they generate, it very largely exceeds any other policing activity.

However tentative may be the notion of an intensive quantity, it stresses that an event cannot be reduced to its statistical inscription. Claiming, for instance, that policing is safe on the basis of its low rate of fatalities ignores the perception that there is a basic difference between the significance of an accident and of an intentional killing. Building theories on such ignorance is as vacuous as attempting to give a scientific account of magnets without taking magnetic fields into consideration. The notion of intensive quantities will be used throughout the book, particularly in chapter 3 on police images.

Summary

The main purpose of this chapter has been to explore what should be included in the content of a theory of policing that aims to cover the full spectrum of policing activities. We began by arguing that a theory of policing aiming to be (relatively) complete should provide an account of what is being referred to when we use the word "police" as a common noun (the police), as a verb (policing), and as an adjective (as in police apparatus). This discussion tried to articulate the relationship between policing conceived as a broad type of activity and the various agents—the police—engaged in performing this activity. This discussion led to the conclusion that a notion of "plural policing" had to be developed to account for the fact that many agencies besides the public police were involved in policing. This conclusion has also been reached by several other researchers. However, our exploration of the meaning the word "police" used as an adjective uncovered the pejorative connotations associated with the terminology of policing, which are essentially the result of our ambiguous attitude in relation to the use of coercion. This ambivalence is captured by the phrase "necessary evil," often applied to the most ominous of policing tactics (infiltration, covert surveillance, roundups). Although one of the pioneering books on the police (Westley, 1970) focused on this less consensual aspect of policing, there is presently a dearth of research of the aspects of policing that are threatening to democracy.

The second and third part of this chapter tried to map out the diverse components of the police assemblage. These components were divided into two categories according to whether they could be unequivocally referred to as forms of policing. The first category briefly presented the features of the various organizations involved in public and private policing. The second category listed forms of social control that were either unregulated or plainly delinquent. Although it would be counterintuitive to refer to these fringes of social control under the name of policing, they nonetheless belong to the spectrum of policing actions. In the final chapter of this book, they will be discussed as forming the edges of policing. The last part of this chapter was devoted to highlighting some of the theoretical underpinnings of the analyses to be presented in the next chapters of this book.

As was seen at the beginning of this chapter, the various meanings of the common noun "police" are first to be found in history. The next chapter reviews the history of policing and describes the evolution of the meaning of "police" and of "policing."

History

Although there is an impressive body of literature on the history of policing, only part of this literature qualifies as historical research; a great deal of the writing idealizes various police forces such as the British bobbies or the Canadian Mounties, whereas other forces, such as the early French police, are demonized.

With respect to the history of the police, who were created as a distinct institution during the seventeenth century, there are three basic "models," although the contemporary models of policing are more numerous (Mawby, 2003). These models are, respectively, the French, the Prussian, and the British models. The Prussian model of the *policey*, which referred to a particular science (*Policeywissenschaft*) and to the form of government that corresponded to it (an early version of the welfare state), never applied to actual police forces and does not survive today as an autonomous paradigm of policing (Stolleis, 2000; Napoli, 2003). A fourth model was developed in North America, but it is to a certain extent a derivative of the British one. For all historical purposes, the key contrast is between the French (later, continental) and the British models of policing.

Within the limits of this chapter, a detailed account of the birth and development of these models of policing cannot be provided. The chapter has two limited aims. First, the history of the police will be briefly discussed with a view to highlighting features and themes that shed light on contemporary aspects of policing. Second, although the answers given to the problems of policing may vary across time and space, some of these problems have an intractable character and allow for solutions that are merely incomplete and provisory. An attempt will be made to identify these persistent problems, which define the conditions that have to be met by a policing scheme in order to be successful for a time.

There is as much to be learned from what endures in history as from what changes.

This chapter is divided into three parts: the birth of policing in France, the British model of policing, and policing in the United States and Canada. These three parts will be followed by conclusions on recurrent features of policing throughout history and on the main differences between the policing models.

The Birth of the Police: The French Model

As a public institution, the police were born in France in 1667. Policing before the birth of the police was studied by Schwartz and Miller, who concluded, after studying fifty-one different societies across time and space, that the recourse to police ("a specialized armed force used partially or wholly for norm enforcement") and to counsel ("specialized non-kin advocates in the settlement of disputes") was found only in association with a substantial degree of division of labor, and that mediation by nonspecialized parties was the habitual noncoercive way of settling disputes in the simplest of societies (Schwartz and Miller, 1964: 166; also see Johnston, 2000: 6–7). Although the police institution was created anew in England with decisive and permanent modifications that superseded the French model, there are continuities among the French, British, and indeed all models of policing.

An extract from Montesquieu's *The Spirit of the Laws* illuminates the fundamental aspects of the general idea of the police. This extract is frequently cited in eighteenth-century policing doctrine. For instance, Lieutenant General Jean Charles Philippe Lenoir begins his memoir on the police of Paris for the empress of Austria by quoting this extract from Montesquieu. In this quote, the word "police" is almost never used to refer to a group of persons (police officers). Except for the mention that "the actions of the police are quick," the extract should be read by supplying the word "regulations" after the word "police" in all occurrences of the latter.

> There are criminals whom the magistrate punishes; there are others whom he corrects; the former are subject to the power of the law, the latter to its authority; the former are withdrawn from society, one obliges the latter to live according to the rules of society.
>
> In the exercise of the police, it is the magistrate who punishes rather than the law; in the judgments of crimes, it is the law that punishes rather than the magistrate. Matters of police are things of every instant, which usually amount to but little; scarcely any formalities are needed. The

actions of the police are quick and the police is exerted over things that recur everyday; therefore, major punishments are not proper to it. It is perpetually busy with details; therefore great examples do not fit it. It has regulations rather than laws. The people who belong to it are constantly under the eye of the magistrates; therefore it is the fault of the magistrate if they fall into excess. Thus, one must not confuse great violations of the laws with the simple violations of the police; these things are of different orders. (Montesquieu, 1748: 5.26.24.)

This excerpt from *The Spirit of the Laws* quickly found an echo in England just a few years later, in 1773.

Police is the second general division of jurisprudence. The name is French, and is originally derived from the Greek "politeia" which properly signified the policy of civil government, but now only means the regulation of the inferior parts of government, viz: cleanliness, security and cheapness or plenty. Carrying dirt from the streets, and the execution of justice, so far as it regards regulations for preventing crimes and the method of keeping a city guard, though useful, are too mean to be considered in a general discourse of this kind. (Adam Smith, *Lectures on Justice, Police, Revenue and Arms*; quoted in Radzinowicz, 1956: 421)

Major themes of police studies can be connected to the different parts of these quotations from Montesquieu and Smith, including the following five.

Police discretion. In distinguishing between the cases where offenders are punished by the laws and other cases where they are directly subject to the authority of the police magistrate, Montesquieu points to the enduring issue of police discretion. Although the police would eventually lose their judicial status, their discretionary power to invoke the law and file criminal charges is quasi-judicial, as Skolnick emphasized in his classic *Justice without Trial* (1966).

Variety of duties. In insisting that matters of police are "things of every instant," that policing is thus dealing with small incidents recurring every day at any time, and that the police magistrate is perpetually busy with details, Montesquieu foreshadows the insistence of later police scholars on stressing the infinite diversity of events in which police intervention is required. For Bentham, the idea expressed by the word "police" seemed "too multifarious to be susceptible of any single definition" (Bentham, 1996: 198, note u). This position was to be echoed in all further research on the police. Montesquieu also provides an early illustration of the ambiguity of the role of the police. Police have, on the one hand, to attend to a myriad of events that are so different in kind that this diversity is said later by Bentham to preclude a single definition of their role. However, Montesquieu begins his remarks on the police by making a distinction between two kinds of criminals, thus implying that despite the diversity of its functions, there is a special relationship between the police and the prevention and repression of crime. The centrality of law enforcement in defining the police mandate is still one of the most controversial issues of policing.

Lowly status. Adam Smith's position that the police were responsible for the inferior parts of government is in line with a tendency among important police theorists to view policing as a "tainted occupation" (Bittner, 1970/1990: 94).[1] Smith also agrees with Montesquieu and Bentham in conceiving of police activity as a series of menial tasks driven by the unpredictable occurrence of various incidents and amounting to little. In contrast to Montesquieu, Adam Smith barely mentions crime control. He also gives an unusually low rating to security among human needs. There is in this regard a sharp difference between him and Bentham. For the latter, security is the basic human need from which everything else flows.

Surveillance. Montesquieu makes a cryptic remark on the responsibility of police magistrates. Since people subject to police regulations are always under the eyes of these magistrates, it is the policing authorities who should be blamed if their wards misbehave. He is thus hinting at the responsibility of police magistrates to prevent crime through constant surveillance. This is one of the most insistent leitmotifs of French thought on the police.

Infralegality. Montesquieu asserts that scarcely any formalities are needed in policing, where speed is of the essence. In a similar vein, he believes that policing rests on regulations rather than on laws. Like the previous themes that we have singled out, the issue of legality in policing is a key matter of concern, the French having a dichotomous view of policing and of formal criminal justice. Legal formalities are seen as a hindrance to policing, whereas all legal guarantees must be provided to someone who is charged with a crime that carries "afflictive" penalties.

The five themes that I have extracted from Montesquieu extend beyond the French historical model of policing and are still relevant for thinking about policing today.

The early French model of policing will now be examined; it has been the subject of abundant literature (Clément, 1866; Chassaigne, 1906; Saint-Germain, 1962; Pillorget, 1978; Williams, 1979; and L'Heuillet, 2001). However, one of the main available sources has so far been untapped: it consists of a

---

1. See note 1 in chapter 1 for the format of the references to Bittner's work.

Mémoire sur la Police en France, et particulièrement sur la Police de Paris that was presented in 1779 to Maria Theresa, the empress of Austria, by the French general lieutenant of police, J.C.P. Lenoir (Lenoir, 1779).[2] A second version of this memoir was presented to her daughter, the queen of Naples.

The Meaning of the Word "Police"

The word "police" is defined by Boucher d'Argis in Diderot and d'Alembert's *Encyclopédie* as "the art of providing a comfortable and quiet life" to all of the earth's inhabitants, but particularly to city dwellers (Boucher d'Argis, 1765). Boucher d'Argis's definition is greatly influenced by Nicolas de La Mare's *Traité de la Police*, a compendium of all legislative texts on the police which, despite its great shortcomings, was the work of reference at the time (La Mare, 1722).

The basic underpinnings of La Mare's concept of the police are that policing is part of the king's service and that it aims at the common good. It is therefore a branch of public law (La Mare, 1722: preface). It follows that for him "police" has three basic meanings. In its widest sense, it simply means *government*, whether referring to the government of the whole state or to the government of a narrower domain, such as the clergy, the military, and so forth (La Mare, 1722: 2). In its ordinary and most current sense, "police" refers to the *public order of a city*, so that saying, for instance, that the "police of a city" is not respected is equivalent to saying that there is no order in that city. In its technical sense, which goes back to Loyseau's work on the structure of French society at the beginning of the seventeenth century, the word refers to the special *power of a police magistrate to establish all regulations* needed to promote public order in a city (La Mare, 1722: 2). In exercising this power, the police magistrate partakes in the authority of the sovereign and acts more as his commissioner than as a judge. In short, "police" both means order and the power to establish it.

La Mare assessed that urban order was composed of eleven elements, that is, religion; morality; public health; food supplies; public roads, bridges and public buildings; public safety; sciences and liberal arts; commerce; factories and mechanical arts; servants and laborers; and the poor. This enumeration of the objects of policing became a standard, and is to be found in Lenoir and in many other works (1779: 7; also see Foucault, 1981: 249). It must be stressed that all of these aspects of order are to be understood in their relation to the king's service and the public good. For instance, commerce is a proper object for the

---

2. Only two manuscript copies of the memoir exist; one of them is to be found at the University Library of Cambridge University (the classmark is Add. 4651). All citations from this manuscript and other texts written in French were translated by the author.

police insofar as merchants have to be kept honest in their dealings with the public. In *Omnes et Singulatim*, his classic analysis of the meaning of the word "police," Michel Foucault focused on one of the early texts on the police (Foucault, 1981: 243–254). The author of this work was Turquet de Mayenne, who presented his program of policing to Dutch parliamentarians in 1611. For Turquet, "police" meant "government" and was an all-inclusive notion. The prime object of the police was "Man" in his relationships with the state.

Lenoir (1779: 34) sums up this conception of policing: it is "the science of governing men and to do them good." This meaning of the word "police" came to be accepted throughout Europe, as Samuel Johnson's *Dictionary of the English Language* testifies. Dr. Johnson defines the word "police," which he says was borrowed from the French, as "the regulation and government of a city or country, so far as regards the inhabitants" (vol. 2 of the 1806 edition). As Paolo Napoli stressed in his book on the birth of the French police, the French police theorists essentially limited their conception of policing to urban government (Napoli, 2003). It was left to the Prussian thinkers such as Christian Wolff, and in particular to von Justi, to develop a theoretical synthesis where the science of policing (*Policeywissenschaft*) was the second part of a crowning trilogy of political sciences (*Staatwissenschaften*)—economics, administration and fiscal policy—that formed the knowledge base of the Prussian welfare state (Napoli, 2003: 259).

Nevertheless, Joseph Fouché, Napoleon's minister of police, explicitly established the connection between policing and governing a country—indeed, a whole empire. "The police," Fouché wrote to the Duke of Wellington in 1816, "is a political magistracy which, apart from its special functions, should co-operate by methods, irregular perhaps, but just, legitimate and benevolent, in augmenting the effectiveness of every measure of government" (Fouché, 1816; quoted in Radzinowicz, 1968: 555). This citation raises the issues of political policing and of whether the operations of the political police are legal (in contrast with being "legitimate" in the eyes of the state). These issues will be addressed further on. For now, it is important to stress that the police of the Revolution and of the Napoleonic empire did not break with the early French tradition, according to which policing is a general form of governance through the executive branch of every department of government (Madelin, 1930: 451, vol. 1).

The Creation of the French "Lieutenance générale de police" and Its Context

The office of the general lieutenancy of police was created by an edict of Louis XIV in March 1667. The maître des requêtes, Gabriel Nicolas de la Reynie, was the first person to hold this office. This edict followed a previous edict of

December 1666 on "the safety of the city of Paris" (see L'Heuillet, 2001: 53, note 13). Alan Williams has argued that the most significant period for the Old Regime police of France was the eighteenth rather than the seventeenth century, when it was originally created (Williams, 1979: 2). Indeed, it is easier to say what Louis XIV did not create in 1667 than what he did establish. What he did not create was a whole new body of men to undertake policing tasks—a police force. As was said, Louis created an office with a dual purpose. First, he wanted to integrate the policing duties, particularly with respect to the policing of Paris. These duties were until then divided between a *lieutenant civil* and a *lieutenant criminel*. This division generated confusion and inefficiency: "murders, assassinations, and thefts were committed with impunity [in Paris] day and night" (Lenoir, 1779: 40). While centralizing policing in the hands of one general lieutenant, the March 1667 edict also declared that since there was some incompatibility between the judicial and police functions, no officer would be responsible for both. The edict redefined the duties of the officer responsible for the administration of justice (the *lieutenant civil* of the prévôt of Paris; Buisson, 1950: 49; L'Heuillet, 2001: 51, note 5).

There is no single historical factor that accounts for the creation of the lieutenancy of police in the context of the 1660s. This period was characterized by high-profile events such as the arrest of the finance minister Fouquet, charged with corruption, and by the murder by poison of prominent members of Louis XIV's court (the mysterious *affaire des poisons*, in which the first lieutenant general, La Reynie, played the part of a special royal commissioner; see Clément, 1866: 224–225). Although individual historians tend to emphasize one feature of the context at the expense of others (such as food riots), historical sources such as the wording of Louis XIV's 1666 and 1667 edicts, pamphlets, and satirical poems on the lack of safety in Paris in the 1660s (quoted in Buisson, 1950: 16–17), and Lenoir's later memoir, all stress the general need for more safety and urban order in Paris.

Whatever may have been the acuteness of these problems, there is a fundamental point about policing that was made in 1754 by Guillauté in a project to reform the police. He writes: "Citizens must be submitted to authority, disarmed internally, and externally peaceful, without great alarms and pressing needs, before we may undertake to police them" (Guillauté, 1754: 34). The general pacification of a community is a precondition for the establishment of a police force. Such a force is the product of a lengthy historical evolution; it is an instrument used to consolidate a previous transition from a general state of lawlessness and violence to a peaceful society. When Louis XIV created the French police in 1667, France had known nearly a century of religious wars and open rebellion against the central power by its nobility. It had finally been subdued by the sovereign's power, and enjoyed internal peace. The advent of the police marks the end of war.

The System of Policing

We stressed that Louis XIV did not create the police as a body of men, but rather originally established the office of the lieutenant general of police; this office was to become a ministry during the Revolution and the Napoleonic empire. Needless to say, the lieutenant general could depend on a force of men, some of whom had already been part of the earlier policing apparatus, such as the Paris Guard and the Night Watch. The police of the French Old Regime, which operated mainly in Paris, was headed by a lieutenant general, as we have said. He had under his direct command forty-eight commissioners responsible for the various Paris neighborhoods and who "multiplied, as it were, his presence throughout the city" (Lenoir, 1779: 69). Being surrogates for the lieutenant general, they had judicial powers and could conduct criminal court proceedings, generally in the case of petty crimes: Lenoir referred to them as the "people magistrates." They were assisted by twenty inspectors, whose main task was surveillance; they were to observe everything that happened in Paris and report crimes, misdemeanors, and all disorders to the commissioners (Lenoir, 1779: 110). Although they had to buy their office, as all other state functionaries did, they did not enjoy the status of public officers and had no institutional power; the lieutenant general could use in this capacity whomever he wanted (Lenoir, 1779: 118). The true power of these inspectors is, however, revealed by the price they had to pay for their office: the cost of inspectorships was four times as high as commissionerships and, at times, as high as a government minister (Williams, 1979). An inspector actually ruled over his given territory (for example, with respect to publications, gambling, or brothels).

To summarize, the command of the police of Paris comprised a lieutenant general, forty-eight commissioners, and twenty inspectors. These sixty-nine officials could depend on a force of 1,028 armed men who formed the Guard; some of these men were mounted on horses and had military training (Lenoir, 1779: 124–125). Estimates of the size of the Paris police force vary greatly. According to Williams, who includes everybody connected with the eleven standard objects of policing enumerated by La Mare (such as garbage collectors, firemen, and persons in charge of street lighting), the whole organization numbered 3,114 in 1788, one year before the Revolution. It should be noted that less than a century later, the Paris police force would number 7,638 officers and 874 plainclothesmen, according to an estimation by the prefect of police for the capital (Andrieux, 1885: 284 and 292).

Several features of this system deserve brief discussion. First, it was a loosely integrated, hybrid system composed of persons of very different status, competence, and training. Within this system, it was the military component that wore uniforms and actually used force. This must be borne in mind when the French Declaration of Human Rights later acknowledged the need for a "public force" (*force publique*; see article 12); this public force was more likely to have been conceived as a military force (the *Garde nationale* or some similar organization) than as a police force in the specific sense of the word (Napoli, 2003: 195–202).

A second crucial aspect of the system was the concentration of all powers into the sole hands of the lieutenant general. He had legislative powers that enabled him to enact regulations that carried such heavy sanctions that they were to all practical purposes criminal laws. He possessed vast judicial powers and acted as a judge in all matters that were not required by law to be referred to a formal court of justice (for instance, homicide by negligence could be prosecuted in a police court, whereas murder had to be referred to justice); for some of the offences under his jurisdiction, he could impose imprisonment and even the death penalty. He was also endowed with the widest executive power, as the head of the police. Furthermore, he added to these executive powers the ancient powers of the royal governors of the provinces (*intendants*), and as such he was a special commissioner of the king and acted in the name of the sovereign (Lenoir, 1779: 51–53). In this respect, he could not have been vested with higher authority. This concentration of all powers in the hands of the police magistrate begat an administrative culture of top-down centralization characterized by its rigidity, which has lasted until this day in France. In his memoir, Lenoir describes how the police magistrate operates through bureaus "where everything is registered" (Lenoir, 1779: 66). He claims that the police magistrate "is aware of all details, whatever their nature ... [that] he knows every dossier in all of its extent ... [that] he alone makes all the decisions and gives all the orders that are issued in his name" (Lenoir, 1779: 68–69).

Without getting into the differences between the French inquisitorial and the English adversarial legal systems, it must be said that the French did not experience the same difficulties as the British with respect to the prosecution of offenders. As all policing was a matter of public law and the king's service, the courts did not depend on victims to press criminal charges as much as the British did (Beattie, 2001): all offences against police regulations were also offences against the king's edicts and the common good. Police magistrates could then assign the various cases to the courts of a highly differentiated judicial system according to the seriousness of the offence. Although the various judicial levels changed in name, police tribunals consisted of courts for "simple or ordinary police" offences, courts of criminal police that processed cases falling in between criminal police regulations and criminal justice, and courts for civil or "contentious" police, which regulated commerce, factories, and so forth (Lenoir, 1779: 27–30).

The last feature that should be highlighted concerns the inspectors. Three of the twenty police inspectors were responsible for the general safety of Paris, and they formed between them the official staff of a criminal investigation department (CID) and a street crime unit. Lenoir claimed that the three inspectors in charge of safety (*la sûreté*) arrested more criminals and more suspects in Paris than the Guard and all other uniformed companies devoted to security taken together (Lenoir, 1779: 154). How could three men be more efficient in this respect than a thousand? According to Lenoir, these inspectors had recruited several crews of irregulars to assist them; these irregulars belonged to the criminal milieu. There was first a score of "observers" (*observateurs*) acting in the traditional capacity of informants. However, these observers also ran an array of subobservers (*sous-mouches*—"flies," the French equivalent for snitches) for themselves; this network of informants encompassed prostitutes, who had an obligation to inform the police, innkeepers, and persons running all kinds of gambling houses. Twice a week during winter (once during the summer), a safety inspector would roam the streets with his crew of informers and thugs and proceeded to arrest all those who had a suspicious demeanor (Lenoir, 1779: 147). The number of informers and irregulars thus in the pay of the police has been deliberately exaggerated by the various lieutenants general of police for the purpose of intimidating the public and destabilizing potential opponents. Williams, who is critical of these exaggerations, estimates the number of subinspectors and spies to be between 360 and 460 at the end of the Old Regime (Williams, 1979: 68–69, table 2). There is no doubt that this system of policing through a network of spies radiating throughout all walks of society gave birth to what came to be known during the Revolution and after as "high policing" (*haute police*; on this, see Brodeur, 1983).

Goals and Priorities

There is no more hotly debated question in police studies across countries than what the police are actually doing with their time; the debate heats up whenever the issue of the time devoted to law enforcement and crime control is raised. The difficulty in resolving this issue is illustrated in exemplary fashion when it is discussed in relation to the early French police. As we saw previously, it was a multipurpose agency that had some eleven official functions. Furthermore, it was also a hybrid organization, its various components being involved in considerably different tasks. Nevertheless, it is possible to shed some light on the issue of its priorities and main targets.

In the most systematic study of the Paris police before the revolution, Alan Williams concluded that the provision of security and the maintenance of order were the overriding concerns of the police, with deterrent patrol as its main activity (Williams, 1979: 202; also see table 2, p. 68). This is in part confirmed by Pierre Clément, in one of the earliest historical studies of the Old Regime police: crime and street disorders are cited as prime concerns, with deterrent patrol as the main police activity (Clément, 1866: 72). In his memoir, Lenoir declares that crime control is the "most immense and most important" of all police functions (Lenoir, 1779: 159–160).

However, Clément also says that control of public opinion was as high a police priority as was safety and order (Clément, 1866: 72). Most studies of the French police share this view (Napoli, 2003: 111–117). It is borne out by an examination of seventeenth- and eigtheenth-century police documents. René d'Argenson was one of the most celebrated lieutenants general of police (1697–1718). Parts of his notes were published in 1866 (d'Argenson, 1866). They consist of an enumeration of 160 incidents that were brought to his attention. According to my examination of these cases, a plurality of incidents concerned the repression of religious dissent, most of them having to do with French Protestants who were outlawed by Louis XIV by the 1685 revocation of the Edict of Nantes: thirty-one cases were of a religious nature, thirty cases were criminal, seventeen concerned violent disorders, and fifteen concerned prostitution, gambling, and like matters. This emphasis on the repression of religious dissent is consistent with the portrait of d'Argenson made by the great diarist Saint-Simon: "he was for a long time responsible for the police and the *inquisition*" (quoted in d'Argenson, 1866: preface, p. ix; see Saint-Simon, 1986: 4: 591–594). The previously mentioned author of the celebrated treatise on policing, La Mare, was also a police commissioner. When he was awarded a pension by Louis XIV, his most noted actions in the service of the king were acknowledged (Bondois, 1936: 21, note 1). No action in relation to common crime is mentioned. La Mare intervened in six cases of economic fraud, three cases of failures to supply food to the population, two cases involving religion, two cases involving matters of the state, and one case of censuring books. It would then appear that crime control and the maintenance of order were not the sole priorities of the police. However, the control of opinion was seen as the main strategy to maintain order, since the belief that troubles stemmed from the spread of "dangerous ideas" was prevalent in France and later on the Continent (Williams, 1979: 220). In consequence, the control of opinion may be seen as a general means to achieve order throughout the realm rather than as a priority among others.

This conclusion is confirmed by an examination of who the targets of policing were. For La Mare, religion is "the first and foremost object of the police" (La Mare, 1722: 287). However, except for rather brief periods during the seventeenth century when Catholic heretics (the *Jansénistes*) and, later, the Protestants were persecuted by the French state, it does not seem that policing religious nonconformists was the main concern of the police. From 1667 to 1789, the nonworking poor were their obsession. For Servan, a member of the Parliament of Grenoble, an idle man has begun to surrender to evil (Servan, 1767: 18–19). Lenoir sums up the police mood when he says that "the vilest of occupation is that of beggars; the worst plague for a nation is begging" (Lenoir, 1779: 267). The populace that was the prime target of the police consisted not only of beggars—their number in Paris was estimated to be 10,000 during the eighteenth century (Williams, 1979, chap. 5)—but of persons of various conditions, who lived a precarious existence at the fringe of the labor market. For the police, this fringe also comprised some 50,000 to 100,000 servants, poorly paid if at all, who acted as strong arms for their master, as well as discharged soldiers, unskilled laborers (often unemployed), and prostitutes. The greater part of this population were not natives of Paris, and two-thirds of the offenders prosecuted by the police were from the provinces or foreign countries (Williams, 1979: chap. 5). This lumpen proletariat was the prime target of the police for an obvious reason: it was believed to be responsible for most crimes. More crucially, it was an available pool of violent elements that could be easily stirred to rioting. There was also an incipient reason that was to be increasingly prominent during the nineteenth century all over Europe. As Fouché wrote to the Duke of Wellington, "the repose of the State depends on the state of mind of the working class, which constitutes the people and form the basis of the social edifice. This state of mind must be, if I can so express myself, the principal object of the care and vigilance of a good police" (Fouché, 1816; quoted in Radzinowicz, 1968: 556). The state of mind of the working class had to be preserved from contamination by the unemployed poor.

Lawfulness of Police Operations

We have stressed that the word "police" did not at first refer to an organization but to the power that was vested in the general lieutenant to make regulations on all aspects of public life. Since the "police" was a type of norm unto itself (Napoli, 2003: 212), it would follow that the behavior of the officers charged with enforcing these norms was self-regulatory. They were either above the rules or supported by them. This was in fact largely true, albeit in different ways.

Emergency. For Montesquieu, as we saw, police matters recur daily, need to be solved quickly, and are averse to legal formality. This contrast between policing and doing justice pervades the early French model of policing, and one can still find traces of it today in the notion of a "state of emergency." This contrast is most vivid when policing is viewed as the direct emanation of the sovereign's executive power. Speed is then of the essence, and police operations must proceed unhindered by formal rules (Lenoir, 1779: 53). Such political operations performed in the name of raison d'état were later to be called "high policing" under Napoleon's imperial regime and other European autocratic regimes, most notably in Austria and Russia. As is argued in a later chapter devoted to the distinction between high and low policing, this conception of political policing as occurring in a legal vacuum has endured until today.

Legalization. Lenoir also describes night arrests that were carried out by police inspectors and their civilian assistants. They were accompanied by a judicial officer—a commissioner—who granted them the authority to use burglars' tools to break into houses where a suspect was sleeping. This procedure foreshadowed the various legal warrants that are granted to the police to perform operations that would otherwise break the law.

Illegal detention. In his brief to the empress of Austria, Lenoir mentions that "hospitals" served as prisons for holding persons that "have been tried for crimes, but not convicted for lack of sufficient evidence, whereas there are presumptions strong enough against them to be considered guilty" (Lenoir, 1779: 164). This practice did not coincide with the infamous *lettres de cachet*, which were secret orders by the king to hold some of his subjects indefinitely in prison, often in the Paris Bastille. There were no judicial proceedings of any kind in the latter cases. These detention orders were in many cases issued by the king following a request by a family from the aristocracy to incapacitate a delinquent member. Much later, in his instructions to his subordinates, Napoleon's minister of police, Fouché, requested that suspects should not be held by the police any longer than it takes to deliver them to justice for their trial (Madelin, 1930: 490, vol. 1). However, individuals incarcerated pursuant to a measure of high policing (*haute police*) were not protected by this habeas corpus rule. Fouché's language in this respect closely parallels Lenoir's, thus testifying to the persistence of the previous customs during the First Empire.

Taxing vice. Lenoir and Fouché speak in identical language with respect to financing the clandestine operations of the police and paying the informants needed for these operations. Whereas Lenoir invokes the "indispensable necessity" of suffering prostitution (Lenoir, 1779: 186), Fouché claims that "the legal exploitation of vice is a bitter necessity" (Fouché, 1993: 175). Since gambling and prostitution could not be eradicated, the police should at least profit from

it. These activities were in fact submitted to a police tax that was used to provide funds for high policing operations. To prostitution and gambling, Fouché
added taxation on the delivery of passports and weapon permits (Buisson,
1930: 188).

In his portrait of the Marquis d'Argenson, one of the most famous police
lieutenants general (with Sartine and Lenoir), Saint-Simon writes: "Courageous,
hardy, and audacious during riots, and thereby master of the populace, his
behavior was much alike that of persons cited to appear before him" (Saint-
Simon, 1986: 6:591). This mirror-image relationship between the police and its
targets is an important topic that will be returned to later.

Prevention

At least since Plato, the (theoretical) priority of crime prevention over crime
repression is the most recurrent theme in the history of policing. In his eulogy
of d'Argenson, delivered before the French Academy of Sciences, the literary
luminary Fontenelle declared that it was the duty of the head of the police to
punish only rarely and "usefully" (quoted in Clément, 1866: 334). In the presentation of his memoir, Lenoir talks about tying all individuals to the public
order by the "softest and most artistically fabricated chain" of their common
interests and duties (Lenoir, 1779: vi; for crime prevention, also see pp. 34 and
84). The real issue, then, is not to determine which model of policing gives
priority to prevention but how it does this. In the case of the French model,
prevention was to be achieved in four ways.

Leniency. French magistrates stressed the need for warnings and nonpenal
remedies for most offences against police regulations (Lenoir, 1779: 33). In fact,
most of the penalties imposed were fines (Lenoir, 1779: 4), and the need to
show understanding toward offenders believed to be guilty of negligence rather
than anything else was often stressed, in line with Montesquieu, who in this
regard favored public education over punishment.

Root cause prevention. Since idleness was believed to be the main factor
underlying deviance, finding work for the unemployed poor was in theory the
choice remedy (Napoli, 2003: 62). However, there was a significant gap between
theory and practice, and the repression of begging was actually severe (Lenoir,
1779: 26).

Surveillance. The main instrument of prevention was surveillance. In his
eulogy of d'Argenson, Fontenelle gave an early expression to the Benthamian
strategy of panoptic surveillance when he wrote that one of the functions of the
police chief magistrate was "to be present everywhere without being seen"
(Clément, 1866: 334). One of the most recurrent words in the literature on

policing, from Louis XIV to Napoleon, was "vigilance." Writing during the second half of the eighteenth century, Servan sums up the prevailing theory of policing, which Fouché later continued to apply:

> Let us not judge of the [police] magistrate's vigilance by the number of his actions....A vigilant magistrate is not heavy-handed in using of the law's bridle, which he makes into a light and almost imperceptible burden for the citizens. He watches rather than he acts and the more he watches and the less he needs to act. (Servan, 1767: 17)

Within this model, the police magistrate is much more of a pair of eyes than of a pair of arms. As Servan makes clear, surveillance, which makes its target actually feel that he or she is a suspect, is essentially a form of intimidation that impedes deviance: evil persons "repress criminal conceits as soon as they spring to mind and still they fear that the Magistrate will see through them by surprise" (Servan, 1767: 23).

Control of public opinion. The need for prevention is in proportion to the magnitude of the risk. The absolute rulers of continental Europe did not fear individual crime as much as collective violence. Riots were a constant threat taken with utmost seriousness by absolute monarchs. Riots were often generated by external conditions such as the lack of food supplies that resulted in famine. However, it was generally believed that subversive ideas stemming either from religious heresy or from political agitation were the catalysts of mass disorder. The police tried to keep these events from occurring through the preventive custody of potential troublemakers. However, this was far from being the only strategy of high policing, which tried to shape public opinion through the censure of dangerous ideas and the spread of rumors that would counteract their effect.

The notion of high policing, to which we have alluded several times, will be the subject of a separate chapter. A different concept of prevention, however, eventually gave birth to the modern model of policing, initially developed by British reformers.

The British Model of Policing

There exists a wealth of documentation and a rich research literature on the birth of the British model of policing. The body of research literature is now increasingly divided between the "traditionalists" and the "revisionists" (Reiner, 1985: chap. 1; Hay and Snyder, 1989: 6, note 8; Emsley, 1991: 4). For the traditionalists, the creation of the public police was an overdue solution to an increase in property crime and in disorder, which was welcomed by all segments of British society (Ascoli, 1979; Critchley, 1967; Reith, 1952, and, to a lesser extent, Radzinowicz, 1956). The revisionists stress the resistance that the police met at various levels of British society, and they view the police institution as the new instrument for the "disciplinary enterprise," in line with Foucault (Gatrell, 1990; see also the seminal articles by Storch, 1975 and 1976; Philips, 1980, and the other contributors to Gatrell, Lenman, and Parker, 1980; Hay and Snyder, 1989; Emsley, 1983, 1991, 1996, and 2003). To the extent that the revisionists put a political reading on the birth of the British model, their findings tend to highlight linkages between the French and the British models of policing, despite the assertion by prominent revisionists such as Hay and Snyder that the history of English policing is sui generis (Hay and Snyder, 1989: 11). Although, I generally agree with the revisionist perspective, I will not try to arbitrate between the revisionists and the traditionalists, nor will I examine to what extent the history of English policing is contained within itself. The history of policing is the history of relative break-ups within a deep-seated continuity. In line with this perspective, the British will be shown to have been faced with problems similar to those of the French and to have initially been driven to answers that were also similar to the French ones. However, they finally created a model of policing that fundamentally changed the way in which policing was understood, although the changes were not as radical in practice as they appeared in theory.

Policing in England from 1660 to 1785

A sketch of the early history of policing in England can be found in Critchley (1967). Critchley was actually following in the footsteps of Colquhoun (1802: ix–xiii), who had reviewed the duties of the various peace officers—high constables, constables, headborough, thirdborough, boroughead, borsholder, tithing man, and chief pledge—in his *Treatise on the Functions and Duties of a Constable*. Skipping the very earliest history, I will briefly scan the period that extends from the creation of the French police in 1667 to the first ill-fated bill to reform the police presented by the Pitt government in June 1785. The greater part of this period was thoroughly examined by Beattie (2001).

Many aspects of policing in England during this period closely parallel similar developments in France, although, as the word "parallel" indicates, they sprang up and evolved on their own. The main similarities are the following.

Urban context. Although there was a certain degree of policing outside London, the "Metropolis" was the main policing field and the impetus for reform originated in London, as previously in France it had stemmed from Paris.

Hybrid police. The policing forces of London were diverse and consisted of constables, the night watch, the beadles, and the city marshals (Beattie, 2001: 122 and ff.) They were superseded by the military in the case of riots.

Thief-takers. According to a 1699 dictionary, thief-takers "made a Trade of helping People (for a gratuity) to their lost Goods and sometimes for Interest or Envy snapping the Rogues themselves, being usually in fee with them and acquainted with their Haunts" (quoted in Beattie, 2001: 232). Their role became increasingly prominent in criminal prosecution when the London authorities decided to increase the number of arrested and convicted criminals. Thief-takers compare to the various species of French *mouches* in several important respects. First, they created a tainted interface between police and criminals in law enforcement. Second, they provided a common ground where public authorities and private individual entrepreneurs were in league for purposes of crime control and the maintenance of order. Third, thief-takers demonstrated how much the police were dependent on informers for criminal detection. In all three respects, thief-takers show how much having recourse to criminals used as "spies," as the French did, is difficult to avoid in solving the problems of detecting who the perpetrators of a crime are and in securing their conviction.

Discretionary imprisonment. Although the reasons may not have been political, the lord mayors of London committed significant numbers of suspects to detention without trial (Beattie, 2001: 97–98).

Despite these similarities, which show that policing problems are common to different legal traditions, there were also crucial differences. The first of these concern the hybrid character of the policing systems in France and in England. However hybrid the policing system may have been in France, its different components were integrated under a centralized command, that of the lieutenant general of policing. This was not the case in England, the lack of integration later becoming one of the mainsprings for reform. The second crucial difference was that "England was almost unique among nations...in not having a bureaucracy staffed by lawyers with the responsibility to charge and proceed against those accused of crimes" (Hay and Snyder, 1989: 4; also see Rudé, 1985; Emsley, 1996: 178 and ff.; Beattie, 1986 and 2001). Prosecution was undertaken by the victims or their relatives and by nonstipendiary magistrates. This problem has wide ramifications that fall outside the scope of this book. However, its impact on policing was to be significant as the police became substitutes for private prosecutors (Gatrell, 1990: 20; Hay and Snyder, 1989: 37). This role of the police had lasting effects. According to Hay and Snyder (1989: 3, note 2), the police were responsible for some 80 percent of decisions to prosecute in the 1960s. This situation may have changed after the enactment in 1985 of the Prosecution of Offences Act (Hay and Snyder, 1989: 4).

The Context of the 1829 Reform

By "context" of the police reform of 1829, I not only mean the events that impelled the reform of policing, but I am also referring to the debate that took place on the nature and desirability of this reform and that became the permanent background of the practice of policing in Anglo-Saxon countries. The French police was created by a royal edict within the political context of an absolute monarchy, where the sovereign was accountable only to himself. Hence, there may have been a debate on whether there was a need to reform policing, but it was conducted within the government and did not filter outside. The situation was totally different in England, where a previous attempt to reform the police had failed in the House of Commons in 1785. The contrast between the French and British contexts obviously owed much to the difference between an absolute monarchy and a parliamentary regime, but cannot solely be explained on the basis of this political difference.

In Britain, private advertisements concerning criminal offences and offenders were printed in provincial newspapers and offered rewards for information about stolen property or fugitives from justice, and these played an increasing role in the detection of crimes (Styles, 1989). Not only did this practice show that the dissemination of criminal intelligence was crucial for the detection of crimes but it also underlined the importance of the printed press in all matters of policing. It prompted Edwin Chadwick to formulate one of the basic axioms of the new policing in his influential 1829 article in the *London Review*: "complete and speedy publicity of all acts of delinquency would effect far more good *without a police*, than a police could effect *without publicity*" (Chadwick, 1829: 285, my emphasis; this key statement is quoted in Radzinowicz, 1956: 460 and in Styles, 1989: 55 and 57). Publicity was to be the new stage on which the police were called to perform, and also the cage from which they tried to escape. They used their visibility as an instrument to further their own ends, but it was also used against them as a means of control. Paradoxically, the public character of the debate on the police did not enhance its transparency, as discourse fell under the sway of political strategy. Political strategy allows for some policing goals to be openly disclosed, whereas others must remain covert. Crime statistics were fed into the rhetoric of law enforcement, and they focused public opinion onto the tip of the policing iceberg (Gatrell, 1990).

Although there is very broad consensus on the fact that erty crime was repeatedly alleged to justify a reform of the Colquhoun (1796 and 1802), the 1828 *Report from the the Police of the Metropolis* (House of Commons, 182§ Chadwick (1829) all devote the greater part of their writ crime statistics—the actual role played by the need for order and for controlling riots has been a subject of debate. Arguing that the last major riots had occurred in 1821 (in relation to the Queen Caroline affair), Emsley concluded that there was no serious incident of disorder (or even crime) that provided any spark for establishing the police (Emsley, 1983: 61). Hay and Snyder (1989: 10, note) judged this position untenable. Many other historians shared their position. Emsley brought nuance to his position, and said in his later work that whether or not crime and disorder had actually increased was less important than the contemporary belief that they had.

As has been seen, England was unique in its system of private prosecutions and non stipendiary magistrates. According to a report of the 1817 *Select Committee on the Police of the Metropolis*, there were two impediments to prosecutions. First, there was no allowance to compensate prosecutors for their loss in spending time on a private prosecution; and, second, the severity of punishments deterred potential private prosecutors from launching proceedings that might have resulted in the infliction of death for a property offence (Rudé, 1985: 88). Both difficulties were remedied before long. In 1826, a Criminal Justice Act extended the system of recovering expenses to the most frequently occurring misdemeanors. By 1837, the death penalty had been repealed for all property offences, including burglary (Rudé, 1985: 90). Although these measures did not have the desired effect in multiplying private prosecutions, they opened up the door to prosecution: the police and stipendiary magistrates eventually rushed into the vacuum. The traditional division between summary hearings for petty offences and community disputes, on the one hand, and quarter sessions and assizes for the more serious offences, on the other, had applied in England for centuries. However, the court system was a maze riddled with discretionary power (King, 2000). Following the 1820 legislation extending the powers of summary trials by stipendiary magistrates, the advent of the police, who were to play a key role in the prosecution of summarily tried offences, further eroded the former discretionary procedures and ushered a modern and bureaucratized criminal justice system that, in part, looked back to the police courts of continental Europe (Gatrell, 1990; Philips, 1980).

In order to usher in this new bureaucratic order, the police themselves had to be integrated into a unified organization operating under a single command. The 1828 report of the *Select Committee on the Police of the Metropolis* stresses

"manifest advantage in considering the whole force…as one united establishment" (House of Commons, 1828: 32). It thus acknowledged a demand for
integration that had been repeatedly formulated in Jeremy Bentham's work at
the end of the eighteenth century and later. In his 1821 Constitutional Code,
Bentham had called for the establishment of the office of a preventive service
minister (Bentham, 1821: chap. 11, sect. 5, 439). In various forms, reformers
such as Colquhoun, Chadwick, and Wade had echoed this need for integration,
however controversial it was perceived to be.

We have emphasized that from the earliest time police was synonymous
with prevention, particularly in France. This is also reflected in Jeremy
Bentham's work, which is entirely focused on prevention when addressing
problems of policing. Bentham's work was so germane to French ideas on policing that he was made a French citizen by the revolutionary government of
France in 1791 (or 1792—accounts vary on the exact year) following the publication of his *Panopticon*. For him, "police" was a French word naturalized in
German, but not in English. He believed, as we have said, that the word was too
"multifarious" for any single definition. Accordingly, he proceeded to divide
policing into two branches: *phtano-paranomic* or crime-preventing and *phtano-
symphoric* or calamity-preventing (Bentham, 1996: 198–199). Bentham's ideas
were spread through British society by various conduits, one of them being
Edwin Chadwick, the police reformer, who was Bentham's secretary from 1831
until the latter's death in June 1832 (Brundage, 1988: 8). There was, however, a
second reason for stressing prevention, which is also implied by the idea of
policing. In his *Treatise on the Functions and Duties of a Constable*, Colquhoun
stresses that his endeavors to reform the institution of constables will "benefit
society, by lessening the demand for punishment" (Colquhoun, 1802: iii).
England, which had made an intemperate use of the death penalty, would particularly welcome this benefit.

The English Police

The assertion that the history of British policing was sui generis needs to be
qualified in several respects. Nevertheless, it should be recognized that the creation of the English police in 1829 marked a new departure and that it changed
forever the core meaning of the word "police." "Police" had chiefly meant the
governance of a territory in all of its aspects, as Dr. Johnson had acknowledged
in his dictionary. Being a form of urban government, the police coalesced into
a self-contained system that possessed all the attributes—legislative, regulatory,
judicial, and executive—to exercise governance. The scope was narrowed down
in England in two crucial ways. First, it was no longer to be conceived as a

self-sufficient system but as a branch of the criminal justice system, which purveyed offenders to the judicial powers.

> The police is a branch of that extensive system instituted to protect the
> community from fraud, annoyance, violence and depredation. While the
> courts of administrative justice ascertain the guilt and prescribe the pun
> ishment of actual delinquents, the business of the police is more specially
> directed to prevent the commission or apprehend the perpetrators of
> offences." (Wade, 1829: 2; note that "the police" is used in the singular)

Wade went on to declare that the functions of the police were not limited to the
handing over of criminals to the judicial powers but extended to whatever
interferes with internal security, order, comfort, and economy. This wider conception of policing that for some time still prevailed in France and Germany
was to wither quickly in England and, later, on the Continent.

Second, "the police" now began to refer to the body of men entrusted with
policing duties, which were strictly focused on the provision of security ("the
prevention and detection of crime," A.D. 1829, 10 Geo. 4. chap. 44, Preamble)
and the preservation of the peace. This switch in the meaning of "police" from
a system of governance to an organization devoted to the prevention and detection of crime reflected a transformation in the conception of the nature of
policing.

The New Police Organization

Various numbers are given for the number of men that composed the police
force created by Sir Robert Peel in 1829; some estimates were as low as 800.
According to the report of a 1908 Royal Commission that reviewed the history
of the force, it was originally led by two commissioners (Colonel Charles Rowan
and Mr. Richard Mayne, a barrister), and in May 1830, it numbered 17 superintendents, 68 inspectors, 318 sergeants, and 2,892 police constables, the number of police constables having reached 2,968 in 1834 (House of Commons,
1908: 22–25).

The crucial feature of this organization was its homogeneity and its unity of
command, since, beyond its two head commissioners, it was under the immediate authority of the home secretary himself. The men wore the same blue
uniform, designed to contrast with that of the military, and were armed with
only a wooden truncheon. Cutlasses were available under special circumstances,
and members with the rank of inspector and above could carry pocket pistols
(Emsley, 1991: 25). No men were initially mounted on horseback, in contrast to
the police of Paris, and the Horse Patrol was amalgamated with the Metropolitan

Police only in 1839. A Criminal Investigation Department (CID) with detectives in plainclothes was only established in 1842, so great was the fear that the new police system would rely on spies, as the French police was reputed to do (see Wade, 1829: 358; Chadwick, 1829: 304; White, 1839; for comments, see Radzinowicz, 1956: Appendices; and Hay and Snyder, 1989: 33).

Most important of all, perhaps, Peel followed the recommendation of the 1828 *Select Committee on the Police of the Metropolis* (House of Commons, 1828) to proceed *gradually* in establishing a new system of police and not to interfere immediately with the powers exercised by the municipal authorities of the City of London. The process of transforming the old police offices into thirteen police courts was cautiously steered over a period that extended from 1829 to 1908, when all thirteen courts were finally in operation. In the end, England would still be in the grip of a sufficiently pervasive police system for the country to be described by a noted historian (Gatrell, 1990) as a "policeman-state." However, this system fell far short of the centralized authoritarian model first envisaged by Bentham, Colquhoun, and Chadwick, who were still influenced by the French model of generalized surveillance (Philips, 1980: 189).

The Members of the Organization

At the juncture of the eighteenth and nineteenth centuries, there emerged a momentous innovation in the discourse on policing. The French lieutenant general of police Lenoir describes the qualities of a good police inspector thus: "They have to use much skill, and be somewhat sophisticated; be able to play all kinds of characters and often stand for what is false in order to learn the truth; they should appear to greatly malign or greatly praise, according to the circumstances, who they have to inform on" (Lenoir, 1779: 119). This description is pragmatic and totally unconcerned with ethics and with image. The inspector being a covert agent, he did not achieve his purposes by setting a moral example but by being skilfully manipulative.

In contrast, the English police reformers began to hold a discourse on the skills, but, more important, on the moral requirements of being a police officer. In his *Treatise on the Functions and Duties of a Constable*, Colquhoun says in the preface that constables should be "able, prudent, and intelligent individuals" (Colquhoun, 1802: ii). He goes on to stipulate in his "Preliminary Observations" that stipendiary constables should possess qualities relevant to their pursuit of the public interest, the first one being honesty, followed by knowledge and ability (Colquhoun, 1802: xiii). His whole treatise is devoted to identifying a constable's duties and to developing in constables a greater awareness of their duties. Other reformers such as Wade and Chadwick similarly insisted on the moral qualities of the future members of the police force (see Wade, 1829: 7–12).

When the new English police force was created, the implementation of these standards first resulted in very high turnover rates of personnel, 80 percent of the dismissals being caused by drunkenness (Taylor, 1998: 89–95). The staff of the forces eventually stabilized, but these demands on police personnel were the first signs of a genuine revolution in policing, which resulted in four important developments: first, the dawning of the professional police force, with its attendant consequences, such as unionization; second, increased public scrutiny of police behavior and a call for more accountability; third, the establishment of bodies, such as government commissions of inquiry, to report on allegations of police misconduct; and fourth, the use of the police image and of the symbolic power increasingly vested in the police as an instrument of discipline for the wider population. The London Metropolitan Police was already the object of a wide investigation by a Royal Commission on how its members dealt with drunkenness, disorder, and street prostitution (House of Commons, 1908; see also *The Times*, December 24, 1908). This was the beginning of the long-standing Anglo-Saxon tradition of investigating how the police fulfilled its duties in the repression of "vice" and what came to be known as "victimless" crime. This field of policing is notorious for generating police corruption.

Allan Silver's use of the adjectives "policed" and "unpoliced" provides a paradigmatic illustration of the change of meaning that the word "police" underwent after 1829 in Anglo-Saxon societies. For instance, Silver writes: "In unpoliced society, police functions were often carried out—if at all—by citizens rotating in local offices (sheriffs, constables, magistrates) or acting as members of militia, posses, Yeomanry corps, or watch and ward committees" (Silver, 1967: 9). For Allan Silver, the "policed" society is not only a society in which order prevails through the action of diverse agents but also a society in which police functions are carried out by a public, unified, and presumably professional police force. In other words, only police can do policing in the proper sense of the word. This is a far cry from the original meaning of the word in France, where a policed society was an ordered society, no matter how this order was enforced. It is also strikingly at odds with the current notion of plural or multilateral policing. We are presently just rediscovering the original meaning of the word "police" as governance and the fact that many agents, besides a professional public police force, can be involved in policing.

Prevention

Prevention is at the core of policing. Models of policing do not differ on whether they favor prevention or not but rather on how they propose to prevent crimes and disorder. The French, as we saw, had an embryonic root-cause theory of crime, and they relied in great part on covert surveillance. Edwin Chadwick, a disciple of Bentham, developed the most articulate doctrine of prevention to be proposed in England (Chadwick, 1829). In his article for the *London Review*, Chadwick quotes excerpts from the autobiography of a repeat offender and finally concludes that "in by far the greater number of cases the motive to depredation is not necessity but...the 'easy guinea,'—an impatience of steady labour, an aversion to the pain of exertion, a proportionally strong appetite for the pleasure of ease" (Chadwick, 1829: 271). In his search for the "easy guinea," the scheming criminal balances the chances of succeeding in a projected theft against the chances of being caught, in true Benthamite fashion.

To counter such a calculating offender, Chadwick devises a dual strategy of crime prevention (to deter potential offenders) and of crime detection (when offences have been successfully perpetrated). Crime prevention rests on the principle of "placing difficulties in the way of obtaining the objects of temptations" (Chadwick, 1829: 272) and blends elements that would nowadays belong to situational crime prevention: increased public vigilance (failure to report a crime would be criminalized), surveillance of potential receivers, better lighting, and selective deployment of police forces. Some of Chadwick's proposals for making crime detection more efficient were also forward looking, such as the establishment of criminal modus operandi and the use of press advertisements for collecting information on crimes and criminal fugitives. Wade, another important reformer, still retained a belief in the deterrent value of public punishments and wanted them to be "solemn and appalling in the Exhibition" (Wade, 1829: chap. 1).

Targets

After providing an estimate of the value of property lost to crime, Colquhoun concludes that it is not the loss actually sustained which is so much to be deplored "as the mischief which arises from the destruction of the morals of so numerous a body of people; who must be directly or collaterally engaged in perpetrating smaller offences, and in fraudulent and criminal pursuits" (Colquhoun, 1796: 605). As we saw, Fouché also believed that the mind-set of the working class was the prime concern of the police. The powers of the police to arrest persons living outside the labor market were continuously increased from 1814, the most important being fostered by the 1824 Vagrancy Act (Philips, 1980: 184). Despite an explicit reference to offences against property, the 1829 bill creating the police made it lawful for any men belonging to the new police "to apprehend all loose, idle and disorderly persons whom he shall find disturbing the public peace, or whom he shall have just cause to suspect of any evil designs" (Metropolitan Police Act, 10 Geo. 4. chap. 44, sect. 7).

This broadening of the police overreach was to have long-term effects. The 1908 Royal Commission provides crime statistics on arrests summarily dealt with. In 1905, 59.84 percent (76,199 out of 127,317) of these arrests were in relation to three classes of offences: drunkenness, disorderly conduct, and solicitation in the street. The proportions for previous years were similar. In his examination of who usually experienced legal disciplining, Gatrell found that most proceedings were against poorer people for street offences, such as drunkenness; the kind of persons arrested for indictable offences in various parts of England in the second half of the nineteenth century were laborers, servants, vagrants, paupers, artisans, lesser tradesmen, and unskilled manual workers (Gatrell, 1990: part 2). Although these English categories of suspects do not strictly coincide with the targets of the French police from 1667 until the early nineteenth century, there is enough overlap to warrant the conclusion that to all practical intents the targets of the two systems of police were almost the same.

Spies and Watchmen

Despite deriding the French police system, which "had mingled [its] myrmidons through every grade of the community" (Wade, 1829: 358), the English reformers did not shy from using its most criticized methods. In 1833, a police sergeant named William Popay had infiltrated a working-class political union— the National Political Union—where he played the role of an agent provocateur (Bunyan, 1976: 62–65; Philips, 1980: 187; Emsley, 1991: 28). The select committee that investigated the case vilified Popay, but exonerated his police bosses. Wade illustrates the ambiguous attitude of the police reformers toward police informers in his 1829 treatise. On the one hand, informers and thief-takers were for him a nuisance and an instrument of individual extortion, caprice, and tyranny (Wade, 1829: 16). Yet, on the other hand, he held that "a parish or district is indeed badly policed if there is not one officer, at least, acquainted with every brothel, every disorderly house, and every suspicious person and place it contains" (Wade, 1829: 10–11). A historian as prudent as John Beattie concluded his book on English policing by saying that the Metropolitan Police Act, although forward-looking in some ways, "reached back to an older ideal of policing in its total dependence on the prevention of crime by surveillance" (Beattie, 2001: 422).

Indeed, the New Police Instructions of 1829 stated that crime prevention would be best attained by making it evident to "all suspected persons...that they are known and strictly watched, and that certain detection will follow any attempt they may make to commit a crime" (the *Times*, 1829; quoted in Philips, 1980: 188). This notion of prevention as being achieved through the intimidating effect of perceived surveillance is quite close to an argument developed by the French advocate Servan, which we presented earlier. Within both the French and the English model of policing, it is realized that surveillance has a freezing effect on delinquency. Yet the conception of surveillance that underpins these two models is different.

For the sake of contrast, I shall say that the "spy" emblematizes the early French conception of police surveillance (Dewerpe, 1994). Surveillance is panoptic: the many are being spied on by the few and do not know whether they are targeted; it is exercised covertly and proceeds through infiltration; its aim is strategic, and it collects intelligence that is actionable in the long term. Finally, the spy is inimical to all, because anyone is either a real or a potential object of spying.

It is the "watchman" who is emblematic of the conception first developed in England by the police reformers. The watch is synoptic: the watchman is actually on display and it is precisely through his conspicuousness that he deters the potential offender; the watch is therefore a fully overt exercise and proceeds through the establishment of a security perimeter rather than through infiltration (one watches at the periphery rather than from the center); its aim is essentially tactical, and action is triggered at the first sign of anomaly. Finally, the visible watch is intimidating for offenders, but it is a factor of reassurance for potential victims. Hence, in contrast with the spy, whom no one follows, the watchman is a dual figure, threatening for those he guards against and friendly for those he protects and for whom he sets an example that may be imitated.

The Importation of the English Model in North America

There is a developing body of research in the history of policing in North America, particularly in the United States (Monkonnen,1990; for reviews of the literature, see Lane, 1980 and 1992, and Monkonnen, 1992). Following Miller (1975, 1977), a great deal of this research compares the U.S. version of the English model of policing to the original and discusses how the English model was skewed on key aspects when it was imported into the North American context. Policing in the United States is generally seen as a distortion of the English model rather than an original configuration. However, there is, I believe, a sense in which we can speak of an early U.S. model of policing. Treading in the footsteps of North American police historians, after acknowledging some of the initial similarities between English and U.S. policing, this account emphasizes their differences. In a third section, illustrations of the intertwinement of public and private policing in the United States is presented, which in the author's view, is a new development. Finally, the structure of Canadian policing is briefly characterized.

The Reluctant Importation of the English Model in the United States

In the late-eighteenth and early-nineteenth centuries, policing U.S. cities and the countryside was the responsibility of a mixed group of officers, such as constables, sheriffs, marshals, and various auxiliaries such as thief-takers and bounty hunters. The equivalent of the British hue and cry—a process by which members of early English medieval communities were summoned to assist in the apprehension of a criminal who had been witnessed in the act of committing a crime—was the rounding up of a posse to give chase to criminals. At the end of the War of Independence, in 1783, several eastern cities such as Boston, New York, and Philadelphia greatly increased their population. There is general agreement among historians that they were the scene of frequent large-scale riots (Rudé, 1964; Lane, 1967; Richardson, 1970, 1974; Lane, 1980: 6–7; Monkonnen, 1992: 553). Riots were, then, the first cause of the creation of urban police forces, together with waves of felonious crimes (Weiss, 1986: 87) and spectacular crimes, such as the 1841 murder of Marie Rogers in New York, which was the subject of a novella by Edgar Allan Poe. It thus seems that the context of the creation of urban police forces in the United States was reminiscent of the early situation in England.

Colquhoun had at least one imitator in Charles Christian, who published in 1812 *A Brief Treatise on the Police of New York* (quoted in Senior, 1997: 50). However, British institutions were viewed critically in the former colonies after the War of Independence. Although it was acknowledged that the creation of police forces on the English model were a potential instrument for bringing peace to U.S. cities, such a creation generally met with fierce opposition in the United States as it had been previously in England. After police forces were established, they were not quickly accepted, either.

Police forces were established in Boston (1838), New York (1844), and Philadelphia (1854). As in England, they did not carry firearms; the New York police were only issued service revolvers on a systematic basis in 1895, although officers unofficially carried pocket revolvers in the 1850s (Lane, 1980: 11). The idea of a detective force was also strongly resisted, as in England. The New York criminal investigation department comprised only twenty-four detectives in

1857 (Senior, 1997: 56), and several states actually enacted anti-detective legislation (Morn, 1982: 91–109).

The Flawed Realization of the English Model

An examination of the facts reveals that it was an abstract idea of the police rather than an operational model that was imported from England. Not only was this idea emptied of much of its content but what remained was misinterpreted. For the British, the police were an alternative to the military, although they kept some aspects of a military organization, most notably uniforms, hierarchical structure with ranks similar to those of the military, close supervision, and direct accountability to the central government (the home secretary). For the U.S. politicians, the integration of these military features into police organizations was enough to qualify them as full-fledged military forces, which they viewed with utmost suspicion. Wearing a uniform crystallized the opposition to what was perceived as a militarization of law enforcement, and it took nearly ten years to get the New York police to wear blue uniforms in 1853. Uniforms (deemed to be a servant's "livery") made the police more visible both for their supervisors and for the most aggressive of the criminal elements (Lane, 1980: 11-12). The resistance to "militarization," as symbolized by uniforms, was only the sign of much more deep-seated differences.

Control of the Police
None of the big U.S. cities where police forces were first created were metropolises in the sense of London, the seat of national government. New York was not even the capital city of the state, Albany was. Hence, both the political structure and the political culture in which the first U.S. police forces were established was local in the narrow sense: whereas their London counterparts were controlled at a distance by the home secretary, who was a minister seeking the public good of the nation, the U.S. police operated in close proximity to their municipal political masters—the mayor and aldermen—who tended to see the police as an instrument to promote their policies and their partisan interests. The New York police were under the control of state authorities from 1857 to 1870, as were at different times twelve other major urban police departments (Senior, 1997: 56), but the municipal authorities eventually all regained the control of their respective police forces. Hence, policing was from the start a highly politicized activity (Richardson, 1970: 284).

This entanglement of policing and of politics colored all aspects of policing. Although they were to relinquish their comprehensive functions during the twentieth century, the U.S. police were again associated with general urban administration, as they were initially in France (Johnson, 1979; Lane, 1980: 14; Monkonnen, 1992: 555; Senior, 1997: 8). Whereas police reformers and leaders came from the military or from the legal profession in England, they generally were politicians in the United States (Miller, 1975: 81–82). The higher ranks in some police forces were elected offices, as was the office of public prosecutor. The men were recruited from the district they had to patrol, in contrast with the British bobbies, who often came from outside of London (Miller, 1975: 84). The most disrupting consequence of the politicization of urban policing was that the notorious political corruption festering in U.S. municipal administrations spilled over massively to the police forces (Richardson, 1970 and 1974).

Police Authority

One of the main criticisms directed before 1829 against the policing system in England was its lack of integration. In consequence, there was a series of measures taken in London to mold the police into a cogent and independent institution. For instance, the recruitment of police tried to be territorially exogenous, as was just mentioned, to preserve them from partisan interests. London constables could not vote until 1885; members of the force had to meet various standards and would be dismissed if they failed to do so; they were issued directives and orders governing their action; bobbies were generally deployed in teams, which made their supervision easier. More important, the first British police commissioners sought to identify the police force with the legal system (Miller, 1975: 338), thus generating that most English (and problematic) notion that the police are only accountable to "the law," and not to any particular person or authority embodying it. They were not only accountable *to* the law but also *for* its full enforcement, and they played a much more active role in the prosecution of offenders than their U.S. counterparts (Monkonnen, 1992: 550).

The end result of this process was beneficial to the British: it meant that a police person's authority was that of the whole institution rather than that of the person who happened to have been recruited into the force. In brief, it was impersonal and institutional rather than personal. Wilbur Miller has made a convincing case that none of the measures listed above were implemented with any seriousness in the United States, and that the U.S. officer's authority was "*personal*, resting on closeness to the citizen's and their informal expectations of his power instead of formal or legal standards" (Miller, 1975: 339, and note 19, emphasis in text; more generally, Miller, 1977). The immediate consequence of this emergence of personal authority is the incomparable extent of police discretion that is the hallmark of U.S. policing (Skolnick, 1966; Miller, 1977: 85–86).

Police Legitimacy

In England, the great social and economic divide crossed between the proper-tied elite, which numbered comparatively few individuals, and the rest of the populace. Whatever may be the view on the class bias in using the police, there is agreement that the British ruling class had to be cautious in having recourse to them, because there the ruled population was so large and the rulers so few. This imbalance impelled the British style of quiet coercion and of policing by consensus. Although the application of this British doctrine of policing has lately been questioned by numerous researchers (Reiner, 1992c), it actually refers to something real when British policing is contrasted to U.S. policing. In the United States, the persons that were most perceived to need being disci-plined were the latest immigrants, and at no time were they ever a majority (Miller, 1975: 82–83; Lane, 1980: 18; Schneider, 1980). Hence there was no need to placate them, and force was used without much restraint; the police could be confidently violent, knowing that they always had the majority of their side.

The comparatively violent character of U.S. policing was thus generated by two factors: first, the rioters and criminals that they were facing were constitu-tionally licensed to have weapons, and they had to respond in kind; and second, they had unconditional majority backing in violently putting immigrants in line, not to say anything of former black slaves. Their heavy-handedness and the negative reputation that it begat stood in the way of their acceptance by the minority groups thus targeted and, more generally, hindered their legitimacy for the whole population that they claimed to protect.

With the exception of the unique U.S. prosecutorial structure, these distortions of the British policing model point to differences in degree—for example, the U.S. system was less centralized, more discretionary, and more heavily armed—rather than to differences in nature, and they do not amount to the generation of a truly new model of policing. In order to find this new model or, at least, its embryo, one must look outside the sphere of public policing. It must be added that police sociologists like Manning (1977) and Bayley (1985: 59), focusing on the current situation, do not see as much continuity between the British and the U.S. models of policing as historians do.

Public and Private Policing

In all the models of police whose history has so far been reviewed, private entrepreneurs played an important part. In France, they were recruited as informants and strong-arms, and in England they acted as thief-takers. One can also view early bodies of police, such as the Bow Street runners, as a cross between the public and the private sphere. In the United States, such private entrepreneurs also thrived as police informants recruited by detectives among criminals willing to talk for money (Lane, 1980: 10). Furthermore, off-duty police were willing to offer their service to private clients; there were also public officers appointed and employed solely by private organizations (Monkonnen, 1992: 564, citing Rebecca Reed's unpublished findings on the Detroit police). This practice of moonlighting by the public police was later studied by Reiss (1988).

The interpenetration of public and private policing was to reach an unprecedented scale realtively early in the history of the United States, where the first big private security agencies, such as Pinkerton and Burns, were founded in the second half of the nineteenth century. This development was precipitated by two factors. First, there was a conspicuous need for crime detection, since the public mistrusted the establishment of public CIDs and, as we saw, the law in some states prohibited their creation. Second, although the New York Metropolitan Police had performed better than the military or the militia in squashing the 1863 Draft Riots (Senior, 1997: 59–60), the police had local political allegiances by virtue of their funding. Consequently, they could not always be relied on to break strikes by the local population, whose taxes provided their salary (Monkonnen, 1992: 562). Well aware of these shortcomings because of their position within the public police establishment, Allan Pinkerton (deputy sheriff for Kane and, later, Cook counties; first city detective in Chicago) and William J. Burns (retired member of the Secret Service in 1909) established their own private security agencies (Weiss, 1986: 88 and 98). These agencies intervened in four kinds of situations.

The covert policing of labor. The Pinkerton agency was first hired by railroad companies to ferret out criminal behavior by testing the integrity of potentially dishonest conductors (Weiss, 1986: 356; Pinkerton, 1870). The agency soon extended its activities beyond detection and covertly gathered information on employees who voiced criticism of their employers. This, it must be emphasized, was precisely the sort of covert surveillance and infiltration that Anglo-Saxon countries professed to despise.

The covert policing of radicals. There is but a short step from monitoring the opinions of employees to infiltrating a group of labor activists. Pinkerton recruited James McParlan, an Irish Catholic from Ulster, to infiltrate the Workingmen's Benevolent Association (WBA). McParlan was elected secretary of the Shenandoah Lodge of the Ancient Order of Hibernians, which was at the center of the guerrilla warfare pursued by the Mollie Maguires, protesting exploitation in the coal mines. With the help of another Pinkerton operative, P. M. Cummings, who held office in the WBA, he gathered evidence that led to the arrest and conviction to the death penalties of nineteen people accused of being Mollie Maguires (Pinkerton, 1877 and 1878). They had been arrested by the Coal and Iron Police, who were nothing other than deputized Pinkerton agents, and they were tried by Benjamin Gowan, the president of the Philadelphia and Reading Railroad Company, acting as special state prosecutor (Weiss, 1986: 91–92). As a noted historian of labor unions wrote, this operation was "one of the most astounding surrenders of sovereignty in American history. A private corporation initiated the investigation through a private detective agency; a private police force arrested the alleged offenders; the coal company attorneys prosecuted them. The state only provided the court and the hangman" (H. W. Aurand, quoted in Weiss, 1986: 92).

Breaking strikes by violence. In an incident that occurred in July 1892 and ultimately led to the public blame of the Pinkerton agency as being a private army, some three hundred armed Pinkerton men engaged in battle with strikers of the Carnegie Steel Company at Homestead, Pennsylvania, and killed ten of them, losing three men of their own. This was the highest-profile incident among many similar ones.

Political policing. During the U.S. Civil War, the New York Metropolitan Police acted in conjunction with the Pinkerton agency in a secret service capacity. They uncovered and foiled a plot to kill President Lincoln in 1861, as he was travelling from Baltimore to Washington (Senior, 1997: 57). This cooperation between public police and private security agents reached the point of a practical symbiosis between the Bureau of Investigations—which was to become the FBI—and the Burns Detective agency. Burns was a former head of the Secret Service, who retired and established his own detective agency in 1909. He was recalled to federal service in 1921, leaving his two sons at the head of the agency he had founded. This was the start of joint ventures against labor organizers, union activists, and eventually "communists." These joint ventures "involved nearly all the possible types of private/public interpenetration and collusion." The parties in league were the Bureau of Investigation's General Intelligence Division and the William J. Burns International Detective Agency. They broke every rule and were involved in corruption scandals. Mr. Burns resigned from the federal service in 1924, when it was known that he had his agents spy on Senator Wheeler, the main critic of the Department of Justice, ransack his office, and entice him into a sexually compromising situation (for this episode, see Weiss, 1986: 100–102).

This interpenetration of public police and private security agents was both an innovation and a regression into the most objectionable police practices. The use of spies and double agents, and the establishment of a symbiotic relation between police detective and the underworld, were as old as the invention of the police by the French in 1667. Yet, the novelty was twofold. First, the relationship was no longer asymmetrical, involving the police institution with individual informants and interlopers. It was established on an equal footing between public and private organizations that acted as institutions. Second, the private agencies were not delinquent agencies staffed with criminals or exoffenders. There is no doubt, however, that these agencies were used as means to outsource police operations of dubious legality and of obvious immorality. A consequence of this reliance on the private sector to do its covert internal political policing is that the United States never developed an internal public internal security service that was distinct from the police, as the United Kingdom did with Military Intelligence (MI5). At the time of writing this book, it is still a branch of the FBI that plays, inadequately, the role of a public security service.

A Hybrid System in Canada

Like Australia and New Zealand, Canada never severed its ties with the United Kingdom (the Queen of England is still the nominal head of the Canadian state, which is otherwise completely independent from England). As expected, its policing institutions reflect in great part those of the United Kingdom and were in fact established by the British, after the conquest of New France in 1760 (Senior, 1997: 63). As regards the history of policing, Canada is noteworthy in three respects.

The historical core of the Canadian territory consists of the central provinces of Ontario and Quebec, which used to be called, respectively, Upper and Lower Canada. It is in these two provinces that the police institutions are most similar to the British model. However, as the Canadian population expanded toward both the east and the west of the two central provinces, the Canadian government had to provide policing to the new developing territories. In order to do that, it created in 1873 the North-West Mounted Rifles, which eventually become the Royal Canadian Mounted Police (RCMP). As its first name indicates, the RCMP was created as a military force and was first led and staffed by exmilitary. As an organization, it was similar to the Royal Ulster Constabulary, which was originally patterned after the French Gendarmerie.

To all practical purposes, Canada has implemented two models of policing: an English, largely decentralized, model that is applied in Ontario and Quebec; and a highly centralized continental Europe model embodied by the RCMP, everywhere else in Canada, with the exception of large cities in the other provinces. These models have contrasting features in many respects. For instance, the RCMP is a nonunionized, militaristic, and highly centralized police force. The many police forces operating in Ontario and Quebec are unionized, nonmilitaristic, and decentralized. The Canadian example shows that policing models with divergent features can be applied side by side and that they are largely compatible in practice.

We have claimed that Canadian police, including the RCMP, were closer to English than to U.S. policing. Although they have firearms, they are less prone to use lethal force than their U.S. counterparts and have not been afflicted by as many corruption scandals. There is not enough space within this book to conduct a detailed comparison. However, the Canadian example should be reflected upon by all of those who believe that the Americanization of criminal justice is the inescapable fate of the Western world. Although no two countries share such a long common border as the United States and Canada, and although the ties between the two countries are very close, Canadian criminal justice institutions are vastly different from those of the United States.

Finally, it is doubtful whether any other country has endowed one of its police forces with enough legitimacy to make it a national symbol. With the maple leaf, the RCMP is undoubtedly a symbol of Canada. This testifies to the symbolic power that can be vested in a police force.

To Conclude

The historical emergence of six models of policing was reviewed in this chapter. The models that were discussed were mediation in primitive societies, the French and German continental European models, the British model, and, in North America, the U.S. and Canadian models. Mediation in primitive societies and the German and the Canadian models were very briefly discussed; more space was devoted to the U.S. model. A contrast between the French and British models of policing provided the main focus of this chapter.

Policing in its specific sense was first invented by the French in 1667 and was reinvented by the British in 1829. The British conception of policing as the prevention and detection of criminal activity prevailed over the more comprehensive French model and was eventually adopted by all democracies, including France, with strong local variants such as a high degree of centralization in continental Europe. I refer to this model as "low policing." The French model provided the template for the creation of security intelligence agencies and for political policing. I refer to this template as "high policing." A separate chapter will be devoted to the distinction between high and low policing. The extent to which these doctrinal models were actually applied on the ground—for instance, the amount of police time effectively devoted to crime control—is still a much-debated question.

The French and the British models were created sequentially. The advent of the British model crystallized several changes in the concept and practice of policing. These changes represented an evolution rather than an historical breakup. Five important transitions should be emphasized: (1) policing evolved from a form of all-encompassing governance to a more specific form of governance: crime control and the preservation of order; (2) the French focus on the abstract notion of governance was superseded by the British concern for the qualifications of the police low-level agents of governance; (3) high policing, which was intelligence-intensive and shaped public opinion, gave way to low policing, which emphasized conspicuous action and was much more labor-intensive (police staff multiplied in every country of Europe in the nineteenth century); (4) the uncontrolled diversity of policing agents was in great part replaced by integrated public police organizations; and (5) the qualifications imposed on the police emphasized morals rather than efficiency and favored means over ends.

Together with these changes, there were repetitions and continuities. The basic repetition consists in the recurrent features of the social and political context that spurred the establishment of police forces. This context displays a certain complexity. On the one hand, the establishment of the police cannot occur unless a territory has been previously pacified, generally by the military. Indeed, the creation of police organizations is the result of a search for alternatives to military heavy-handedness that is perceived to be counterproductive. More precisely, an army requires an open space to be deployed and use its fire power; it is hindered by its operational rules when called upon to perform in the cluttered urban space, where the need for policing was especially acute. Narrow city streets are not the ideal ground for a cavalry charge. On the other hand, there is no denying that a mixture of disorder (caused by rioting), of spectacular violent crime, and of rampant property crime cause a great deal of insecurity for the state and for civil society. These elements, which were present in Paris in the second half of the seventeenth century and in London at the beginning of the nineteenth, stressed the urgency of creating a new force of order. They can also be found in contexts as different as eighteenth-century Germany and nineteenth-century United States.

There were also marked continuities. Economists like Adam Smith, philosophers such as Jeremy Bentham, and reformers like Colquhoun and Chadwick channeled the French idea of police in England. After the Napoleonic wars, everything French became understandably unpopular in England, notwithstanding the fact that British heroes, such as the Duke of Wellington, exchanged ideas on policing with Fouché, the emblematic figure of French high policing. The reformers had to be cautious in advocating French policing ideas, and what they ended up proposing was markedly different from Fouché's "despised" political police. Nevertheless, there were profound continuities between the French and the British model of policing. First, the overwhelming continuity related to the main targets of policing: the non-working poor; and second, the other overarching continuation was the emphasis on surveillance as the main tool of policing. Surveillance was conceived differently within each model: it was covert in France and overt in England. Yet both forms of surveillance strived to intimidate, with the crucial difference that all the populace was to be intimidated in France, whereas only the criminal elements were to be in England. However, the definition of the criminal element was shown to be extensible enough in England to encompass organized labor.

There were historical evolutions, recurrences, and continuities. There was also a legacy of ambiguities, which we have not yet succeeded in dispelling. The first unresolved question relates to the assessment of the success of a preventive police: it is difficult to devise measures for what does not happen. The proverbial decreases in crime rates were never convincing because of the difficulty in isolating the action of the police from other determinants and the facility of manipulating crime statistics. The evaluation problem is still with us.

The second problem concerns the legality of police operations. For all the models examined, with one exception, there is no doubt that the police operated in great part outside the law; it is as if the law, which they often made themselves, did not apply to them. The exception is the British model, which purported to make the police accountable to the law. This ideal coincided with the birth of a tradition of inquiry into the police that has shown how difficult it was to realize this ideal. Furthermore, the British kept using means of dubious legality such as the infiltration of labor movements and the use of active criminals as informants and occasional assistants.

Finally, there are few clues from our historical review that would lead us to define the police by their use of physical violence and coercion. For primitive societies with a weak pattern for the division of labor, it would seem that mediation preceded force as the main tool of conflict solving. The police models elaborated in Europe—including the French and the British—rested much more on the exercise of surveillance than on the use of armed force. This also applied for a time in the United States and Canada. Actually, the mainspring of an unbridled use of armed force was the policing of labor by private agencies in the United States. The Pinkerton and Burns hired hands used their weapons against the workers with the same murderous nonchalance as the Blackwater thugs now do in Iraq. All three questions—prevention, lawfulness, and violence—will be thoroughly discussed in the next chapters.

Police Images

3

This chapter on representations of the police and their work should be read not only as a stand-alone chapter but also in conjunction with chapter 6 on police criminal investigation. This chapter focuses on *police* images and not *crime* images, which is an altogether broader subject that was covered in great part by Ericson and his colleagues (1987, 1989, and 1991), and more recently by Reiner (2002). Researchers have also examined specific questions, such as the dramatization of crime in television shows (Sparks, 1992), the growing number of television reality programs (Fishman and Cavender, 1998), and the effect of media violence on aggression (Freedman, 2002).

Needless to say, there is a considerable amount of overlap between the images of policing and the images of crime. Since I am trying to set the scene for establishing a contrast between media depictions of criminal investigation and my own empirical findings, a significant part of this chapter will be devoted to police fiction. As we shall see, police fiction is almost wholly dedicated to criminal investigation and to the work of detectives. More generally, police fiction, particularly in its written form, has received less attention than it deserves in a general theory of policing. No profession has been nearly as highly fictionalized as the police, except the military, who are the object of high art rather than genre literature.

This chapter is divided into three parts: the police and the media; police fiction; and, to conclude, a summary of the findings together with a discussion of their implications.

The Police and the Media

This area has recently become a growing focus of research (recently, Reiner, 2003; Leishman and Mason, 2003; and Mawby, 2002). There is one feature of these studies that is noticeable in almost all research on the press: the most conspicuous output of the written and the electronic press being news, researchers tend to focus on the content of the news rather than on the process of producing it (Ryan, 1997; Howe, 1998). In my own experience, I have been official spokesman to the press for three Canadian commissions of inquiry into the police and criminal justice. One of these commissions scrutinized security services abuses in the prevention and repression of terrorism in Canada and had a very high media profile (Quebec, 1981a). Another reported on large-scale riots in Montreal, after the Montreal hockey team had won a championship (Quebec, 1993). Following on from this, I became a regular commentator of criminal justice events for the press and was a columnist for a radio program (1998–2001) and for a Montral newspaper, *Le Devoir* (2001–2003). Finally, I was a member of the civilian review committee of the Quebec provincial police force (QPF), which automatically reviewed all media allegations of misconduct by members of the QPF. On the basis of this experience, I came to the conclusion that process—news making—was just as important as content—news content—in reporting on the police, although the process was in great part shielded from the public's eyes. I shall consequently present some observations and hypotheses on the news process, after briefly addressing the issue of content.

Media Content

Robert Reiner has published two extensive reviews of research on the media, crime, and the police, not limiting himself to the British media (Reiner, 2002 and 2003). In both papers, he summarized the characteristics of the content of crime and policing news stories. In Canada, Aaron Doyle studied the images of crime caught on camera and published by the media (Doyle, 2004). Reiner's studies of the media are more comprehensive, since they focus on both crime and policing, and a great deal of what Reiner says on crime is consistent with Doyle's study. I will now comment on the characteristics that Reiner identified. They are as follows.

Frequency. Stories about crime are abundant in all media. This is actually true regardless of the fluctuations in crime rates. For instance, a decrease in violent crime is not reflected by fewer stories in the press, as was shown in the United States after homicides started to go down after 1992. Thus, the reading public is under the impression either that crime increases (when it does) or that its level remain unchanged (when it goes down).

Serious crime. Unsurprisingly, the media concentrate on the most serious crimes, such as homicide and aggravated sexual assault, which also happen to have the highest clear-up rates because of their high profile. The strength of the link between the seriousness of a crime and its clear-up rate is subject to many qualifications. The percentage of unreported sexual offences of the most serious nature is very high. Depending on the social climate (whether there exists a moral panic), the media will run feature stories on unresolved and unreported sexual offences, such a gang rape among juveniles. Within the category of homicide, there are offences with low clear-up rates, such as contract killings related to organized crime warfare and acts of terrorism against persons, the latter cases being much fewer in Western-type democracies. Regardless of their clear-up rate, these offences are extensively reported in the media. Offenders with the highest media profile are still the serial killers, their closest competitors being terrorists. By definition, when a string of murders are categorized as serial, it implies that they have not yet been solved. The identification of one or several serial murderers can take years, as was shown in Vancouver with the 2003 Pickton case involving the killing of many prostitutes over a nineteen-year period (1983–2002).

Bias. Offenders and victims reported in news stories are disproportionately older, white, middle or upper class, when compared the offenders actually processed by the criminal justice system. The exception to this general rule is asymmetric offences, that is offences where there is a great difference of age between offender and victim or where offender and victim do not belong to the same ethnic group (particularly when a member of the white majority is the victim of a minority offender; cases where minority youths are beaten or killed by white offenders, such as Skinheads, do not get the same publicity).

Violence. The media have always overplayed the risk of being a victim of a violent offence and underplayed the risk of being victimized by a property offender. However, fraudulent financial operations involving corporations, prominent investors, or celebrity offenders are generating a great amount of media attention in the volatile economic climate provoked by the worldwide recession of 2008. Some of the frauds perpetrated have been on a massive scale. This type of crime and related misbehavior such as corruption will remain high on the media agenda. One can only speculate on whether these news reports will have an impact on the behavior of small investors.

Police stories. On the whole, the media present a positive image of the success and integrity of the police. Although generally true, this assertion by Reiner is the most problematic. From a police perspective, the media will never be positive enough. In my own experience, many police believe that the media are strongly biased against them, to which the title of books written by journalists bear witness (McShane, 1999: *Cops under Fire: The Reign of Terror against Hero Cops*; see also Lawrence, 2000: *The Politics of Force: Media and the Construction of Police Brutality*). As we shall see, depending on their politics, some news channels give a prominent role to stories on police deviance.

These characteristics borrowed from Reiner are no doubt interesting. However, they mainly apply to only one type of publication format, that is, the news story. Researchers generally acknowledge the differences in the kinds of medium used by the press—written press, radio, TV, and the Internet. However, they generally do not take into account the different constraints that apply to the various publishing formats in which the same basic news content is presented.

There are four kinds of publishing formats in the written press, which have provided the template for all other media: the news stories themselves, the headlines (arbitrarily) capping them, the columns, and the editorials. It is the news stories that are the main focus of research, because they share common semantic characteristics. Generalizations about headlines, columns, and editorials are much harder to make because these formats are much more dependent than stories on the ideological line of a news organization. It is well known that certain newspapers or television channels follow a definite ideological line, some of them actually being the voice of a particular political party, as *Pravda* used to be in the former Soviet Union. Although in the West the ties between a news organization and a political or ideological position are not as official as in the case of *Pravda*, there is no such thing as a completely "neutral" public reporting enterprise. Neutrality is particularly elusive in respect to matters relating to criminal justice. The normative perspective that is strident in headlines, columns, and editorials is in a lower key in news stories. However, it is also reflected in the sort of news stories that a media outlet decides to run or to emphasize. These differences between the ideological perspectives undermine the value of generalizations about the press when considered as a whole and on its willingness to report certain topics, such as police deviance.

Process

By "process" is meant the sequence of actions taken in order to publish a news story. For instance, news stories, their headings, columns, and editorials may be viewed as different sorts of publishing formats. They may also be seen as interactions, at times conflicting, between reporters, headline writers, columnists, and editorialists. Here is a series of constraints on the production of news, within which I have had to work in my past experience.

Time Cycle

News stories have an essential relationship to time—the time an event occurs, or the time of its discovery and public revelation. Anecdotes about individual reporters scrambling to meet deadlines are all too familiar. These time constraints vary from media to media and have wide-ranging implications. First, not all journalists are subject to the same time constraints. Reporters that write features in weekly or monthly magazines are working under different conditions than journalists working for the daily press or TV journals. It has not been sufficiently acknowledged that the most influential reporters are spared the chore of having to meet deadlines on a daily basis. With the exception of investigative reporters, the most basic constraint for a journalist working for the daily press is to have something to say for the next issue of his newspaper or of the evening news. This cannot be too strongly emphasized. The more a government agency moves closer to a journalist's deadline in issuing a press release (in writing or orally through a public spokesman), then the more it can dictate the following day's headlines, which are often literally lifted from the press release for lack of time. Conversely, this constraint also affects government agencies, which strive to stage events to meet—or, in the case of bad news, to avoid—the evening news deadline. The point of these remarks is that a significant part of what goes into print or on the air is uncontrolled, each side—the press and the criminal justice administration—trying to manipulate the other, with the result that the reputation of innocent persons is often inadvertently damaged.

Time also constrains the different players within the media system. Research correctly stresses the differences between the written and the electronic press. Nevertheless, all news organizations are part of a system that echoes stories published in other media, according to a daily time cycle. For instance, radio journalists begin the day very early by reading newspapers, which they follow up in their own news programs; they are then listened to by TV journalists for midday and evening news. Depending on how big a splash a story makes on television, the written press will follow it up. The important research question is not how these different media independently communicate news but how they echo the same events according to their internal rules.

Lowest Denominator

The press has been often criticized for flouting the presumption of innocence (Press Council, 1983; Friendly and Goldfarb, 1967) and for needlessly staining reputations. The high number of civil suits against various news organizations bears witness to the press's apparent lack of respect for privacy and human rights. These criticisms are often justified, but they point to a systemic issue rather than to a generalized disrespect for ethics shown by reporters. In my work as the spokesman for a high-profile commission of inquiry, I witnessed meetings of journalists where they agreed, out of fairness, not to report events that would ruin the reputation of innocent persons who were called before the commission. However, it only took one journalist to break this agreement for these events to become a matter of public record. Then all the other journalists had to follow up on the story in order to keep up with their less ethical colleague. The problematic result of this rule stemming from media competition is that the news-covering press must adjust to the lowest standards applied by any one of its members in a high-profile criminal case.

Dominance

The question of who is the "dominant party" in media relations involving crime reporting has been raised by several authors, the orthodox view being that it is the police (Leishman and Mason, 2003: 42–45). There is no unequivocal answer to this question, dominance or control being largely a matter of negotiation, which depends on many circumstances (Ericson et al., 1989). Nevertheless some rules can be formulated in this respect, which take into account the differences between press organizations. First, the more a news medium is dependent upon visual representations rather than text (tabloids and TV), then the more it must defer to the police, who have the power to grant access to crime scenes or their vicinity and to approach suspects. Second, the more a news medium is specialized in covering crime stories, then the more it must rely on the police and pay heed to their views. Finally, in every local journalistic community, there are reporters known to be "police journalists." Not only have they made crime stories their own special beat, but they also strive to present positive images of the police.

Conflict

The issue of dominance is closely linked to the issue of conflict between the media and the police, as such conflicts contradict the orthodox view of police dominance in its relationship with the media. In contrast to continental Europe, English-speaking countries have a tradition of appointing independent commissions of inquiry that investigate serious allegations of police wrongdoing. These commissions are generally appointed in the wake of media campaigns calling for a public inquiry (Brodeur, 1984a, 1984b, and 2004). There are several newspapers that have developed in their respective countries a long-standing tradition of disclosing police misbehavior and of calling for the appointment of these commissions. Such vigilance has not ingratiated these newspapers with the police. It has also had an unintended effect: by making police organizations over-conscious of the link between their media image and their public legitimacy

(Mawby, 2002), media criticism has driven police organizations to undertake cosmetic rather than actual reforms. In a notorious incident that occurred in Canada in 1990, the Quebec provincial police force (QPF) was so brutal in forcing a crowd to evacuate a bridge on which it was staging a demonstration—the whole incident being recorded live on TV—that the chief of the force felt obliged to apologize publicly to the Quebec population the following day on television. Never before had a Canadian police chief felt obliged to apologize to the population for the misconduct of his men. This incident was only one among the many that occurred during an ethnic crisis in which the Canadian army had to intervene.

The crisis was later investigated by a government board of which I was part. It found that the only measure that the QPF had taken following the biggest crisis in its history was to change the officer who was in charge of its media relations. In interviewing senior staff of the QPF, I was repeatedly told that the only thing that went wrong was that the officer in charge of media relations had not done a proper job. In the wake of its investigation, the board of inquiry recommended that disciplinary proceedings be taken against senior officers charged with dereliction of duty, and that systemic reform be undertaken with respect to the control of collective violence. None of these recommendations was followed. The QPF is far from being the only Canadian police organization that tends to view its lack of experience in dealing with the media as the only reason for the criticism directed against it.

The Media as Police

The role of the media in social control has generally been examined from the standpoint of their contribution to the definition of deviance and the part they play in generating moral panics (Critcher, 2003). Their contribution is actually much more concrete: in several aspects of their functioning, the media are an actual and active part of the police assemblage.

Investigative journalism. The media play an increasing role in revelations about the "crimes of the powerful": corporate crime, environmental delinquency, and political corruption. Investigative journalism is, however, a risky business that also implies the exploitation of leaks from the police. Investigative journalists can thus be manipulated by the police for their own ends. However, it cannot be denied that investigative journalism often independently ferrets out police deviance, and more generally, serious violations of human rights.

Police informants. Journalists may act as registered police informants, referred to by their own individual code. Little is known about this, since the whole field of police informants is cloaked in secrecy. In an unexpected move—according to official doctrine police are supposed to go to extreme lengths to protect the identity of their sources—the RCMP disclosed in 2004 not only the name of a star investigative reporter in Canada, who was one of its sources, but also gave out her code name.

Information channels. In an increasing number of ways—crime-stoppers programs and their many variants, TV reality shows (Fishman and Cavender, 1998), the publication of police ads of wanted suspects, and the broadcasting of live police media conferences—the media are playing an active part in assisting the police in identifying and apprehending criminal suspects.

Technological surveillance. In the case of collective violence, the TV networks may become efficient substitutes of CCTV, their footage being used by the police to identify people who destroy and loot property. The latter are well aware of this use: during the 1993 Stanley cup riots in Montreal, the rioters began by systematically smashing all TV network trucks that were parked near the arena where the final game was to be played. During the following public inquiry, for which I was director of research, we heard media witnesses testifying to having been intimidated by rioting thugs (one female TV reporter had her wallet and house keys taken from her and was warned that there would be reprisals if her reporting led to the identification of rioters). There were similar cases in other Canadian cities, such as Toronto and Vancouver, where there were major riots following a sporting event.

We know much less about these aspects of media action, where the press plays a role through means other than the publication of stories with a specific content. I think that the process by which the media ultimately arrive at the publication of a story deserves more attention than it has so far been accorded, because it is mainly through this process that the media are evolving into being policing agents in their own right, particularly with respect to intentional or unintended visual surveillance. Coupled with the posting on the Internet, the media that use visual technology of any kind are powerful contributors to the advent of the total panoptic society. Certain features of this process, such as becoming a police informant, are only tangentially connected to the production of news stories.

Crime and Police Fiction

Two authors have published a bibliography of essays in various languages on police fiction in writing and in film (Spehner and Allard, 1990). It lists such classics as Benjamin (1972), Bloch (1962), Orwell (1946), and Wilson (1950). This bibliography, nearly twenty years old already, has 731 pages. Its length not only testifies to the amount of research on police fiction but, more important perhaps, on the vastness of police fiction itself, which is the object of so many essays.

More recently, the Oxford (Herbert, 1999) and Cambridge (Priestman, 2003) companions to crime and police fiction have provided excellent surveys of the field, which are completed by Bourdier's history of the genre (Bourdier, 1996). There are also several dictionaries of crime and police fiction (Henderson, 1991, and Jakubowski, 1991), to which the monumental international dictionary of crime literature recently published in France must be added (Mesplède, 2003).

Tales of crime are pervasive in all literature, and they cannot be confined to a particular genre, although crime fiction does constitute a particular literary genre (Ruggiero, 2003). Researchers use various names to refer to crime fiction: gothic and horror stories, private-eye books, thrillers, mysteries, murder stories, police procedurals and, more recently, spy stories. With the possible exception of spy stories and early gothic, all crime fiction includes private or public police among its main characters.

Crime fiction has a prominent place within all media—written, radio, television, film, and video games. It is produced on a mass scale. As early as 1984, the Marxist economist Ernest Mandel, who was a murder story fan, listed nine authors who had sold more than one hundred million books, Agatha Christie having sold more than 500 million at that time. According to recent press releases, Dame Agatha has now sold over two billion books, and crime fiction is a genre that is second only to general fiction, an all-encompassing category. According to figures tabulated in Brooks and Marsh (1995), 268 new crime serial programs playing on U.S. prime-time TV were created from 1949 to 1994, with an average of some six new programs billed every year. In 1987, these crime programs accounted for 22.5 hours per week (out of a total of 28 hours of prime time). In 2004, both CBS (in the United States) and CTV (in Canada) showed eleven hours of crime fiction per week, in prime time.

Although the mass audience of film and TV police fiction may be larger than the readership of written police novels—this not being altogether certain—this chapter focuses on written texts. Not only have they defined the basic rules of the genre, but film and TV police fiction have brought to the screen stories that were first published in writing, this being particularly true of film. The aim of this brief review of police fiction is not to analyze it for its own sake, but to contrast it with some of the findings of police research, particularly in the case of criminal investigation.

Police Fiction: General Features

Police fiction belongs to the category of crime fiction, which has its early beginning in the gothic tale (Bell, 2003; Tompkins, 1932). Crime and police fiction make up a particular literary genre within the novel. In contrast with artistic literature, genre literature such as fairy tales and folk narratives follow a strict pattern; the narrower the genre, the stricter the pattern. In a groundbreaking study, Vladimir Propp has shown that nearly all Russian folk tales followed a similar pattern: an initial state of harmony is broken by the theft or disappearance of a precious object and is reestablished at the end by its recovery (Propp, 1975). We must therefore be cautious in our analysis of police fiction: the fact that TV crime stories are moral tales that give viewers reassurance (Sparks, 192: chap. 6) may be given a sociological interpretation or it may simply result from the formal rules of a particular genre that generally favors happy endings (with the notable exception of noir crime fiction).

Although its formal structure is generally predictable, police fiction may vary from one country to another, particularly with respect to its heroes. The avuncular police constable George Dixon, who embodied on TV a caring rather than a controlling style of policing, was for a time a quintessential image of the British bobby (Reiner, 1994: 21); in U.S. movies, it was rather the gun-toting inspector Harry Callahan—Dirty Harry—who "made the day" of U.S. film audiences. This contextual feature of police fiction is another reason to be cautious in our conclusions. With these reservations in mind, some recurrent traits of police fiction will be discussed.

Constables and Investigators

Edgar Allan Poe is generally credited with the invention of crime and mystery writing in three tales featuring the Chevalier C. Auguste Dupin—*The Murders in Rue Morgue* (1841), *The Mystery of Marie Rogêt* (1842), inspired by the New York "cigar-girl" murder that was never solved, and the *Purloined Letter* (1845). Poe's amateur detective provided the template for nearly all future private sleuths who solved crimes in their armchairs by reflecting upon clues. The dominance of the investigator over the uniformed constable is so overwhelming in written literature and in film that it has given police fiction one of its current names—detective stories.

Although the imbalance is not as blatant on TV, such characters as *Dixon of Dock Green* and programs like *Z-Cars* having enjoyed a wide popularity on British TV, the prevalence of plainclothes policepersons is still evident on U.S. TV. Of 268 different crime and law-enforcement programs shown on U.S. TV from 1949 to 1994, only sixteen featured cops in uniform as their main characters (another sixteen featured lawyers, prosecutors, or judges, who were generally assisted by detectives playing a prominent role). Depending on how you categorize programs featuring lawyers, investigators starred in between 88 and 94 percent of U.S. TV programs for that period (Brooks and Marsh, 1995; also see Perlmutter, 2000). The preeminence of investigators is in part due to a formal trait of narratives: they tell stories that must extend in time. As uniformed officers deal with short-term events, the work of detectives to solve crimes over time lends itself much more to storytelling than does quick police crisis intervention. As we shall see in chapter 6, the lengthy investigation is also a myth, most murders being solved in a matter of hours by the intervening uniformed police.

The nearly exclusive focus of police fiction on crime investigation stands in stark contrast to the focus of research. According to recent research conducted in main police research databases from 1967 to 2002, criminal investigation is the least researched topic of all (National Research Council, 2003a). It would then seem that, in the English-speaking world, criminal investigation falls almost totally within the bounds of fiction, whereas policing in uniform is an area restricted to research.

Private Eyes and Public Investigators

This dichotomy, even opposition, is also at the core of police fiction. It neatly follows from the previous one: at a time when there were few police detectives, the primacy of the investigator first translated into the prominence of the private eye. As was seen in the preceding chapter, public investigators were a late and limited increment to the public police. Working in plainclothes, the private eye filled in for the missing public investigators and thus reinforced the dominance of detectives in police fiction. Until the relatively late advent of the "police procedural," police fiction was widely dominated by gifted eccentric amateurs in Europe and by tough private eyes in the United States. Among the first generation of detectives, the French Commissaire Maigret is the only public police character to have achieved the mythical status enjoyed by Sherlock Holmes, Lord Peter Wimsey, Hercule Poirot, Nero Wolfe, or Philip Marlowe, to name just a few private investigative celebrities.

Private investigators and public police have often been presented in pairs by writers, the public officer acting as a foil for the much cleverer private detective (for example, Inspector Lestrade vis-à-vis Sherlock Holmes). In its celebration of the private sleuth, police fiction provided a background for criticisms of the public police (slow-witted, bureaucratic, and corrupted). One can consider the shift in favor of the public police that is displayed in police procedurals as an indication of its professionalization and heightened status.

Insiders and Outsiders

This contrast takes many forms, all of them securing the predominance of the outsider, which is a general rule of fiction: heroes must stand out. By definition, all private eyes are outsiders, particularly if they belong to a police minority. So are, to a large extent, women investigators such as Thomas Harris's Clarice Starling, whose career is fledging before taking on the case of a serial killer in *Hannibal*. In spy thrillers such as those of Tom Clancy or even, at times, John Le Carré, the hero is not a member of the organization, being recruited as an outside analyst (Tom Clancy's Jack Ryan) or being manipulated by insiders, such as in Le Carré's *The Honourable Schoolboy*. In recent times, forensic experts (Dr. Kay Scarpetta) and criminal profilers (Starling's mentor, Jack Crawford) who are viewed with suspicion by their police colleagues have assumed an increasing importance.

The most frequent illustration of this in-group/out-group polarity, however, is the investigator who is in conflict with his own organization, either because he flouts legal procedure and takes justice into his own hands (the Dirty Harry prototype, by far the most frequent; see Lenz, 2003: 176), because he is critical of police bureaucracy (Wahloo and Sjöwall's Martin Beck or Ian Rankin's John Rebus) or because he is an unreachable loner (Connelly's Hieronymus Bosch). In police procedurals, the heroes are often persecuted by their department's internal affairs unit, and suspension of the main character (who resolves the murder on his own) is a familiar occurrence (for example, Jimmy McNulty in the television series *The Wire*). One of the most persistent themes of police fiction is that you cannot be a successful investigator by applying the rules in the book. The only true organizational hero is Simenon's Inspector Maigret. Despite the fact that his methods of blending into the environment are perceived as unorthodox, Maigret is venerated by his colleagues and is a strong team player with his closest associates. In his fictitious memoirs (*Les mémoires de Maigret*, 1951), Maigret himself claims that "with all due respect to novel writers, a policeman is above all a professional. He is a civil servant" (quoted in Mesplède, 2003: 2:254). There is an ironical twist to the fact that the fictional celebrity detective best integrated in his organization is French, the French being notoriously critical of their police establishment.

Super-Sleuths and Great Criminals

Describing how crimes and criminals are represented in police fiction falls outside the scope of this book, except when the representation of criminals is a direct consequence of the way the police themselves are shown. Whether they are private eyes, gifted amateurs, police detectives, or international spies, police characters are depicted as heroes in the sense that they have qualities and skills that set them apart and allow them to prevent or solve crimes. A literary genre cannot rest on losers. As was stressed by many researchers, it is the great criminal—the great collar—that makes the great police officer. It therefore follows that from Professor Moriarty to Dr. Hannibal Lecter, most criminals appearing in police fiction are super-criminals because of their cunning, their energy, and, more generally, the great danger that they pose to society. Although historians agree that the level of internal violence in Western-type societies has decreased since the end of the nineteenth century, and although murder statistics have been going down in most of these countries since 1990, the current fad for serial killers has resulted in unprecedented violence in crime fiction, which seems to be regressing toward gothic horror. The pairing of super-sleuths with great criminals reaches its apex when both extremes coincide. Such is the case with the TV character named Dexter, who is a serial killer who eliminates serial killers, and the hero of *24*, who unabashedly uses torture to find the "ticking bomb" before it explodes. According to the Parents Television Council based in Los Angeles, the number of incidents of torture on prime-time network television in the United States was 110 from 1994 to 2001. This number increased to 897 for the period 2002 to 2007. The repercussions of such crass TV serials on the popular conception of policing should not be underestimated.

Police Fiction: Criminal Investigation

Criminal investigation is, as was seen, the main subject of police fiction, although not the only one. The main features of criminal investigation, as it is represented in police fiction, will now be examined.

Murder Investigations

Various offences such as rape and theft may be the subject of artistic literature. One thinks of Faulkner's *Sanctuary* for rape and of Gogol's novella "The Overcoat" for theft. Murder plays a large role in world literature, particularly in theatrical plays. However, crime is almost never approached in the general literature through a narrative of its investigation: the author is known from the start, as is the case in Dostoyevsky's *Crime and Punishment*, which is a study in the evolution of psychological guilt. The investigation of crime, as we have seen, has created its own genre literature, which is referred to by different names, such as "detective stories." Detective stories are almost exclusively murder stories. *The Purloined Letter* by Edgar Allan Poe is perhaps the most famous exception to this rule, the low seriousness of the offence—the theft of a letter—being in this case compensated for by the fact that its victim is a member of royalty and the offender a cabinet minister. Here, the contrast between police reality and crime fiction reaches one of its highest points: in most countries, murder represents the smallest proportion of all offences committed and later investigated by the police.

Reactive Policing

Criminal investigation generally takes place after a murder or some other serious offence has been perpetrated. The reactive nature of police fiction goes against the claim that police should above all be preventive. Therein lays the biggest difference between police fiction and spy thrillers. To the extent that they involve a struggle against terrorism, the plot of spy thrillers generally consists of the prevention of mass murder (for example, *Black Sunday* by Thomas Harris), of political assassination (for example, *The Day of the Jackal* by John Forsythe or *The Terrorist* by Wahloo and Söjwall), or the foiling of large-scale conspiracies (such as Robert Ludlum's novels). Few crime stories bear on finding the perpetrators of a terrorist act after it has been successfully committed; the hunt for the perpetrators would only appear in fiction as an anticlimax compared to the magnitude of the offence perpetrated.

Lengthy Inquiries

In real-life policing, homicides are either solved very quickly (within one day) or not at all, the probability of success for the investigation decreasing dramatically with each passing hour. In great part because of the rules governing narratives, murder investigations have to extend over several days for the story to be written. This constraint is compounded by the fact that in many murder stories the interest of the reader is sustained by the committing of a sequence of murders that thicken the plot (not to mention the outright serial murder thrillers that have invaded the market).

The Tools of the Trade

As Ernest Mandel perspicaciously stressed, the detective story is about the restoration of rationality against the disorder created by the perpetration of a murder (Mandel, 1984: 44). Indeed, the path followed in a detective story is a progression to a state of knowing from a state of ignorance, through the resources of reason. These resources are the following.

Deduction. The first incarnation of reason is the *deductive mind*. Historically, all the great detectives could reason impeccably, Poe's Chevalier Dupin having initially set a pattern that was set in stone by Sherlock Holmes. At the beginning of the twentieth century, author Jacques Futrelle created the character of Professor Van Dusen, an armchair detective known as the "thinking machine" (*The Thinking Machine Investigates* is the title of Futrelle's second book). Until the advent of the hard-boiled characters of Raymond Chandler and Dashiell Hammett, all sleuths were deductive automatons.

Physical clues. The deductive mind works from clues. Physical clues may be conspicuous and readily available for examination at the scene of the crime, as they were in Poe's seminal short stories. However, forensic medicine and forensic science rapidly developed from the middle of the nineteenth century with the work of Bertillon (criminal anthropology), Tarde, and Quételet, in France (Kaluszynski, 2002). It spread throughout Europe and begat momentous inventions such as fingerprinting. Physical clues had to be scientifically processed in order to reveal their true secrets. From Conan Doyle to Patricia Cornwell, police fiction was quick to capitalize on forensics, which is now taking such an increasing place in crime fiction that it is giving birth to a new subgenre—the forensic thriller. The forensic thriller exaggerates so much the power of technologies such as genetic fingerprinting, biometrics, and the various "crime scene identification" gimmicks that it is increasingly overlapping with science fiction.

Data banks. The storage of information in criminal files is as old as the birth of the police in France. However, it has been the object of an exponential growth in the computer age. Researching data banks of all conceivable sorts ("data mining") is now as much part of police fiction as was looking at physical evidence with a magnifying glass in Sherlock Holmes's times. The cult of computerized intelligence has now become so intensive that, like mythologizing the power of forensics, it is creating a convergence between police fiction and science fiction.

Criminal profiling. All the resources and instruments of the fictional detective—deductive mind, physical clues, forensic medicine (including psychiatry) and science, data banks, and even geography—are pooled together in the practice of criminal profiling, which in reality is a fragmented field involving a score of overlapping yet different practices: criminal and psychological profiling, crime scene analysis and profiling, behavioral profiling, criminal personality profiling, statistical profiling, profile analysis, investigative psychology, and geographical profiling (Ainsworth, 2001: 8). In crime fiction, these distinctions do not need to be made, as criminal profiling is essentially defined as the opposing correlate of serial killing: a profiler is someone who uses his or her brain to catch a serial killer. Such a person performs in crime fiction a role similar to that of a diviner in antique tragedy: the decoding of signs, whatever their nature may be. Crime profiling has attained a mythical status through two of Thomas Harris's books: *Red Dragon* and the *Silence of the Lambs*. It is now featured in films and TV series (*The Profilers* in the United States and *Cracker* in Britain). The present fashion enjoyed by serial killers and criminal profilers is transforming police fiction into a populist exercise in semiotics (the study of signs; Simpson, 2000: 76). Ironically, the only kind of profiling that is current in police work—racial profiling—is seldom mentioned in the research on profiling and in crime fiction because of its political incorrectness.

This brief enumeration is not exhaustive and has focused on standard crime fiction. In spy thrillers and in police science fiction, a wide array of complex surveillance technology is also used by the main characters.

Finally, there are two other features of murder stories that stand in utter contrast with police investigative practice. The first one concerns the relationship between detection and conviction. As we shall see in chapter 6, scientific policing tools play almost no part in the solving of actual cases. However, forensics plays an important role, ex post facto, in securing the conviction of offenders—more specifically murderers—in court. Offenders charged with first-degree murder have nothing to gain by entering a guilty plea. Proving their guilt in court can become a complex undertaking, and scientific policing is called upon to persuade magistrates and juries of the guilt of the accused. With the exception of courtroom thrillers, which are but a fraction of crime fiction despite their considerable popularity, most detective stories end before the trial. In many cases there is good reason for this, when the death of the offender provides a fitting end to the book. More usually however, it is a general assumption of crime fiction that the person finally designated as the perpetrator in the book is in effect the guilty party. The outcome of an investigation is never flawed. Unless it is from the beginning the subject of a book (for example, the Perry Mason thrillers), the presumption of innocence plays no part in crime fiction with respect to the solution provided by the police investigation. In consequence, securing a conviction is viewed as a technical matter of little narrative interest.

The second contrasting feature relates to the efficacy of team work. In police procedurals such as the *87th Precinct* series of novels (which were also adapted for TV), there is an emphasis on team work, which misrepresents the fiercely competitive nature of the profession. Unless an author wants to make a point against the police, police fiction generally stresses cooperation and the sharing of information between different forces and between the police forces of various countries, generally through Interpol. For instance, the FBI makes it a point to share its information with local police forces in police fiction (notably in Thomas Harris's work). This runs contrary to the conclusions of various official inquiries into the behavior of this police agency (for example, in the inquiries that followed 9/11). As for Interpol, it is the product of an informal agreement between police forces and has never received any government sanction (Anderson, 1989). Its action is therefore very limited. Although it is developing, international cooperation between police agencies still has many obstacles to overcome (Bigo, 1996).

Looping in and Looping out: The Low-Definition Environment

Peter Manning has worked extensively on the relationship between policing and information technology (Manning, 1988 and 1992). This work has led him to write a series of studies on the media and policing, which are brought together in a paper—entitled "Media Loops"—that spearheads many current trends in the study of media and police (Manning, 1998). This paper studies the making of three media events or series of such events: the broadcasting of the 1991 video recording of the beating of Rodney King and the ensuing events, the proto-reality show *Cops* (1989–1991), and the live coverage of the hours following the 1995 Oklahoma bombing. Manning formulates six reality rules describing "the cognitive work necessary to convert the flickering of television onto a believable mini-portrait of society" (Manning, 1998: 29–30). These media portrayals of society become, in certain dramatic instances, "media events" that are *looped back into* reality to define the political agenda or provoke further events, such as the Los Angeles riots that followed the acquittal of the police charged with beating Rodney King. Manning's paper exemplifies an important trend in accounting for the links between media and policing. The account is produced from a standpoint where the media are in the driver's seat, as one of the subtitles of the paper testifies ("A media-driven society," Manning, 1998: 28). Within such an account, the structural sequence is the following: first, an external event; second, its portrayal and making into a media event; and third, the looping back of the media event into reality. What is now referred to as the "CSI effect" is a spectacular illustration of a media artefact looping back into reality. The CSI effect was generated by a highly popular TV serial entitled "Crime Scene Investigation," which fictionalizes the work of forensic scientists. According to various studies, the CSI effect is a phenomenon whereby television-"educated" jurors are more likely to not convict an accused because procedures and techniques they observed from the fictional television show were not applied to the case (Heinrick, 2006: 59). The alleged existence of such a CSI effect on jurors who are persuaded of the infallibility of forensic evidence has spurred a lot of controversy among legal scholars.

Serial killings, such as the ones perpetrated in the Washington, D.C., area by Lee Boyd Malvo and John Allen Muhammad at the beginning of 2003, are huge media events that feed the fad for "criminal profilers." An ex-FBI agent—Robert Ressler—credits himself for having popularized the expression "serial killer" (also see Douglas, 1996). He is the co-author of a homicide primer (Ressler et al., 1988), from which this quote is excerpted:

> Although Lunde has stated that the murders of fiction bear no resemblance to the murders of reality…a connection between fictional detective techniques and modern profiling methods may indeed exist. For example, it is an attention to detail that is the hallmark of famous fictional detectives; the smallest item at a crime scene does not escape their notice. [This] is stated by the famous Sergeant Cuff in Wilkie Collin's

1868 novel *The Moonstone*, widely acknowledged as the first full-length detective story.... [A]ttention to detail is equally essential to present-day profiling. No piece of information is too small; each detail is scrutinized for its contribution to a profile of the killer. (Ressler et al., 1988, quoted in Simpson, 2000: 79)

As Simpson correctly remarks, the writings of professional profilers is "a particularly empty or hollow style of writing...almost offensively self-lauda-tory...[that] fits within a long literary and cultural tradition" (Simpson, 2000: 79). Despite their smugness, these writings point to an important fact: the inversion of the historically expected sequence of fact and fiction. We now have: first, a fictional portrayal of detection (Collin's); second, its framing of crime detection practices (crime profiling); and third, the loop back of reality into fiction—most notably the Lecter novels of Thomas Harris, who makes no mystery of his FBI acquaintances. The subversion of reality by fiction is unmistakable in Ressler et al.'s assertion in the quote given above that "No piece of information is too small" (for the fiction-inspired profiler). With today's forensic technology, the smallest piece of information can be compared to the particles in the physics of quanta: it is not a given, but "a fact in progress" that depends on the development of our measurement technology (DNA signatures would have escaped famous Sergeant Cuff).

Looping in and looping out can be sequenced into an integrated series, where each moment is summarily identified: first, the fictional "Sergeant Cuff" and similar characters; second, the true-life FBI profilers seeking recognition; third, the looping out of their doings to serial killer fiction (for example, the Thomas Harris novels); fourth, real-life serial killing events (for example, the Malvo-Muhammad killings); fifth, their framing on "live" TV with repeated interviews of crime profilers acting like fortune tellers; and sixth, the looping of the TV frame back into reality—the Malvo trial, the issue of whether to execute juveniles, and so forth. This sequencing of media looping into reality and of police work looping out to crime fiction should be the subject of more exploration.

I also want to introduce another concept, however. It could be hypothesized that media looping in and looping out produce what could be called a low-definition environment, when they are functioning as a system, as they are increasingly doing. "Low definition" does not mean a relative failure of our effort to provide scientific or semantic definitions of diverse aspects of the environment. What is meant is "low-definition environment" in a sense similar to what is said when photo and TV images lack definition and are blurry: a low-definition environment blurs the difference between the external environment and its representation in the media, including fiction. It blends fact and fiction into a mixture where the original ingredients can no longer be distinguished. In the famous U.S. television series *Dallas*, there was an attempt on the life of the main character "JR" (John Ross Ewing Jr.) by another (yet) unidentified character. The press ran numerous stories asking "who shot JR?" as if he were a real person. In the same way, many people believe that Sherlock Holmes was a detective who actually lived in nineteenth-century London, where a replica of his apartment can be visited. It is important in this regard to differentiate between individual and mass perceptions. As was said at the beginning, reality imposes itself on the individual (who is not mentally deluded). However, the law of necessity does not impose itself with the same force on individuals and on populations, which are prone to mass-movement irrationality. When all perceptions of reality are mixed together, the end result may be a systemic social inability to react differently to reality and to its images.

Summary and Discussion

Researchers are justifiably cautious in drawing inferences from their findings on crime reporting and on police fiction (Ericson et al., 1989, Sparks, 1992, and Leishman and Mason, 2003). Caution is especially warranted when trying to assess the effect of representations on reality. In this respect, there are recurrent issues such as whether violence in the media affects actual behavior or to what extent the press succeeds in framing reality (Manning, 1998). These issues will not be addressed directly; the examination here will be limited to the meaning for a theory of policing of the representations of the police in the press and in police fiction, focusing, as was said earlier, on police fiction rather than on the press. Since factual and normative issues are intrinsically linked within a theory of the police, the question of police reform must be discussed. To this extent, the impact of representations of the police on policing reality and also on the possibility of changing it ought to be addressed, at least in part.

Police Reality and Its Representation

A few general statements on the significance of policing representations, whether they claim to be true, as in the press, or indeed make no such claim, as in fiction, ought to be made in order to properly frame the issues.

First, although one should not forget the difference between images and reality, which in any event imposes itself upon us in respect to the concrete necessities of life, one makes no scientific gain in dichotomizing them. Whereas images ought not to be substituted for reality, they are in themselves an important part of the social environment in which we all live. Producing and selling images is, for instance, a powerful and lucrative industry. What needs to be stressed even more is that media events are events of the world and cannot be disregarded, as if they belonged to some lesser reality.

Second, fiction is a way to explore reality (Banks and Banks, 1998) and, within its specific narrative rules, it must be accurate in its depiction of reality. Characters in novels may be fictitious but their psychology, their behavior, and the settings in which they evolve must have some degree of correspondence to reality; good novelists actually spend extended periods of time researching their subject and making sure that they paint "a true picture" of certain aspects of reality. Karl Marx said that he learned much more about economic reality from Balzac than from the economists of his time.

Third, there is probably no field other than policing where the notion of intertextuality has a broader application. In police narratives, intertextuality transcends the written text and links all media (writing, film, TV, and video). It bridges the gap between press reporting and fiction writing through many authors who have been first police press reporters and then best-selling crime novelists (George Simenon, Michael Connelly, and Patricia Cornwell, to name a few). Celebrated authors were once professionally involved in the world that they describe (Ian Fleming and John Le Carré both had a stint in an intelligence service). Most important, crime and police fiction have played a key role in generating a hybrid genre that amalgamates fact and fiction and that is variously referred to under the appellations of "infotainment," "faction," and "docudrama."

The gist of the previous remarks is to stress that the degree of truthfulness to be found in policing representations and, more specifically, in the press is greater than usually believed and ought to be taken into account—the crime stories based on the use of forensic science are quite knowledgeable about it, except for the fact that it very rarely solves cases by itself. This conclusion leads to a paradox, which stems from the disproportion between the very limited trust vested by the public in the press and the great power attributed to the media. In all Western-like democracies, public opinion is surveyed every year on the basis of the trust it invests in some twenty-five professions. I have researched these public opinion polls (1998–2006) through various Web sites, in Australia, Canada, France, the United Kingdom, and the United States, and concluded they all consistently say the same thing: the press is always listed among the five professions enjoying the least trust (politicians are generally in the last position); competing with journalists as the least trusted professions are car dealers, real estate agents, business leaders, and trade unionists. Whatever the reservations we may have toward public opinion surveys, these results are too consistent over time and space to be ignored. These findings raise two issues. The short-term and immediately obvious issue is that the "power of the press" may have been greatly exaggerated, and that people read the news according to Lord Beaverbrook's dictum: news is just what separates the various pieces of advertisement. The same rule would apply to commercial radio and television. The long-term issue, which cannot be addressed here, is that trust and legitimation make no difference with respect to power: either you have power or you do not, and if you do, you simply exercise it without any second thoughts. This issue springs directly from the fact that all professions that wield the most power—politicians, business leaders, and the press, not to mention trade unionists—are the most discredited with respect to trust, according to polls that were reviewed.

Police Fiction and Police Research: A Contrast

The contrast between police fiction and crime investigation will become obvious in chapter 6, which looks at criminal investigation. Nevertheless, we can already note a persistent decoupling of police research and police fiction. First, police research is almost exclusively focused on police wearing uniform and intervening in very different contexts. Second, as was seen in the previous chapter on history, the variety of incidents that the police are dealing with is said to be such that it frustrates any attempt to provide a single explicit definition of policing. One of the most general features of police research is, as we shall see, to try to figure out what police constables are actually doing and, more specifically, what proportion of their working time is devoted to law enforcement and crime detection, this proportion generally being assessed as rather low (between 15 and 30 percent of their working time). Finally, not only is police research focused on officers in uniform but criminal investigation is the least researched topic of policing research. This appraisal of research is probably even truer in the field of private security, where researchers focus on some very general concerns, nearly all of them related to the growth of private policing in Western-type democracies. With the exception of historical works on particular agencies such as Pinkerton's, there is almost no research on private investigation.

Although there are notable exceptions, such as David Simon's TV serial entitled *The Wire*, police fiction is, in almost in every respect, the reverse image of policing research. First, its almost single focus is criminal investigation, presented as an activity that can be conducted from a private eye's armchair or from a crime lab. Second, criminal investigation is not only concentrated upon crime but it also centers on one type of crime, namely murder. Finally, the problem of professional time allocation is easy to solve within police fiction: the greater part of it—if not all—is actually devoted to the investigation of a murder. This is in part the result of narrative and commercial constraints. A popular narrative is linear and cannot afford to meander at random without jeopardizing its selling potential. Good escapist literature must be filled with exciting events: the best praise that a critic can shower on a murder story is that it is a compulsive "page-turner" and that one cannot stop reading it, so gripping is its story. The word "thriller" that is also used to refer to crime fiction indicates that this kind of fiction implicitly begets its own notion of time: the pace is fast, time is compressed by action, without breaks and idle periods. The car chase, with its high level of adrenalin, is a fitting symbol of the representation of time.

Media Impacts

As was stressed previously, the question of media—press and fiction—is a difficult one, and it is preferable to begin with what stands out most clearly. The bond joining policing and law enforcement is pervasive and overwhelming; crime fiction and press coverage speak with one voice in this regard. The connection between policing and crime control is constantly reinforced by two factors. First, crime fiction plays infinite variations on almost a single theme: homicide. The particular challenge that must be met by an author is to be original within a narrative framework that is both rigid and sparse in the elements allowed to define a plot. The efficiency of police fiction in articulating stereotypes that condition both public and professional opinion relies for a significant part on the recurrent features of its message. Despite appearances, the same is true of the press, where being given the police beat is not a prize assignment because of its relative monotony; as soon as a crime story makes the front page because of its wider implications, it is generally taken out of the hands of police reporters.

Both crime writers and reporters try to compensate for the repetitious content of their message by sensationalizing the most shocking features, which generally means hyping the violence involved in the press or fictional stories. Therein lays the second impulse boosting the power of the dissemination of stereotypes by the media (press and fiction): they are infused with an intense emotional resonance because of the macabre and at times horrific twist given to them in order to single them out. The mobilizing force of criminal events is not exclusively due to their frequency, but also to their singularity, as is shown by the shock following events such as the 1993 murder of the child James Bulger by two underage boys in England, and the Dutroux affair, which involved the widespread sexual abuse and murder of young girls and sent hundreds of thousands of demonstrators to the streets of Brussels in 1996.

How do these stereotypes connect with reality? This connection is rarely direct, that is, joining images to real-life behavior. Rather, it tends to generate a cascade of mindsets that ripples through society and the criminal justice system and affects various groups such as the respondents to public opinion polls on security, police recruits, and politicians involved in policy making.

Four issues can be singled out in this respect. The first concerns the definition of the police mandate. Press reports and police fiction narrow down the definition of the police mandate to law enforcement and crime fighting. Although it is at odds with what the police are actually doing or will be asked to do, the younger police rank and file and police recruits tend to accept this definition of their mandate, and among their tasks they value those closest to the media stereotypes (Zhao and Thurman, 1997). These images also tend to affect recruits, in that it leads them to believe that they are joining a profession that offers a life full of action. According to my frequent teaching experiences in police academies, the "car chase" mythology is the first that instructors have to debunk. They never completely succeed, as the stereotype factory weighs much more heavily with respect to policing than the police academy, in which they spend limited time.

A second issue relates to expectations toward the police. Press coverage and police fiction raise expectations with respect to police efficiency. As we saw, Reiner argues that the crimes most likely to be reported in the press are those that have a high clear-up rate. In detective stories, the police clear-up rate is optimal. The police seem to be caught in a circle in this regard: the media raise expectations with respect to the efficiency of crime investigation, and they apply pressure by whipping up public opinion against the police when these expectations are not fulfilled in high-profile cases. This two-pronged attack has two unintended effects. It increases the number of wrongful arrests and convictions, which is now shown to be much higher than originally believed. It also fosters conspiracy theories undermining the credibility of the police, when high-profile crimes, such as political assassinations, are not solved at all.

Shaping the answers given to pollsters is a third issue, which is connected to political decision making. Sparks (1992: 153 and ff.) offers a thoughtful discussion of the relationship between police drama series on television and public fear, and although he is reluctant to assert a causal relationship between TV drama and public fearfulness, he nonetheless agrees that dramatizations of crime are a prime arena for the discussion of social anxiety. Despite being cautious about the relationship between TV crime fiction and fear, he does commit himself in the end to a description of how such fear may influence overt behavior. This illustrates the predicament that was described above: media images may influence mental representations and emotions, but reaching beyond the gap that separates images and behavior appears to be as difficult as jumping over one's shadow. Yet the notion of a cascading of representations toward "reality" suggests that there may hypothetically be a point where the media rubber hits the policy road.

According to research on media-induced fear, this kind of anxiety rarely translates into a change into one's daily behavior (Skogan, 1986). It does, however, translate into one kind of behavior that is politically quite influential: answering public opinion surveys. Even the most scientifically conducted surveys—such as *Policing for London* (PFLS), undertaken on behalf of several private foundations—replicate in their findings the content of media messages. The survey just referred to asked what people wanted from police on patrol: 65 percent of the sample answered deterring or preventing crime, and 49 percent said providing reassurance; the rest of the options—working with schools, gathering local intelligence, dealing with disturbances, and providing advice on crime prevention—elicited the assent of merely 25 percent of the respondents (Fitzgerald et al., 2002: 43). As governments tend to rely heavily on public opinion surveys to determine their policies, opinion polls may be the oblique way in which police and crime representations are channeled into the political agenda.

There is finally the issue of police reform. Starting from the 1980s, there were strong movements for police reform, the most strongly advocated reforms being community-oriented policing and problem-oriented policing. In the PFLS survey quoted above, two of the key components of community policing—striking partnerships (for example, with schools) and reacting against disorder (dealing with disturbances) were not favored by the majority of respondents. Minorities (Pakistani, Bangladeshi, and blacks) were more supportive of community policing methods than the white majority. Gathering local intelligence, which is a crucial tool for intelligence-led policing, was only supported by 24 percent of the sample surveyed by the PFLS. It would then appear that when police reform is driven by research, it does not find popular support on its own merits, if it has a low media profile. The much-hyped NYPD CompStat program was used by politicians and police media personalities to promote their careers. It could boast of a scientific/statistical approach to law enforcement understood in its most traditional sense and therefore met with greater media success than community-oriented policing.

Elements of a Theory of Policing

The definition of "police" proposed by David Bayley in the *Encyclopedia of Crime and Justice* is: "In the modern world, police generally refers to persons employed by government who are authorized to use physical force to maintain order and safety" (Bayley, 1983a: 1120; also see Bayley, 1985: 7–11). This formulation is based on Egon Bittner's definition of the role of the police through their use of force (Bittner, 1970/1990: 131).[1] Bittner's influence on the definition of the police function was pervasive from the beginning of the 1970s and has grown ever since. Jones and Newburn (1998: 258) correctly remarked that "sociologists have not improved upon this [Bittner's] definition in the past twenty-five years." It is quoted, paraphrased, or expanded in works as diverse as Monjardet (1996: 16–17), Bayley (1985: 7), Newburn (2003: 5), Loader and Mulcahy (2003: 106), Manning (2003: 41–42) and, for Brazil, Proença Junior and Muniz (2006).

Having written on Bittner (Brodeur 1984b, 1994a) and been instrumental in the translation of parts of his work into French (Bittner, 1991; Brodeur and Monjardet, 2003), I met with him in Berkeley in May 2000 for a two-day interview that was based on a list of questions that I had previously submitted to him. The present discussion of his work is based on a reading of his publications and on the clarifications that he provided in May 2000. I published an edited version of the interview under the title "An Encounter with Egon Bittner" (Brodeur, 2007, with an introduction by Peter K. Manning; in this chapter, the interview will be referred to as "Bittner/Brodeur, 2007" to underscore the fact that I only asked the questions and Bittner provided the answers).

---

1. See note 1 in chapter 1 for the format of the references to Bittner's work.

Bittner's perspective on the police is encapsulated in two basic propositions. The first is the definition of the role of the police: "the role of the police is best understood as a mechanism for the distribution of non-negotiably coercive force employed in accordance with the dictates of an intuitive grasp of situational exigencies" (Bittner, 1970/1990: 131). The second is the characterization of the typical circumstances in which the police are called to act and which are summed up in the following description: "something-that-ought-not-to-be-happening-and-about-which-someone-had-better-do-something-now" (Bittner, 1974/1990: 249).

Variations on these two themes were provided by Bittner himself and are also widely circulated throughout the scholarly literature on policing. Bittner thus articulated the template for the current definitions of the role of the police. In laying the ground for this definition, based upon his conception of the typical situation where the police intervene, he also developed the core elements of a theory of the police on which a large part of subsequent police studies were premised. Would it be justified to claim that Bittner outlined a paradigm for thinking about the police, which would be referred to as the "police-use-of-force" paradigm? This question requires careful examination.

First, although he later disclaimed any ambition to having provided a theory of the police (Bittner/Brodeur, 2007: 110), Bittner's *The Function of the Police in Modern Society* (1970) and its classic 1974 follow-up, "Florence Nightingale in Pursuit of Willie Sutton," are the closest thing we have to an explicit theory of the police. Both pieces are fairly extended, the first one being an essay of nearly 150 pages, and they cover a wide range of issues. Klockars's book entitled *The Idea of Police* (1985) is essentially a synthesis of Bittner's ideas; the chapter devoted to police theory in Bayley's *Patterns of Policing* (1985: 3–19) builds on Bittner's emphasis on the use of physical force in defining the unique competence of the police (7–8). Bittner's main assumptions are to this day still unquestioned, even by researchers who view the police as knowledge workers (Ericson and Haggerty, 1997: 69 and 133).

If theory is understood to mean the account of a scientific object in all of its manifestations, then Bittner has not developed such a theory. Many crucial aspects of policing are not addressed, such as the great diversity of policing organizations. However, if we mean by theory a consistent set of closely connected assertions ranging over a number of core issues about the police, then Bittner has without doubt formulated such a theory, despite its limitations in scope. It should be noted that the full title of the most thorough formulation of his thought is "Florence Nightingale in Pursuit of Willie Sutton: *A Theory of the Police*" (Bittner, 1974/1990: 233–268, my emphasis).

Second, the most salient elements of this theory are widely incorporated into the body of police research (for instance, the police use of force, the subsidiary role of law enforcement in policing, the wide diversity of the situations where the police are asked to act, and so forth). In most cases, this integration takes the explicit form of quotations or direct references to Bittner's work (see the opening paragraph of this chapter). In other cases, the initial attempt of Bittner at defining the police is expanded and transformed, although its core element—the use of force—is retained (Manning, 2003: 41–42). Although alternative perspectives are developed—for instance, the police as knowledge workers—they are said to complement Bittner's stance rather than to contradict it (Ericson and Haggerty, 1997: 133).

It should be said that the key importance of force in defining the police was recognized in continental Europe quite independently of Bittner, although his contribution to the theoretical development of the use of force by the police is explicitly acknowledged (Monjardet, 1996; Loubet del Bayle, 1992; Jobard, 2001 and 2002). Indeed, the need for an impartial "public force" is proclaimed in article 12 of the 1789 French Declaration of Human Rights (quoted in Monjardet, 1996: 24). It would thus be preferable to refer to a general "police-use-of-force" paradigm rather than to a narrower Bittner paradigm, so long as it is kept in mind that the body of assertions making up the paradigm was developed by Egon Bittner. Needless to say, not all police researchers accept this perspective (Johnston, 1992 and 2000; Johnston and Shearing, 2003); nonetheless, they all feel that they have to position themselves in relation to it.

Third, there are implications of the police-use-of-force paradigm that have had a practical impact on police research. The most important of these implications, as was already intimated, is that this paradigm mainly reflects the characteristics that are specific to public constabularies. This limitation also shaped the focus of police research, which still largely studies public constabularies. There are other implications of the use-of-force paradigm, such as the distinction between the potential and the actual use of force, which is also pervasive in police studies. To review Bittner's work is at the same time to examine the foundation of the current definition of the role of the police and, most important, to clarify the implications of this definition.

There is one last reason for treating Bittner's work as the key contribution to the development of a police-use-of-force paradigm. In many cases, the adoption of Bittner's definition of the role of the police seems to be a perfunctory move made in order to dispose conveniently of the thorny issue of defining the police. In fact, the classic formulations excerpted from Bittner's work are often quoted out of the context of his thought, which is indispensable to illuminate their true meaning. This practice can lead to serious misunderstandings. There is in this respect a tendency to introduce into the police-use-of-force paradigm elements from Weber's theory of the state's monopoly of legitimate force that do not really fit in the paradigm.

In summary, Bittner's analysis of the use of force as the unique police competence can serve as a standard against which other less explicit police theories based on the use of force can be measured. It can also be considered as the "standard theory" that serves as a starting point for defining the role of the police through the use of force (Manning, 2003). Although it is not a paradigm in the Khunian, natural sciences sense of the word (Kuhn, 1970: 10 and 23), it can heuristically be construed as a model for testing the validity of defining the police through the use of force. In the remainder of this chapter, the acronym PUFP refers to the "police-use-of-force paradigm" (the word "perspective" can be substituted for the word "paradigm" by readers objecting to the use of the latter).

Bittner's thought deserves a more thorough examination than is offered in this chapter. Technical questions such as whether Bittner proposed a functionalist as opposed to a "capacity" definition of the police (Reiner, 1992b: 458) will be only briefly touched upon. The purpose of discussing his work is not to engage in a thorough textual commentary but to use this discussion as a tool to shed light on the issues connected with defining the "specific nature of police competence," in Bittner's own terminology (Bittner, 1974/1990: 255). Consequently, the presentation of the main features of the PUFP, as articulated by Bittner, will be generally followed by critical comments.

Minimal State and Minimal Force

As he stressed during our encounter, Bittner had not provided us with a theory of the relationship between the state and its police, saying that he "did not spend time thinking about it, how it is that the state authorizes the existence of the police" (Bittner/Brodeur, 2007: 110). As I raised questions on this relationship, he decided to address the issue in the following way. He began by stripping the state of all its current functions, to generate what he called a minimal state, which went back to the antique city-state of Greece (the *polis*):

> And now, what is left is essentially what was present already in the city of antiquity. That is, it's a "polis" that already redefines the minimal state where it literally consists of the organization of conditions of urban life...What then the state provides in its minimal function is creating conditions for the orderly coexistence of strangers....The provision for the orderly coexistence of strangers already contains within it the

implication of control of predatory violations of those conditions. Something needs to be done about that. A good deal of legality starts with that, with the control of predatory exploitation, and for the longest time...that's entrusted to the private pursuit of remedies. The state yet lacks the resources to become an independent agent for the control of what I refer to as a predatory exploitation. [The control of] predatory exploitation prominently includes the control of violence and the pre-emptive control of risks of violence. That, then, is the context within which I think about the use of force. (Bittner/Brodeur, 2007: 111)

Several consequences are seen to follow from this preliminary clarification.

The Need for Force

The immediate consequence of Bittner's characterization of the minimal state puts the emphasis on the need for force. On the basis of the text quoted above, the need for force follows from the nature of what is to be controlled in the city-state, that is, predatory violence undermining the possibility of coexistence among urban strangers. Since the police are to be viewed as "the fire it takes to fight fire" (Bittner, 1970/1990: 96), they represent the force opposed to preda-tory violence. This justification of the need for force is ultimately based on a deeper ground, which is expressed in the well-known hyphenated clause quoted above ("something-that-ought-not-to-be-happening-and-about-which-some-one-had-better-do-something-now"). Acting in the context of an emergency or a crisis where people might get hurt (such as the aftermath of a natural disaster), the police need to impose coercive solutions because there is no time for nego-tiation. Stopping violent predators is not the only feature of the general police mandate to engage into micro-crisis management with a potential for violence.

Minimal Force

The first such feature is the requirement that the force used by the state to secure the orderly coexistence of strangers be minimal. The limitation of police force to the minimum needed to deal with a problem situation is a recurrent theme of Bittner's work (1970/1990: 187, 190; 1974/1990: 262; 1983/1990: 27; Bittner/Brodeur, 2007: 4) and of all subsequent police doctrine. In his pub-lished work, Bittner usually bases this requirement upon the historical develop-ment that resulted in the creation of the police institution as the unique instrument for limiting the internal use of force. A similar argument was also made by the German sociologists Max Weber (1978) and Norbert Elias (1996 and 1998). The same limiting logic that gave birth to the police institution compels their members to restrict their own use of coercion to the unavoidable minimum (Bittner, 1970/1990: 192).

The reason for this requirement can also be framed in more practical terms, as Bittner does in the text of our encounter: within the city-state, strangers have to control predatory violations in order to live side by side. However, Bittner is quick to point out that to control is not to annihilate: "In war, we destroy the opponent, but in controlling whatever situation we control within the boundaries of the state, we do what is absolutely minimally necessary" (Bittner/Brodeur, 2007: 112). In contrast to predatory situations, where the police are protecting one party against another, a great deal of police crisis intervention involves protecting all parties involved (for instance, keeping onlookers from getting too close to a fire scene for their own safety and providing firemen with enough space to operate—Bittner, 1974/1990: 258). Since it would be self-defeating to use more force than is necessary to protect people from themselves, managing a crisis is not equivalent to clamping down on it. Using minimum force is not merely incidental to the police mandate, but constitutive of it.

The requirement that police force be minimal is not only based on ethics and on pragmatics. It is also based on the epistemological principle that a definition must identify the distinctive feature of its object. The use of force appears to be specific to the police in comparison to softer internal controls, such as social work, which are superseded by police coercion in the context of developing crises. The police are who you call when all else is failing. However, the specific nature of the definition may be jeopardized when the police are compared to stronger controls, such as military intervention in an officially proclaimed state of internal emergency. The definition of the police through its use of force might then equally apply to the military, if it were not for the minimal force imperative. Confusing the police and the military is one of the most basic mistakes that can be made within the PUFP.

Consent

Bittner is very critical of the performance of the police in controlling civil disorders and, more generally, collective violence. He suggested accordingly that the handling of mass upheavals should be left to the military (Bittner, 1970/1990: 190–191). This is an unexpected limitation on the action of an institution defined as "nothing else than a mechanism for the distribution of situationally justified force in society" (Bittner, 1970/1990: 123). Bittner's position is premised upon a crucial distinction between general threats to the social order and limited violations of that order, which do not threaten to break it down as a whole.

I think that the reason why the intervention by the military forces, the reasons that bring forth the use of military forces, is the risk of the total breakdown of the order. That is, *anomie*. Hence rioting is often controlled by invoking the militia in the USA. *What the police do is act on the presumption that generally speaking the order is intact. And what they take care of are occasional breaches of certain parts of the order.* (Bittner/Brodeur, 2007: 117, my emphasis)

The police deal with emergencies that involve individuals or small groups or, as I use the word, "microcrises." They can also be deployed to keep the peace in the context of large events, such as mass demonstrations, when it is reasonably assumed that the crowd is not gathering for the purpose of bringing down the established order. This feature of policing—micromanagement of individual contingencies within the context of an established order that remains unchallenged—is a fundamental feature of Bittner's view of policing. The controversial notion of policing by consent, which is not used by Bittner, can be interpreted as reflecting his assumption that the police act on the presumption that breaches of certain parts of the established order do not signify that it is rejected as a whole. This interpretation does not make Bittner into a consensualist. On the contrary, one of his most profound observations is that consensus and dissensus can coexist within society, providing that they are allocated to different levels of ordering (macro and micro).

It could be objected that this limitation of policing to individual conflict is only effective—if at all—in countries influenced by the Anglo-Saxon tradition of policing. Almost everywhere else (for example, in continental Europe, in Latin America and in Asia), public constabularies are deeply involved in policing public demonstrations and collective violence that now erupts whenever several heads of states are meeting for an international conference. This objection should be granted, but only in part. On closer look, the forces deployed against collective violence are police forces only in name. By their tradition, culture, training and life conditions, these forces are closer to the military than the police (for example, the French Compagnies républicaines de sécurité).

Polis and police
The fact that the police operate inside a circle of public order that is not challenged as a whole does not mean that they play an incidental part in upholding this order. Actually, Bittner attributed interchangeably to the minimal city-state and to the police the basic function of providing the conditions for the coexistence of strangers ("I'm convinced that the idea of police is an urban phenomenon and that the maintenance of orderly and peaceful relations among

the city brings into existence"—Bittner/Brodeur, 2007: 129;

7). If we schematically depict the minimal state by a circle

uous line, policing could then be represented as another

.....ng the first circle that depicts the minimal state. In other

...οrds, the state and the police institution are coextensive and replicate each other at the macro and micro levels. This relationship is at the core of the definition of the police, as will tentatively be shown.

Critical Comments

There are three features of the minimal or city-state that are critical for understanding the PUFP and that are closely intertwined. The first of these features is presumptive compliance. According to Bittner, the police only act on the presumption that order is on the whole intact within a community. This presumption is crucial for understanding the police use of force. The police use force in a context where they do not expect organized resistance (presumption of compliance), or where they are certain to quickly overwhelm any opposition that they meet (presumption of superior force; see Keegan, 1994: 386). Both presumptions are equally fundamental for policing and, taken together, they provide a factual account of the key notion of minimum force. If the use of force were all there was to policing, there would not be an outcry to train ever more police in occupied countries such as Iraq and Afghanistan, where the military have the advantage of overwhelming force.

When people are compliant and do not test the power of the police, there is little need to resort to actual force. However, we can question whether these presumptions apply in all policing contexts, including those of emergent countries, and even whether they are even still valid in Western democracies. Robert Reiner (2000a and 2000c) is the most vocal critic of the notion of policing by consent. A distinction should be made between policing *by* consent, policing *on the basis* of consent, and policing *without* consent. These distinctions can be illustrated with respect to crowd control. In the hypothetical context of policing by consent, a crowd of demonstrators would disperse upon being ordered to by the police. When policing is exercised on the basis of consent, the police may have to resort to forceful action to break the demonstration. However, this result is achieved without a major and lasting confrontation with the demonstrators. When consent to be policed is completely lacking, the demonstrators may entrench themselves, be reinforced by bystanders siding with them, and oppose the police with all means available. The military has then to be called in. Policing *by* consent may be an outdated notion that should be justly criticized. However, when there is no more consensual basis on which the police can stand, it is policing itself which is in jeopardy.

The second feature of the minimal state may be conceived as the precondition for correctly assuming that the community is on the whole compliant: the original state being characterized by demographic homogeneity. The urban territory is conceived in terms of its population: a large number of people living in the same place. It is thus a human rather than a physical space. Its (tribal) population is presumed to be homogeneous in terms of ethnicity and culture. The homogeneity of the population feeds back into the conception of the territory, its unity being a given that mirrors the relative sameness of its inhabitants. Admittedly, the *polis* or the *urbs* is populated by people who are strangers to one another. However, they are not strangers in the sense of being foreigners, who would be coming from different states to coalesce into mutually exclusive communities potentially in conflict. Excepting slaves and other noncitizens, the city-state population is endogenous, and the fact that the citizens do not know each other by name does not keep them from having a collective identity (as "Athenians" or "Romans"). Bittner remarks in this respect: "Members of tribes are the opposite of strangers. They become strangers when they need to live together in the same social context" (Bittner/Brodeur, 2007: 111). In other words, they are strangers as individuals but not as members of groups, and their rapport is one of anonymity rather than estrangement. There is no wish to imply that Bittner is insensitive to differences among groups. He explicitly acknowledges that before World War I, "it was literally understood that the cops were hired to bash the heads of immigrants," but also believes that there has been a radical change in this respect since World War II (Bittner/Brodeur, 2007: 115). Since the police operate under the presumption that the established order is on the whole intact, there are however few elements within the PUFP that would allow us to analyze situations where clashes between ethnic groups threaten this order as a whole.

Although much research is devoted to the consequences for police authority of the increasing fragmentation of late modern societies (Reiner, 1992a: 763; Reiner, 1992c: 37; Loader and Mulcahy, 2003: 100), the assumption of population homogeneity that defines the minimal state is still widespread, although it is now increasingly programmatic and at odds with actual demographics. The cosmopolitan policing culture advocated by Loader and Mulcahy reasserts, albeit in a flexible way, the connection between police, state, and nation (Loader and Mulcahy, 2003: 323). According to this perspective, the police operate in a relatively homogeneous anthropological and cultural space, in line with the first feature of the minimal state. However, they also perform in a territorial space, where the advent of the cosmo-polis may be precluded by the spread of what these authors call the schizo-polis, that is, the splintering of the national territory through legal devolution or through physical retreat into defiant ghettos that provide a reactive identity for their inhabitants. In a country like Canada, Aboriginal territories are both de facto and de jure self-(de)regulating enclaves, where opposing factions often resort to violence against each other without Canadian police interference. In other countries, slums and "favellas" (Davis, 2006), the "new ghettos" (Vergara, 1997), and "ethnic suburbs" (Donzelot et al., 2003) are no man's lands where police refuse to venture and which have surrendered to anomie. Is there a role for a civilian police using minimum force in these contexts, or will they be increasingly policed by the military or paramilitary organizations, as they already are in many South American countries? These questions will be addressed in chapter 9.

Finally, the minimal or city-state making up the setting for Bittner's theory of policing is entirely defined by its internal function of providing the conditions of urban life, that is, the peaceful coexistence of strangers. Of decisive importance is the fact that Bittner chooses "to disregard the very influential formulation of the function of the state by Carl Schmitt, namely that the state is defined by the presence of its enemies" (Bittner/Brodeur, 2007: 111). Bittner's minimal state does not have enough substance of its own to have internal or external enemies. It is by definition transparent and does not wage war against its citizens, as a police state does in order to enforce a dominant order. This postulated transparency is a critical limitation of the framework provided by Bittner and one that vindicates his claim that he did not want to formulate a comprehensive theory of policing. It does not provide us with the conceptual means to elucidate the role of the police in the context of a general social and political conflict.

The Non-Monopoly of Legitimate Force

Several authors working within the PUFP have introduced Weber's notion of the monopoly of the legitimate use of force into Bittner's theory (Newburn, 2005: 5). This external imposition of Weberian elements into his thought was in part fostered by Bittner himself through his positive review of Muir's *Police: Streetcorner Politicians* (1977). Muir develops a theory of policing based explicitly on Weber's essay on politics as a vocation (Weber, 1946). When questioned about it, Bittner answered that he did not consider this notion of the monopoly of legitimate force to be a key aspect of his theory of policing.

> It is not that the thought about the monopoly of the legitimate force is wrong, it's just that it's too confining for me to think about. In some particular way, the creation of the city, the "polis" again, abolishes the private

use of force or delegitimizes it. So, in certain ways, the definition about the monopoly, state monopoly, is sort of a residual definition. (Bittner/ Brodeur, 2007: 119)

Nonetheless, it cannot be doubted that the notion of a state monopoly of the legitimate use of force is compatible with the drift of Bittner's thought, as he is ready to acknowledge. However, it can generate a basic misunderstanding of what the specific nature of the police use of force really is. As critics of Bittner have argued, the police do not actually have the monopoly of the legitimate use of force, either directly or through deputizing special constables, as would be the case in North America (Brodeur, 1984b; Johnston, 1992). For instance, parents and teachers are legally authorized to use force to discipline children; as the population is aging, we learn more about the considerable amount of physical coercion exercised in institutions for the elderly, not to mention the mentally ill; private security companies—particularly those specializing in the transport of money—use personnel who are heavily armed and allowed to circulate with their weapons drawn. More examples could be added to this list.

While such examples do not invalidate Bittner's definition of the role of the police, they may be conducive to finding what uniquely qualifies the police mandate to use force. Bittner readily acknowledges that, for instance, prison guards are legally authorized to use force, but stresses that the police authority is in this respect radically different from that of a prison guard. "Whereas the powers of the latter [the prison guard] are incidental to his obligation to implement a legal command, the police role is far better understood by saying that their ability to arrest offenders is incidental to their authority to use force" (Bittner, 1970/1990: 122–123). The easiest way to interpret this rather dense sentence is to add one word to it: the police role is better understood by saying that their ability to arrest offenders is incidental to their *general* authority to use force. Therein lays the crucial difference between the police use of force and the authority enjoyed by any other group: the police can use their capacity to overpower resistance to their intervention in *any* situation where the use of force can be justified (Bittner, 1970/1990: 125). All other groups have limited authority (for example, parents have authority over their own children, teachers over their pupils, surgeons over their patients, prison guards over inmates, and so forth). The police use of force should be minimal in its intensity, but it *is* unlimited in its scope.

The second feature of the police authority to use force is a direct consequence of the fact that the police institution and the minimal state are coextensive, as was emphasised above. In my interview with him (Bittner/Brodeur 2007: 130–131), I asked Professor Bittner what the legal basis was for his view that the use of force was the core of the police mandate. He first answered that he had not found it in the law of any democratic country, and that he did not know that there was such a legal basis apart from many judicial decisions upholding the police authority to use force. With respect to the sentence quoted above, he declared, "All I can say in justification of that quote is: I took it from observation. I can't cite any authority for it or authorization for it. Whatever I can add to [it] is that it is subject to challenge, but apparently not challenged" (Bittner/Brodeur, 2007: 131).

Critical Comments

This defining feature of the police authority to use force—that it is all-encompassing rather than monopolistic—explains several aspects of the PUFP.

To Whom Does the Paradigm Apply?

Bittner found that the general scope of the police authority to use force was its defining feature in his ethnographical fieldwork. His basic observation was the huge diversity of the situations in which the police were called in. His insights into the limited weight of law enforcement in policing played an important part in the later development of the problem-oriented approach in policing, as has been explicitly recognized by Goldstein (1979: 27). The kind of police that fit this description of being call-answering generalists are actually the rank-and-file uniformed patrolpersons. It is to them that the PUFP primarily applies (Bittner, 1974/1990: 241).

It also tangentially applies to detectives who, according to Bittner, tend to avoid involvement with offences in which it is assumed that there will be no need to apprehend fleeing suspects by using force (Bittner, 1974/1990: 242). This assertion, made more than thirty years ago, is becoming more questionable as, for instance, the fight against money laundering and economic crime is growing in importance. Economic crimes are generally not perpetrated by violent offenders. To all practical purposes, the PUFP applies almost exclusively to public uniformed field officers. It sheds little light on the work of their supervisors and leaders, which is a neglected field of research, with the exception of Reiner's study of chief constables in the United Kingdom (Reiner, 1991). Not only does this limitation appear to exclude the greater number of policing agents (who were listed in chapter 1), but it goes against the present trend toward plural policing.

Public and Private Police

In all of his work, Bittner is sensitive to historical developments. When he defined the *polis* as providing the conditions for the coexistence of strangers, he was careful to say that these conditions were actually provided by "private armies" up to the end of the feudal period, pointing to the difference between *polis* and the true birth of the "state" after the Renaissance. However, the dawning of the state entailed for him the delegitimization of private force (Bittner/Brodeur, 2007: 119), in great part because "the commodified police cannot be impartial" (Bittner/Brodeur, 2007: 120). The implication of this reasoning is that efforts to bring together public and private policing into integrated networks (Bayley and Shearing, 2001; Johnston and Shearing, 2003) are not concordant with the PUFP, at least as it was developed by Bittner. This is obviously not an argument against these endeavors, but an indication that the integration of public and private policing is for now a program resting essentially on practical considerations that may play in favor of parties that can afford the services offered by private policing. The policing of labor relations in the United States by private security agencies can hardly be said to have benefited the workers.

Legislative Hollowness

Although it is in theory unlimited, the police mandate to use force is in reality submitted to an increasing number of legal constraints. The police can roam and operate freely in public spaces, but as soon as they want to invade privacy, they are in theory under judicial supervision and have to apply for various warrants, which they almost invariably obtain. The legal constraints on the police use of force are of a dichotomous nature. On the one hand, there are a number of formal constraints on specific instances of the use of coercion (search and seizure, arrest, forfeiting of assets, interception of private communications, and so forth). These constraints usually apply to criminal investigation, which has a subsidiary role in the PUFP and was not studied by Bittner. On the other hand, legislators have resisted, for good reasons, the idea of conferring by statute an unrestricted mandate to use force on any kind of state agents. I probed this question with Bittner only to receive the renewed answer that there is no enabling statute granting the police the general authority to use force in all circumstances that may require it. This legislative hollowness compounds the problem of police accountability, since it appears to grant them unfettered discretion in their use of force. It is also in line with the fact that police authority rests on an informal presumption of acquiescence to the established order. This presumption reflects our ambivalence toward policing, which Bittner was fully aware of. "In sum, the frequently heard talk about the lawful use of force is practically meaningless.... Our expectation that policemen will use force, coupled by our refusal to state clearly what we mean by it (aside from sanctimonious homilies) smacks of more than a bit of perver⸱⸱⸱" (Bittner, 1970/1990: 122).

The Police Unique Competence

The results of the previous analyses can be summarized thus: the police use of force should be minimal, although the scope of police authority is all-encompassing. The first part of this summary implies a trend toward contraction and the second one toward expansion. This apparent divergence is resolved in Bittner's notion of the police's unique competence, which means that the police use of force is potential rather than actual. Its potential nature is what reconciles, in theory, the fact that it is all-encompassing with the requirement that it be minimal.

Supply and Demand for Force

Bittner always emphasised that force was much more visible on the demand than on the supply side: "citizen demand is a factor of extraordinary importance for the distribution of police service" (Bittner, 1974/1990: 252). This was reiterated by Bittner at the beginning of our meeting: "[the use of force] becomes much more visible on the demand side than on the supply side" (Bittner/Brodeur, 2007: 111). When people call the police, they want them to forcefully impose a solution upon an emergency situation, although this interpretation of their will "probably conflicts with what most people would say or expect to hear, in answer to the question about the proper police function"(Bittner, 1970/1990: 123).[2]

This contrast between supply and demand is important in several respects. First, it provides essential support to the assertion that the police's capacity to use force applies without restriction to all situations. In truth, police proaction is severely limited, since it is framed by the distinction between public space, where police operate without restriction, and private space, where they have to obtain special authorization to intervene. They do not need to have such an authorization, however, when they are called into a private habitat by its owner or lessee. Hence a theory of policing developed from the standpoint of demand would be in a stronger position to argue for the extensive nature of the police's capacity to use force than a theory developed from the supply angle. Second, it also explains the almost exclusive theoretical focus of the PUFP on uniformed patrol. They are the police officers answering calls. Members of plainclothes

---

2. What Bittner implies here is that people would not dare speak their mind, a reasonable assumption under the circumstances. Yet it raises the methodological issue of whether some of his key assertions can be empirically tested. Once suspicion is cast on the truth of people's answers to questions, all we have left is the ethnographer's word as to their real intention in calling the police.

units practically never react to direct calls from the public. Third, theories of policing that emphasise the role of trust are by implication oriented toward demand: there cannot be any demand if there is no trust. This dimension of the paradigm was not explicitly developed by Bittner, but was highlighted by the work of Manning (2003).

Finally, the symbolic function of the police was rediscovered by empirical research into police calls, which reveal public expectations about the police (Shapland and Vagg, 1988: 149); it was also recently stressed by research into public attitudes toward them (Loader and Mulcahy, 2003). Although symbols are created at the juncture between supply and demand, they are endowed with their special meaning from the outside by the public.

From Response to Responsibility

It is not unthinkable that at some future date the police might operate without ever resorting to force (Bittner, 1970/1990: 187). This might happen if there was no demand for force and if the police were able to bring about the desired outcome of any problem without having to resort to physical force. Even if this became the case, the police would still bear the responsibility for using force, if it were exceptionally called for. In other words, Bittner does not claim that police work actually consists of using force to solve problems, but rather that it consists in coping with problems in which force may have to be used. This distinction between actuality and potentiality is said by Bittner to be of extraordinary importance (Bittner, 1974/1990: 256).

Police Competence

Bittner's reasoning follows a path along which the use of force seems to be progressively vanishing. It begins with a definition of the police role through the use of force, then branches into minimal force, and ends up stressing that the use of force fundamentally refers to a capacity rather than to actual use. Thus the notion of a unique competence bridges the gap between the scope of the police mandate to use force and the requirement that force be used according to the necessary minimum. In the course of our exchange, Bittner tried to elucidate this notion of competence by using the analogy of priesthood.

> 95% of what constitute the routine of police work has nothing to do with force. Perhaps 99%—nevertheless, the unique competence remains as [being] its outstanding feature albeit rarely employed. . . . What I'm trying to suggest is that the sacramental duty of the priesthood is defining of it even though it's only a small part of it and most of the time is taken up by other things. (Bittner/Brodeur, 2007: 113).

Critical Comments

The critical comments address the previous issues in the same order.

Demand-Side Theory

There is no doubt that the foundation of Bittner's theory of the use of force lies in his field observations of the demand for the imposition of nonnegotiated solutions. This one-sided foundation raises a question: is the use-of-force paradigm dependent upon the demand for force? In other words, must all definitions of the police through their use of force be based on demand?

The answer to this difficult question should be a qualified "yes," the emphasis being put on the qualification. The need for a "public force" can surely be asserted independently of civil society's demand. As was seen in chapter 2, this need is unconditionally proclaimed in section 12 of the 1789 French Declaration of Human Rights. However, this proclamation remains within the ambit of a demand-side explanation, as it really amounts to giving priority to a demand emanating from the state over a demand originating from the citizens. Bittner himself comes very close to acknowledging the historical primacy of the state demand when he writes that "the police were created as a mechanism for coping with the so-called dangerous classes" and "thus to contain the *internal* enemy" (Bittner, 1974/1990: 260, my emphasis). Here, Bittner is endorsing a position expressed by Silver (1967). The position that he embraces here may not be wholly consistent with one of the tenets of his thought, which claims not to consider Schmitt's notion of enemies of the state (Schmitt, 1927). Be that as it may, there would seem to be two kinds of demands for coercive policing: the state demand, which accounts for the birth of the police as an institution, and the public demand, which accounts for day-to-day mobilization of individual police intervention. The existence (without further qualification) of a demand for "a public force" is a trivial observation. The thorny question is whether police force can be justified on the supply side, independently of any demand. I think not.

Bittner provided a classic formulation of this question: "the question, 'What are policemen supposed to do?' is almost completely identical with the question, 'What kind of situations require remedies that are non-negotiably coercible?'" (Bittner, 1970/1990: 125). Notwithstanding exceptional circumstances like natural disasters, such a question cannot be answered outside a normative framework that spells out what values are to be respected by the police. In contrast to people, situations do not call out by themselves for a particular kind of resolution and need to be interpreted in the light of the values that we hold in order to decide upon a course of action. In spelling out these values, taking various kinds of expectations and demands into consideration cannot be avoided. When the naked imposition of force on behalf of particular interests is deemed unacceptable, all justification of force must be based on a critical examination of demand.

Selective Policing

Bittner is fully aware that it is "exceedingly rare" for policemen to make decisions that affect the life of members of the middle and upper classes, with the exception of traffic control and low-level service (1970/1990: 159). The policeman is, however, a figure of awesome power for the poor, the powerless, the immigrant, the ghetto and slum dweller, not to mention the deviant, the devious, and the criminal (Bittner, 1990: 159). The PUFP would appear, at first, to provide an explanation for such selective policing without resorting to class or ethnic bias. It can be argued that the demand for policing the predatory elements among the poor and the powerless originate mainly from these very segments of the population. This line of reasoning is problematic in several ways.

First, it implies that the poor are simultaneously the trigger of selective enforcement and its victim. Second, it overlooks that people calling for the police make a critical difference between forcibly ending a crisis (stopping a husband from beating his wife) and following up on the coercive implications of the crisis (arresting and charging the husband). According to my own research, many demands focus on the short-term provisional resolution of the conflict, while rejecting its long-term judicial consequences as enforced by the police. Third, Bittner's argument conflicts with other observations that he made. He repeatedly stressed, as we saw, that the police, including detectives, tend to neglect crimes perpetrated by offenders who will not try to escape and to resist arrest (Bittner, 1974/1990: 242). If this is the case, the police would now avoid responding to a public demand, indeed a clamor, to be protected against fraud and other crimes involving deception rather than violence, and thus supply force on their own through their targeting of offences that may satisfy their craving for action.

Competence

The concept of competence is generally opposed to the actual realization of a capacity, and it is used to solve the apparent paradox involved in defining a group of practitioners by what they do the least often and in the last resort. It also offers an important clue to meeting an objection against the kind of definition offered by Bittner, namely, that it does not state for what purpose force is used (Cain, 1979; Marenin, 1982; Reiner, 1992b). It first seems that the diversity of situations that may justify the use of force is so overwhelming—"the duties of patrolmen are of a mind-boggling variety" (Bittner, 1974/1990: 250)—that it defies any attempt to provide a functionalist formulation adjusting means to ends. On a deeper level, a functionalist formulation may obfuscate the meaning of a definition using the notion of competence, as is shown by this quote:

> Q. Do you think that one can formulate ends of policing which are more precise than simply saying [that] they [the police] have to do what must urgently be done to stop situations that should not be allowed to happen?
>
> A. Well I don't know whether one can. But my objection to describing the physician who operates, who does surgery, [and] that somehow or other it is necessary to mention that he does it for the benefit of the patient [my objection to this is that] this disregards one very important thing: namely, that others are not entitled to cut for the benefit of the patient. The physician alone is licensed to do surgery, which among others things, means that he has a certain margin of being entitled to make errors. Now, if I were to find that my neighbour has a bellyache, and I go and say, it is right here, that's were the appendix is, do you happen to have a knife around? Give me a knife and I'll cut it out for you. Can I? I'd do it for his benefit. No. I'm not a licensed physician. But the licensed physician can do that. That's the whole point of the matter. Now, that he does it for the benefit [of the patient]—and I think that's implied in what we're talking about, the police too, that does it for the benefit of maintaining social order. (Bittner/Brodeur, 2007: 131–32)

Reiner may be right when he contrasts defining the police in functional terms, on the one hand, with defining them, like Bittner, as "the institutional repository of the use of legitimate force," on the other (Reiner, 1992b: 458). The fact that it becomes unnecessary to add that the police will use force for the public good, indeed the obscuring nature of such a statement, illustrates in a striking way how Bittner developed a whole set of closely related ideas that must be considered in their interconnections.

One last thing should be said with respect to the previous quote. It uses the familiar metaphor of the surgeon to illustrate the kind of competence conferred upon the police. But the analogy of the priest is closer to the police competence in one respect. Both the priest and the police enjoy a unique competence (respectively performing sacraments and using force) that they are called to exercise rather infrequently, whereas a surgeon actually devotes most of his or her time to the practice of surgery. The analogy between medicine and policing is misleading in other ways that will be discussed more fully later on.

Features of the Police-Use-of-Force Paradigm

The PUFP, as I have been using the notion, can be described in two ways. First, its features can be summarized, as is usually the case. Second, an attempt can be made to show the dichotomous nature of this paradigm by expounding the theoretical oppositions on which it rests. I shall begin with the features, which will be both discussed and critically appraised.

Progressive Orientation

Although various forms of ordering the polity can be found throughout history, the police are for the PUFP the specific outcome of a trend to limit violence by concentrating it in state agencies. This genetic perspective is shared by Weber, Elias, and also clearly by Bittner, who presents a sketch of the development of the police idea in early-nineteenth-century English society (Bittner 1970/1990: 102). The birth of the police institution represents a significant progress of civilization over the ordering of societies by private feudal armies that "offered pretty much the kind of protection that the Mafia offers in American cities today" (Bittner/Brodeur, 2007: 129; also see Chesnais, 1981). This orientation of the PUFP toward progress implies that the PUFP is not value-free: it does not so much embody a generalized theory of policing as an account of the police in a particular setting that can be broadly described as democratic. What seems to contradict the core of the paradigm—such as non-minimal use of force, political repression, and discrimination—is reduced to being practical deviations from the theoretical model, which are of interest only for evaluative research. The existence of police brutality, for instance, does not question the theoretical notion of minimal force as such, but rather its practical translation into reality.

Depoliticization

As he makes clear, Bittner's ethnographical methodology was not conducive to the development of an explicit conceptualization of the wider physical, political, and legal context in which the police operate. In this minimal context, the *polis* and the police are not sufficiently differentiated to allow for a study of the relationships between the state and its police. Even if most researchers working within the ambit of the PUFP are not ethnographers, the linkage between politics and policing has not been the focus of most research in police studies, despite notable exceptions (Banton, 1964; Cain, 1973; Reiner, 2000a), and has mainly been studied by historians (Liang, 1992: 4). Due to the highly centralized structure of policing, more attention has been devoted to this topic in continental Europe (Monjardet, 1996; Loubet del Bayle, 1992; Dewerpe, 1994).

Police Visibility

Uniformed field officers who belong to public constabularies are the prime object of the PUFP. If it were applied to private security, it would focus on guards. This is not only true because of their greater number and visibility but also because they are the original embodiment of the modern police idea when it came of age in nineteenth-century England. To a large extent, the focus of the PUFP on uniformed officers is a consequence of its historical perspective. This focus clearly excludes key actors of policing—such as crime investigators, intelligence officers, the political police (deemed a perversion of the model), paramilitary forces deployed to control collective violence, police informants (hired by contract), and private security organizations—or pushes them into a distant background.

Virtual Force

The core feature of the paradigm is that the use of force is not conceived as force in action but as a power or capacity to act. The most conspicuous examples of the use of force—the policing of mass demonstrations—are in theory excluded from the PUFP. The ambiguous nature of police force is one of the PUFP's most problematic features. The concept of power is one of the most difficult to analyze, as the work of thinkers as diverse as Aristotle, Hegel, and Foucault testifies. Although power cannot be observed as such (only its actual exercise can), it cannot be reduced to an abstract construct of the mind. It hovers in between the virtual and the actual. Its problematic nature is enhanced within the PUFP, where it vanishes into a competence that may never be exercized. When the capacity to use force is coupled with the requirement to use minimum force, empirically testing the model becomes a challenging task. Finally, it is also unclear whether the capacity to use force is an adequate tool to account for the increasingly important police practice of surveillance. In some of their aspects, surveillance practices are preliminaries to actual intervention and can thus, albeit in a very general sense, be associated with a capacity. However, surveillance is no mere potentiality and is actually exercised through an array of police activities that are now growing exponentially.

Fragmentation

The unique nature of the police capacity to use force is that it can be exercised in all situations that justify it, with the exception of collective violence, as we have just seen. With respect to solving conflicts, the general police competence is in practice broken down into a myriad of micro-performances occurring in the context of confrontations between the police and individuals. At first sight, the exclusion of the situations calling the most urgently for police action— collective violence that often leads to an official proclamation of a "state of emergency"—would appear to be inconsistent with the general character of the police mandate to use force when and wherever necessary. Upon closer examination, this exclusion is revealing of the prerequisites for the *police* to use force: that is, the presumption of general compliance and the presumption of superior force. Both presumptions are suspended in the context of collective violence.

Demand-Side Theory

The PUFP is in great part based on the public demand to use whatever force is necessary to put a stop to a crisis situation. Although police mobilization through public calls can be the object of empirical inquiries, Bittner's contentions have not been the object of systematic verification. It is not even certain that they could be falsified by empirical research, since what police callers would say about their motivation is open to doubt on the part of the researcher (Bittner, 1970/1990: 123). Individual fragmentation was just described in the previous paragraph as ruling out police action against collective disorders. This feature also underpins demand-side theory, as demands from the state or corporate agents have not really been scrutinized within the PUFP. This orientation of the paradigm toward individual demand is far-reaching, as it impacts on police theories that stress the importance of trust in policing (Manning, 2003).

This presentation of the main features of the PUFP also highlighted what is not explicitly addressed within the paradigm. This procedure was meant to reflect a fundamental aspect of the PUFP, which is that it attempts to balance opposing perspectives in thinking about the police. Thus, the use of force is balanced by the requirement that it be minimal. However, the most striking manifestation of the conflict of perspectives is Bittner's assertion that police work is a tainted occupation (Bittner, 1970/1990: 94). This assertion is made in a section of *The Functions of Police in Modern Society* entitled "Popular Conceptions about the Character of Police Work." For Bittner the taint that attaches to police work first "refers to the fact that policemen are viewed as the fire that it takes to fight fire" (1970/1990: 96). On a deeper level, it stems from the fact that the need for quickly solving human situations that display complexity and drama invests police activities "with the character of crudeness," the need to disregard complexity being structurally built into the occupation (Bittner, 1970/1990: 97). The public demands that violence be fought by violence, and at the same time it stigmatizes the violence workers. Duality may not be just a conceptual feature of the PUFP, but an unavoidable trait of thinking about the police. As claimed in chapter 1, policing is not a tidy object of knowledge but a sprawling field full of conflicting strands.

Conceptual Oppositions within the Police-Use-of-Force Paradigm

The title of this section in no way implies that the PUFP is inconsistent. It simply means that there are justified conceptual tensions within it. The polarities that are referred to are for the most current distinctions (such as between public forces and private agencies), and do not require discussion beyond what was devoted to them in the preceding pages. However, there are others sources of conceptual tension deserving of closer attention. Discussing them will lead us in the direction of an alternative formulation of the unique police competence.

Opposite Terms within the PUFP

The conceptual opposites to be listed refer to various aspects of policing. Although theoretical constructs, they are firmly grounded in fact.

1. Policing agents
   public police vs. private security agencies
   constabularies vs. military forces
   uniformed patrolmen vs. plainclothes details
   holders of general mandate to use force vs. holders of limited
       authorization to use force
2. Policing situations
   urban settings vs. rural settings
   emergency crises vs. routine incidents
   individual conflict vs. collective violence
3. Policing activities
   coercive reaction to demand vs. proactive supply of force
   police mobilization by civil society vs. police mobilization by the state
   public order vs. law enforcement
   unregulated vs. regulated by law

Generally speaking, the PUFP gives priority to the first term of each listed pair of notions. This list is not exhaustive. It refers to my reconstruction of the

PUFP. There are, however, other alternate notions in the PUFP—such as policing as a craft and as a science—that were not mentioned, since they play no part in the development of the present argument. Second, not all conceptual oppositions in relation to policing are dual. There are hybrids (such as alternatives in between public and private policing) and there are also "other possibilities" (such as Aboriginal territories, which do not fit on either side of the city-country distinction).

Substantial Oppositions within the PUFP

The two substantial oppositions—or tensions, as Bittner used the word—concern the core of the paradigm, that is, the use of force.

Competence and Performance

As Bittner often stresses, the use of force by the police is primarily a capacity (Bittner, 1970) or, in the terminology that he later used, a unique competence (Bittner 1974; Bittner/Brodeur, 2007). The two terms are not equivalent, as the notion of competence can also be construed as an institutional empowerment to have recourse to force.

Competence is also widely used in linguistics, where it refers to a capacity to communicate in a particular language, used in the actual performance of speech acts. In linguistics, the notion of competence and performance are intrinsically linked, a competent speaker of English normally performing in this language in order to communicate. The situation is noticeably different in respect of the PUFP, where the competence to use force is all but disconnected from actual police performance. As was previously stressed, Bittner deems it even possible that at a future date, the police may be able to solve any problem without ever resorting to physical force, which would keep its threatening power of being the tangible "or else," if all other options failed (Bittner, 1970/1990: 187). The corresponding situation in linguistics would be the need to be competent in a language, with the tacit understanding that it should be used as little as possible. As all analogues, this one should not be taken at face value. It nevertheless serves its purpose to make the point that in the PUFP there is such a gap between competence and performance (actual use) that it leads to an uncoupling of the capacity and its use. The public belief that the police are continuously involved in the imposition of force is in great part generated by the flow of media images that exclusively focus on the implication of the police in dramatic situations and violent conflict. In fact, such coercive episodes only occur infrequently in a given jurisdiction and they are separated by long intervals of relative peacefulness.

Dynamics of the Physical Struggle

The normative requirement of using minimal force leads to a relative divorce of police competence from police performance. Conversely, the practical difficulty of actually meeting this requirement is another source of tension, highlighted by Bittner during our meeting. Bittner described two features of the actual use of physical force that were in conflict with the principle of minimal force. The first is the result of what he called the natural dynamics of the physical struggle: "once you start punching, it's very hard to stop it." The second feature mentioned by Bittner reveals a deeper insight.

> The second aspect has to do with making sure that the use of force will prevail. So that almost, if you want to make sure that this will be satisfactorily done, the last blow is so [to speak] beyond necessity....What I am proposing is that these two things are in conflict: the idea, the human ideal of minimal force, and the practical aspect of doing it create tensions that are inherent in the work and very difficult to control. (Bittner/Bodeur, 2007: 112)

Bittner's insight is starkly illustrated by firearm training in police academies: once a police officer decides to draw his gun, he should shoot until his target is down, making (often lethally) sure that armed force prevails. This was the explanation given for the fact that Amadou Diallo, in an infamous incident that occurred in the New York Bronx in 1999, was shot forty-one times. It was claimed at the police trial that the collar of Diallo's coat became tangled with the door knob of his apartment, keeping him from falling to the floor, and that the police continued firing until he was down. Such tragedies are not specific to the United States and happen elsewhere, as the 2005 lethal shooting of Jean Charles de Menezes in Britain reminds us. Mr. de Menezes had no connection whatsoever with terrorism; he was shot seven times by the British police, who suspected him to be part of the bombing of the London public transportation system.

The requirement to use minimal force means at least two things. It first means that force should be used in as few instances as possible. The need to curtail the frequency of the recourse to force is what generates the tension between police competence and actual police performance. This tension is usually resolved in favor of restraint, the ratio between the number of police interventions and the use of physical force being small (Bayley and Garofalo, 1989; Brodeur, 2003). Second, the requirement for minimum force also means reducing the intensity of the forced used, once it is decided to trigger the process of having recourse to force. Whether this second form of tension is likely to be revolved in favor of restraint is far less clear. The tension between competence and performance refers to physical force before it is used. The tension between the dynamics of physical struggle and the prescription to minimize force refers to force after it has begun to be used.

Formal Oppositions within the Police-Use-of-Force Paradigm

Formal oppositions are conceptual tensions arising with respect to the process of knowledge itself rather than in relation to the objects of knowledge ("the facts"). Two of these are discussed below, the second of which plays a central role in the ensuing argument.

Definition and Description

The overwhelming fact that strikes any researcher studying police operating in the field is the mind-boggling variety of activities that they perform. Hence the search of a common thread running through activities as diverse as foot-patrol officers looking for the parents of a lost child and a SWAT team liberating a hostage is bound to fail if one looks for an empirical feature that can be actually observed in everything that they do. The PUFP brings a brilliant solution to this problem in defining the police through their unique capacity or competence: although this capacity is not manifest in all their activities, it can always be activated, activation thus providing an opportune middle ground between power and action.

Despite its elegance, this solution creates a gap between the definition of the police and the empirical account of their activities. For instance, although Shapland and Vagg (1988: 39) first assert that Bittner's notion of using coercive force to solve problems runs across the various public demands on the police, the actual use of coercion is only briefly discussed in one paragraph of their book, which concludes that the most important police role demanded by the public is the symbolic one of proclaiming a state of order by "their very presence" (Shapland and Vagg, 1988: 108 and 149). Starting with Goldstein (1979: 27), the considerable body of literature on community and problem-oriented policing acknowledges the crucial nature of Bittner's contribution, but barely mentions the use of force in policing (and mostly to criticize it.) Given the variety of police activity, it is less than certain that the gap between definition and description can ever be satisfactorily filled.

Description and Evaluation

Within the PUFP, there was actually an attempt to fill this gap by a distinction between what is and what ought to be (Rumbaut and Bittner, 1979: 267; Klockars, 1985). On the one hand, defining the police as a mechanism for the distribution of nonnegotiated force is giving a factual description of what they do or might have to do. On the other hand, determining whether the police are respecting the requirement to use only the minimum force necessary is undertaking evaluation research. According to this logic, a police officer who brought about a desired outcome without ever resorting to physical force could still be described in theory as an "a mechanism for the distribution of force," on the one hand, while being positively evaluated on his ability to satisfy the requirement to minimize force, on the other. Paradoxically, the better a police department performed in generating results with a minimum use of force, the less its activities would conform to its definition as a mechanism for the distribution of force. Conversely, failing the test of being restrained in its use of coercion would imply closer correspondence to its uniquely defining competence to use force.

Although the formal tensions discussed above result in the rather awkward situation that the description and the evaluation of police performance seem to be jointly involved in a zero-sum game, there may be nothing wrong in this result, which just reflects a unique feature of policing: it uses for the common good violent means that are reputed to be otherwise evil. This paradox, which has deliberately been formulated in a provocative way, will now be discussed.

Toward a New Definition of Policing

Manning (2003: 33–43) provides a thorough discussion of the definition of policing. He proposes his own definition, which rests ultimately on the use of force and thus remains within the PUFP. Another tack at the problem of defining the police will be taken here. Bittner's definition of the police could be used as a template for defining other professions. Using it in this way is not very revealing of other professions, but it brings out critical features of the PUFP definition of policing.

A first testing ground would be teachers. For the sake of making my point, they will be defined à la Bittner as "a mechanism for the distribution of knowledge, nonnegotiably recognized as science, in accordance with the dictates of the transmission of culture." Obviously, it makes no sense to say that according to this definition the best teacher is the one that distributes the least knowledge. Even if there is an obvious need for adjusting the sum of information transmitted to the capacity of the learners, this balance is never struck in favor of minimizing knowledge; the teacher tries to transmit as much knowledge as possible "in accordance with the dictates of an intuitive grasp of situational exigencies." The disconnection observed in the case of policing between the definition of the profession and the assessment of individual performance does not occur in relation to teachers. The reason for this is obvious: knowledge is unanimously believed to be a positive thing, whereas there is no such consensus in the case of force; within the PUFP, the principle of minimal force rests on the assumption that coercion, although at times unavoidable, is not in itself a positive value.

A second testing ground would be surgeons, with whom the police are often compared by authors working within the PUFP. The common ground between surgeons and police is that both professions use extreme remedies. However, the discrepancy between the theoretical definition of surgeons and the actual description of their activities is not nearly as strong as with the police: as we already noted, surgeons spend the greater part of their working time operating on patients or preparing to do so. Also, despite Bittner's objection, it would be counterintuitive to define surgery as a mechanism for the distribution of surgical cuts without at least mentioning that these are inflicted to improve the patient's health.

There are two additional differences that are even more important for framing a definition of policing. First, surgeons discuss with their patients what they propose to do and, under normal circumstances, the patient must give his consent in order for the surgical intervention to proceed. The police do not ask for consent when they use force. Second, although it involves cutting the flesh of a patient, surgery is performed by highly trained professionals operating on consenting persons in a complex set of conditions meant to protect the life and well-being of the patient (for example, anaesthesia, sterilization of instruments, monitoring of life signs, and so forth). Notwithstanding the moral gulf separating surgeons and predators, there is no physical common ground between a surgical incision and a switch-blade wound except for the bodily cut. Surgeons are not duelling with their patients, and a surgical operation is not simply a wound inflicted for a good purpose. By contrast, the police are generally (but not always) in conflict with the persons against whom they are applying force. Their training to use force is negligible compared with the training of surgeons to practice their profession. Most important, the use of physical force by police and by criminals is in many cases almost identical. For instance, when a police car is chasing another car, both show similar disregard for traffic regulations; when plainclothes police and members of gangs exchange fire, it is hard to tell who the police are. During demonstrations, riot police and demonstrators often use similar tactics (clubs, gas masks). These examples could be indefinitely added to: when the dynamic of physical struggle is triggered, opponents use the same kind of blows.

The comparison between police and teachers shows that police use potentially harmful means and are thus perceived to be "tainted." The comparison between police and surgeons reveals how much police make use of these problematic means in an environment that is not professionally controlled and that is the basically the same as the one in which nonpolice use these means. To illustrate: when plainclothes police exchange fire with criminals, they do so in a context that is common to both police and criminals, and where the difference between them is not immediately apparent. Because the use of violence and other forms of coercion is harmful, their use has generally been defined as a criminal offence or a statutory violation. Since the use of these harmful means by the police does not differ in kind from their illegal use by the population, the police could be said to use illegal means, if it were not for the fact that they are authorized by the law, custom, or some other authority to use them—it is assumed—for legitimate purposes. Building upon this observation, I propose this tentative definition of policing agents. (In line with my inventory of persons professionally involved in policing, I prefer the expression "policing agent" to the word "police," which generally refers to public constabularies.)

> Policing agents are part of several connected organizations authorized to use in more or less controlled ways diverse means, generally prohibited by statute or regulation to the rest of the population, in order to enforce various types of rules and customs that promote a defined order in society, considered in its whole or in some of its parts.

This tentative definition is a starting point that will be discussed and tested throughout the next chapters of this book. For now, a preliminary discussion of its meaning and justification is given.

An intrinsic feature of governance by rule is that rules cannot be enforced on one level without breaking some of them on a higher level. This feature reveals itself in the analysis of police practice. One of the oldest police practices is physical surveillance, which is generally a covert practice that avoids rousing the suspicion of its target(s). It is thus very different from emergency or crisis intervention (such as chasing a get-away car). The Canadian Commission of Inquiry Concerning Certain Activities of the Royal Canadian Mounted Police—the McDonald commission—scrutinized the scope of the legal violations that could potentially be committed by policemen carrying out physical surveillance, which is one of the most elementary police operations. Physical surveillance was performed by a special RCMP unit ("the watchers"), which undertook it, at the behest of the RCMP Criminal Investigation Department and for its Security service (Canada, 1981a: 279–293; also see Canada, 1981b). The potential violations identified by the commission were of four kinds (the mention of "CCC" indicates a criminal offence, which was in most instances identified by a section number):

1. Rules of the Road
   criminal negligence (CCC)   dangerous driving (CCC)
       illegal U-turns   failure to stop
       unnecessarily slow driving   following too closely
   proceeding the wrong way in one-way traffic
   failure to yield right of way
   improper turns or signals
   failure to obey traffic lights
   failure to drive in proper lane
   improperly overtaking other vehicles
   failure to yield to emergency vehicles
   failure to stop at railway signals
   failure to obey instructions on traffic signs
2. Laws Governing the Identification of Persons and Property
   forgery (driver's license and vehicle registration, CCC, s. 324)
   use of forged document (CCC, s. 326)
   false pretence (CCC, s. 320)
   fraudulently impersonating a person (CCC, s. 361–362)
   supplying false statement for obtaining driver's license
   possession and use of a fictitious license
   dual registration of a surveillance vehicle
3. Laws Relating to Trespass
   trespassing at night (CCC, s. 173)
   willful damaging of property [CCC, 387(1)]
   willful destruction or damaging [CCC, 388(1)]
   "violations of petty trespass legislation are inherent in surveillance
       operations" (Canada, 1981a: 288)
4. Laws Relating to Violations of Privacy
   attaching a beeper to personal effects or clothes of a person (such
       offences have potentially increased since 1981 because of the growth
       of surveillance technology)
5. Criminal Offences (Nonancillary to Physical Surveillance)
   intimidation (CCC, s. 381)

Although this enumeration makes for rather tedious reading, it illustrates forcefully that the resort to means that would be illegal or illicit to nonpolice is deeply embedded in some of the oldest and most banal policing activities, such as physical surveillance. This study of police physical surveillance was under-taken by the McDonald commission at the request of the RCMP in order to show the commissioners, who were at first tempted to take a legalistic approach, the magnitude, if not the impossibility, of the task of bringing all aspects of policing under the strict rule of the law.

The definition formulated above builds on the use of means-that-are-illegal-to-all-but-policing-agents and appears to be less precise than Bittner's, although it is not incompatible with it (the use of violence being in most instances a crime when resorted to by nonpolice). Indeed, it could be argued that the main weakness of the definition is that it does not substantially identify the core competence of the police (the use of force) as the PUFP does. Table 4.1 shows that there is such a great diversity of competences specific to policing agents and defined as crimes or as statutory violations for other citizens that they defy being categorized under any single substantive heading, such as the use of force. The first column of the table identifies a criminal violation, the second one the corresponding authorized police practice, and the third one lists some of the policing agencies resorting to these practices, which are not limited to public constabularies.

This survey is in no way exhaustive. If statutes other than the criminal code are taken into consideration, the scope of the means used by policing agents that are prohibited to other citizens becomes even more impressive.

In summary, the elements of the proposed new definition are the following.

Legalization

There are several misunderstandings that may be generated by the proposed definition of policing agents. They should be dispelled from the outset. The most grievous one would be to believe that policing is an activity that is largely illegal, because it makes use of means prohibited to the rest of the population. The police have been granted in several ways the full authority to resort to these means. In a large variety of instances, they enjoy this authority through the explicit legalization of their practices (for example, electronic surveillance). In democratic countries, such legalization is not arbitrary and occurs in most instances after much public and political debate. Furthermore, the legalized practice is often exercised under judicial surveillance.

In other instances, their authority derives from their being provided with a specific legal defense for violating a particular statute. This legal defense is almost never tested in court, because police are very seldom prosecuted for the kind of violations that are listed in relation to physical surveillance. Thus the provision of a legal defense to policing agents amounts in practice to legitimize their systemic violation of numerous legal statutes.

Finally, their authority derives from certain exceptional powers given to them, often in relation to obtaining confidential information (such as medical records, lists of commercial airline passengers). Other members of the population almost

Table 4.1 The Scope of Extralegality in Policing

Offences against Persons	Physical Force	Policing Agencies
Criminal Law and Other Statutes	Police Legalized Authority	Policing Agency
Murder	Lethal force	Public police, security service, militarized police, some private security agencies (money carriers)
Assault and battery	Reasonable use of force	Public police, riot squads, security services, militarized police, some private security agencies
Possession/use of firearms and prohibited weapons	Submachine guns, taser guns, tear gas, pepper spray, plastic bullet-firing guns, etc.	Public police, riot squads, militarized police
Kidnapping	Arrest and detention	Public police, private security
Robbery	Use of force to make seizure	Public police, security services
Offences against Persons and Property	Search and Seizure	Policing Agencies
Sexual assault (aggravated)	Strip and body cavities searches	Public police, riot squads, militarized police
Sexual assault	Body searches	Public police, private security
Burglary (break and enter, trespass)	House, office search	Public police
Theft inside vehicle	Car, boat, etc.	Public police, customs officers
Violations of Post Office Act, trespass, theft	Searching luggage, purse, mail opening, computer hard disk search	Public police, security services, private security (e.g., in transportation)
Offences against Property	Seizure and Forfeiture	Policing Agencies
Theft	Seizures	Public police, security services
Theft, fraud	Confiscation and forfeiture of assets	Public police, security services
Mischief	Damage to and destruction of property during searches and seizures	Public police, security services

(*Continued*)

Table 4.1 Continued

Offences against Persons and Privacy	Surveillance	Policing Agencies
Invasion of privacy	Electronic surveillance (audio, video)	Public police, security services
Harassment, stalking, intimidation	Physical surveillance	Public police, security services, private security
Harassment, intimidation	Interrogation	Public police, security services, private security
Interception of communications	Mail opening, interception of e-mail messages	Public police, security services
Various Criminal Offences	**Undercover Operations**	**Policing Agencies**
Drug offences	Sting operations	Public police, security services
Offering bribes	Sting operations	Public police, security services
Assault	Protecting cover	Public police, security services
Technical Offences	**Patrol, Physical Surveillance and Undercover Operations**	**Policing Agencies**
Violations of traffic regulations	Chasing (tailing) car	Public police, security services, private security
Forgery	False identification	Public police, security services, private security
Impersonation	Infiltration, testing	Public police, security services, private security

never attempt to exercise these powers, because such attempts would be futile; there is consequently no real need to criminalize them explicitly.

In this definition, reference is made to "diverse means generally prohibited by statute to the rest of the population." The qualification expressed by the word "generally" means two things. First, there are instances where members of the public may resort to these means, for instance in self-defense. Second, not all of what policing agents are doing is prohibited to other citizens. Many activities undertaken within the framework of community and problem-oriented policing could be legally performed by any citizen. It should be noted in this respect that many police do not view these activities as real policing.

Diversification

It was previously noted that my definition of policing agents was not incompatible with Bittner's, as the use of force is, as a rule, prohibited to the rest of society. One could even argue that my definition is a generalization of Bittner's. Dominique Monjardet, for instance, uses the notion of "noncontractual means" to refer to many of the practices listed in table 4.1, which he would view as derivative from coercion and, by implication, from force (Monjardet, 1996: 21). I strongly disagree with the assumption that all "noncontractual" policing activities are ultimately derivative from force. Surveillance is now an increasing part of policing. One could make a case that overt surveillance (such as CCTV cameras) is effective only because it is a warning that the police may forcefully intervene when surveillance detects something wrong. There is merit in this claim. However, since a significant part of surveillance is covert, it has no such deterrent effect. More crucially, one should stress that people strongly react to being under observation, independently of whether they will later be the object of a police intervention. The practice of observation generates by itself feelings of uneasiness, as any field observer can testify. Reducing surveillance to a mere threat to use force is to miss some of the most important aspects of this practice, particularly when it is being generalized, as it now tends to be. The same argument could be made for other policing practices, which are increasingly diversified. Even if they imply an element of coercion, it does not follow that these practices can be reduced to being mere instances of the use of force.

Political Neutrality

The greater part of police studies is devoted to democratic policing, since undemocratic countries do not allow research on their respective police apparatuses. In defining "democratic policing," one might attempt to provide a normative set of requirements that the police apparatus should meet in order to be democratic (Liang, 1992: xx). This procedure defeats in part the purpose of a definition, as the object is defined as it should be and not as it is. One can also proceed in a more factual way and define democratic policing by focusing on the kind of policing that is actually practiced in the current context of democratic societies (for example, Anglo-American societies; see Manning, 2003: 41). This procedure is more epistemologically satisfying, although it uncritically assumes that the police operating in a democratic society are democratic as a result of that. This assumption may be at times controversial in relation to certain components of the police apparatus in a democratic society, such as Edgar J. Hoover's FBI in the later part of Mr. Hoover's tenure or George W. Bush's domestic surveillance apparatus.

In proposing an alternative definition, I tried to make the questions of description and of evaluation distinct. However, the proposed definition is not based on the assumption that the means it refers to should be used minimally, and it does not generate the paradox that description and evaluation are underpinned by divergent logics. However, the proposed definition does not carry the implication that the requirement of minimal use would be altogether dropped. The need for restraint would be adapted to the policing means to be used. For instance, minimal use takes a different sense depending on whether this standard is applied with respect to surveillance, to the use of force, or to speeding when giving chase to a getaway car. The question of restraint in the use of the means of policing is a complex one and will be discussed further in the following chapters.

To Conclude

I will conclude by briefly reviewing the general features of the PUFP and position my own definition in respect to them.

Progressive orientation. The proposed definition asserts that the means legalized on behalf of the police are statutory violations for the other citizens and hence forbidden to them. Furthermore, the police exercise their powers in a controlled way, the stronger controls being external. According to these two features, the alternative definition that I submit is consistent with the PUFP's perspective of an historical evolution toward a lesser usage of harmful or noxious means in society. However, the scope of these means has been much widened by their diversification. There is a risk that the broadening of surveillance could upset the balance established by the limitations placed on the use of police coercion.

Minimal context. The alternative definition is not compatible with the notion of a minimal political (state) context. The notions of legalization, legitimization, and legal empowerment all imply an explicit reference to the modern state. The additional specification in the proposed definition that society may be considered in its whole or in some of its parts entails the existence within the total society of sectarian or private orders.

Uniformed public staff. One of the key contentions against the PUFP is that it basically only refers to public constabularies, from which the rest of policing is considered as derivative. Not only is the alternative definition incompatible with this reductionism, but it is intentionally formulated to overcome it.

Virtual force. The potential nature of the police use of force generates in the PUFP an acute tension between virtual competence and actual performance. Although the alternative definition also refers to a policing competence, it is not as distanced from actual police performance as the use of force. For instance, even when it is not focused on a particular case of physical surveillance or responding to an emergency, car patrol is a general police activity that traditionally takes great liberty with the traffic regulations to which the rest of the population are submitted. This license is not viewed as police deviance but as a requirement for efficiency (which is actually much abused). This issue of a gap between competence and performance is also linked to the requirement for minimal violence that is crucial for the PUFP. Because the use of legalized means is subjected to a variety of controls, the requirement of a minimal use of the specific police competence is adapted to the diversified nature of this competence and to the type of control applied to it. The aim of these controls is not to minimize certain practices but to provide structure to their exercise. For instance, almost all police applications to the judiciary to obtain warrants for electronic surveillance (such as wiretaps) are granted to them (Brodeur, 1997b).

Individual fragmentation. This is a key feature of the PUFP—indeed, of the whole police idea that it embodies—and it reflects its almost exclusive focus on public constabularies. However, when the action of criminal investigation departments, security services (high political policing), and special units such as riot squads are taken into account, action against forms of collective deviance such as rioting, or network delinquency such as organized crime and terrorism, are not inconsistent with the police idea.

Demand-side theory. This feature of the PUFP can also be traced back to its focus on public constabularies, which spend a significant proportion of their time answering calls from the public. In contrast, some the components of the public police apparatus that have previously been listed are largely proactive (they are either self-triggering or responding to a demand originating from the state). Furthermore, if we take into account private security, as indeed we should, the supply side aspect of policing then becomes more prominent, as new services and new products are offered and promoted.

This characterization of the PUFP proceeded in two steps. First, some of its main features were discussed and, second, an attempt was made to articulate the core oppositions that underpinned this paradigm. The alternative definition that was proposed has been so far discussed only with respect to the main features of the PUFP. How the alternative definition stands in relation to the core oppositions underpinning the PUFP is not yet elucidated. Such a positioning of the alternative definition will be undertaken in the subsequent chapters. There are also two further questions that need to be addressed. Does the new definition simply amount to redefining the police as mere delinquents operating under the cover of the law? The same question can be reformulated thus: is the alternative definition precluding the possibility of police deviance, any kind of police behavior being countenanced by the law? These questions will be answered after the actual behavior of the various components of the policing web have been examined in the following chapters.

Police in Uniform

The previous chapter ended with a definition of the police as agents authorized to use diverse means prohibited to the rest of policed society in order to uphold a particular kind of sociopolitical order. This characterization was said to be less specific than defining the police by their capacity to use force. However, this open-ended feature of the proposed definition should not be seen as a shortcoming, since it allows us to take into account crucial differences between the function and behavior of the various components of the policing web. Thus the general nature of my characterization of a policing agent is intended to provide a stepping stone from which it will be possible to identify the specific extralegal means used by different policing agents.

When all democratic countries are taken into account, the public police in uniform—they will henceforth be referred to as constables—still make up the greatest part of policing agents, despite the accelerated growth of the private sector. They generally account for more than 80% of the police personnel of law enforcement agencies, with the exception of forces such as the FBI or the German Bundeskriminalamt (BKA), which are wholly composed of plainclothes investigators and analysts. This study of the various components of the police apparatus will begin by focusing on public constables, who are the most visible element of this apparatus.

Conflicting Synecdoches

As previously mentioned, uniformed police make up the largest part of public police forces. In much the same way, the biggest part of private security agencies is composed of uniformed guards. But although they are the backbone of all policing organizations, constables are just one part of a public police force. Uniformed personnel within a police organization also include members of a diversity of units—riot squads, SWAT teams, and various other specialists. Despite being much less numerous, however, nonuniformed detectives have shaped the quintessential image of the police officer presented to the public by the media and by crime fiction. The police are, in fact, generally viewed through two basic and conflicting synecdoches, the detective and the constable.[1]

The synecdoches of the detective and of the constable do not operate at the same level. The first one plays a decisive part in the field of popular, fictional, and media representations of the police. Academic research on policing, however, is anchored in different waters. As Bayley (1985: 114) noted, with many other researchers, police research essentially focuses on patrolling as it is performed by personnel in uniform. This observation applies as much to descriptive as to prescriptive and evaluative research. A great deal of descriptive empirical research has addressed the question of how the police actually spend their time. This question was narrowed down to what patrolmen and women were in fact doing.

From the 1970s on, there was a considerable body of reform literature that examined what the police should be doing. Ranging from community to evidence-based policing, Weisburd and Braga (2006) enumerated no fewer than eight new models of policing, this enumeration not being exhaustive. For the most part, these models applied to uniformed constables. With the exception of a few controversial evaluations of criminal investigators (Greenwood et al., 1975 and 1977) that were not replicated, the question "What works in policing?" was asked in relation to the performance of police working in uniform (Bayley, 1998). Patrolmen and women thus provide the window through which most researchers observe policing. The same remark is true of guards in uniform in the private sector. Police in uniform also provide the basis for generalizations encompassing the whole of policing, the work of Bittner being a paradigmatic example of this process. Although authors such as Klockars (1985) and Reiner (2000a) distinguish between patrol and detection in their work, there are few researchers who have conducted separate inquiries into constables in uniform and plainclothes investigators, with the notable exceptions of Ericson (1981/1993 and 1982) and Manning (1977, 2004, and 2006a).

---

1. A synecdoche is a figure of speech in which the part is made to represent the whole or vice versa (for example, one speaks of a "new face" to refer to a new person). With the metaphor, it is probably the most common figure of speech in all languages. The use in scientific language of figures of speech like synecdoches and metaphors has been criticized.

Despite their separate realms, the synecdoches of the detective and the constable are connected in critical ways. Viewing all policing through the lens of detective work implies that the importance of law enforcement and crime fighting are overestimated. One of the initial mainsprings of academic research into policing has been to remedy this imbalance and to stress the great variety of situations in which the police were asked to intervene. Media and academic presentations of the police conflict to the extent that they do not focus on the same type of police officer nor on the same type of policing situations in order to, respectively, mythologize or to demythologize the police. Although this clash of representations will not altogether cease, we might develop a clearer picture of policing if we were more specific in the kind of policing agent we are studying and if we tried to integrate into a comprehensive theory the findings of diversely focused inquiries. This is what we will attempt to do in the following chapters, beginning with the uniformed police.

This chapter on the work of uniformed constables focuses on a discussion of the notions of *force* and of *visibility*, which are presented as the core elements of a theoretical account of public constabularies. As previously argued, defining the police by their use of force implies in practice that the scope of policing is narrowed down to the work of public constables. The role of force in policing and, more particularly, the kind of force that is used by the uniformed police will be examined here, and the concept of visibility will also be linked to the work of the uniformed police. The notions of wearing a uniform and of being visible are nearly equivalent: the uniform is an instrument of visibility, and identical visual appearance signifies membership in the same organization.

This chapter is divided in four parts. First, basic demographic information is presented and leads to a discussion about the increasing proportion of women in the composition of police forces, which I regard as a key development. Second, the numerous studies of what uniformed police do and how they spend their time on duty are analyzed. In the third part, various aspects of police visibility are examined, and it is argued that visibility is a key source of police impact on the social environment. Finally, the issue of force is addressed, with an attempt to find what is specific in the police use of force, in addition to the normative requirement of using minimal force. Insofar as force can be used to characterize policing, policing can be retrospectively used to assess the nature of force, which is a vague and ill-defined concept.

Who the Police Are

This section will provide data on basic demographical variables such as age, sex, ethnicity, and level of education. Despite being scattered and indicative, these data are presented here for two reasons. They provide an occasion to address some of the theoretical issues connected with police demographics and, more important, they highlight the importance of one development: the growing place of women in policing.

Age

It is difficult to find national data on the age of constables. In their general portrait of local U.S. police departments, Hickman and Reaves (2003) do not present data on the age of the police. I have conducted two surveys of large samples of police in the Canadian province of Quebec. The first survey, conducted in 1991, collected data from a sample of 656 constables who were part of the city of Montreal Police Department (MPD). All sergeants and lieutenants were included in the sample and filled out a questionnaire; the sample also comprised rank and file constables chosen at random. It was found that 30.5% of all respondents were aged between twenty-one and thirty, and only 5% of respondents were aged between fifty and sixty. Since the sample included a majority of middle-rank supervisors (52%), the relative youth of the surveyed constables was all the more remarkable. The other survey was conducted in 1992 over a random sample of 852 constables drawn from various Quebec police forces. Of the respondents, 46% were between nineteen and thirty years of age, and fewer than 4% were over fifty. In its 2006 annual report, the MPD reported that 40% of sworn agents were aged thirty-four years or less and that 4% were over fifty. These findings are in line with the quoted median age of thirty-five for police (constables and plainclothes) in the international literature.

The first issue raised by the relative youth of the police workforce is that people with a limited experience of life and the unformed judgment that often accompanies this are called to intervene in the context of complex crises involving a tangled web of human relationships. Not having the experience to resolve such crises peacefully, they tend to impose a coercive solution that exacerbates the conflict rather than resolving it.

A second issue is that a great number of police are in a position to have two careers, one following the other. In North America, many police are entitled to a retirement pension after having spent some twenty-five years in a public police force. Being retired at an early age—between forty-five and fifty years old—they undertake a second career. In English-speaking countries, there are two careers of choice for a police person retiring after having enjoyed several promotions during his or her initial police career. One is to become chief of a smaller force, often policing a country township. Another favored option is to be part of the management of a private security agency. This option is also available for retiring police in centralized countries, who cannot move from a bigger to a smaller force. This career mobility of police officers results in a blurring of the distinction between urban and rural policing and, more significant, between public and private policing. This undermining of the distinction between public service and private enterprise is also increasingly occurring in the military and the intelligence communities.

A third issue raised by the involvement of police in two back-to-back careers concerns their legitimacy, when both careers are undertaken in the public sector. Police retire with a comfortable pension to which they may add the substantial wages that they earn in their second career. Having two sources of income may not sit well with the public.

Sex

Gender studies have assumed an increasing importance in the social sciences. Police studies are no exception. There is now a large body of literature on women in policing, which dates back much further in time than is usually thought (Allen, 1925; for more contemporary work, see Fielding and Fielding, 1992; Martin and Jurik, 1996; Brown and Heidensohn, 1996 and 2000). Heidensohn (2005: 752) gives an account of the pioneer days of women in policing. National and international conferences on women police are now regularly held, and their proceedings are published (Pagon, 1996; Canadian Police College, 1997; Institut de Police du Québec, 2000). There are also several associations of women police such as the International Association of Women Police and the British Association for Women in Policing.

Women in policing thus have a long history, which was overshadowed by the masculine character of police culture (Heidensohn, 1994: 294; Young, 1991: 191). Marie Charpentier is generally cited as being the first policewoman; she was sworn in during the French Revolution in 1792. It is also claimed that Rose Fortune, a former black slave who escaped from New York City to the town of Annapolis Royal in Nova Scotia at the end of the eighteenth century, was the first policewoman. Her memory is honored by the Canadian Association of Black Law Enforcers. A police matron was hired by the New York police in 1845. The year 1910 can be considered as a landmark. In that year, Alice Stebbins Wells was hired by the Los Angeles police department and became the first policewoman given powers of arrest. Shortly after that, Edith Smith was also sworn in with powers of arrest in Grantham, in the United Kingdom. By the end of the First World War, more than two hundred U.S. cities had women working as police (House, 1993). In Canada, women were hired by various municipal police departments—Vancouver, Edmonton,

Toronto, and Montreal—between 1912 and 1915. Women had to wait until 1974 to gain entry as sworn police officers in the RCMP.

The current data on the number of women in the police refer not only to women constables but also to women in all areas of public policing. However, since some 90% of police women are to be found at the level of constable, overall statistics can be interpreted as mainly referring to police in uniform (Lebeuf, 2000: 21). According to the U.S. Bureau of Justice statistics, female police in local police departments comprised 10.6% of police officers—441,000 full-time sworn personnel—in 2000, up from 8.1% in 1990 (Hickman and Reaves, 2003). This represented an increase of some 17,300 officers, or 59% of their number in 1990. In 2001, the proportion of females in all U.S. police forces was 12.7%. There is a great deal of variation from one local department to the other. For instance, women comprised some 30% of the Philadelphia police force, according to its latest annual report.

In the United Kingdom, the proportion of women police increased from 12% in the 1990s (Heidensohn, 1994: 301) to 17% in 2000 (Heidensohn, 2003: 568). In Canada, the proportion of female police officers increased from 4% in 1985 to a current 18.5%, according to the official figures released in 2007 by Statistics Canada—Juristats. As in the United States, there is significant variation between the different municipal forces. According to Juristats, women now comprise 29% of the police personnel of the MPD, an unusually high percentage. All police candidates in the province of Quebec must have a college degree earned in a special program of police studies in order to be recruited by a police force. Female students vastly outperform their male counterparts in school, particularly at the secondary level. The police studies program being highly competitive, only the students with the best marks at secondary school can enrol in this program and thus obtain the college degree that is required for being hired by a police force. It follows that there is a growing imbalance between female and male students who have the necessary educational requirements to pursue a career in the police. Such explanations can account locally for the fast rate of increase of women in police organizations, but should not hide the general fact that this growing proportion of women in policing reflects a growing openness of public police forces. With respect to its masculinity, the police culture is in great contrast with the culture of the fire brigade. The number of firewomen is as yet insignificant, for instance making up 1% of the personnel of Montreal fire department as compared to 29% of the MPD.

Raffel Price (1996) noted that in respect to the feminization of policing, the situation was similar in North America, Europe, Asia, and Latin America. France is in this respect an interesting case. The French public police establishment is notably conservative. Save for a brief episode that spanned less than a year (1999–2000), the French police were impervious to any of the policing innovations described in Weisburd and Braga (2006), and remain so. This conservatism naturally extended to community policing, which is believed to have been instrumental in the integration of women into police forces (Heidensohn, 2003: 571). Yet, the French police are open to change in other important respects. The percentage of female public police stands at 14% in France, which is above the international average. Geneviève Pruvost (2007 and 2008) examined how women fared in such an environment, which is at the same time open to the integration of women and yet otherwise reluctant to change its ways. Her detailed findings are consistent with other studies, while at times going beyond them. The findings of Pruvost (2007) that challenge the stereotypes of women in policing are the following:

A taste for action. Women do not apply to become sworn officers in the Police Nationale or the Gendarmerie for different reasons than men do. They view policing as fulfilling their sense of adventure and their need for action (Pruvost, 2007: 279). In short, they are no Florence Nightingales in pursuit of Willy Sutton, to quote the title of a famous article by Bittner (1974/1990).[2] In Susan Miller's study of gender and community policing in Jackson City in the United States, police women attracted to high-crime neighborhoods were said to act as "Dirty Harriets" (Miller, 1999: 217). Race riots that erupted in 2008 in a Montreal suburb were said to have been caused by "Dirty Harriets."

Involvement in all police duties. Women are not confined to doing "police social work" such as policing juveniles and attending to female victims. The greatest proportion of policewomen is to be found within the emergency units—called *Police Secours*—and that are the most exposed to unpredictable violence (Pruvost, 2007: 281). They are also posted in squads fighting serious and organized crime, and work as crime investigators. Women are even part of units that specialize in maintaining order and crowd control. However, the women recruited into these special units are submitted to a process of overselection, which means that the criteria applied to women joining these units with respect to fitness, training, and other qualifications are higher than those required of male applicants.

Promotion. Females constitute 14% of police personnel and 17% of commanding officers (329 women and 1,576 men). According to the latest available projections made by the Police Nationale in France, one-fifth of the police ranking officers will be composed of women in the years following 2005. The downside of this upward mobility is that promoting women is also a means of pigeonholing them in administrative duties. Fielding et al. (2002: 216) mention

---

2. See note 1 in chapter 1 for the format of the references to Bittner's work.

a parallel development in the United Kingdom. Women can also rise to the highest rank, the chief of the national police of Norway being a woman. Some of these developments favor the complete integration of women in policing systems, despite being at odds with the traditional "caring" images associated with womanhood. Unfortunately, they are undermined by other organizational trends that show how resistant police forces are to change.

Quotas. What we previously noted on the better performance of women at school in Canada is also occurring in France. Women perform better in written recruitment exams and also exams for promotion in France. This is why the two French police administrations—Police Nationale and Gendarmerie Nationale—have imposed quotas limiting the recruitment of female police. Interviews with high-ranking police officers in the MPD lead one to believe that the same will happen in Montreal.

Exclusion. There are several kinds of units involved in crowd control in France, and women can be part of some of them. However, the emblematic antiriot specialists are the Compagnies républicaines de sécurité (CRS), who are the toughest police in France, with a reputation to match. Although part of the civilian police apparatus, the CRS are militarized units, and their members live in barracks. Women are excluded from CRS field operations, although they can be part of the organization in an administrative capacity (as commissaires). Hence, to quote the title of Heidenshon's article (1994), it is not believed in France that women "can handle it out there" in all kinds of situations.

Tutelage. There is an unwritten but closely followed policy in the French police requiring that at least one man be part of a team of police answering a call or intervening in some other capacity (Pruvost, 2007: 284). That is, women police cannot intervene on their own without being accompanied by at least one male policeman. It is not so much that women are excluded from using force as police, but that they allegedly cannot do it alone. As Pruvost (2007: 284) notes wryly, "two women don't add up to one police."

Locker-room culture. According to Pruvost (2007: 282), the true test of the integration of women is their willingness to join the boys in their ways of relaxing: drinking on the premises of the precinct, sexual innuendo, and even physical harassment. The current wisdom is that a woman who is the victim of sexual harassment should have avoided the kind of situations leading to it.

Anyone familiar with the literature on women in policing organizations will recognize that these features of the predicament of females recruited into the police are widely shared. The common features are sometimes quite specific. For instance, more than 50% of women police choose a companion among their police colleagues, the female often outranking her companion in the organization (Pruvost, 2007: 280). Similarly, more that 50% of policewomen in the Montreal police have a male colleague as a life partner (Meloche, 2000: 60). The overall conclusion of Pruvost is that the feminization of police organizations represents a potent example of the divorce between gender and sex: the partial or complete masculinization of policewomen is a precondition for their professional recognition by their male peers and for their progression through the police hierarchy (Pruvost, 2007: 283). The upshot of her analyses and of similar research conducted in other countries is that the power of the police organization to change the individuals belonging to it is much greater than the capacity of these individual members to change the police organizational culture. Miller (1999: 226) argues that the structure of community police capitalizes on the skills that have been culturally designated as feminine and believes that "a crucial issue for community policing involves how best to attract 'masculine' men to perform 'women's work' in a masculinist police subculture" (1999: 214). As Miller is aware, this is a programmatic statement that does not yet apply to the evolution of policing. Its very formulation would deter most policemen from even applying for the job.

Ethnic and Racial Minorities

The quantity of research on the integration of racial and ethnic minorities in public police organizations has not grown at the same rate as the research on police women. Seminal research on black police in the United States (Alex, 1969; Alexander, 1978; and Leinen, 1984) and in the United Kingdom (Holdoway 1993 and 1996) did not grow into a large body of literature. This problem is now being revisited by researchers in the larger context of the policing of minorities, which attracts greater attention (Bowling and Phillips, 2003: 541–544).

Only a few countries collect statistics that differentiate among the ethnic origins of the police. Based on the 2000 general census, it is estimated that in the United States racial and ethnic minorities comprised 22.7% of full-time sworn personnel of local police forces, black police accounting for 11% of this total (Hickman and Reaves, 2003: iii). The black minority grew by 35% from 1990 to 2000, as compared to 93% for Hispanics during the same period (female police grew by 59%). According to a 2009 press release, a majority of the NYPD recruits are curently nonwhite (Powell, 2009). In the United Kingdom, ethnic minorities constituted 3% of police in 2001–2002, according to Home Office figures (Bowling and Philips, 2003: 541). In Canada, the 2006 annual report of the MPD stated that "visible minorities" (blacks and Asians) accounted for 2.5% of police staff.

The early U.S. research on minorities in the police focused exclusively on the black community and painted a gloomy picture. Blacks were first hired in the

NYPD at the end of the nineteenth century as doormen. Their situation got progressively better, and Leinen (1984: 244) believed that it was safe to say that institutional discrimination had been all but eliminated in the 1980s. The civic rights movement and black police militancy leading to the creation of a black police union (the Guardians Association) were said to have driven the positive changes in the conditions of black and other minority officers. The number of black police grew through policies of positive discrimination that imposed quotas in recruitment and promotion to the lower levels of the hierarchy. Although minorities gained access in all police units, this access was in practice limited in relation to some preferred assignments in the NYPD (Leinen, 1984: 249). Whether in the United States, the United Kingdom, or Canada, police extracted from minorities are still underrepresented in certain choice assignments and at the higher levels of command (Bowling and Phillips, 2003: 542).

Despite the symbolic resonance of the fact that people from ethnic minorities have succeeded in becoming police chiefs, there are still some intractable problems. First, even if institutional discrimination has been successfully fought off, discriminatory and even racist behavior from officers belonging to the ethnic majority toward their colleagues from ethnic minorities is still rampant (Leinen, 1984: 255; Bowling and Phillips, 2003: 541). Second, police from minorities are still the object of multilevel marginalization: they are partial outsiders in the eyes of their colleagues from the majority, are unwelcome in all-white affluent neighborhoods, and are often scorned by the minority to which they belong. Finally, the implicit motivation leading to their recruitment—acting as a buffer between the white police force and the alienated minority communities—has not produced the desired outcome. It is well documented that some minority officers tend to overcompensate for their ethnic origins by being tougher on their own people than their white counterparts. In a disturbing study of the use of firearms by white, black, and Hispanic police in the NYPD, Fyfe (1981: 370; also see Fyfe, 1988) found that rates of involvement in fatal interracial shootings by black and Hispanic officers (black versus black shooting rate per 1,000 = 19.6; Hispanic versus Hispanic rate = 9.9) are more than twice as high as the rates for white officers versus members of those same minority groups (8.3 and 3.6, respectively). These higher rates of shootings are in great part explained by the fact that black and Hispanic officers are deployed among their own community. Nonetheless, they provide no evidence that minority groups are better off being policed by constables from minority groups.

The general conclusion that follows from research on minorities—including gay police (Leinen, 1993)—and women points to the great difficulty of transforming police organizations from within. The argument that previously excluded groups such as people from minorities and women would inevitably bring new perspectives and become catalysts for changing police organizations and their occupational culture just by "being there" (Bowling and Phillips, 2003: 543) seems prematurely optimistic. Members of an organization can change it, or be changed by it themselves. The transformational powers of the organization on its members should not be underestimated. This sober perspective is based on one overriding fact: whoever they may be, people join the police much more because they want to belong to it than because they want to change it. Thus, they are more prone to being changed by the organization than to be agents of its transformation.

Education

There is enormous variation among countries with respect to the training and educational requirements for entering police service. This can be shown by comparing the two neighboring countries of the United States and Canada. In 2000, 15% of U.S. local police departments, employing 32% of all officers, required new recruits to have completed at least some college education, up from 6% of departments employing 10% of officers, in 1990 (Hickman and Reaves, 2003). In the Canadian province of Quebec, no one can be recruited by a police organization unless they have completed two years of college in a special program of police studies (older recruits are exempted from this requirement, but their numbers are swiftly dwindling). Applicants to the RMCP need to have a secondary school diploma and succeed at tests on policing aptitudes developed by the force. In addition to this, 23.7% of the sworn officer staff of the MPD have university diplomas ranging from a certificate to a Ph.D. This already significant variation would become overwhelming if the police forces of all democratic countries were taken into consideration.

There are other issues than educational levels meriting consideration. An important question was recently raised within the European Union (EU). The Council of the European Police College (CEPOL) established a project group on a European approach to police science, which issued its final report in 2007 (CEPOL, 2007). The report proposes to make a distinction between police training and police education. According to the CEPOL glossary, training is defined as "a process of gaining knowledge, skills and attitudes, which are needed to perform specific tasks" (CEPOL, 2007: 141). The same glossary also defines education as "a process and a series of activities which aim at enabling an individual to assimilate and develop knowledge, skills, values and understanding that are not simply related to a narrow field of activities but allow a broad range of problems to be defined, analysed and solved. Education usually provides more theoretical and conceptual frameworks designed to stimulate analytical and critical abilities" (CEPOL, 2007: 141). Training concerns the tactics of policing in a narrow sense, whereas education is more oriented toward strategy. The report was launched in October 2007 during a conference, where it became clear that there was a great deal of dissent between EU countries as to whether the police should have both training and education, or just limited training. Norway spearheaded the countries arguing for the wider requirements, whereas Slovakia did not believe that police needed training that went beyond the specific (physical) skills needed to be a uniformed constable. Whether training and education are defined in the manner of CEPOL (2007) or not, the pressing issue remains the scope of police instruction. Closely related to this question is whether police instruction should be exclusively delivered within specialized policing academies, as in France, or acquired in civilian educational institutions where police recruits mingle with other students, as in Canada.

Whatever the answers to these questions may be, two things are clear. First, the trend is toward a police education defined in a broader sense than practical police training. Second, it is no less clear that police recruits first join the police to fulfill a quest for action (or economic security) rather than a quest for knowledge. Attempts to mold them into knowledge workers—to use Peter Drucker's much-abused phrase—go against the grain of the profession and the motives of those who embrace it, which does not necessarily imply that they are bound to fail.

What the Police Do

The question of what the police actually did and how they spent their time was perhaps the most topical issue for police research in the 1970s and 1980s. With few exceptions, it was raised exclusively in relation to uniformed police. The research on this issue is still relevant and, despite a limited consensus on some of its findings, the nature of police work is a question that is far from having been settled. However, the focus of police research has shifted from descriptive to prescriptive and evaluative research after the 1980s. The question "What works?" has thus superseded the former interrogation on what the police did, which is still unresolved.

Before looking at these research findings, important features of the question itself—what police do—should be stressed. No professional activity has been the object of as much investigation as what the uniformed police spend their time on. This is due in great part to our fascination with the police; it is also due to the peculiar difficulties of answering the question. The question itself is not as straightforward as one would expect: "What is it that the police do?" What is really being asked is: "Are the police spending as much time fighting crime and enforcing the law as is implied by their popular image?" The answer to this question is potentially demystifying (Reiner, 2000a: chap. 4) and consequently controversial. There are three specific aspects of policing that continually feed the controversy.

Competence vs. Performance

As we have seen, one of the most fundamental aspects of the PUFP is its definition of the police by their capacity to use force rather than by their actual use of it. Even if the police never used force, they still should be defined by their licence to use it (Bittner, 1972/1990: 187). Such playing upon potential and actual behavior can be turned on its head. Bittner (1974/1990: 240) argues that criminal law enforcement is "not at all characteristic of day-to-day, ordinary practices of the vastly preponderant majority of policemen." This statement is based on an examination of actual police performance: "when one looks at what police actually do, one finds that criminal law enforcement is something that most of them do with the frequency located somewhere between never and very rarely" (240). This fact eventually leads Bittner to exclude law enforcement from the core definition of the police function.

Once the use of a distinction between potential and actual police behavior is agreed upon, however, we cannot exclude law enforcement any more than force from being at the core of the police function on the weak ground that the police do it infrequently. If we disregard actual police behavior by granting force a defining role with respect to public policing, why not apply the same reasoning to law enforcement, which intuitively is as much entitled to make up the core of the police function as the use of force? This is essentially what Shearing and Leon (1977: 341) have concluded: "In our view, both law enforcement *and* physical force are essential features of the police licence and capability, and, therefore, of the police role.... *Everything* a policeman does takes place within the context of the police licence and capability [to enforce the law and use physical coercion]." Bittner would have made the objection that Shearing and Leon were wrong in believing that law enforcement was a specific trait of policing, law enforcement being "in our times... the task of a host of law enforcement bureaucracies" (Bittner, 1974/1990: 237; also see Mawby, 2000). Nevertheless, their reasoning was quoted approvingly by Cordner (1979: 58–59) in a paper critical of the alleged demystification of the role of the police as well as in subsequent editions of his influential work on police administration (Cordner, 1989: 69; Cordner and Sheehan, 1999: 39; Cordner,

Scarborough, and Sheehan, 2004: 43). The gist of Cordner's position was to argue that crime- and enforcement-related work far exceed service-related work (Cordner, 1989: 69).

The option to argue either on the basis of what the police are actually doing or on the basis of what they are licensed to do precludes any definitive answer to questions concerning the true nature of their activity. False alarms, which comprise 90% of all alarms, illustrate the problem: in terms of actual police action, they do not count as crime-fighting incidents; with respect to potentiality, they should be classified as crime incidents.

Committed and Uncommitted Time

Reiss (1971: 95, table 2.5) estimated that 14% of patrol activity was spent answering calls and 85% on routine patrol. With the exception of tiny percentages of various kinds of activity (always less than 1% according to Reiss, 1971), routine patrol is uncommitted time. Following the Kansas City patrol experiment, much work was devoted to assessing what part of patrol officers' time was committed to specific assignments and what part was uncommitted and spent on unfocused patrol (Kelling et al., 1974a and b; Kelling, 1978).[3] In Cordner's dense formulation, "police patrol work might best be described as the handling of situations and the self-directed use of uncommitted time under circumstances of ambiguity" (Cordner, 1979: 59). Thoroughly reviewing this kind of research, Whitaker (1982: 16) concluded that officers assigned to patrol spent about one-third of their time on specific tasks and that the remaining two-thirds was uncommitted and variously used by patrol officers (traffic stops, citizen-initiated encounters, personal business of the officer, and driving around).

Cordner (1989: 69) revisited the issue years later and once again reached a similar conclusion: "the biggest portion of patrol officers' time is uncommitted, and officers vary greatly in how they utilize this time." This conclusion also

---

3. The Kansas City preventive patrol experiment is the most famous experiment that has been carried out on the impact of police routine car patrol on the community.

> The Kansas City, Missouri, Police Department conducted an experiment from October 1, 1972, through September 30, 1973, designed to measure the impact routine patrol had on the incidence of crime and the public fear of crime. This experiment...accurately determined that traditional routine preventive patrol had no significant impact on the level of crime or the public's feeling of security....A great deal of caution must be used to avoid the error of believing that the experiment proved more than it actually did. One thing the experiment did not show is that a visible police presence can have no impact on crime in selected circumstances. The experiment did show that *routine preventive patrol in marked police cars has little value in preventing crime or making citizens feel safe.* (Kelling et al., 1974: Preface, vii; emphasis added).

applies to the findings of Canadian research (Griffiths et al., 1999: 116). The large amount of uncommitted time makes it difficult to produce a precise assessment of what the police are actually doing, the verb "to do" generally meaning in this kind of assessment "doing something." The records used to determine how the police spend their time, such as, for instance, the kinds of calls received and answered, refer to specific assignments. In order to evaluate what the constables are doing during their entire daily shift, one needs observational studies, which are fewer in number and require the police to consent to being subject to observation. The strong impact of uncommitted time is shown in Comrie and Kings (1975:11), one of the paradigmatic studies of a constable's work in urban settings. In relation to calls made to the police and the time spent by patrolmen answering these calls, crime-related work accounts for 34% of calls (only service calls rank higher, at 35%), while 35% of incident-driven man-hours are spent answering crime incidents (the highest percentage of time devoted to incidents). Crime-related work thus appears to be a significant part of police work. However, if the denominator used to assess how police time is spent is neither the number of calls received nor the man-hours devoted to follow up on incidents, but the whole daily tour of police duty—eight hours on average—the figures become drastically lower. Only 11% of police working time is spent on responding to incidents (Comrie and Kings, 1975: 11), the time devoted to dealing with *crime* incidents falling to a low 4% of a tour of duty (12; also see Tarling, 1988: 10). By comparison, 9% of a tour of duty is spent on refreshment periods (Comrie and Kings, 1975: 20).

Reactive and Proactive Mobilization
Several findings suggest that fewer than 20% of police mobilizations are proactive (Black, 1968; Webster, 1970; Reiss, 1971; Cordner, 1979). These findings were confirmed by the community and problem-oriented policing research, which stressed that one of the key shortcomings of traditional policing was its reactive nature. Ericson (1982: 75) is one of the few authors to have found that proactive mobilizations were nearly on a par with reactive ones (47.2% compared to 52.6%). Ericson (1982: 74) explains this huge discrepancy with previous research by the fact that he excluded from his computations all mobilization data that did not produce police-citizen interaction. Although far from being as significant as uncommitted time, police proactive work is also a problem for the assessment of what the police do. Reactive mobilizations generally leave a paper trace, whereas a portion of self-initiated police action is only accessible through observational studies.

Despite these limitations, many studies of police work were conducted, mainly from 1965 to 1995, although there was also influential research undertaken after 1995 (for example, Knox and MacDonald, 2001). These studies were largely impelled by the depiction of the public constable as "philosopher, guide and friend" proposed by Cumming et al. (1965), which challenged the crime focus usually attributed to police work. Thus, the great majority of them tried to estimate the part of police work dealing with crime incidents and the part relating to other situations, with a particular emphasis on service duties. With very few exceptions, all studies reviewed in this chapter base their structure on the criminal work/noncriminal work dichotomy. One of them replaced this dichotomy by the distinction between conflict and non-conflict situations (Smith and Gray, 1985). I reviewed ninety-five of these studies and excluded eighteen of them on methodological grounds. Most of the seventy-seven studies that I retained were conducted in either the United States or the United Kingdom; a few studies are international in scope, and others originate from Canada or the Netherlands. The number of studies quoted in the research literature is greater than the number of studies that are reviewed in this chapter. However, many of the former are unpublished reports with a narrow circulation within a particular research community. I excluded all reports to which I did not get firsthand access.

The studies included are based on a variety of sources: records of calls from the public, dispatch reports, computerized assignment records, police incidents reports, individual officer logs, activity files maintained collectively by police units, surveys of police officers (questionnaires and interviews), observational reports (from researchers), police department annual reports, and national crime surveys, such as the British Crime Survey. The studies were classified according to their sources: outside calls, various sources and surveys, and observational studies. A category for review articles and chapters was also added. The purpose of adding this category was twofold. First, it was to include, albeit indirectly, studies that I could not access but which were discussed in the review essay. Second, it was to show how the empirical studies were integrated into the general research literature. These review essays generally conclude by giving an overall assessment, which is quoted. Except for classifying the studies in relation to their basic sources, a detailed evaluation of their methodology was not performed. On the one hand, the data and methods used are rather disparate and would require a lengthy analysis. On the other hand, the general conclusions of these studies point in the same direction despite their methodological disparity. A thorough methodological assessment would thus have made little difference to the general outcome of the meta-analysis.

Tables 5.1 to 5.4 present the main findings of the studies of police work that were reviewed. They are limited to presenting the percentage of police work that was related to crime (and, by implication, not related to it). This procedure contrasts with Jones et al. (1986: 120), who classified the findings of the eight studies he reviewed into three categories (crime related, order related and service related). The number of the categories used in the seventy-seven studies included in my own sample was much too large to be reduced to three or four subcategories without artificiality. More important, there is an irreducible ambiguity in a great part of what the police do, which defies tidy subcategorization (Cordner, 1979: 57). There is, however, no suggestion in the following analysis that the high percentage of noncrime-related police work can be interpreted as some form of "social service." It comprises a significant variety of tasks, in which traffic and administrative paperwork play a dominant role. This issue is addressed in more detail later.

Explanations of the nature of the various items included in tables 5.1–5.3 are first given, and then the general picture that they provide is presented in a summary table.

Table 5.1   Calls Made to the Police

Authors	Estimated Percentage of Calls Concerning Crime
Cumming et al. (1965) – U.S.	5.4% to 23.6%
Wilson (1968) – U.S.	10% (Wilson refers to law enforcement rather than crime)
Black (1970) – U.S.	less than 50%
Bercal (1970) – U.S.	16% in Detroit (39% radioed calls in Detroit; 51% radioed calls in Saint Louis)
Reiss (1971) – U.S.	17% (as assessed by police; 58% as reported by caller)
Punch and Naylor (1973) – U.K.	27% to 50%
Comrie and Kings (1975) – U.K.	34%
Boydstun et al. (1977) – U.S.	43%
Tien et al. (1978) – U.S.	60%
Lilly (1978) – U.S.	32% (all calls answered by police classified as crime calls)
Antunes and Scott (1981) – U.S.	20%
Ekblom and Heal (1982) – U.K.	18% (2% urgent calls)
Jones (1983) – U.K.	43%
Shearing (1984) – Canada	24%
Jones et al. (1986) – U.K.	51%
Sherman (1996, pub. 1987) – U.S.	34% (repeated calls to hot spots)
Shapland and Hobbs (1989) – U.K.	17% (calls processed as crime calls)
Gilsinian (1989) – U.K.	15%
Waddington (1993) – U.K.	"minorities of calls"
Home Office (1995) – U.S.	36%

The studies in table 5.1 are listed according to their order of publication. The country where they were performed is also mentioned. When an estimate had to be made, the rule followed was to give the highest estimated percentage of crime-related items in a study—calls, dispatches, incidents reports, and so forth; this rule was followed throughout all tables. In other words, no attempt was made to minimize the percentage of police activity devoted to dealing with crime incidents. In a few cases, the reviewed study was conducted on more than one site, in which the percentages of crime-related calls did not coincide; in such cases the full range of assessed percentages is given.

Not all of the studies appearing in table 5.1 focus exclusively on whether or not calls to the police are crime-related, but they all address this question in a sufficiently detailed way to permit a reliable estimation of the nature of the calls made to the police. Black (1970) studied the social organization of arrest, but is quite clear that fewer than half of citizens' calls have to do with crime (Black, 1970: 1087). He also refers approvingly to Cumming et al. (1965). This latter study does not explicitly use the crime/noncrime dichotomy, preferring to make a distinction between calls about "things" and calls for support in the case of persistent and periodic personal problems (Cumming et al., 1965: 200). Some of these problems are clearly crime-related and some are not. Dealing with repeated calls to "hot spots," Sherman (1996) has a higher probability of finding crime-related calls. Finally, studies such as Reiss (1971) or Comrie and Kings (1975) address many topics and fit in more than one category. With two exceptions, all the studies found a low percentage of crime-related calls, this being especially true with the studies performed before 1980 (except Tien et al., 1978).

In table 5.2, Reiss (1971: 95) found that the percentage of all police activity dealing with crime was very low (the portion of criminal proaction is 0.2% of routine patrol time). Webster presents the same set of findings, one in article form and the other in book form. In the final analysis, they will be counted as one study (Webster, 1970). As previously stated, Smith and Gray (1985) dichotomize conflict and nonconflict situations rather than crime and noncrime-related incidents. Tarling (1988) assessed the time spent by constables on thirteen activities in ten British police forces. In seven of these forces, 10% or less of the time is spent on crime incidents (public order incidents account for 4% or less of the activity of eight of the ten forces). Assuming that all report writing by constables is on criminal incidents, the range of the time devoted to crime-related incidents increased to between 20% and 33% when the writing of these reports is taken into account, depending on the force being examined by Tarling (1988: table 3.1). Bayley (1985) reviewed a significant number of police forces in different continents. The portion of activity related to crime varies greatly, depending on which cluster of forces he is referring to. On one page, Bayley (1985: 126) concludes that

Table 5.2   Various Sources and Surveys

Authors	Estimated Percentage of Police Time Devoted to Crime
Martin and Wilson (1969) – U.K.	30%
Webster (1970) – U.S.	36% (16.58% crime calls; 19.68% crime "on view": sum total 36.26%)
Reiss (1971) – U.S.	3.04% (sum total of all police activity)
O'Neill and Bloom (1972) – U.S.	5%
Comrie and Kings (1975) – U.K.	4% of actual police time
Hough (1980) – U.K.	33 1/3% (including false alarms)
Southgate and Ekblom (1984) – U.K.	14%
Kinsey (1985) – U.K.	57%
Bayley (1985) – International	66% – 80% of work concerns crime ("overwhelmingly" law related)
Brown and Iles (1985) – U.K.	10.1%
Smith and Gray (1985) – U.K.	51% (conflict solving rather than crime work)
Tarling (1988) – U.K.	7% – 14%
Skogan (1990b) – U.K.	18% – 30%
Greene and Klockars (1991) – U.S.	42.9%, maximum figure – loose criteria; 26.4% – using stricter criteria
Bennett and Lupton (1992) – U.K.	25% – 33% (depending on environment – rural / urban)
Bayley (1994) – International	"the police spend very little time of their time dealing with crime"

66% to 80% of police activity revolves around crime; on the next one (127), he asserts that noncriminal matters dominate police work, according to the bulk of the evidence. His final conclusion is that "the issue of the nature of police work cannot be considered to be resolved" (127), because of the manifold difficulties in comparing data from different countries. The general trend is the same as in table 5.1 above, with most studies resulting in low assessments of crime-related police work. The distance separating the various estimations is extreme, ranging from a low 3% (Reiss, 1971) to a high 80% (Bayley, 1985).

Table 5.3 presents observational studies. Skolnick does not provide percentages but a qualitative assessment. Kelling et al. (1974b) focus on committed and uncommitted patrol time. They found that 60% of patrol time was uncommitted, and that only half of this time was devoted to police work, strictly speaking. My estimation that 15% to 30% of total patrol time is crime-related is rather high.

Table 5.4 presents a summary of the findings of the studies listed in the previous tables. As can be immediately seen, nine-tenths of the studies (46/51) determined that the percentage of police work devoted to crime-related work

Table 5.3 Observational Studies

Authors	Estimated Percentage of Police Time Devoted to Crime
Skolnick (1966) – U.S.	police work "minimally about legal proceedings"
Black (1968) – U.S.	less than 50% of encounters concern crime
Martin and Wilson (1969) – U.K.	30%
Reiss (1971) – U.S.	3.06%
Kelling et al. (1974b) – U.S.	15% – 30% (my estimation)
Cordner (1979) – U.S.	13% crime, 4% noncrime, 44% administration, 39% ambiguous
Punch (1979) – Netherlands	49%
Lundman (1980) – U.S.	33%
Ericson (1982) – Canada	8.5%
Whitaker (1982) – U.S.	38%
Mastrofski (1983) – U.S.	29%
Shapland and Vagg (1987) – U.K.	no % (low rating of crime among identified problems)
Shapland and Hobbs (1989) – U.K.	no % (low frequency of crime among reported incidents)
Knox and MacDonald (2001) – U.K.	22%

was 50% or less, two-thirds of the studies concluding that this percentage was 33% or less. There is no significant discrepancy between the three types of studies examined. The studies with the narrowest basis—citizens' calls to the police—found that the portion of police work dealing with criminal incidents was somewhat higher, even if it generally remained under 50%. Among the more robust observational studies, there are none asserting that criminal work was more than half of the work time of uniformed police. One such study (Galliher et al., 1975) was finally excluded from this review because it exclusively focused on *potential* suspects and hot spots.

As previously said, the inclusion of review articles and chapters, whose authors had access to studies I could not find, increases the scope of my own analysis. The left-hand column indicates whether these researchers tended to

Table 5.4 Summary of Findings

	33%	33%–50%	+ 50%	Total
Calls	12	6	2	20
Various sources	12	2	3	17
Observational	10	4	—	14
Total	34	12	5	51

minimize (MIN) or to maximize (MAX) the portion of police work related to crime, or presented a balanced assessment of it ("middle of the road," Cordner, 1999 and 2007). This MIN/MAX classification does not mean that these authors unduly reduce or increase the time spent by constables fighting crime. It is made in relation to the general conclusions of these review papers. Many authors actually engage in an extensive review of the literature before presenting their own empirical findings; this is why, although they are mentioned in the previous tables, they also figure in table 5.5. I included many review papers by Gary Cordner who, with colleagues, published textbooks on police administration, because this author took an active part in the debate on the nature of police work. This is not the case with other authors of such textbooks, and their review of the literature is more perfunctory than Cordner's. Although there are twenty reviews included in table 5.5, some of these reviews have the same author (Cordner). The number of the reviews undertaken by different authors is seventeen. Of these authors, only two (Shearing and Cordner, with their respective colleagues) tended to maximize the portion of police work devoted to crime incidents. In other words, the proportion of reviews that minimize this portion or take a balanced view of it is 88%. This percentage is virtually the same as the portion of empirical studies included in tables 5.1–5.3 (90%) that present a low estimate of crime-related police work.

In the course of reviewing the studies on police work in its relation to crime, I came upon a finding of research undertaken in the United Kingdom, which is not consonant with our common representation of police work. It should influence the way we think of such subjects as police visibility and the capacity of constables to stop a criminal incident from happening (see table 5.6).

In an early study on uniformed police, Hough (1980: 10) found that patrolling tended to be concentrated in the night shift. This finding had paradoxical consequences: first, police visibility on the streets is greatest when fewest people are awake to see them; second, whether these people are actually able to see the police is even open to question, as visibility is greatly diminished in the dark; and third, most preventive patrol is undertaken when fewest crimes are committed—in the small hours of the morning (most crime is committed during the evening shift). In the light of these facts, Hough (1980: 11) quotes the U.S. Katzenbach Commission (1967) on its estimation that a patrol officer in a large city could expect to intercept a street robbery in progress once every fourteen years. Clarke and Hough (1984: 7) determined on the basis of burglary rates and evenly distributed patrol coverage that a patrolling officer in London could expect to pass within a hundred yards of a burglary in progress once every eight years, without necessarily catching the burglar or realizing that a crime was taking place. As is shown in table 5.6, research undertaken in Britain from 1980 to

Table 5.5 Review Articles and Book Chapters

	Authors	Estimated Percentage of Police Time Devoted to Crime
MIN	Banton (1964) – U.K.	police are "peace officers" rather than "law enforcers"
MIN	Punch (1975) – U.K.	50% – 75% non crime ("secret social service")
MIN	Kelling (1978) – U.S.	Less than 20%
MIN	Walker (1977) – U.S.	service functions have priority over crime fighting
MAX	Shearing and Leon (1977) – Canada	all activity is potentially law enforcement
MAX	Cordner (1979) – U.S.	more crime-related than believed; basic fact is multivalence of calls
MIN	Morris and Heal (1981) – U.K.	much time on noncrime
MIN	Ericson (1982) – Canada	"tiny fraction" of time devoted to crime
MIN	Wilson (1983) – U.S.	"majority of calls are for service"
MIN	Wycoff and Manning (1983) – U.S.	66% service and other maintenance
MIN	Smith and Klein (1984) – U.S.	"most calls do not involve criminal incidents"
MAX	Jones et al. (1986) – U.K.	13% – 57% (figure most often quoted is 30%)
MIN	Moore and Kelling (1983) – U.S.	"small portion devoted to crime"
MAX	Cordner (1989) – U.S.	"crime and law enforcement far exceed service"; most calls radioed to police cars involve crime
BAL	Greene and Klockars (1991) – U.S.	20% (at most); assessment of previous work by others leading to overall balanced assessment
MAX	Cordner and Trojanowicz (1992) – U.S.	same assessment as above (Cordner 1979)
MIN	Bayley (1994) – International	7% – 10% devoted to crime ("very little has to do with crime")
MIN	Stanfield (1996) – Canada	20% crime-related (80% service-related)
MIN	Reiner (2002a) – U.K.	"order maintenance is the core of the police mandate"
BAL	Cordner and Sheehan (1999) and Cordner and Scarborough (2007) – U.S.	"middle of the road position is advisable"; same text in 1999 and 2007 editions

Table 5.6   Time in Station and out of Station

Authors	Estimated Percentage of Police Time in and out of the Police Station
Hough (1980) – U.K.	most time out of station spent during night shift
Brown and Iles (1985) – U.K.	50% general duties (mostly in-station)
Tarling (1988) – U.K.	50% in-station: Northumbria and West Midlands
	56% in-station: Merseyside
	51% in-station: Metropolitan officers
	27% in-station: Lancashire
Bennett and Lupton (1992) – U.K.	36.4% – 43.1% in-station (depending on location)
Knox and MacDonald (2001) – U.K.	43% in-station
Bowling and Foster (2002) – U.K.	more than 40% in-station; based on external sources

2002 replicates the finding that uniformed police spend at least 40% of their time in the police station. According to my own research, detectives spend an even greater portion of their time in their office.

My own survey of the opinion of large samples of uniformed police in 1991 and 1992 collected the answers of 852 police respondents from various forces in Quebec on aspects of their work. These findings dovetail with the previous analyses, as follows.

Police Mandate

The constables were first asked what the police mandate was on the basis on their experience: the majority (44%) answered that it was maintaining order; in the Canadian context, order maintenance is understood as targeting all kinds of incivilities and troubles rather than as riot control, as in continental Europe. Crime-related work was divided in two categories: 12% of respondents answered that crime repression (catching offenders) was the core mandate, and 16% that it was crime prevention, understood in the broad sense of encompassing police visibility. The service functions accounted for the rest of the answers (28%). Crime prevention being a fuzzier category than crime repression, the crime-related work is much less prominent than order maintenance.

Most Frequent Situations

A six-degree scale ranging from "very often" to "never" was used to assess their estimation of the frequency of their intervention in four kinds of situation. The significant answers are at both ends of the scale. For situations requiring urgent intervention, the "very often" and "often" categories composed 57% (26/31) of responses; for contexts involving neither urgency nor criminal violence, they were 64% (40/24); the same scores on the scale for violent crime situations were 36% (11/25); for uncommitted time, they were 39% (22/17). At the bottom of the frequency scale (either "not often" or "rarely") were violent crime situations (35%) and uncommitted time (36%). Thus, the same group of respondents assessed in a dichotomous way the frequency of their interventions in violent contexts and the proportion of their time that was uncommitted, with fewer answers falling in the middle of the scale. The lack of consistency between these answers tends to confirm Cordner's dictum on the ambiguous nature of police activity.

Major Part of Uniformed Police Activity

The respondents were asked to answer this question in two ways. First, they were asked to identify the one activity among six to which they devoted the major part of their time; second, they were asked to assess independently how often they performed each of these six activities. The answers to the two questions were consistent. The percentages with respect to the first question are given in the following list; the respondents' scores for the "very often" option on the frequency scale for each activity are also given (in brackets).

Serious crime: 3.4% (major part of time) and 5.7% (top frequency score)
Petty crime: 10.4% (11.8%)
Order maintenance: 24.6% (28.8%)
Problem-solving (noncriminal kind): 44.8% (49%)
Administration: 13.7% (29.2%)
Testifying in court: 0.2% (3.4%)

Although there is consistency, these percentages also show that selecting a "major part" answer does not always coincide with performing the task that it describes very often, as is shown by the "administration" category.

Most Similar Profession

The police surveyed were also asked which profession was most similar to theirs. Interestingly, the single profession most often chosen is mediator. The least similar professions are identified as lawyers and the military. As both professions are associated with key components of the police idea (law enforcement and use of force), these police ratings are quite significant, as shown in the following list.

Mediator: 18.1%
Social worker: 8.1%
Educator: 2.8%

Doctor/psychologist: 1%
Military: 0.8%
Lawyer: 0.4%
All of the above: 51.4%
None of the above: 12.4

This 1992 list of professions deemed to be close to policing (mediator, social worker, and educator) is unexpectedly consonant with the list provided by Cumming et al. (1965) in their celebrated article (philosopher, guide, and friend).

Despite the reservations made at the beginning of this analysis, several conclusions can be cautiously drawn from it. The supply and demand terminology introduced in the previous chapter is used to formulate some of these conclusions.

First, the data on which the studies of police work are based are generally related to the demand for police services, such as citizens' calls, and the police reaction to these demands. The data on police proactive work are much fewer. A great deal of such work concerns stopping vehicles to perform various checks and searches.

Second, the data on public demand can be reinterpreted by the police. As Reiss (1971) has shown, the number of public calls relating to crime can be drastically defined down by police dispatchers. The vulnerability of such data to reinterpretation is not limited to the police profession.

Third, the most frequently recurring finding is negative: crime-related work plays a limited role for constables. However, there is within this general assessment a great deal of variance in the statistical determination of this limited role.

Fourth, the demand for and the supply of police services is diverse and difficult to categorize when we step out of the category of crime-related work. Although it is difficult to identify a major trend in public demand, order maintenance stands out as the principal request. Contrary to early intimations, service calls and social service work do not compose a substantial part of police work. The primacy of order maintenance is confirmed by the police offer on the supply side (in the police conception of the nature of their mandate). This is the main finding of all the survey work that I undertook in Canada, using a large sample of police.

Fifth, there is an important portion of police work that resists classification, such as uncommitted time and in-station time, not to mention "what-they-might-have-done" time, which is an open-ended construct.

The apparently urgent question of what the police do was superseded at the end of the 1980s by the question of what works in policing. Evaluative research gained its prominence when the literature on policing moved from fact-oriented descriptive questions to prescriptive reform programs. Such programs generated the need for evaluating the extent to which they worked. There is one striking development that occurred as research moved from "what happens" to "what works." Despite the fact that all previous reforms of policing—for example community and problem-oriented policing—were based on research that stressed the significant diversity of the problems that the police were called to solve (Goldstein, 1990), all these research findings appeared to have suddenly evaporated (Bratton and Knobler, 1998). With few exceptions, evaluative research on policing now focused on assessing what worked in terms of lowering the incidence of crime and the level of public insecurity (Sherman, 1986, 1990, and 1992; Sherman et al. 1997; Sherman and Rogan, 1998; and Zhao et al., 2002). Disorder became a prime concern mainly because it fostered crime and feelings of insecurity through the weakening of informal community control (Wilson and Kelling, 1982; Skogan, 1990a).

The Means of Policing

The police perform such a variety tasks that it is difficult to define them by what they do. The previous analyses illustrate this point. An alternative research strategy, advocated by Max Weber in his attempt to define the state (which is also involved in innumerable domains), is to focus on the means used by the police in order to find what is specific to police work. The definition of the police by their competence to use coercion is the best example of such an approach. Building on the elements of a theory of policing developed in chapter 4, we now examine the question of the way in which the police perform their duties. This question is much too broad to be addressed in its full scope. Two issues will be raised. The issue of police visibility is addressed first, and then the issue of force is once more discussed in an attempt to find what is specific in the way the police use force.

Visibility

Police visibility is one of the most pervasive notions of the literature on policing. It was often referred to in the writings of the nineteenth-century British police reformers. It gained a renewed prominence in the writings of the advocates of community policing, who stressed the benefits of foot patrol (Trojanowicz and Bucqueroux, 1989). Three basic points need to be made in relation to the concept of visibility. First, visibility is not to be equated with the more general notion of perceptibility. Perceptibility encompasses the five senses, whereas visibility only refers to the visual sense. Differences in the medium of perception may affect the impact of policing. For instance, the sight of a foot patrol officer may enhance security, whereas hearing police sirens may generate anxiety. With respect to crime repression, smell plays an important role in cases of driving under the influence of alcohol. Second, and most important, visibility is not a thing but a relationship to the environment. Depending, for instance, on how crowded a street is, an officer patrolling on foot may be conspicuous or nearly invisible. The same point can be made in relation to the various periods of the day (for example, nighttime). Third, visibility is also an associative process that leads beyond what is seen. It may trigger strong emotions or act as a signal for something else, and both processes can occur at the same time.

As seen in chapter 4, the existence of public police forces is concomitant to the birth and development of cities. According to urban sociology, the city is defined as a "world of strangers" (Lofland, 1973: 19; also see Simmel, 1970, and Milgram, 1970). Within this shared perspective on the city, Bittner contended, as we have seen, that the minimal function of the state is to create conditions for the orderly coexistence of strangers; he further argued that the police mandate is to control the predatory violations of these conditions through the use of force. It can also be maintained that the notion of visibility is logically prior to the notion of force, and that it begets its own kind of city ordering. Lofland (1973: 18) defines a stranger as "anyone personally unknown to [an] actor of reference, but visually available to him." She further adds that the world of urban strangers is located in the city's *public* space (19).

For city dwellers, urban public space is characterized by overload (Milgram, 1970: 1462). Overload ranges over cognitive capacities and over behavior. Since we cannot identify all persons met in the city on a daily basis or be courteous to them all, there is a need to bring some sort of order into this overload. Lofland (1973) identified two logics of urban public order: the logic of "appearential" ordering and the logic of spatial ordering. According to the former logic, city dwellers are identified on the basis of visual appearance (mainly clothing); according to the latter, their identification rests on which part of a city they are living in, either by choice or by coercion. Both ordering logics rest on visibility: "appearance is most reliable as an indicator when it is linked with location" (Lofland, 1973: 84). Although she stresses that both types of ordering are coercive (Lofland, 1973: 177), she does not discuss the public agencies that enforce these logics of ordering. Police forces play a crucial role in this regard. However, the main point is not that the police enforce an ordering by appearance (for example, a dress code), but that their action is predominantly based upon visual clues. There is a conceptual nexus where the notions of the city, strangerhood, and policing come together under the category of visibility.

The Visibility of Crime and Disorder

As we found before, a crime can be committed within a short distance of patrolling police officers without their knowledge or intervention. In these cases, the visibility gap neutralizes police efficiency. Police are the usual channel through which offenders are charged with a criminal offence and brought to trial. Figure 5.1 shows those offences under Canadian Criminal Code offences that most frequently led to a conviction in a Canadian adult court in the last period for which such statistics are available (1999–2000; Juristat, 2001). The crucial part played by visibility stands out clearly in a discussion of this table.

The offence most frequently resulting in a conviction is impaired driving (driving under the influence of alcohol—DUI). Not only are criminal charges of impaired driving the result of proactive police work but the police are also generally spurred to action by the external signs of delinquent behavior (such as erratic driving, behavior of the stopped motorist, the smell of alcohol). Canadian statistics on adult admissions to custody show that DUI is a determinant factor. In a small Canadian province such as Prince Edward Island, DUI

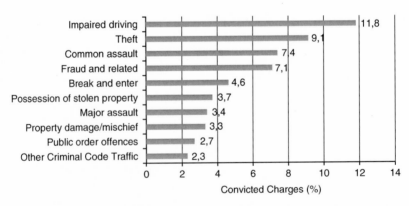

Figure 5.1 Criminal Code Offences Most Frequently Receiving a Conviction in Adult Criminal Court in Nine Provinces of Canada, 1999/2000
Note: Combined, the ten most common offences listed in the chart represent 54% of the total for all offences resulting in a conviction. No other types of offence represented at least 2% of the total, though combined, they represent the remaining 46% of all convicted offences. Data do not include New Brunswick, Manitoba, British Columbia, and Nunavut.
Source: Adult Criminal Court survey, Canadian Centre for Justice Statistics, Statistics Canada.

accounts for as much as 59% of sentenced admissions to custody, as compared to violent crime (18%) and property crime (13%; see Juristat 2005 and Canadian Centre for Justice Statistics, 2005). In the second largest province of Canada (Quebec), DUI accounts for 18% of sentenced admissions to custody, as compared to violent crime (7%) and property crime (18%; see Juristat, 2006). In France, a country very different from Canada, the situation is nonetheless similar: traffic offences account for 41% of criminal convictions, whereas all offences against property comprise only 24% (Bauer, 2007: 166).

Possession of stolen property (PSP) represents 3.7% of all convictions. However, just giving a percentage does not reflect the true importance of PSP in obtaining a criminal conviction. According to the 2007 annual criminal statistics for the city of Montreal, 43,583 cases of theft and 20,383 cases of breaking and entering were reported to the police, as compared to only 700 cases of PSP. This enormous discrepancy is more or less the same across all Canadian cities. Yet, despite its very small number, PSP makes up 3.7% of all convictions, as compared to 9.1% for theft and 4.6% for breaking and entering. Those percentages reflect several things. Obviously, the clearance rate of PSP is incomparably higher than the resolution of other property offences. This nearly perfect clearance rate is explained by the fact that PSP, like other offences of criminal possession (such as drugs), is not "solved" pursuant to an external complaint that leads to an investigation. Reporting a case of PSP and solving it generally coincide, for instance when police check a suspicious car or perform an arrest for another offence (such as a burglary). Also, it must be emphasized that making such a case basically rests on visual clues. For instance, the presence of incriminating objects or substances is discovered in the trunk of a car in the course of a routine check on a vehicle. Many of the offences generating a significant portion of convictions—DUI, PSP, mischief, and public order offences—are the targets of proactive police operations. At the level of the uniformed police, proactivity is essentially triggered by the visibility of certain crimes and acts of delinquency.

This connection between the visibility of offences and the processing of offenders by the police is quite extensive. Most offences appearing in figure 5.1 have a relatively high degree of visibility—with the possible exceptions of theft and fraud, the latter being mainly credit card fraud—and constitute "street crime," such as the many cases of common assault. Criminal outbursts of violence that leave manifest physical traces (wounds, injuries, and dead bodies) are the main cause for the most severe sentences (Juristat, 2001: 6; also see Juristat, 2005 and 2006). This can be verified throughout history (Radzinowicz, 1968: 191) and across countries (Bauer, 2007: 166). By contrast, fewer than 1% of convictions for criminal offences were against a company in Canada for the years 1999–2000 (Juristat, 2001: 1). Similarly, all "economic and financial" criminal violations accounted for fewer than 3% of all convictions in France in 2005 (Bauer, 2007: 166).

Consistent with his definition of the police through their capacity to use force, Bittner claimed that they only targeted offenders who would potentially seek to violently oppose their arrest (Bittner 1974/1990: 242). This would explain why economic crimes, for which perpetrators almost never physically resist their apprehension, have such a low priority on the police agenda. There is some truth in this remark. In view of the observations made above, the low visibility and stealthy character of white-collar crime are probably more important than the nonviolent behavior of economic offenders in explaining the police neglect of it.

The visibility of incidents that trigger police intervention is of four kinds.

Physical visibility. These incidents, such as mischief or street crime, are proactively dealt with by the police. All kinds of disorder—small-time drug dealing, prostitution, defacing of public and private property, loitering—are prime members of this category. Their visibility is not only physical but immediately perceived.

Investigative visibility. As will be seen in the next chapter, the resolution of homicide inquiries depends little on investigative reasoning, cases being solved mainly on the basis of testimony provided by eye witnesses. The ocular nature of these testimonies has not been stressed enough in police proceedings. Many of the offences generating a high level of conviction are cleared through visual clues (such as PSP and the few cases of breaking and entering and theft solved by the police).

Symbolic visibility. These offences correspond in part to what British researchers have called "signal crimes" and "signal disorder" (Innes, 2004a, 2004b), which generally vary from one community to the other. Signal crimes and disorderly incidents, which generally involve violence, resonate with an enlarged significance that is an add-on to their primary visibility. Being perceived as symptoms of a larger social pathology, they impel individual risk-avoidance reactions in members of the community (Innes and Fielding, 2002: 7–9).

Constructed visibility. The symbolic visibility of a criminal incident may be given firsthand. For instance, a crime of intimidation or of retaliation may convey by itself a message that can be immediately perceived by a community without any further processing. In many cases, the visibility of a crime is enhanced by the media, which build on its original resonance to give it an aura that has a life of its own (Innes, 2004b). All terrorist incidents represent cases of enhanced media visibility. The action of the media is not limited to the enhancement of visibility. In some instances, the visibility of incidents is wholly fabricated by the media (Altheide, 2002) and may spur "moral panics" (Cohen, 2002). The disappearance of children provides particularly volatile material for the construction of visibility. Constructed visibility is a prime example of the phenomenon that we described under the name of "intensive quantities" in chapter 1. Constructed visibility and symbolic visibility overlap in many instances.

Taking place against the backdrop of statistical data, the discussion has so far proceeded in terms of the visibility of incidents. There is yet another kind of visibility that is of paramount importance:

Offender visibility. Many individual offenders and groups of offenders have a high visual profile. Criminal motorcycle gangs (such as Hells Angels) provide a paradigmatic example of offender visibility. These gangs are composed of criminals following a dress code that is both so conspicuous and so formalized—with specific "colors" and badges indicating their standing in the gang hierarchy—that they may be described as criminals in uniform. All offenders do not have a visual profile as high as that of criminal bikers. Nevertheless, delinquent milieus such as, for instance, prostitution and drug trafficking are populated by people that stand out because of their dress, the vehicles they drive, and their lifestyle. The various distinctions made with respect to visible crime incidents also apply to offenders with a high visual profile. Flashy offenders eventually become choice police targets because their conspicuousness is perceived over time as an act of defiance of police order. White-collar criminals generally have a very low visual profile and receive little attention from the police.

The visibility of criminal offences and offenders does not have the sole effect of triggering police action (on a selective and discretionary basis). It also impacts on communities, where it generates mixed feelings and reactions. The most frequently quoted feeling or reaction is fear. The study of the fear of crime has generated a huge body of research, reviewed by Hale (1996) and Zhao et al. (2002). The concept of fear of crime is open to criticism and should be superseded by the notion of insecurity, which refers both to a feeling and to a contextual probability of victimization. The concept of fear of crime was early criticized by researchers on the basis that criminal victimization appeared to be negatively related to fear (Box et al., 1988: 352). Box et al. also argued that victimization increased fear only when it interacted with disorder in neighborhoods plagued with high levels of incivility. The connection between fear and disorder was definitively established by Skogan (1990a). A crucial difference between crime and disorder is that the latter has a greater potential for effects through its visibility; a significant volume of crime may occur in a neighborhood without being perceived by the community. Finally, Ditton et al. (1999) have shown that the threat of criminal victimization was as likely to cause anger as fear. It does appear, on the one hand, that community fears are not primarily related to crime and that, on the other hand, the risk of victimization provokes other feelings than just fear.

Hale concluded his review of the research of fear of crime—or, to use a better word, insecurity—with the acknowledgment that insecurity was "a problem in its own right" (Hale, 1996: 131). Police researchers had also reached this conclusion. Referring to papers published in 1978 and 1981, George Kelling wrote that he had "suggested that the primary problem regarding crime in the United States [was] not crime itself but the exaggerated fear of crime and the consequences of that fear" (Kelling, 1983: 163). This conclusion followed his observation that while foot patrol did not have a significant effect on crime, it "consistently and systematically" affected citizens' fear of crime. Kelling's perspective has two far-reaching implications. First, it implies that police strategies devoted to reducing insecurity may be "strategies in their own right" and that the perceptual problem they are trying to address is no less real than the actual occurrence of crime. Second, these strategies—such as foot patrol, which is explicitly referred to by Kelling—are grounded, to a significant degree, in police visibility. On the basis of these implications, policing may tentatively be conceived as a chain reaction process in which visual appearances feed back into each other: the uniformed police are spurred to action by visual propellants, and they use their own visibility as a basic problem-solving device.

Police Visibility

An account of police in uniform should begin with what makes them visually distinct, that is to say, their uniform. In her essay on ordering the city, Lofland (1973: 85) did not fail to stress the part that uniforms played in the logic of appearances. The uniform is only one of three kinds of identifying clothing, the others being livery and armor. Livery used to be worn by servants and was the mark of an inferior condition. In the United States, the police first perceived the uniform as a kind of livery and were initially reluctant to adopt it (Walker, 1992: 12–13). When standardized in appearance, armor can be said to be a kind of uniform, although its primary function is not to identify but to protect. One of the clearer trends in the evolution of police uniforms is their progressive transformation into body armor. This transformation is now completed with special units such as SWAT teams, whose physical appearance is indistinguishable from that of soldiers. In many Western countries, bullet-proof vests are now part of the police uniform.

In addition, since the uniformed police have become motorized, they drive police cruisers with distinctive markings.

The police uniform's most general function is to provide a solution to the urban problem of perceptual overload and to enhance police visibility. When the new system of policing was created in England in 1829, putting constables in uniform solved several problems. It provided the new body with a collective identity and, more important, the uniform was an instrument of uniformity and a sign of unification. One of the main problems identified by the police reformers was that the "present police [consisted] of disjointed bodies of men governed separately, under heterogeneous regulations, and acting...under the earliest set of expedients" (Chadwick, 1829, quoted in Taylor, 1997: 148). The men wearing the uniform were also to be "conspicuously marked" with the letters of their divisions and their own numbers, so that they could be easily identified and complained against if they failed to perform their duties properly (Radzinowicz, 1968: 162). Through personal identity markings, the uniform was a means to promote individual accountability. A great deal of care went into making the new uniform as distinct as possible from that of the military, who had been the butt of severe criticism for their brutal repression of public disorder. At its deepest level of meaning, the uniform thus became the symbol of a whole style of operation and of its potential efficiency.

During the formative years of the RCMP (1872–1873), Alexander Morris, the chief representative of the federal government in the Canadian North-West, wrote to Prime Minister Macdonald that "the police should be under military discipline and if possible be *red coated*—as 50 men in red coats are better here than 100 in other colour" (quoted in Macleod, 1976: 14). The color red has always been a dramatic symbol of power and heroism, and still is. The efficiency of the police uniform in "conspicuously marking apart" groups and individuals is demonstrated *a contrario* when it is perceived in some communities as a public stigma. In his pioneering research on blacks in the NYPD, Nicholas Alex asked black police officers what the police uniform meant to them. He found that they looked at the uniform "as a target of ridicule, scorn, abuse, derision from both the Negro and white communities and from whites in the department," and referred to it as a "bag" or a "monkey suit" (Alex, 1969: 172).

In a prescient article, Bahn (1974) identified three general functions of the police patrol. The first two—preventing crime and disorder through randomized deterrent patrol and answering calls in the shortest time possible—are traditional. He also identified a third function of patrol: "This is the simple function of citizen reassurance—the feeling of security and safety that a citizen experiences when he sees a police officer or police patrol car nearby" (Bahn,

1974: 340). This quote encapsulates two of our previous observations: that experiencing feelings of insecurity is a problem in its own right, and that this problem is tentatively solved through a perceptual intervention that is also a strategy in its own right.

What is now called reassurance policing was developed in the United Kingdom through the work of Jason Ditton, Nigel Fielding, Jane Fielding, Martin Innes, and Ian Loader, among others (for a review, see Ditton and Innes, 2005). It is implemented in several locations in Britain (for example, in Surrey). Reassurance policing is no windfall, and its development builds on previous reforms of policing, the Chicago Alternative Policing Strategy (CAPS) being explicitly mentioned as the forerunner of reassurance policing. CAPS is a resilient community policing initiative that was implemented in Chicago by a team led by Wesley Skogan in 1993. As its name implies, CAPS does not consist of a loose set of unrelated programs, but is defined by a comprehensive organizational strategy resting on three pillars: citizen involvement, decentratization, and problem-solving. These core elements are bound together by leaving the setting of priorities and the means of achieving them largely to the residents and the police who serve in their neighborhood for a significant amount of time (Skogan, 2006: 27–28). The concerns of the community are aired in monthly beat meetings. The Chicago Police Department is working with the University of Illinois at Chicago to develop a geo-based Internet survey that will measure what really matters for the community, including indicators of hot spots and disorder, fear and strained police-community relations (Rosenbaum, 2006: 258). This effort to bridge the gap between the true concerns of the community, as based on the citizens' perception of what threatens them most, and their unwarranted redefinition by the police according to their own purposes was integrated into reassurance policing. There can be no successful reassurance efforts without trust in the police. Building trust and legitimacy implies taking seriously the community's input and acting upon it.

Reassurance policing brings together several strands of the analyses previously undertaken in this chapter and elsewhere in the police research literature. The detailed examination of how uniformed police spent their time impelled a critical review of the traditional functions of the uniformed patrol and questioned the strength of the connection between police patrol and criminal law enforcement work. These interrogations fostered challenging findings, such as the relatively small portion of crime-related calls made to the police, their nonurgent character, the consequent limitations of a system of motorized police that was geared to answer urgent calls, the discovery of police working time that was either uncommitted or spent in-station, and the attendant low probability of solving property crime in progress through roving patrol. These questions also led to a more thorough examination of the impact of police visibility. Following the famous Kansas City police experiment, it was held that motorized and foot patrol had markedly different impacts on crime and insecurity, foot patrol being more reassuring (Kelling et al., 1974a and 1974b). Furthermore, police visibility was not always associated with a reduction in insecurity; a sudden and uncontrolled increase of police presence had an adverse effect on public feelings of security (Ditton and Innes, 2005: 601). However, the sum of these research findings failed to result in the production of a common body of policing doctrine. The only finding on which everybody agreed was that foot patrol increased feelings of security (Ditton and Innes, 2005: 601). Despite some reservations on the effect of police visibility, the demand for it remained acute and was a key feature of all innovations in policing.

The overall result of those developments is the gradual acknowledgment that the police operated on two distinct levels. The first of these is the actual environment in its various dimensions—physical, social, and so forth. The second is the public perception or reconstruction of this environment, which is a complex process that involves the decoding of signals embedded into the environment. Not only do the police operate on two distinct levels, moreover, but they also operate in different ways at each of these levels. They try to modify the environment—for instance, the actual rates of victimization—through the exercise of their powers and through various strategies for action. These instrumental attempts are increasingly the object of systematic assessments. After an auspicious beginning, these assessments generally end up indicating the limited impact of specific police initiatives on the environment over an extended period of time. On the level of the perceived environment, the police act through interventions that aim to change the way that the environment—for instance, a particular neighborhood—is perceived by the community. These interventions are pursued through communications with the public, such as carefully laying out for the media a display of drugs and weapons seized during a raid. Interventions aiming to change public perceptions can also occur at the street level. In the course of research on drug dealing in downtown Montreal, I interviewed the area commander of a busy downtown police district. For him, there was little to be gained in arresting small-time dope peddlers. Prosecuting a small-time dealer was costly and time-consuming, and another street dealer would immediately take his place. The precinct commander instructed his uniformed staff to clean up the downtown area by pushing back the dealers into the numerous drinking establishments that lined the downtown streets. Drug dealing was not to occur in plain view on the streets. He explained that this operation had no impact on the amount of drugs that were sold. However, people taking a stroll downtown could now do so without bumping into drug dealers, and tourists were under the impression that the downtown area was relatively clean. The century-old debate on prostitution in Quebec was couched in exactly the same terms. Since prostitution could not be eradicated, the question was how to drive it underground and make it invisible (Brodeur, 1984a). This area commander was essentially involved in the policing of appearances.

The Circle of Policing Appearances

In a paper that foreshadowed reassurance policing, Shapland and Vagg studied the capacity in which the public wanted to use the police. They found that the most important role that the public wanted the police to assume "was the symbolic one of, by their very presence, proclaiming a state of order" (1987: 60). This insight was confirmed by a thorough review of the research on the effect of police presence on public fear reduction and public satisfaction (Zhao et al., 2002). This review concluded that police presence did have a strong effect on public fear reduction and also, by implication, on public satisfaction with the police, the latter being strongly associated with successful fear reduction programs. Shapland and Vagg built on previous work by Manning (1977/1997: 24–26), who articulated a conception of policing as the performance of a symbolic ritual before an audience of citizens; Manning further developed this perspective in *The Narcs' Game* (Manning, 2004; also see Dorn and South, 1991 and 1992). The notion of "policing appearances" (Brodeur, 1994b) is also an attempt to capture the insight underpinning reassurance policing and similar models.

The notion of policing appearances can change its meaning, depending on which word is stressed. It refers both to the policing of appearances and to the appearances of policing. Its reversibility can be used to summarize the preceding line of argument. Far from being mere fictions contrasting with reality, appearances, as they are understood here, refer to these aspects of reality that perceptually impose themselves upon us and bring out our attention to them.

Policing appearances first refers to the external object of policing, this object being understood as the target or the focus of police intervention. Whether it is crime, disorder, or the host of problems that present themselves, the police act on whatever problematic incident "that may announce itself in various manners" in the public space (Bentham, quoted in Radzinowicz, 1956: 435). Problems that do not "announce" themselves, like white-collar crimes or political corruption, are generally left unattended. Following the crash of financial markets in 2008, the situation is now changing in respect to white-collar crime, and it can be expected that white-collar criminals will be the new public scapegoats. Many of the usually self-announcing problems, such as the provision of illegal substances and the varieties of disorder, are recurrent and defy any permanent solution. Consequently, what the police are aiming to achieve is an ordering of appearances so that they are perceived as normal enough so as not to generate intolerable levels of insecurity.

Policing appearances also refers to interventions where the police build upon their own visibility in the public space to normalize appearances. There are two kinds of "perceptual" interventions that must be distinguished from one another. Deterrence is aimed at potential offenders, whereas reassurance is aimed at potential victims. Although they may use the same means—for instance police presence saturation—they may have opposite effect. There are situations of high deterrence and low reassurance, the reverse also being possible. All police perceptual interventions stem from the radical assumption that the perceived deployment of a police force is in itself the greatest proof that an environment is secure. In relatively consensual democracies, the police constitute the self-accomplishment of security. So-called failed countries where the policing system has collapsed are highly insecure, in spite of being saturated with heavily armed military and mercenaries. Countries such as Iraq and Afghanistan feature an extremely high rate of police casualties. The police are not killed for what they are doing, but for what they are standing for: the promise of a civilian order based upon the securization of appearances.

Force

It was previously stressed that the police operated on two distinct levels, the first being the actual environment and the second one the public perception of this environment. Depending on what level they operate on, the police use different means. Beginning with the perceived environment, the role of police visibility and the targeting of public perceptions was examined. We now turn to physical intervention, with a focus on the use of force. Visibility and force are not opposite means of policing. In many instances they are complementary, as is suggested by the phrase "a show of force." Legitimate force is often exercised with great effect within the realm of the visible. Police brutality, however, shuns visibility. The pivotal role of the concept of force in defining the police function was thoroughly examined in chapter 4. This chapter now looks at concrete aspects of the use of force by the police in specific contexts.

As we have seen, Bittner was very reluctant to include within the police mandate the control of collective violence. Nevertheless, riots played a crucial role in the history of the establishment of public police forces. British historians are divided on the extent to which the need to exercise political control over the emerging working class in England was influential in the creation of the new police in 1829 (Reiner, 2000a: 11–56). They agree, however, that fears generated by perceived increases in the level of crime and the failure by the parish constables and the military to control public riots acted as the immediate causes for the police reform. The military forces were the target of two opposite lines of criticism. On the one hand, they were reproached for using indiscriminate violence against the rioters, as when they killed at least eleven civilians and wounded over one hundred others during the Peterloo riots of 1819; on the other hand, their loyalty to the government was questioned, and it was feared that they might side with the rioters, with whom they shared a common social background. The most recurrent criticism, however, was expressed on the tactical level: the military could forcefully put down disorder but they could not follow up on their action by arresting the leaders (Stallion and Wall, 1999: 4; Emsley, 1996: 55).

This difference between military force and police force runs much deeper than merely arresting the leaders of a demonstration to prevent its repetition. Although its use can be perverted, force is instrumental and generally not exercised for its own sake. Clausewitz's famous dictum that war was nothing but a continuation of politics through other means is the classic expression of this view. However, the connection of military operations with politics is much less formalized than the integration of the police within the larger whole of the criminal justice system. This integration does not mean that all police use of force must be followed by subsequent court proceedings or indeed that it is, nor does it imply that law enforcement is the core of the police function. It means, however, that the instrumental character of the use of force by the police is not merely the result of practice or of morals, but is compelled by the law. Beyond a certain discretionary threshold, the use of force must be accounted for through the successful prosecution of arrested offenders. Police force is the major premise of a penal reasoning that must be concluded through due process. Needless to say, this logic can be turned against itself, as when a (wrongful) conviction provides a post hoc justification to an unwarranted arrest. In spite of the possibility of miscarriage of justice, it is crucial to realize that the police are, to a significant extent, compelled to exercise their powers within the framework provided by the criminal justice system. As will be shown in chapter 7, police become undemocratic when they overwhelm the whole system of which they are only one part.

The new police were then created with a view that they would provide a more efficient and a more controlled alternative to the military in suppressing public disorder. Over the years, the police function of maintaining order was greatly expanded. It reaches beyond riot control and accounts for a significant amount of police work. The police are called upon to supervise most public events. For instance, the MPD supervised over one thousand public events and demonstrations from 2002 to 2006. This supervision implies more than merely dispatching a few officers to provide a visible police presence; it proceeds according to a plan for maintaining order that is tailored to the specific needs of every event.

One of the questionable implications of defining the police by their capacity to use the amount of force necessary to stop the progress of a threatening situation is the general belief that the police will prevail and cannot "be beaten" (Monjardet, 1996: 20). This belief is embodied in the popular notion of the police as providing the tangible "…or else" to an injunction, as it is assumed that the police alternative to immediate compliance will be both unpleasant and final. This belief is partly wrong, as it can be shown through a discussion of one notorious case of collective violence in Canada, which represents one of the major Canadian crises in the history of policing. The purpose of this discussion is to give a concrete illustration of two presumptions that were noted in chapter 4 as being crucial for an understanding of the police use of force. These presumptions are, respectively, the presumption of compliance and the presumption of superior force. Testing these assumptions should allow us to draw out more specific features of the police.

The Oka Crisis of 1990

On March 11, 1990, Mohawk Aboriginals erected barricades to preserve what they believed to be sacred ground in a small community, called Oka, near the city of Montreal, in Quebec. This sacred ground, which comprised an Aboriginal cemetery, was to be transformed into a golf course by the municipal authorities. The provincial police were called in to dismantle the barricades, and in the early morning of July 11, 1990, a large police contingent of one hundred police from the Quebec provincial police force (QPF) charged the Mohawk stronghold. They were met by entrenched Mohawk "warriors" using submachine guns, and fled in disorder, after an exchange of fire. One police officer—Corporal Marcel Lemay—was killed. These events escalated into a major political crisis in Canada, and the military were sent in with armored vehicles on August 20 to take over from the police (Hornung, 1991). The crisis only ended at the end of September 1990, and had lasting effects: the police were never to confront Mohawks "warriors" in the future, and the Aboriginal reservations have now become safe havens for organized crime. In 2004, when another confrontation with Mohawk "warriors" was building up, the chairman of the QPF union declared that the police would refuse to be "cannon fodder" should a new crisis arise, and would not intervene on Mohawk territory (McCann and Turbide, 2004: 15). The death of Corporal Lemay was never solved, despite the most extensive police investigation undertaken in the history of Quebec policing. The situation in respect to policing U.S. Aboriginals is just as bad in the neighboring state of New York, where the police also lost a battle against the Mohawks in their reservation of St. Regis. Mohawk reservations straddle the border between Canada and the United States across the St. Lawrence River, and provide the basis for extensive smuggling between the two countries.

Reflecting upon the Oka crisis several years later, the public spokesman for the QPF wrote:

> Insofar that their action was to dismantle barricades to answer a legitimate request from a municipal council, the police were fulfilling their proper responsibilities....From the moment that an armed faction decided to counter a police intervention and, above all, to fire back against the police carrying this action, a new situation arose that went largely beyond the usual police mandate. (Gagnon, 1999: 78, my translation)

Although such incidents are infrequent and brief, exchanges of fire between the police and people resisting their apprehension do occasionally occur. During the Oka crisis, however, the two presumptions underpinning the police use of force were suspended, thus creating a new situation "that went largely beyond the usual police mandate." The presumption of superior force did not apply any more, the Mohawk "warriors" being numerous, well organized, and possessing as much fire power as the police. The Mohawks were also ready to use their weapons against the police, and indeed did so. Canadian Aboriginals enjoy a special legal status in Canada and view themselves as independent nations who must defend their territories and ways of life against external aggression. When their fundamental customs are violated, they feel themselves under no obligation to condone these violations. In other words, they are not constrained by a general presumption of compliance with Canadian law and the dictates of Canadian law enforcement.

According to this example, the demise of the presumption of general compliance is overtly political. In Canada, Aboriginal nations claim to live autonomously by their own customs and rules. It would, however, be wrong to believe that the suspension of the presumption of general compliance only occurs in political contexts. As historians of U.S. policing have noted, the police were initially used in that country in great part to control the arriving immigrants. The same is true of other countries, such as Canada and Australia. Immigrants arriving in the "new countries" wanted to partake of the national "dream" of a better life that these countries seemed to embody, and there existed real hopes that they would be able to integrate into their chosen society, if they complied with its rules. These hopes of joining the mainstream of a new country have been progressively dashed. The ethnic and cultural gap between the new immigrants and the countries they are moving to—often illegally—has never been so great and often results in exclusion. Instead of integrating, these arriving populations are segregated into various kinds of no man's lands—ghettos, depressed suburbs, and refugee camps. There is no presumption of general compliance that applies in these troubled zones, and the police either desert them or move into them in great numbers to perform sudden crackdowns with short-lived effects.

When the presumption of general compliance no longer applies, the attendant assumption of superior force is also lifted. Defiant people tend to seek the means of their defiance and arm themselves. When they venture into their territory, the police meet resistance and are increasingly the target of armed attacks. This development is destructive of policing. The police can only operate in a context of radical asymmetry, where the balance of force is tipped so much in their favor that their opponents do not dare to fight back. What is called by the military "asymmetrical conflict" is wholly different from this radical kind of asymmetry. Despite the disproportion of forces, an asymmetrical conflict remains a form of warfare where both opponents are fighting each other. What characterizes the radical asymmetry of policing is the very limited capacity of the police to cope with armed resistance. After the devastation left in 2005 by hurricane Katrina, bands of looters armed with automatic weapons started to operate in New Orleans. Reporting on this situation, the *New York Times* capped its story with the following title: "Police Quitting: Hundreds of Officers, Feeling Outmatched, Have Left Force" (Treaster, 2005). Such policing failures occurred in Naples in November 2006, when various Camorra factions started to fight each other in the streets, and in Brazil in May 2006, when incarcerated crime bosses ordered outside riots to pressurise prison administrations.

The most misguided metaphor to represent the police is the "thin blue line." Battle waged across drawn lines of combat is characteristic of military operations, not policing. Police forces are embedded within a generally peaceful public space and do not normally divide it along territorial lines. When lines are being drawn, the police have already lost control of the situation and must fall back on the military. The prototype of a policing operation is an action that normally leads to the arrest of one or several individuals, who are later submitted to criminal prosecution. Arrests can only be performed under the presumption of compliance and in conditions of relative peacefulness. The idea of performing an arrest on a battlefield is simply spurious. The contrast between military and police force will be further developed in chapter 9, which deals with military policing.

Summary and Conclusions

This chapter has presented basic demographic data on uniformed constables, with a focus on the growing number of women joining the police. It also analyzed the answers that were provided by research on the nature of the work performed by uniformed police and examined the means that they used, with special emphasis on police visibility and the use of force. Here are the main conclusions that can be drawn from the previous discussions.

The regular uniformed personnel of police organizations are on average young. Between 30 and 40 percent of the constables surveyed are under the age of thirty-four, and only a minority of some 5% are over fifty years old. Of more importance, however, is the fact that police qualify for retirement at a relatively early age and undertake a second career, often in the field of private security. This is particularly true for the retired ranking officers of the public police forces. The involvement of public police officers in private security should be the focus of more study.

The accelerating recruitment of women as sworn officers in police forces is one of the major developments of the last twenty years. The proportion of female officers reaches one-third of the staff of some police organizations in Western-style democracies. The access of women to the police profession is not likely to subside (unless quotas are enforced), since it is the result of structural causes, such as the better performance of female students in school and the fact that police forces increasingly require recruits to have college degrees. It is too early to assess to what extent policing is going to be transformed by the recruitment of women. Research so far indicates that a potential feminization effect on the police is largely offset by the partial masculinization of female officers.

The strong resistance of police culture to being changed by the recruitment of new types of personnel is shown by the weak effect on police organizations of recruiting members from ethnic minorities. The assumption that recruiting ethnic officers to join police organizations would defuse racial conflict proved largely unfounded. Moreover, the integration of these officers into a police force has remained problematic, despite noted progress, as is the case with women. The diversification of the makeup of police forces raises the issue of whether the alleged homogeneity of the police culture is not a screen behind which considerable strife and fragmentation are present.

There is a huge international discrepancy in the training and education requirements for joining a public police force. As might be expected, the requirements vary according to the conception of the police function. In this respect, it is far from clear that the conception of the police as expert problem solvers has made substantial inroads outside a few English-speaking countries. On the other hand, all inquiries into the motivation of recruits joining the police have shown that they were seeking either an action-filled profession or job benefits, rather than an occupation where the production of knowledge and the use of intelligence as a basis for action played a decisive part.

The research on the nature of uniformed police work has produced two general findings. The first concerns the substance of police work: activities related to duties other than crime control take up the major part of actual police time. The second finding relates to the form of police work: it revolves around the occurrence of incidents treated as unconnected. As was demonstrated by the Pickton affair in Vancouver, where a serial killer operated unhindered over many years, there can be active resistance from the police to establishing connections. The quintessential police (paper) form is the "incident report," which provides the basis of the research on the nature of police work. The consequences of the disjunctive police way of operating cannot be overstated, as it is the major impediment to progressing from an incidental to a situational form of policing.

It has proven difficult to reach a consensus on precisely quantified assessments of how uniformed police spend their time because empirical research is undermined by two tendencies. There is first a tendency to split police work between what is actually done and what might have been done if an incident spun out of control. In this case, the dramatization of virtual reality leads to a reconstruction of what is actually happening. Second, assessments of what is working in policing consist in great part in interpreting upward or downward variations in the occurrence of crime. Crime-focused evaluation research inevitably feeds back into descriptive research and overstates the importance of crime-related police work.

Although the police are defined by their authority to use force, it was argued that force is but one of two fundamental means of policing. The other is police visibility. Police visibility is the immediate instrument of policing, whereas force is the ultimate recourse (in democratic countries). There is no obvious theoretical reason to give primacy to what is ultimate (force) over what is immediate (visibility) in the definition of a public organization (comparably, medicine is not defined by surgery but by health care).

Using the participle "policing" in order to refer to the object of police study has several theoretical advantages but also some drawbacks. It tends to dramatize the dynamic features of policing, while obscuring the fact that the ends of policing are also achieved passively by just being at the right place. Public policing is triggered by conspicuous incidents and explicit demands for police presence. The police also promote their own visibility as a problem-solving strategy. To the (significant) extent that it relies on sheer police presence to generate security, policing is a self-fulfilling initiative. Another important consequence of the reliance of the police on the logic of appearances to generate order is that discrimination—against "visible minorities"—is a structural feature of the business of policing. Anything that visually stands out is the clue of a potential offence and is initially viewed with suspicion.

Three points were argued in respect to the use of force. First, despite the fact that they have the authority to use force, the police are not the proper instrument to pacify a territory torn by conflict or slipping into chaos. The police intervene in the narrow context of particular incidents, and they succeed in upholding social order only when it has previously been firmly established through other means and is not questioned as such. As has been argued, they operate under a presumption of general compliance. In this respect, their use of force is intermittent and tightly located in space rather than sustained and spread out over large expanses of territory. Second, it was also claimed that police use concentrated force in situations of radical asymmetry. Radical asymmetry not only means that there is a disproportion that favors the police in the distribution of force but also that this disproportion is so overwhelming that their adversaries are expected to surrender rather than to fight it out. This expectation is generally fulfilled. And third, once they are overwhelmed, offenders are put under arrest, with the expectation that they will be brought to trial. Thus, the use of force by the police is in many cases the first step of an ongoing process that is regulated by legal rules.

Finally, I want to introduce at this point a distinction between two kinds of policing—low policing and high policing—which will be elaborated on in chapter 7. The word "criminology" was coined in Italian (*criminologia*) by Raffaelle Garofalo (1914). Garofalo developed a theory of the "natural crime" (*mala in se*): natural crimes are the most harmful of crimes and they are allegedly found in all societies (for example, homicide and theft). They are opposed to criminal law and other regulatory constructions (*mala prohibita*), which are dependent on culture (for example, polygamy). This second category is quite wide: it includes most forms of incivilities, disorderly conduct, and victimless deviance.

Despite the terminology in which it is couched, Garofalo's distinction does not promote an obsolete form of naturalism in criminology. His basic insight is the following: there is a hard core that pervades the kinds of behavior that are prohibited in most human societies. These generally prohibited acts are based on either violence or deception. This insight actually goes back in time at least as far as Hobbes. He noted in *Leviathan* that "force and fraud are in war the cardinal virtues" (Hobbes, 1651/1985, part 1, chap. 13; also see part 2, chaps. 21 and 27). Such warlike virtues were to become crimes after the establishment of the political covenant that put an end to the war of "every man against every man" from which Hobbes sought an escape. When it focuses on crime, the kind of policing that was described in this chapter is mainly directed at the most visible forms of predatory behavior and at overt manifestations of disorder. Actual or potential violence is a recurrent feature of such behavior, although it does not characterize all forms of misconduct that generate insecurity. In the context of a general theory of policing, the word "violence" can be used as shorthand for overt and individual (or small-group) misbehavior that generates insecurity in communities, even if it is agreed that not all such behavior—prostitution, for example—is intrinsically violent.

Even if we extend the meaning of violence in this way and consider policing as a system of counterviolence, we still have to account for the other half, so to speak, of the hard core of crime, which is grounded in deception. The expression "low policing" is now introduced to refer to policing considered as an overt system of counterviolence. What will be called "high policing" is a covert activity that targets socially harmful forms of behavior based on deception and fraud, which may result in political violence like terrorism or collective forms of insurgency. Deception is not only instrumental in a significant number of serious crimes, but it is also the main factor undermining trust—its arch-enemy, as it were. A society completely devoid of trust regresses into the chaos of the war of every person against every other person. Both forms of policing will be discussed in chapter 7.

Police Investigation

According to a report written under the auspices of the U.S. National Research Council, the topics that were the least researched in the field of police studies were human rights, riot control, police discretion, the use of firearms and deadly force, and, finally, criminal investigation (National Research Council, 2003a: chap. 1). The researchers identified twenty-two research topics and sifted through seventeen sources of data from the period 1967–2002—two journals of abstracts, twelve criminal justice scholarly journals, and three professional publications on policing—to determine which of these topics were cited with the most (or the least) frequency. Crime, drugs, women (as victims), police and community relations, performance evaluation and police effectiveness, and police organization were the most frequently cited topics. The researchers took other measurements of the most and less researched topics according to their sources of data, and criminal investigation was always listed among the six least researched topics, often coming in last place.

This rating is comparative, as all ratings are. Although criminal investigation is at the bottom of the list, it does not mean that there has been no research on criminal investigation. There is an early body of unconnected findings that was brought together in the seminal work of Kuykendall (1982 and 1986) and Klockars (1985). There are some good review articles of the recent criminal investigation literature (Maguire, 2003; Sanders and Young, 2002); many of the chapters of Newburn (2005) also cover part of the research into police investigation. The main publications on criminal investigation fall into five types: (1) general textbooks (Newburn et al., 2007, and Stelfox, 2009, to cite the most recent publications); (2) manuals and primers on special techniques of inquiry—for instance, electronic surveillance; (3) studies of crime investigation itself, which focus on homicide investigations (Camps, 1966; Riedel, Zahn, and Mock, 1985; Maxfield, 1989; Simon, 1991; International Association of Chiefs of Police, 1995; Wellford and Cronin, 1999; Innes, 2003; Mucchielli, 2004 and 2006; Brodeur, 2005b) and narcotics (for instance, Wilson, 1978, and Manning, 2004); (4) studies of the judicial process; and (5) evaluation studies. However, the total body of empirical work on criminal investigation is in no way comparable with the impressive output on uniformed patrol. This dearth of research could not be in greater contrast with police fiction: as we saw in chapter 3, almost all police fiction focuses on police investigation and especially on homicide investigation.

This chapter, devoted to criminal investigation, is divided into four parts. The first part assesses the state of knowledge on criminal investigation, identifying main assumptions and assertions. In the second part, the powers of public police investigators are discussed in light of the definition of the police proposed in chapter 4. The third part develops a classification of the various kinds of police inquiry. Finally, some of the results of my own empirical research on criminal investigation are presented. The chapter concludes with a discussion of the significance of this research for building a theory of criminal investigation.

The State of Knowledge

Although there is a meaningful body of research on criminal investigation, it is still possible to give a brief account of the literature, as it is much smaller than the mass of writings on the public police in uniform, mistakenly identified with the whole of policing. The main focal points of research and the principal assertions made by researchers will be discussed in turn. Finally, a classification of the various kinds of writings on police investigations will be presented, followed by brief comments on landmark books.

Focal Points of Research

A research focus is a topic or a particular problem that draws together a significant amount of work. It is also, as we shall see, the result of implicitly choosing one side of an alternative, and it carries several implications that become, over time, unquestioned assumptions. We will discuss five basic focal points of research, which provide the assumptions underpinning a large part of research on criminal investigation. Although these assumptions are to some extent grounded in fact, they refer mostly to current theoretical trends in the research on criminal investigation rather than to actual features of criminal investigation itself.

Criminal Investigation as a Reactive Process

In one of the few attempts to develop a truly encompassing conceptual framework for understanding the investigative process, Kuykendall (1982: 138) makes a crucial distinction between proactive and reactive investigative subprocesses. The proactive process covers the initial stages of the criminal act continuum (concept, plan, and the incipient act); the reactive process corresponds to the later stages of the continuum (completion of the act, escape, and disposal of evidence or stolen property). The first "detectives" started to operate at the beginning of the nineteenth century and were aptly described as "secretive rogues," who blended with the criminals and acted proactively (Kuykendall, 1986: 179). By so doing, they played various unsavory roles, such as informers, thief-takers and even agents provocateurs, and were increasingly scorned by the police, by public opinion, and by police reformers (Klockars, 1985: 66). In order to gain legitimacy, modern detectives had to break away from being associated with these badly reputed operators. They achieved this result by publicly distancing themselves from proactive investigation and redefining themselves as reactive post factum crime solvers.

Although its scope was much reduced, proactive policing did not so much disappear as it went underground. This change in investigative practice was reflected in research, which essentially focused on the reactive investigative process that is casework. Such a change had wide-ranging implications. It implied by definition that all investigative processes that preceded the perpetration of a crime and aimed to prevent its commission or to neutralize an offender by catching him in the act were repudiated as legitimate objects of research. As policing evolved in its proactive tactics, the near exclusion from research of crime instigation—to refer to a classic distinction between crime investigation and crime instigation drawn by J. Q. Wilson (1978)—had wider consequences than merely excluding police entrapment as it was initially practiced by thief-takers. The work of agents operating in the fields of narcotics (Wilson, 1978; Manning, 1980/2004), organized crime, and counterterrorism rely significantly on proactive policing and undercover policing. With a few notable exceptions—Manning (1980/2004) and Marx (1988)—these fields have attracted almost no research, counterterrorism being for now nearly a terra incognita for research, although we are allegedly at war against terrorism. The assumption that all criminal investigation is reactive to a criminal event has been criticized by Maguire (2003: 367) as leading to a "highly misleading impression" of the actual business of investigative work, which centers more on (known) offenders than on individual offences. Maguire (2003: 369) is also critical of the proactive-reactive distinction, which may generate confusion when proactive methods (for example, introducing a police informant as the cell companion of a suspect in preventive custody) are embedded within a reactive major crime inquiry.

The Orientation of the Criminal Investigation: From Crime to Perpetrator

If criminal investigation is seen as an inquiry that is triggered by the perpetration of a crime, it then follows that its essential goal is to find who committed the crime and to bring this person to justice. This orientation of the criminal investigation, which proceeds from the commission of a crime toward the discovery of its author, is the most unquestioned assumption of research on police investigations. The most widely used, if not the only, performance indicator of criminal investigation is the clearance or "clear up" rate, which is an estimate of the frequency of linking a type of crime with its actual perpetrator(s). Investigating a crime is then seen as synonymous with solving it through the arraignment and eventual conviction of a suspect.

This assumption of the orientation of a criminal investigation encompasses the direction in which most criminal investigators are working. However, it also misses the other ways in which they proceed. With respect to a growing number of offences—terrorism, racketeering, corporate crime, fiscal fraud, environmental crime, sexual aggression, and professional (political) corruption—the investigative challenge is to link conclusively a person who is under serious suspicion with the actual commission of a crime. Such investigations, which begin with a suspect and work their way toward the perpetration of a crime, are of two basic forms. The most frequent case is where there are allegations that a person is involved in criminal activities, these allegations not being specific enough to pin a particular crime on that person. The suspect is then put under surveillance—for example, an organized crime boss—with the hope of building a case against him in relation to the commission of a specific offence for which he can be prosecuted.

There is another variant of this type of investigation, which often concerns cases of alleged political corruption. For example, an elected official is publicly criticized for engaging in certain practices deemed to be reprehensible. This official may acknowledge his actual involvement in these practices but dispute that they constitute a crime. The police are then called upon to determine whether criminal charges can be laid against the denounced official in relation to these practices. This type of investigation is also frequently performed with respect to sexual deviance. The suspect and his act being known, it remains to be assessed whether he should be criminally prosecuted for what he did. These criminal investigations that move from a suspect to a crime are presumed to be much less frequent than those proceeding in the opposite direction. However reasonable this presumption may be, we are not in a position to know with any precision how much investigative time is devoted to criminal inquiries that begin with a suspect instead of a crime, since this question has yet to be studied. It should also be added that some of the offences requiring this kind of suspect-centered investigations now have a much higher profile than was previously the case (for example, in corporate crime).

The Centrality of Homicide

Although classic studies of criminal investigation did not especially focus on murder (Greenwood et al., 1975 and 1977; Sanders, 1977; Lévy, 1987; Manning, 1980/2004; Ericson, 1981/1993; Burrows and Tarling, 1987; Hobbs, 1988), homicide is assuming a growing importance in the research literature on criminal investigation. Research on the history of detective units has highlighted the importance of high-profile murder cases in spurring the creation of independent investigative squads staffed by plainclothes police, despite considerable public reservations against the setting up of such units (Klockars, 1985: 70–71; Kuykendall, 1986: 176). The bulk of the literature on criminal investigation is still composed of textbooks intended for practitioners (for example, Palmiotto, 1994; Osterburg and Ward, 2000; Bennett and Hess, 2001). The presentation and discussion of forensics, crime scene techniques, and scientific policing have a prominent place in these textbooks, such topics being mostly relevant for homicide investigation.

The investigation of murder has been the object of more research than other crimes, although there are not many published studies (Havard, 1960; Camps, 1966; Maxfield, 1989; Simon, 1991; Wellford and Cronin, 1999; Innes, 2003; Brodeur, 2005b; Mucchielli, 2004 and 2006). The crime of murder has, itself, been researched more thoroughly than any other crime (Daly and Wilson, 1988; Polk, 1994; Leyton, 1995; Lane, 1997; Zimring and Hawkins, 1997; Knox, 1998). There is a scholarly journal devoted to the study of homicide (*Homicide Studies, An Interdisciplinary Journal*). Studies of homicide occasionally blend research on the offence of murder and on its investigation (Riedel et al., 1985; International Association of Chiefs of Police, 1995). Combined with the overwhelming cultural influence of murder fiction, the research literature on homicide and murder investigation had an impact on policing that is disproportionate to its importance. Investigating murder is seen as confronting evil in its most violent manifestation (Hobbs, 1988: 206) and "has been constructed as the apotheosis of the police mission" (Innes, 2003: 276). In their attempt to identify the skills needed to be an effective senior investigative officer, Smith and Flanagan (2000) draw some of their conclusions from a discussion of various cases of investigation presented as paradigmatic, three of which exemplify homicide investigations. Failed homicide investigations, whether leading to wrongful convictions (Donald Marshall, Guy-Paul Morin, and David Milgaard in Canada) or allowing prime suspects to escape justice (the Lawrence inquiry in the United Kingdom: see Macpherson, 1999, and Hawkins, 2003), have shocked public opinion and have been the object of extensive scrutiny by public commissions of inquiry.

The Emphasis on the Clearance Rate

Undertaking empirical research on criminal investigation requires a much stronger institutional backing than does studying the uniformed patrol. Most police reform having focused on the patrol since at least the 1950s, police organizations were eager to show what had been accomplished and welcomed researchers. Except for the introduction of new technology, investigative work was little affected by these reforms. Cohen and Chaiken (1987: 2) found that as late as 1985 not one of the 940 standards of police organization and management formulated by the Commission on Accreditation for Law Enforcement Agencies discussed how to identify qualified officers for investigative assignments. Criminal investigation departments conducted their operation in relative isolation from the broader changes affecting police organizations. Their prestige buttressed their independence, and they were reluctant to admit academic outsiders to their midst, unless they were ordered to do so by the higher police management. A significant amount of research was commissioned at different levels of government and by organizations such as the various national and international associations of chiefs of police. These institutional sponsors were much less interested in developing a theory of police investigation than in increasing the overall performance of the police investigators. The clearance or clear-up rate of criminal cases being the most widely used performance indicator of criminal investigators, researchers were authorized to conduct empirical research on criminal investigation on the condition that they would submit proposals to improve the clearance rate for various categories of offences.

The measurement of investigative performance through clearance rates is fraught with difficulties, however. Clearance rates do not apply to all cases that may end up in a criminal court. In order to speak meaningfully of solving a case, this "case" must be generated independently of police practice—through the discovery of a corpse or the external report of a property crime. But when cases stem wholly from police action—for instance, police crackdowns on drug dealers or prostitutes—recording a case coincides with solving it. Applying a clearance rate to such police-generated cases is devoid of meaning, as it is by definition equal to 100 percent. It must be stressed that these police-generated cases for which the application of clearance rates is a meaningless procedure

represent a sizeable amount of investigative time, as they generally target transactional consensual crimes, that is, all kinds of illegal services and traffics. Even
when it is properly applied, the clearance rate is an organizational term that is
context-dependent and that should not be confused with solving a case by
arresting and eventually convicting a perpetrator (Maguire et al., 1993;
Manning, 2006a). Cases can be solved by an arrest, but they can also be closed
by putting an end to inconclusive investigative efforts; they can, in addition, be
administratively terminated by the issuance of a warrant not specifying the
name of an individual, by transferring the case to another agency, and by the
occurrence of various exceptional circumstances (a suicide note; a plea bargaining deal whereby an offender is willing to clear the police files by pleading
guilty to offences that he did not commit, and so forth).

Practical research that addressed the different problems raised by the clearance rate generated three kinds of proposals. First, researchers took a methodological approach and proposed to develop a more sophisticated performance
indicator than the clearance rate as it is currently used by police organizations
(Maguire et al., 1993). Maguire and his collaborators proposed using different
performance indicators for high-detectibility crimes (major violent offences)
and for low-detectibility property offences. Second, researchers tried to identify
the factors associated with solving a crime through arresting its perpetrator
and formulated recommendations to build on these elements to solve cases
(Wellford and Cronin, 1999; Brodeur, 2005b; Mucchielli, 2006). Finally, research
tried to describe the different skills needed for solving cases (Smith and
Flanagan, 2000). There is one wide-ranging question that stems from this
research that focuses on the clearance rate: to what extent does a theory of
crime-solving coincide with a theory of criminal investigation? It will be argued
later on that these undertakings do not coincide.

Solving Cases by Targeting the Individual Perpetrator
With the exception of research on the work of narcotics squads (Wilson, 1978;
Manning, 1980/2004), the study of criminal investigation is in line with traditional crime inquiry as it is represented in police fiction. It focuses on the individual perpetrator, despite the fact that a growing share of criminal investigation
is devoted to network crime (such as organized and corporate crime, youth
gangs, and terrorism). There are several reasons accounting for this situation,
such as the police tradition and the fact that casework still involves, in the main,
dealing with individual offenders. There is a further reason for this prominence
of the individual perpetrator (with occasional accomplices) that can be hypothetically singled out. A notion such as the clearance rate can be intuitively
associated with linking a case to be solved with an individual suspect on the

basis of a one-on-one correspondence—crime A is matched with perpetrator A1. As we move away from this one-on-one matching, the clearance rate becomes a more ambivalent notion, and its calculation is fraught with technical difficulties. For example, there is no easily quantifiable connection between a crackdown against a criminal gang to disrupt the functioning of an illegal market, on the one hand, and clearing up specific criminal cases, on the other. Such a connection can be construed, but it requires statistical skills generally not possessed by members of police organizations. As research on criminal investigation is urged to propose ways of improving the clearance rate of individual offences, it is reluctant to address the much greater complexity of collective offending in this respect.

As stated at the beginning of this discussion, a research focus acts as a practical assumption and should not be confused with an explicit assertion. For instance, researchers on police investigation do not make the theoretical claim that crimes are perpetrated by lone individuals rather than by several offenders loosely or tightly coordinated. For reasons that I tried to suggest, their research practice uncritically reflects some of the actual features of criminal investigation in focusing on individual perpetrators. In contrast with these practical assumptions, we now review the main assertions stemming from research on crime inquiry.

Main Assertions

Criminal Investigation Was First Practiced on a Private Basis

In early medieval England, crime victims and their family had the prime responsibility of bringing the person who had caused them injury to justice (Radzinowicz, 1958; Beattie, 2001). The wealthier of these victims eventually resorted to thief-takers to recover their stolen property and to arrest the offender (Klockars 1985; Kuykendall, 1986). In the United States, private detective agencies such as Pinkerton's were used by individual customers, private corporations, and by local government before the first criminal investigation departments started to operate on a systematic basis. The situation was different in continental Europe—notably in France—where public police forces that comprised investigative units were created by the state. However, as we have seen in chapter 2, these investigative units relied on a large number of informants and private auxiliaries that bore much resemblance to thief-takers and other private clandestine operators, who were as close to habitual criminals as they were to the police. The institution of public criminal investigation departments met with strong resistance, as the practice of investigation was twice tainted as a profession. First, it was uncomfortably close to the criminal milieu and, second, the plainclothes detectives were perceived as infiltrators that were a threat to the full exercise of civil liberties.

The Efficiency of the Criminal Investigation Is Limited

This claim is variously stressed, depending on which authors make it, and depending also on the type of crime that they examined. The clearance rates for high-detectibility violent crimes are much higher than for low-detectibility crimes against property (Maguire et al., 1993). The claim that crime investigation is much less efficient than depicted in the crime fiction literature and in the memoirs of famous investigators, however, has a larger basis than an examination of the clearance rates. As much as crime fiction mythologizes the investigator, research demythologizes the practice of criminal investigation.

This debunking of the crime inquiry takes several forms. In an early book on the investigation of murder, Professor Francis Camps advocated a reform of the processing of information on criminal cases to increase the efficiency of murder investigations (Camps, 1966: 138). Peter Greenwood and his colleagues were perhaps the worst iconoclasts in asserting that suppressing half of what investigators do in trying to resolve cases would make no perceptible difference on outcomes, as they keep repeating actions that were ill performed (Greenwood et al., 1975 and 1977). In work that was replicated in Japan, Richard Ericson basically argued that criminal investigation consisted of processing further down the criminal justice system suspects that were, for most part, already arrested by the patrol (Ericson, 1981/1993; Miyazawa, 1992). Bruce Smith had already noted in 1925 that 85 percent of the cases processed by detectives had been solved by patrol officers (Smith, 1925, quoted in Kuykendall, 1986: 184, note 6).

Detectives classify cases according to the expected difficulty of solving them. At one end of the spectrum are cases where the suspect is caught in the act or gives himself up, which are self-solvers, and at the other end are the "mysteries," where there is no available clue as to the identity of the perpetrator. There are various categorizations in the literature that reflect this polarity: "walk-throughs" (or "walk-arounds") as opposed to "whodunits" (Sanders, 1977: 174; Ericson, 1981: 136); routine "pork chop burglaries," which are suspended cases, as opposed to nonroutine burglaries that are investigated because of an expected payoff (Waegel, 1982: 454); killings that are only perfunctorily investigated, as opposed to murders that become major cases (Waegel, 1982: 463); "walk-throughs," "where-are-theys," and "whodunits" (Kuykendall, 1986: 191); "self-solvers," "whodunits," and "hybrids" (Innes, 2003: 198 and appendix B); "dunkers" ("smoking guns") and "whodunits" (Manning, 2006a). Some of the oppositions admit intermediary cases that fall in between the extremes. As is stressed by Kuykendall (1986: 193), it is the complexity of the case rather than the skills, methods, and techniques of the investigators that determines the probability of solving it. Hence, detectives concentrate on the problems with easy solutions and screen out for investigation the cases most likely to result in an arrest, this practice being known as "skimming" (Waegel, 1982: 453; Greenberg et al., 1977).

Time Spent on Post-Case Work Is Considerable

Research undertaken by various authors such as Reiner (1985), Morris and Heal (1981), and Kuykendall (1986: 177) highlights the fact that detectives spend a significant amount of time preparing cases for the prosecution. This finding runs contrary to all police fiction and murder stories, which generally end with the discovery of the assassin, who is shamed into a public confession. It is consistent with the practice of investigative "skimming" and with the fact that a majority of cases are swiftly solved by the uniformed patrol persons, or not at all.

Crime Investigation Is Information Processing

This assertion is so frequent in the research literature that it is difficult to identify who first made it. An early expounding of this perspective can be found in Sanders (1977); also see Kuykendall (1986: 191). Innes (2003: chap. 5) articulates a theory of criminal investigation that is based on this premise. This theory dovetails with the influential characterization of policing as knowledge work developed by Ericson and Haggerty (1997) and is now the dominant perspective (Manning, 2006a).

Investigative Powers

We have defined the police by their authority to use powers that violate the law when used by other citizens. The powers exercised by detectives under the warrant system provide what is probably the best formalized illustration of this assertion. A warrant is a written authorization to exercise a particular form of power, which is granted to public investigators. This authorization is generally issued by a judge to an investigator, pursuant to a formal application explaining the reasons for soliciting such an authorization. This system is now evolving in three directions. First, authorizations equivalent to warrants are given in certain countries by state ministers rather than magistrates, as is the case in the United Kingdom for intercepting private communications. The countries of continental Europe, where a number of such authorizations are granted on an administrative basis, have long been familiar with this practice. Second, emergency warrants (telewarrants), which are given electronically without a detailed application made by an investigator appearing in person, are used increasingly. A peace officer may in fact exercise many of his powers without a warrant "if the conditions for obtaining a warrant exist but by reason of exigent circumstances it would be impracticable to obtain a warrant" (subsection 487.11 of the Canadian Criminal Code). Finally, the police may requisition a significant volume of private information from telecommunication companies without having a warrant. In Canada, section 16 of Bill C-47—An Act Regulating Telecommunications Facilities to Support Investigations, 2009—obliges telecommunications services to provide to the police twelve kinds of subscriber information without a warrant. This bill of law has yet to be passed in Parliament, but there is a large consensus in its favor.

The warrant system is quite extensive, as is shown by a study of the warrant system in Canada. We will first list the various kinds of warrant already in use, and then comment on the system. Most of the legal provisions for these warrants are to be found in the Canadian Criminal Code (CCC), where they are classified more or less on an ad hoc basis.

The original type of warrant is probably the *arrest warrant* (subsection 83.29 of the CCC). A second type of warrant is *search and seizure* [487(1)], with the following subcategories: a warrant to search the building, receptacle, or place for any such thing and to seize it [487 (1) (d)]; a warrant to search a computer system [this warrant is extensive, covering searching a computer system, reproducing its data, seizing the print-out and other output and copying the data; see 487 (2.1)]; a warrant to take bodily substances for forensic DNA analysis [487.05]; warrants to obtain blood samples (256); and warrants for the seizure of things not specified [489.1]. A third type is the *general warrant* "authorizing a peace officer to…use any device or investigative technique or procedure or do any thing described in the warrant that would, if not authorized, constitute an unreasonable search or seizure in respect of a person or a person's property" [487.01 (1)]. A fourth type of warrant is the *authorization to intercept private communications*, which takes a great diversity of forms (Part VI of the CCC); *warrants for video surveillance* [487.01(4)] are often obtained in conjunction with authorizations to intercept private communications. Bills C–46 and C–47 (2009) against cybercrime will be shortly enacted by the Canadian Parliament. They create still new types of warrants (referred to as "orders" in this legislation): preservation of computer data order (487.013), general production order (487.014), production of transmission data order (487.016), and production of financial data order (487.018). The security intelligence community has its own warrant system enshrined in the enabling legislation that created the Canadian

Security Intelligence Service and the Communication Security Establishment (the Canadian counterpart of the U.S. National Security Agency—NSA).

The following comments apply to the Canadian warrant system.

Criminalization-legalization. Part VI of the CCC provides an exemplary case of the coupling of criminalization with legalization. It begins by stating that anyone using an electronic device to intercept a private communication is guilty of an indictable offence and is liable to a maximum term of five years of imprisonment [184(1)]. It then immediately adds a "saving provision" to the effect that section 184 does to apply to peace officers intercepting a private communication in accordance with a judicial authorization [184(2)].

Warrant refusals. Brodeur (1997b) studies the number of authorizations granted by judges for intercepting private communications as compared to the number of refusals. From 1974—the year when the law on the interception of private communications was passed—to 1994, the Canadian judiciary received 14,505 applications for authorizations to intercept private communications or for the renewal of such authorizations. It refused to grant an authorization in only 19 instances. After 1994, the number of refusals became even lower, the official statistics showing no refusals for most years.

Power without warrant. Unsurprisingly, detectives tend to view the submission of an application for a warrant from a judge as a mere formality. They generally claim to weed out the applications that would not respect the conditions of authorization themselves. Nevertheless, there have been notorious cases in Canada, when detectives or intelligence officers have been caught making false assertions to a judge for the purpose of obtaining a formal authorization to intercept private communications. A significant proportion of such applications are based on information provided by informants, which are notably unreliable. Studies of detective work have revealed that they often convince suspects and witnesses to submit to their demands without producing a warrant by claiming that they will get this authorization in any event, and that the suspect is only wasting their time by resisting them. Persons with little experience of criminal justice are the most vulnerable to this kind of intimidation.

A value-free framework. This last comment goes beyond the traditional issue of police warrants. Dershowitz (2002: 158) recommends that judicial warrants be issued "as a prerequisite to nonlethal torture." Such warrants are intended to "decrease the amount of physical violence directed against [the ticking bomb] suspects," although Dershowitz is quite clear on the fact that such judicially authorized torture should cause excruciating pain to extract information from the "ticking bomb terrorist." These proposals could only be implemented through a judicial warrant system that would have forfeited any obligation to defend values based on the respect of human rights.

The sum of these powers should be profiled against the background of table 4.1, to which they provide a concrete legal illustration. Needless to say, this illustration is an important step for confirming the validity of the definition of the police formulated in chapter 4.

An Evidence-Based Classification of Criminal Investigations

From 1999 to 2004, I conducted empirical research on criminal investigations (Brodeur, 2005b). I first developed a research project and submitted it to a large urban police force in the Province of Quebec. After protracted negotiations, I was finally authorized to have access to the police investigation files for the period extending from 1990 to 2001 and to conduct interviews with the investigators.

In my research, I wanted to answer two questions. The first was empirical: what were the determinants in the resolution of a case, defined as the identification and arrest of the perpetrator(s) of a crime? The second question was more theoretical: what was the part played by knowledge—understood as true information—and by the technological means of collecting it in policing? Criminal investigation qualifies as one of the best testing grounds for the claim that policing is knowledge work (Ericson and Haggerty, 1997). Following the seminal work of Ericson and Haggerty, the assertion that crime investigation is information processing became dominant in the research literature (Innes, 2003: 27 and chap. 5). Consequently, the role of knowledge factors such as forensics, data banks, and criminal intelligence in the clearing up of criminal cases was scrutinized with special care.

With regard to method, a two-pronged approach was followed. First, a content analysis of a random selection of investigation files on resolved cases from 1990 to 2001 was undertaken, leaving for a later stage the comparison with unresolved cases. There was also a relatively small number of unresolved cases in my sample, which were compared with the resolved cases in some of their aspects. Twenty-five resolved cases for each of the following offences were initially selected: homicide (including attempted homicides and murder conspiracies), sexual assault, robbery, fraud, and narcotic offences. The 125 individual cases were chosen according to a random procedure that avoided sample biases with regard to year and territorial district. As I began my analysis, I realized that only the homicide cases produced sufficiently detailed files for my purposes. For the other offences, a "file" usually consisted of a few pages recording a complaint or, in a minority of cases, describing the swift arrest of the perpetrator by uniformed patrol or by a civilian. For instance, in one of the cases involving rape, the rapist was identified by the victim and located by her mother, who walked the neighborhood streets with her daughter in order to find him. With the exception of a few large-scale operations, nearly all the narcotic files consisted of a short narrative of a sting operation targeting a street drug peddler, this operation being often conducted by patrolpersons wearing plainclothes rather than by investigators.

Upon my examination of the police files, most of the nonhomicide cases vindicated Ericson's perspective that "the detectives' work was to deal with suspects delivered to them or otherwise identified through the work of others" (1981: 136). Knowledge production viewed as a process that extended in time and that was underpinned by scientific methods played almost no role in these inquiries. There was one type of inquiry, however, that did not fit Ericson's description of an individual case. It brought together several incidents that exemplified the same modus operandi and targeted offenders that were known to operate in this way; this type of inquiry was suspect-centered and often focused on criminal gangs and organized crime rather than on one individual perpetrator. These inquiries were called by the police "concentration inquiries" or "integrated investigations." I shall call them by their second designation. Integrated investigations often involve the members of several police forces, and they are an independent object of research. Because of their specific complexity they are touched on here only briefly.

Because of the dearth of material in the nonhomicide files, I decided to focus on resolved murder investigations. The number of files recounting a typical murder investigation filled at least one storage box for police archives. Approximately half of the homicide cases generated enough files to fill several boxes. In the end, an extended sample of 153 homicide cases involving 193 suspects was collected (depending on how the data was processed, the maximum figure of 153 cases was scaled down for statistical purposes). The cases were broken down into 163 variables that were computerized. Most of the variables referred to the investigative process, but several represented features of the case itself (such as information on the victims and perpetrators).

The work in police files was combined with lengthy interviews with key informants from the homicide squad (supervisors and best practitioners). This procedure was completed in three steps. A first draft of the archival analysis was put together. These findings were then submitted to selected investigators in the course of interviews to check whether they corresponded with their practices. The analysis was fine-tuned in the light of their comments. This three-step procedure was the result of past experience in police research. I am convinced that it is courting failure to interview criminal investigators (and intelligence officers) without being thoroughly acquainted with their work and without being in a position to question, albeit in a nonconfrontational way, the claims they make in the course of an interview. The procedure of discussing their own files with investigators proved to be rewarding for both parties.

A Typology of Criminal Investigation

There are many types of criminal investigation. The proposed typology is based on my empirical research and resulted in a categorization of nine kinds of investigation. It is not exhaustive, as it does not fully take into account certain types of highly specialized investigations in the field of national security (for example, security clearance investigations) or organized crime, which will be discussed later. Furthermore, the typology is not fully integrated, as it does not encompass in one table all the important distinctions that need to be made. It is based in part on distinctions previously made by Kuykendall (1982: 139–141) and by Maguire (2003).

Two pairs of crucial distinctions are initially taken into account in my typology. The first pair distinguishes between proactive and reactive inquiries; the second pair separates suspect-centered investigations from event-centered investigations. To the proactive-reactive distinction, the category of "retrospective inquiry" was added; to the suspect-event distinction, the notion of "hybrid inquiry" was also added. The meaning of these building blocks of the typology will be first discussed and then the various types of investigation generated by their combination will be presented.

In its basic meaning, the proactive-reactive distinction refers to investigations occurring respectively before and after a criminal event. Occurring before a criminal event, a proactive investigation is often—but not always—internally triggered by the police, whereas the reactive inquiry is pursuant to external information from various sources (such as a citizen complaint). Each of these types of investigation uses specific techniques: the proactive techniques involve stealth and deception (such as undercover policing), whereas the reactive techniques have visibility and at times even a high public profile. This high profile is meant to provide public reassurance that the police are taking action following a major criminal event.

The category of the retrospective investigation has generally been neglected. Its aim is generally to assess whether a past event or a current practice that is perceived to be potentially criminal was in fact of a criminal nature. In my previous discussion of the orientation of the criminal investigation process, I gave examples of retrospective investigations—political corruption, economic crime, and terrorist plots. In most retrospective investigations the potential offender is known, the aim of the inquiry being to determine whether his (or her) behavior is actually criminal. In contrast to the "whodunit," which focuses on identifying the perpetrator of a crime, the retrospective investigation tries to answer the question "what is it?" (is this behavior a crime?). Such inquiries are a mix of interpretation and of fact-finding. In other cases, which have a high profile but are few in number, a retrospective inquiry centers on a convicted offender and investigates whether this person was wrongfully convicted. In such investigations, fact-finding outweighs fact interpretation. These investigations are a kind of retrospective "whodunit."

The meaning of the distinction between suspect- and event-centered investigations is self-evident. The category of "hybrid investigations" was added to cover the numerous cases where the focus of an inquiry was split or constantly shifting.

Crossing these distinctions one with the other, we produce a small matrix with nine cells that represent various types of investigations. Each type of investigation will now be briefly described.

Proactive and suspect-centered. This is the prototypical preventive investigation. It uses covert tactics (infiltration, physical surveillance, communication monitoring) to prevent identified suspects from carrying out a planned criminal action. This kind of investigation is prevalent in the fields of organized crime and national security (counterterrorism).

Proactive and event-centered. This kind of investigation presents several variants. In its best-known variant, it relies on risk assessment and uses all available means of surveillance to prevent the perpetration of crimes in places and at

Table 6.1   Type of Investigations

	Suspect-Centered	Event-Centered	Hybrid (Status-Centered)
Proactive	preventive investigation (e.g., counterterrorism)	special high-security events (e.g., state visit; Olympic games)	instigation (e.g., sting operation: carreer criminal; special type of offence)
Reactive	individual denunciation reactivated cold cases	current case solving (most frequent investigations)	postcase processing
Retrospective	security clearance immigration check	assessment of suspicious events (e.g., suicide; fire; fraud; terror plots)	high-profile suspect (e.g., politician; business leader)

events that may be targeted by offenders, such as a gathering of heads of state or the Olympic games. A proactive investigation may possess this characteristic only in part, as when proactive techniques are used within a major reactive investigation (for example, a high-profile murder or kidnapping).

Proactive and hybrid. In many cases, both the suspects and the event may be known, as when sports hooligans with a long record of offending plan to disrupt a particular competition. Also, the type of proaction that Wilson (1978) initially called "instigation" and which is now known as a sting (or countersting) operation is of a hybrid nature. It attempts to bridge the gap between high-volume offenders and evidence of their criminal activity, providing them with an occasion to be involved in a crime event under conditions monitored by the police. This type of operation, which may beget a practice known as "framing the guilty" in police parlance, raises legal problems of potential entrapment and police provocation that will not be discussed for now.

Reactive and suspect-centered. This kind of investigation involves a much larger set of inquiries than is usually believed. They belong to two broad subtypes. The kind of investigation that falls most neatly into this category is generated by a piece of external information: an informant, who often wants to remain anonymous, alleges that a person is involved in criminal activities of a special kind—such as tax evasion, to take one of the most frequent kinds of denunciation—without specifying any particular event (which it is up to the investigation to find). The other subtype initially centers on a past criminal event, but shifts the focus of the investigation to potential or actual suspects. Ordinary cases that are not swiftly solved become in this way suspect-centered. Integrated investigations that attempt to solve several events by targeting suspects and criminal gangs or organizations according to their known modus operandi also fall in this category. Once a criminal event has been cleared by the identification and arrest of a suspect, the whole investigative process becomes focused on obtaining the conviction of this person. All postclearance court processing is suspect-centered.

Reactive and event-centered. This is the stereotypical criminal investigation, which in most cases proceeds according to the following sequence: first, an event of a criminal nature is reported by a member of the public; second, detectives inspect the scene of the crime, looking for clues and interview witnesses; third, a suspect is identified, arrested, and finally confesses to the crime. For Maguire (2003: 367), this sequence and its underlying assumptions are part of an investigative mythology far removed from the reality of criminal investigations, which are suspect- rather than event-centered. Maguire nevertheless recognizes that there are real cases matching this sequence, which he calls "hard-to-solve-major-inquiries." As will be seen, the greater part of the murder and murder-related cases that I researched are not "hard-to-solve-major-inquiries", although they follow more or less this pattern, that is, all are after-the-fact externally generated inquiries. Many of these investigations focus on a serious suspect in a matter of a few hours. This would seem to vindicate Maguire's position.

Reactive and hybrid. It could be said that when they are closely analyzed, most criminal investigations fall within this category. As an investigation moves from its initial crime-solving stage to the postclearance presentation of a case in court, its emphasis shifts from event to suspect. With the compulsory registration of certain types of offenders (such as sexual offenders), hybrid investigations are invested with a status of their own. The surveillance of registered offenders focuses on persons rather than events, and is to an even significant extent proactive. However, it is also reactive to the extent that it is externally generated by a legal order, which is itself the outcome of one or several criminal events.

Retrospective and suspect-centered. This kind of investigation is mostly generated by a government department, which directs investigators to revisit a past incident. The best example of a suspect-centered retrospective investigation is the reexamination of a suspicious past conviction. Although this type of inquiry is becoming more frequent because of more powerful techniques to prove innocence such as DNA fingerprinting, it remains relatively exceptional. Its rarity is compensated for by its very high media profile. In Canada, several public commissions of inquiry have been established to investigate a wrongful conviction of murder (see, for example, Ontario, 1998; Nova Scotia, 1989). There are other kinds of retrospective inquiries focusing on persons that are much more frequent. These consist in the assessment of the trustworthiness of persons who will have access to sensitive information. Such inquiries are generally conducted to grant a level of security clearance to a person who is not at this stage suspected of wrongdoing. Immigration checks also fall within this category. In this case, persons being investigated are often considered suspects (of terrorist activities, for instance).

Retrospective and event-centered. The purpose of such investigations is to determine whether an event is criminal and should be the object of further investigation. It could reasonably be claimed that all investigation hinges on such a determination. However, there are huge discrepancies between cases in this regard. For some crimes, such as armed robbery, the criminal nature of the event is self-evident. In other cases, such as suspicious fires or alleged hate crime, the retrospective investigation is elaborate and can get rather technical (for example, chemistry may be used to determine the cause of a suspicious fire).

Retrospective and hybrid. The police reaction to suspicious events and suspects often varies in proportion to the status of the persons involved. In cases such as political corruption, sexual abuse by persons in a position of authority, or police abuse of power, there are serious presumptions that the incident is of a criminal nature; the person(s) that would qualify as suspect(s) are also fully known. However, because of their status, a retrospective investigation is ordered to reassess whether the suspects' behavior actually constitutes a criminal offence. The hallmark of these investigations is that they take a much longer time than they would with suspects who do not possess a special status. For instance, investigations into suspicious police shootings often take months. This type of inquiry is retrospective rather than reactive, because the issue to be decided is whether there are grounds for a formal police reaction. The inquiry is hybrid, because it involves the status of both a potential offender and a suspicious event, which is to be reassessed.

This typology is not exhaustive and does not attempt to match a kind of investigation with the corresponding investigative techniques that it makes use of (Kuykendall, 1982: 138). In order to make the typology more complete, one new category—integration—will be added to the nine that were just discussed. Subtypes within the main categories previously generated in table 6.1 will also be discussed.

Integrated investigations. Integrated investigations essentially focus on clusters of criminal events that display the same pattern and are suspected to have been perpetrated by the same individual suspect (for example, serial murders) or the same group of suspects (for example, a gang involved in drug trafficking). In Canada, they are often conducted by task forces in which investigators from several police organizations work together. These police forces operating at various levels of government (municipal, provincial, and national) pool their resources to solve crimes that display the same modus operandi or to neutralize a particular criminal organization. A very high-profile operation undertaken in 2001 in the province of Quebec against a criminal organization involved thirty-six police forces. These investigations are in the main proactive in their scope, although they may be triggered by a criminal event that has deeply shocked public opinion. Integrated investigations may be international in scope, in the case of organized crime or terrorism. The cost of integrated investigations may reach astronomical proportions. According to the solicitor general of the Canadian province of British Columbia, Rich Coleman, the cost of the investigation that resulted in the 2007 conviction of Robert Pickton, a serial killer who allegedly operated between 1983 and 2002, was in excess of 70 million Canadian dollars.

Differentiation. As was previously said, all cases of murder generate reactive investigations, which are event- or suspect-centered, depending on the circumstances of the case. In the course of my own research on criminal homicide, I was led to distinguish between three kinds of investigation. Kuykendall (1986:

191) also distinguishes between these three types of inquiry, but he does not elaborate on these distinctions. The *identification* inquiry aims to find out who is the perpetrator of a crime. If the criminal investigation process is conceived as a knowledge-producing undertaking, then the identification inquiry is its most important stage. This is borne out by the fact that all forensics and scientific policing are focused almost exclusively on suspect identification (crime scene analysis, ballistics, DNA fingerprinting, criminal profiling, and so forth). The *location* inquiry aims to track down and arrest the identified suspect. In many cases identification and arrest coincide in time. However, in other cases suspects take flight and it requires an elaborate operation to catch them. Finally, there is the *case-processing* investigation that takes place after the arrest of a suspect and the laying down of charges against him or her.

It proved necessary to make these distinctions for at least two reasons. First, the techniques involved in each kind of investigation are different. The identification inquiry may be event-centered, but the location and case-processing phases are obviously suspect-centred. The amount of time devoted to each subtype is highly variable. Contrary to what is believed, the case-processing investigation is generally the longer in resolved inquiries. It could be asked whether identification, location, and case processing were not simply different phases of an investigation rather than distinct kinds of investigation. They should be viewed as distinct kinds of investigation because conceiving them as phases of one investigation would generate the belief that all or the majority of criminal investigations go through these three distinct phases. This belief is wrong: solving the identification problem acts as a precondition for trying to locate a suspect and for processing the case further down the line. In many cases, the investigators cannot solve the identification problem, either because of lack of knowledge or lack of evidence (investigators claim to know who the perpetrator is but cannot make a case that would stand up in court).

The case-processing investigation has a crucial importance with respect to organized crime. In Canada (as in Italy, for instance), the prosecution of the members of a criminal organization largely rests on the testimony of police informants (the notorious Italian *pentiti*, or "repenting criminals") who are willing to testify in court against their accomplices in exchange for police protection and a new identity. Some of these informants come forward to the police on their own, often because their life is threatened, and they make extensive disclosures about their organization and its members. In these witness-centered investigations, the work of the investigators is wholly devoted to the staging of a trial that involves at times hundreds of defendants, such as the "maxi-trial" that followed Tomaso Buscetta's confession in Italy, in 1986–1987. Some 344 members of the Mafia were convicted and sentenced to long prison terms. Canada has not witnessed such maxi-trials, but criminal court proceedings against members of the Hells Angels in 2002 involved more than thirty defendants.

Empirical Findings

Clearance Time

I first determined how much time it took the police to identify the perpetrator(s) of a homicide and related offences, the related offences being less than 10 percent of the sample (attempted murder and conspiracy). A distinction between "identification" and "location" inquiries was made because they use different investigative techniques, as emphasized in the previous section. The number of identification inquiries (131 cases) and location inquiries (153 cases) is not the same. When there are multiple perpetrators in a single case, the identification inquiry generally succeeds in finding their respective identity within the same time frame, whereas locating the various suspects varies in time. Notwithstanding that they spring from the same case, I made a separate count of the investigations undertaken to locate the various suspects implicated in one case.

My findings were compared with one of the few research projects on homicide investigations that also attempted to estimate the clearance time and to single out the most influential factors in reaching a resolution (Wellford and Cronin, 1999). Wellford and Cronin collected a sample of 798 murder cases in four U.S. cities for the period 1994–1995 (589 of these cases were solved; 209 had remained unsolved). They coded 215 factors related to the characteristics of the case and its investigation as found in the police files. Their research was limited to the police files, and they did not conduct interviews with investigators or make field observations. Wellford and Cronin compared two cities with high clearance rates to two cities with low clearance rates (the numerical significance of high and low clearance rates is not specified, although we eventually find that they refer, respectively, to 94% (highest clearance rate) and 67% (lowest rate). The municipal police force that I selected had an average clearance rate of 70% of its cases between 1990 and 2001—a little below the aggregated Canadian average of 77%. It is reasonable to believe that the average clearance rate of the four cities selected by Wellford and Cronin would not be very different from 70%, perhaps a little higher. Consequently, the performance of the Canadian force can be compared with the police departments selected by Wellford and Cronin (1999). Table 6.2 compares my sample with the police departments selected by Wellford and Cronin.

Table 6.2   Time Needed to Solve Case

Time Elapsed	Brodeur		Welford and Cronin (1999)
	Identification (N=131)	Location** (N=153)	Clearance = Arrest (N=589)
None*	62 cases	51 cases	169 cases
1h or less	10		
5h or less	13	8	
24h or less	8	16	
Total % (no time to 24 h or less)	**71%**	**49%**	**28.7%**
2–3 days or less	8	19 (12.4%)	125 (21.2%)
4–7 days or less	4		
More than a week	5	18	99 (16.8%)
More than a month	2	11	154 (26.2%)
More than a year	7	15	23 (3.9%)
Total % (1 day + to 1 year +)	**20%**	**41%**	**68%**
Missing values	12 (9%)	15 (10%)	19 (3.3%)

Notes: * The identification and location of the main suspect(s) coincide immediately or nearly immediately with the arrival of the patrol.

** When there is more than one suspect, the number of location inquiries may be higher than the number of identification inquiries. Many suspects may be identified at the same time through only one identification inquiry. It may, however, take several location inquiries to track them down.

Sources: Brodeur: research conducted for this book; no previous source.
Charles Wellford and James Cronin. 1999. *An Analysis of Variables Affecting the Clearance of Homicides: A Multistate Study.* Washington, D.C.: Justice Research and Statistics Association.

These findings lead to two conclusions. First, the overwhelming fact stemming from these findings is the very short time that it takes to identify the suspect(s) who will be arrested and prosecuted. In my own Canadian sample, 71% of suspects were identified in twenty-four hours or less (discounting the missing values, this percentage increases to 78%). This figure dropped to 49% when I took into account the added time needed to locate and arrest the suspect(s). Still, we can conclude that half the cases were cleared in twenty-four hours or less, using the stronger criteria of location and arrest. These high figures impelled me to double-check all my time calculations for the entire sample, and they stood up to the test. The criterion of arrest was also used by Wellford and Cronin (1999) to classify a case as resolved, with the following results: 28.7% of the cases in their sample were solved in twenty-four hours or less, which is significantly lower than what I have found but still impressive, as almost one-third of Wellford and Cronin's cases were solved within twenty-four hours. The difference between the two samples decreases as we move to longer periods of time: some 50% (294) of Wellford and Cronin's sampled cases were resolved in one week or less, as compared to 61% of my own. To conclude, resolving a murder case is accomplished quickly in a significant proportion of cases: adding all cases for the five police forces under consideration, 52.2% of the 742 (153+ 589) cases were cleared by an arrest in less than a week. In respect to my own sample, we see that 55% of the identification inquiries are resolved almost immediately, and that one-third of the perpetrators are also immediately put under arrest.

The second conclusion allows of either a weak or a strong formulation. The weak formulation is that clearing up cases is only part of what investigators do, and that a complete theory of criminal investigation must take into consideration other things they are doing. The strong formulation would be to claim that developing models for case-solving and articulating a theory of criminal investigation are different endeavors, the first being an exercise in pragmatics and the second an exercise in knowledge.

Exploring the weaker formulation, I wanted to interview the best investigator in the homicide unit I was studying. I asked both the unit's supervisors and the detectives that were part of it who was the best investigator. All members of the unit that I interviewed quickly agreed on a name. This investigator did not owe his reputation entirely to his ability to crack difficult cases (which he also had) but also to his skills as a courtroom manager of homicide cases. His crowning achievement was to have avoided a mistrial in a very high-profile case (the Fabrikant case). Valery Fabrikant was a mass murderer who had finally been overwhelmed by the people he had taken as hostages, after killing four other persons. He decided to act as his own attorney and nearly succeeded in bringing chaos to the court proceedings. In this case, the challenge was not to clear the case, which was a self-solver, but to overcome the obstacles that the accused piled up throughout the court proceedings by his spirited defense. In the follow-up to this interview, I asked the detectives whom I interviewed whether they were case solvers or courtroom evidence managers, and they all chose the second alternative.

Identification Factors

I tried to assess which factors proved the most decisive in identifying the perpetrator(s) of a criminal offence. I selected fifteen different factors, whereas Wellford and Cronin (1999), who relied exclusively on computer analysis, listed eight. The determinant factor(s) stands out without any ambiguity upon the reading of a file. Table 6.3 presents, in terms of percentages, the importance of each factor. The percentages were calculated on the basis of the number of suspects. The first number of 144 suspects was computed by adding all the suspects in single-suspect incidents to the first suspect in the remaining several-suspects incidents. The second number of twenty-four suspects refers to all the second suspects in cases with two or more suspects. Finally, the third number of eleven suspects refers to all other suspects in cases with more than two suspects.

The findings are consistent. The fifteen selected variables can be compressed into three sets: first, the external human sources variables: factors one to eight, excepting factor four (patrol), and the last factor; second, the police-centered factors: patrol, routine inquiry, criminal intelligence, surveillance, and instigation; and, third, technical sources: line-ups and photographic identification, scientific policing (including forensics) and "other" (such as computer checks). With respect to identifying the first (or only) suspect, external human sources (including all sources, such as eye-witnesses) were the determinant factor in

Table 6.3   Determinants of the Identification of Suspects

Determinant Factors	Identification: Suspect 1 (N=144)	Identification Suspect 2 (N=24)	Identification: Additional Suspects (N= 11)
Eye witness	22.5%	25%	-
Spontaneous confession	20.5%	3.7%	-
Police informant	12.5%	27%	33%
Patrol	10.6%	-	-
Victim/co-victim	10.6%	12%	16%
Denunciation (friend)	3.3%	16%	16%
Denunciation (relative)	2.6%	-	-
Denunciation (spouse)	0.7%	-	-
Routine inquiry	2%	-	-
Electronic and/or physical surveillance	1.3%	-	-
Instigation	1.3%	-	-
Suspect photograph	0.7%	-	-
Criminal intelligence	0.7%	-	-
Scientific policing	0.7%	-	-
External assistance	0.7%	-	-
Other	1.3%	8.2%	27%
Missing values	8%	8%	8%

73% of the cases; police-centered factors were decisive in 16% of cases, and technical sources in fewer than 3%. All other suspects (columns 2 and 3) were identified through external human sources. The increasing importance of police informants for the identification of suspects in the second and third columns in table 6.3 reflects the fact that the first suspect arrested often turns in the others. These results are consistent with those of Wellford and Cronin (1999: table 9, p. 27). In close to two-thirds of their sample (64%), the offender was identified by witnesses at the crime scene or by some other external source. The role of physical evidence collected at the scene is negligible (determinant in only 1.9% of their cases).

Location Factors

The findings in table 6.4 are also presented in three columns that correspond to the number of suspects in a case, computed in the same way as table 6.3. Since my research focuses on the work of criminal investigators, I make a distinction between the location of a suspect and the arrest of this person. Locating a suspect is an investigative task, whereas the physical arrest may not be—it was actually effected in 6% of the cases by a SWAT team (this is not reflected in table 6.4).

The findings regarding clearance time are confirmed by table 6.4. In half of the cases, the offender is either immediately arrested by the patrol or a witness, or surrenders to the police. Nevertheless, these findings show that the successful outcome of the location inquiry is determined by factors other than those prominent with respect to identification. Routine inquiry and physical surveillance play a larger role, and so does electronic surveillance. Electronic surveillance was increasingly a key determinant in locating second and third suspects. The explanation for this was given to me in the course of my interviews: electronic surveillance is more effective when there is more than one suspect. In these cases, the investigators can use the tactic of feeding back to the various suspects whom they interrogate parts of the intercepted conversations of their accomplices in order to destabilize them.

Three negative findings ought to be stressed. First, computer searches play a very marginal role in locating a fleeing suspect. Second, surveillance technology also plays a very minor role in locating a suspect—the most efficient means are the traditional ones, such as tailing subjects. As we shall see in chapter 8, the British police complain that video surveillance plays a limited role in solving crimes, although it is pervasive in the United Kingdom. Finally, private security played no role in solving the murder cases in our sample, either in relation to the identification or the location of perpetrators. Although it was originally meant to include the private sector, the variable "external assistance" only refers

Table 6.4   Determinants of the Location of Suspects

Determinant Factors	Location Suspect 1 (N=144)	Location Suspect 2 (N=24)	Location Additional Suspects (N= 11)
Patrol (flagrante delicto)	23.5%	14%	-
Suspect surrenders	20%	-	-
Routine investigation and physical surveillance	16.3%	48%	60%
External assistance	5.5%	-	-
Suspect overpowered by witness	3.3%	-	-
Police informant	2.6%	-	-
Thought solving another case	2.6%	-	-
Electronic surveillance	2.6%	10%	20%
Denunciation (relative or friend)	2.6%	-	-
Information from corrections	2%	-	-
Wanted person ad	2%	-	-
Wounded by victim	1.3%	-	-
Instigation	1.3%	-	-
Criminal intelligence	0.7%	-	-
Computer searches	0.7%	-	-
Other	3.3%	28%	20%
Missing	9.7%	-	-

to assistance provided to the police by other criminal justice agencies (such as corrections). Private investigators, it should be emphasized, played no part whatsoever in the homicide cases that we analyzed.

Scientific Policing

The previous tables show that scientific policing and forensics played no immediate role in identifying and locating suspects. The role played by each of the techniques listed in table 6.5 in solving a case (important, average, no role, expertise not performed) was also examined. Even when assessed as being influential, the role of expertise was essentially ancillary: except in one case, it was never a key determinant.

Table 6.5   The Role of Scientific Expertise

Type of Expertise	Number of Cases (N=144; 179 Suspects)	Percentage
Autopsy	3	1.6
Crime scene	0	-
Blood samples	4	2.23
Chemical analyses	5	2.8
Ballistics	3	1.6
Fingerprints	3	1.6
DNA analyses*	4	2.2
Lie detectors*	11	6.1
Hypnosis	0	-
Data banks	7	3.9
TOTAL	40 (40-15=25)	22.3% (40) and 13.9% (25)

Note: * The lie detectors and the DNA analyses played no part in identifying suspects. Their role was strictly exculpatory (15 suspects).

Table 6.5 lists the number and percentage of cases where scientific expertise played an important—but still ancillary—part. It shows that scientific policing played an auxiliary role in the identification or location of some 22 percent of all suspects, the respective contribution of each technique being important in less than 3 percent of the cases. Kuykendall (1986: 193) had also concluded that scientific policing was of marginal value in identifying suspects. The three expert committees recently brought together by the U.S. National Research Council to assess forensic science concluded that the media depiction of forensic science—particularly in the television serial *Crime Scene Investigation*—presented "an unrealistic portrayal of the daily operations of crime scene investigators" (Committee, 2009: 48). Actually, two of the most useful techniques—the polygraph and DNA fingerprinting—exclusively played an exculpatory role (excluding a suspect). Polygraph evidence is not admissible as evidence in Canadian courts. The investigators only use it as a last resort before classifying a case as inactive. For the period that was investigated, DNA fingerprinting was infrequent, and the police had to wait several months to get the laboratory results. No DNA analysis was conclusive in identifying a suspect.

Subtracting the fifteen cases where the polygraph and DNA analyses played a relatively important part, we are left with twenty-five cases (13.9 percent of the suspects investigated). The most useful technique was computer searches of criminal intelligence data banks, which played a significant role in seven cases (3.9 percent). Crime scene investigation and hypnosis were included even though they played no part, because they do play a large role in crime fiction (particularly crime scene investigation). Such staples of crime fiction as "crime profiling," which also played no part, could also have been included. I discussed extensively the role of expertise and scientific policing in the course of my interviews. Their role was generally perceived to be important in setting the stage in murder court proceedings, where they impressed the jury. However, their contribution to solving homicide cases was said by detectives to be modest.

Two Theories of Criminal Investigation

Criminal investigation is a quest for information that can be used as court evidence to secure the conviction of one or several suspects. The claim that to investigate is to process information is less of a finding—that is, the end result of a process of inquiry—than an initial assumption that is the starting point of most research on criminal investigation. This assumption is not only consistent with common sense but it is also rooted in the very meaning of the words "inquiry" and "investigation." Both words are derived from the Latin. "To inquire" comes from a word—*in-quaerere*—meaning to "search for" and "to interrogate." It had already taken the meaning of looking for the perpetrator of a serious crime in the thirteenth century, where it was linked with the expression "blood inquiry." "Investigation" comes from "*investigatio*," which originally meant the process of tracking down (literally: to look for a vestige of) a prey. The claim that criminal investigation "is fundamentally a form of information work" (Innes, 2003: 113) is basically a restatement of what can be found in examining the semantics of the word "investigation." It is to this extent almost a tautology, which nevertheless must be taken into account if we are to carry out research on criminal investigation. This starting point is, however, very broad and allows for contrasting research perspectives that do not stress the same aspects of the investigative process. Two different theoretical approaches will now be briefly reviewed.

The Epistemic Approach

The adjective "epistemic" is generally applied to things relating to knowledge and its validation. The most articulate example of this approach to criminal investigation, albeit not the only one, is provided by Martin Innes's book on the investigation of murder (2003). In his theory of crime investigation, Innes makes a distinction between various kinds of messages according to the degree of their validation. *Information* is relevant data as opposed to "noise"; *knowledge* is information believed to have factual status; *intelligence* opens new fields of police action to generate further knowledge; and, finally, *evidence* is knowledge formatted according to legal standards of proof (Innes, 2003: 113–114). Criminal investigation is essentially viewed as the production of "information," understood as a generic term referring to the four variants presented above. In view of my own empirical findings, this epistemic approach has several distinct features.

First, this approach is centered on the activity of detectives, that is, plain-clothes criminal investigators belonging to special units. Even if all police were to be broadly viewed as knowledge workers à la Ericson and Haggerty (1997), the epistemic approach according to which detectives are conceived almost exclusively as information collators would not fit all police activity. As suggested above, a theory of crime solving is distinct from a theory of what criminal investigators actually do, since a great deal of crime is cleared up by patrol officers rushing to a crime scene, independently of the action of detectives, and catching the perpetrator red-handed. This kind of police action does not require any preceding knowledge work and basically consists in answering a priority call. The practical consequence of this observation is that recommendations to increase the clearance rate should not be directed exclusively at detectives, but should aim to increase their coordination with uniformed police officers.

Second, the epistemic approach focuses on major crimes, such as murder, drug trafficking, and organized crime. If one wants to develop a theory of criminal investigation, understood in the narrow sense of what criminal investigators do to solve a crime, one has to see them actually at work. As Richard Ericson showed in his classic study of two general investigation units, the detectives' task was "to process readily available suspects" delivered to them or otherwise identified through the work of others" (1981: 136; also see Greenwood et al., 1977: 225, and Hobbs, 1988: 186). Such a perspective offers no support for an epistemic theory of criminal investigation. Even if more than half of the homicides in our sample were immediately solved without any detective work, murder investigations are still a fertile ground for observing detectives performing investigative work. Because of the high profile of murder, detectives have no discretion in selecting the promising cases for a speedy resolution while discarding the cases that hold little promise for clearance. Every case has to be investigated. This obligation generates a paradox for the epistemic theory. It cannot be questioned that, once an investigation has started, it is an information-gathering process that is expanding as long as the case remains unsolved. It has been found by research that the probability of solving a case drastically decreases according to the time that must be devoted to solving it. On the one hand, the longer the investigation, the more it is information work. On the other hand, the lengthier the opportunity for information work, then the less chance there is of solving the case. The paradoxical consequence of this reasoning is that the epistemic theory of criminal investigation becomes more accurate as an investigation is failing. The technological paraphernalia is used as a last resort, usually to little avail, when all else is failing.

This puzzling consequence points to a third feature of the epistemic theory: it does not take into consideration the judicial outcome of an investigation—that is, the conviction of the accused. For all research purposes, it stops at the point where a suspect is identified (arrested and charged), leaving outside its scope the conviction process. However, my own findings show that homicide detectives are primarily courtroom evidence managers, and much of their time is spent securing a conviction. Taking postcase court processing into consideration reveals another crucial feature of the epistemic approach. The epistemic approach is deductive: it works from theory to context, applying the abstract conceptual definition of its key concepts to the actual business of criminal investigation as performed by detectives. For instance, it credits police detectives with a knack for intelligence, whereas police organizations have been criticized for their ineptitude at producing intelligence (United States Congress, Senate, 2002; Suskind, 2006; Brodeur, 2008; Brodeur and Dupont, 2008). More crucially, courtroom evidence is defined as factual knowledge formatted according to the canons of legal discourse (Innes, 2003: 114). Although the epistemic theory does admit that the police may exclude part of its knowledge from conversion into legal evidence for strategic reasons reflecting the politics of adversarial justice (Innes, 2003: 114–115), it does not consider the darker side of police information work. When it reaches the courtroom stage, where securing a conviction is of paramount importance, due process requirements are superseded by the imperative to get results, with the emphasis on means giving way to a focus on results (Klockars, 1985). Police evidence presented in court often results from coercion and deception, and it may also stem from lies and perjury that are incompatible with the meaning of knowledge (and, needless to say, justice). The epistemic theory suffers in this regard from a memory lapse as it forgets that detectives were first described as "secretive rogues" (Kuykendall, 1986: 179). Defining the court evidence presented by detectives as knowledge is, at best, ingenuous. Research on the growing number of publicly acknowledged false convictions has shown that the police have produced, as court evidence, information that they explicitly knew not to be factual.

The Pragmatic Approach

According to Klockars (1985: 85–86; also see Kuykendall, 1986: 191), detectives can be divided into those who are either primarily concerned with means or with ends. This distinction may also apply to the scholars who study criminal investigation. The epistemic theory obviously focuses on the means of investigation, and especially on the collection and processing of information, which offers no guarantee with respect to the result of the investigation. The pragmatic approach is result-oriented and mainly accounts for the consequences of an investigative process.

The result-oriented theory of criminal investigation has several features. First, it focuses on the external outcomes. Outcomes obviously comprise clearance rates in their various definitions, but their significance cannot be reduced to statistical measurements. For instance, the conviction of one high-profile crime boss may produce a destabilizing ripple effect throughout his organization. Pragmatists are also more sensitive to the different nature of the means used by detectives to produce results. Mike Maguire and his colleagues were commissioned by the Home Office in the United Kingdom to perform a study of the assessment of investigative performance. Although they had to address at length the issue of clear-up rates to fulfil their commission, they also endorsed the detectives' characterization of their investigative work as "a mosaic of little tasks" (Maguire et al., 1993: 3). Result-oriented researchers such as Greenwood et al. (1977) also tended to see in the diversity of detective work its defining feature. As was found in my own research, many of these tasks have a tenuous relationship to information work, as when detectives establish a stakeout or use decoys in order to catch a suspect in the act and proceed to an arrest.

Second, a theory focusing on external outcomes cannot avoid looking into the postcase processing. Although the clearance rate is generally defined by the arrest of a suspect, such an arrest is not the definitive closure of a case; if the arrested suspect is eventually cleared by the court, the investigative case has to be, in theory, reopened (although this is not always done). Hence, the second feature of the pragmatist approach is that it includes the postcase (postarrest) segment of the investigation. Indeed, I found in my research that this was the stage of the inquiry that required the most detective time; investigators endorsed my description of what they principally did as the presentation and management of courtroom evidence (also see Lévy, 1987; McConville et al., 1991; Sanders and Young, 2002). This kind of work also consists of "a mosaic of little tasks," such as making sure that the witnesses appear in court, summarizing their testimony for the prosecutor, and affording protection for witnesses whose lives are in danger.

Results-oriented investigations are vulnerable to the belief that the end justifies the means. The effects of such a belief on criminal investigation can only be detected through an inductive approach that is the third core feature of a pragmatic theory of criminal investigation. This particular form of induction proceeds from field research to a theoretical elaboration that does not preclude contentious findings from the outset. This type of approach can be called critical induction in order to distinguish it from value-free empiricism.

For all its theoretical sophistication, the epistemic approach to criminal investigation shares with hard-boiled positivism a tendency to be blind to the mistakes of the knowledge workers and more generally to police deviance. The epistemic approach is quiescent theory, which is in stark contrast with the scientific approach that was outlined in chapter 1 (see the section entitled "Antinomies").

The postclearance work takes on a special significance for assessing whether investigative work is information work. As we saw previously, information is a generic term comprising various specific forms, such as knowledge and evidence, not to mention intelligence. In the context of a theory of investigation, both knowledge and evidence have a specific meaning. Knowledge refers in this context to personal identification knowledge (the identification of perpetrators), which is individual knowledge that proceeds by listing names or numbers: names of persons, places, and commercial firms; telephone numbers, license plates numbers, computer passwords—the types of numbers being nearly infinite. It must be stressed that the logic of individual knowledge is still uncharted territory, the theory of knowledge having followed Aristotle's dictum that there is no knowledge but of the general. Evidence is even more individualized. In the context of criminal investigation, evidence is essentially court evidence. An overwhelming case could be made to the effect that epistemic (scientific) and juridical knowledge are governed by different logical rules (Hart, 1994; Perelman and Olbrechts-Tyteca, 1969). I will limit myself to a few points with respect to judicial evidence, which go beyond an abstract theory of knowledge.

Postclearance work is of two kinds: the work immediately following the arrest of a suspect and the evidence presented in court. Postclearance work is subject to different constraints, depending on whether the police are operating within the Anglo-Saxon or the European continental traditions, the latter stressing the role of prosecuting magistrates (*juges d'instruction*, who apparently will be abolished in France by the government of President Sarkozy). Despite these differences, a few points can be made that apply to nearly all investigators.

The investigative work immediately following an arrest concentrates on trying to get a confession from the arrested suspect and on determining under what charges suspects are going to be prosecuted. In some countries such as Japan, the rate of suspect confessions is above 90 percent of all arrested suspects. It has been shown that getting a confession from a suspect is an achievement with little connection to a knowledge inquiry. At its best, it involves good psychological acumen and interrogation skills from investigators. It also involves manipulation, deception, and at its worst, coercion. The means used to get this information defeat at times its value, the number of confessions being challenged before the courts being on the increase. The charging process often has little to do with the merits of the case and, as detectives that I interviewed confirmed, it aims in common law countries to give the maximum leverage to the prosecuting attorney for securing a negotiated guilty plea to lesser charges than initially filed. In this respect, the most harrowing cases in our own murder investigation samples concerned mothers who themselves called the police after having killed their child afflicted with an incurable degenerative disease. For instance, one mother killed her young paralyzed daughter by drowning her in a bathtub and immediately afterward called the police, having slashed her own wrists. She was rescued and charged with first degree murder. Persons suffering from permanent or temporary mental illness typically fare badly when they are subject to a criminal investigation, which generally shows no mercy.

The second kind of postclearance work concerns the criminal trial itself. The holding of a criminal trial does not of itself means that the plea bargaining process is over, as an accused may plead guilty to lesser charges after the start of the trial. As was noted previously, detectives are extensively involved in criminal trials in Canada. Dick Hobbs noted that "the ultimate expression of a police officer's skill as a crime-fighter is located in the courtroom" (Hobbs, 1988: 186). In addition to being key witnesses for the prosecution, police officers act in Canada as court evidence managers for the prosecution. As we have noted, the courtroom juridical logic does not follow the same rules as scientific knowledge. The differences go much beyond the (biased) selection of evidence that supports conviction (or acquittal), which is typical of adversarial proceedings. Basic tenets of the epistemic approach, such as the difference between irrelevant noise and pertinent information are disregarded. Since a landmark ruling by the Supreme Court of Canada—*Stinchcombe* [1991, 3 S.C.R. at 326]—the prosecution is under a unilateral obligation to disclose all of its evidence to the defense. The police often defeat this obligation by submitting so much evidence to the defense—tens of thousand of pages compressed into various computer formats—that it becomes nearly impossible for the defense team to separate the grain from the chaff in time for the trial.

The postclearance work takes on special significance for assessing whether investigative work is information work. All the courtroom tactics used by the prosecution and the police cannot be reviewed here. However, to the extent that they help us decide between an epistemic and a pragmatic theory of criminal investigation, some of these tactics deserve comment. First, the material support of a piece of information (such as an audiotape) is as important for the purposes of evidence as is the information recorded on it. For instance, if the police cannot establish—through a complex "chain of possession" process linking audiotapes to the intercepted communications of suspects—that recorded conversations presented in court are authentic and have not been tampered with, they cannot be admitted as evidence. Second, a witness's credibility plays as big a part as what this person has to say. As we have seen, forensics and what is referred to as scientific policing play almost no part in solving crime. However, they play a crucial role in court, as judges and jury are favorably impressed by expert opinion and scientific procedures and technology. Some of these experts belong to forensics laboratories operated by the state and regularly appear in court. Their scientific competence comes to be taken for granted over the years. However, special experts recruited by the prosecution or the defense are subject at times to a ferocious cross-examination that tries to undermine their credibility. It is also well known that victims of sexual assault have their reputation targeted by the defense, although these destructive cross-examinations have been banned in many jurisdictions. The general point of the preceding observations is that the vehicle of information—be it an object or a person—is subject to as much scrutiny in court as the information it carries.

Police investigators generally assess the credibility of witnesses and of informants before they call them to testify for the prosecution. However, there are situations where the investigators fail to test their sources of information, either intentionally or unintentionally. They may even entice a paid informant to lie on the witness stand in order to get a conviction. This is but one of the means that are used in the context of a general practice of "framing the guilty," which was described by Egon Bittner during the extended interview quoted in chapter 3.

> See, the police very often are convinced that they have the goods on somebody, but those goods don't work in the courtroom.... And they engage in the practice for which they have a very peculiar term, as I heard it. It's called "framing the guilty." Well, the idea of framing is of course framing the innocent, but they frame the guilty. What they mean by that is that they catch somebody, they know that he did what they think he did, but they don't have the evidence. So they lie. Now, the fact that police lie on the witness stand is a well-known fact, everybody knows that, including the judges, I might say.... I spoke to a man I befriended...—he resigned from the New York Police Department with the rank of Lieutenant—and in our conversation turned out to be one of the strongest critics of American policing.... When I brought up this business of

framing the guilty, he says he finds this to be the least objectionable part of policing. He says, in this struggle against crime, circumventing what is a bizarre and baroque system of restraint in the courtroom is not such a terribly great transgression. (Bittner/Brodeur, 2007: 122–23)

In the course of my research, I was in a position to verify the assertions made by Bittner. In June 1995, a Quebec Superior judge cleared members of a notorious Montreal criminal gang of all charges against them that related to their importing into Canada 16.5 tons of hashish when it became obvious that the police had fabricated evidence against them. This spectacular dismissal of a criminal trial because of police tampering with evidence caused a great shock, and so the Quebec government established two commissions of inquiry into the investigating practices of the police force involved in the case (I participated in one of the inquiries as director of research). It came out very clearly that this was indeed a case of framing the guilty, as later police investigations independently showed that this criminal gang was involved in massive operations of importing drugs (these subsequent police investigations later resulted in several convictions). I also learned that lies and false evidence were almost commonplace police practices, and that this fact was well known by judges. What made this case so different was that the judge dared to dismiss the trial in the face of fabricated evidence by the police.

However we may assess the practice of framing the guilty (such as known career criminals), it should not hide the fact that there are also cases where persons without any past criminal history were wrongly convicted of very serious offences and jailed on the basis of flimsy evidence. DNA tests have been hailed as a most significant tool in the police arsenal. It may be an even more significant tool for the exoneration of the wrongfully convicted. From 1993 to April 2007, two hundred persons wrongfully convicted in the United States of offences punished by very long terms in jail—mostly murder and rape—were exonerated by DNA tests and freed, often after having served part of their lives in prison (see http//www.law.northwestern.edu/wrongfulconvictions).

When means other than DNA analysis are taken into account, the number of persons exonerated from wrongful conviction is significantly higher. In Canada, three high-profile cases of wrongful convictions for murder—the Don Marshall case in Nova Scotia, the Guy-Paul Morin case in Ontario, and the David Milgaard case in Saskatchewan—have generated public government inquiries (Nova Scotia, 1989; Ontario, 1998; the Commission of Inquiry into the Wrongful Conviction of David Milgaard was created in Saskatchewan in 2004 and has not yet published its report). The cost of these inquiries is extremely high, running into millions of Canadian dollars. After Milgaard's exoneration in 1999, the real culprit was found and convicted. David Milgaard was awarded $10 million (Canadian) in compensation for his ordeal. The police may, however, also err on the other side when they fail to thoroughly investigate an obvious suspect. The Stephen Lawrence inquiry in the United Kingdom investigated such a case (Macpherson, 1999).

To Conclude

The observations made throughout this chapter are not intended to settle definitively the issue of whether an epistemic or a pragmatic approach should be applied to criminal investigation. Although I recognize that the epistemic approach is more focused than the pragmatic one, I also believe that it is too narrow and overly simplified. For one thing, solving cases is a much broader notion than detective work, as I tried to show through the discussion of empirical findings. The persons immediately involved in solving a case—neighbors identifying the perpetrator, citizens performing an arrest, a police patrol, and other participants—are not performing any information work by any means. In addition, solving a case is, in a great number of instances, a brief process that bears little resemblance to the painstaking gathering of clues and their clever interpretation as depicted in detective fiction. Admittedly, the longer it takes to solve a case, in the narrow sense of the word, the more the awaited resolution is solely dependent on the work of investigators. However, the more resolving a case is dependent upon the extended work of investigators, the fewer the chances that the case will be cleared. Paradoxically, detectives come into their own as knowledge workers when they fail to solve a case.

It must be added that a theory of criminal investigation that leaves out the postarrest processing, leading in most cases to a conviction, misses an essential dimension of criminal inquiries. Detective work extends in time much beyond the simple business of solving crimes, which is generally achieved quickly. For many investigators, real detective work is accomplished in securing a conviction through a guilty plea or a court verdict of guilty, after the case has been solved through the identification and arrest of the perpetrator(s). Finally, a theory of criminal investigation that does not address the issue of investigative fallibility is woefully incomplete. Egon Bitter aptly captured what separates criminal investigation work from the true pursuit of knowledge, as follows:

[The detectives'] reliance on informants about criminal affairs creates an information movement, [in] an information-structuring sense. It's not the kind of information-gathering that is characteristic of science, where the scientist simply keeps his eyes open and, perhaps informed by a theo-retical perspective, takes in whatever he or she sees without any kind of preconceived notion of relevance. Truth is the thing that is relevant, and if things turn out to be the opposite of what a theory led him to expect, well, then that's what he finds. And I think it's not that way in informa-tion-gathering in the police. That is, the police are interested in hearing only particular kinds of things, and if they don't hear what they would like to hear, they will reformulate what they do hear to fit their expecta-tions. (Bittner/Brodeur, 2007: 122)

Theories of policing as information or knowledge work are relatively insen-sitive to perversions of knowledge. Bacon's maxim is not reversible: knowledge is power, but power is not knowledge, however hard it tries to bend facts to fit its designs. The most fitting test for the theory of policing as information work is provided by the activities of security intelligence agencies, which belong to what is called "high policing" in this book. If there is something that should be akin to information or knowledge work, it is surely intelligence work. High policing is the subject of the next chapter.

High and Low Policing

The distinction between high and low policing was referred to at the end of the previous two chapters. This chapter is devoted to an elaboration on this distinction. High and low policing are also discussed by the historian Hsi-Huey Liang (1992: 10–11). His authoritative book is one of the few works to address the issue of undemocratic political policing in regimes such as Nazi Germany. His perspective is, however, markedly different from mine. Liang's approach is evolutionary, as he describes the advent of modern police in five countries of continental Europe. His characterization of "modern police" is essentially normative (Liang, 1992: 4), modern police being defined as synonymous with democratic police. Liang views the rise of modern policing between Metternich's nineteenth-century Austria and the Second World War as the gradual emergence of democratic police systems in reaction to the authoritarian regimes that prevailed in continental Europe at the beginning of the nineteenth century. The emancipation of the modern police came to an abrupt end in Nazi Germany. It was pursued once more after the defeat of Nazism. Liang's evolutionary perspective implies that high political policing and modern democratic police are conceived as alternatives to each other, and they are indeed presented as being mutually incompatible (Liang, 1992: 3–4). For me, high policing and democratic policing are not antithetical, although they have a strained relationship. New developments in policing point to the increasing role of high policing within democracies and to the necessity to monitor closely the uneasy partnership between "cops and spooks" (Brodeur, 2005a: 809).

This chapter is divided into four parts. First, the main elements of high policing are presented and contrasted with low policing. Second, the operational procedures typical of both kinds of policing are briefly highlighted. The use of police informants being one of the defining aspects of high policing, the third part of this chapter will address the issue of police informants. In conclusion, I will propose a model that integrates high and low public policing.

This chapter is exclusively devoted to the distinction between high and low policing as it is embodied in *public* policing. The distinction also extends to private policing, and I shall address this issue in the following chapter.

I reactivated the notion of high policing after having performed first-hand documentary research into the files of the Canadian intelligence services. As director of research for a Quebec commission of inquiry with the judicial powers to demand access to any document pertinent to its inquiry into counterterrorism, I was granted legal access to these classified files, which exceptionally also included the files of police informants. I continued until recently to work for various commissions of inquiry that investigated high policing directly or tangentially.

The modern concept of high policing is not the offspring of traditional academic research, but rather of work undertaken for several commissions of inquiry from 1979 to the present day. One does not always need to exercise legal powers of access in order to conduct research into high policing. However, this research should be measured against exacting standards of accuracy and should not rest wholly on extrapolations from the published literature or from news clippings. Classifying various forms of policing activity in the category of high policing depends on whether it displays several of the features to be presented in this chapter. Fitting all police "knowledge work" into high policing results in inflating the concept to the point where it loses all heuristic value.

High and Low Policing: A Contrast

The distinction between high and low policing is theoretically unbalanced. This distinction was originally drawn from a reading of the history of the French police (Brodeur, 1983), which brought to light a type of policing that contrasted with everyday policing as performed by uniformed agents and detectives. This type of policing was called "high policing," borrowing from the French *haute police*, and it aimed to protect national security. Agencies engaged in such political policing—for example, the British MI5 and MI6, the Canadian Security Intelligence Service (CSIS), the FBI national security units and the CIA, the French Direction de la surveillance du territoire (DST)—are said to belong to the "intelligence community." Most countries have at least two of these agencies, one dealing with internal security and another with external protection (according to the official count, the United States has sixteen of these agencies, 80 percent of them funded by the Pentagon). However, the concept of high policing does not apply only to agencies belonging to the intelligence community. All sizeable police forces have a high policing component to the extent that they are involved in the collection of intelligence. Private security agencies are also involved in high policing.

When it was originally proposed, the distinction between high and low policing tried to remedy the neglect of high policing by research. It was thus focused on the latter, and no explicit characterization of "low policing" in its own right was provided. This shortcoming is in practice remedied in the previous chapters of this book. The chapter on history provided a dual account of the birth of policing as a system. The early French and British models of policing respectively provided a template for high and low policing and their methods. The two previous chapters dealt with low policing, as performed by uniformed police and plainclothes detectives. The main features of high policing will now be described and systematically contrasted with corresponding aspects of low policing.

It is important to stress at the outset that high policing represents an *idea* of policing that is at variance with the notion of a coercive apparatus dealing with situations of emergency, as developed in the PUFP. The early French police evolved into a system of high policing under the leadership of the Marquis d'Argenson (1697–1715), nicknamed "the devil" by the French populace. When he retired in 1715, Fontenelle, who was then president of the prestigious French Académie, pronounced his eulogy. The eulogy encapsulates in striking fashion some of the underpinnings of high policing.

> To perpetually feed in a city like Paris an immense consumption, of which some of the sources can be dried up by an infinite number of accidents; to repress the tyranny of the merchants against the public, while at the same time stirring up their trade; to draw from an infinite crowd all of those who can so easily hide within it their pernicious industry; either to purge society from them or to tolerate their being insofar as they can be useful in performing tasks which nobody would assume or carry out as well; to hold necessary abuses within the precise bounds of necessity which they are always prone to violate; to reduce these abuses to such obscurity as they must be condemned, and not even to retrieve them from it by too glaring a punishment; to ignore what it is better to ignore than to punish, and to punish only rarely and usefully; to penetrate inside families through underground passages and to keep the secrets that they never imparted for as long as it is unnecessary to use them; to be everywhere without being seen; finally, to move or to check at will a vast and tempestuous multitude and to be the ever active and nearly unknown

soul of this great body; these are the duties of the police magistrate. (Quoted in Clément, 1978: 334; translated by the author)

There are parts of this early-eighteenth-century speech that need to be interpreted in a modern context. The emphasis on families has no relation to their well-being. The families targeted by the high police were the great titled families of the realm, always suspected of plotting against the king (as they did throughout the seventeenth century). As was stressed in previous chapters, policing is synonymous here with governance. Providing Paris with enough food was essentially dictated by the political imperative of avoiding food riots that threatened the regime. The striking absence of any reference to crime control—the word "crime" does not occur in this speech on the duties of the police magistrate—points to one of the reasons why political policing was called "high policing." The great practitioner of high policing—Joseph Fouché, Napoleon's minister of police—referred deprecatingly to criminal policing as the "policing of [the] lampposts" (prostitutes stood under lampposts to advertise their presence).

Criminal policing was thus directed against persons of low status, whereas high policing was exercised at the top of the social scale. The "intelligence community" now involved in political policing has retained some of this prestigious halo. Most remarkable is the retroversion of the traditional logic of policing visibility, which morphs into a renewed logic of stealth and dread. High policing is an exercise in covering up, carried to its ultimate consequences.

Although it neatly suggests what the idea of high policing is, one obviously cannot rely on a text written nearly three centuries ago to account for the distinction between high and low policing. The most salient aspects of this distinction are examined below. As they will be characterized, these aspects logically follow from one another, and taken together form a consistent paradigm.

Protection of the Political Regime

In his book on Fouché, von Hentig makes an observation that expresses the fundamental nature of high policing: "A political police is not so much an instrument for the protection of society as a form of political activity through the medium of the police" (von Hentig, 1919: 30; quoted in Radzinowicz, 1956: 572, note 15). In this quote, von Hentig applies to policing what Clausewitz famously said of war in 1853 ("war is nothing but a continuation of political intercourse with the admixture of different means"). As part of the criminal justice system, low police share its aim of protecting society. In contrast, the protection of the political regime is the raison d'être of high policing. This basic aim is sometimes expressed as the protection of the state or the protection of national security. However, the clause "protection of the political regime" is

more comprehensive, as it also covers so-called "failed states," where high policing is devoted to perpetuating the imposed distribution of power, often at the
expense of society.

There are two variants of this feature of protecting the state, which are quite
different from each other. In their democratic incarnation, high policing agencies are tasked with protecting the nation's political institutions and constitutional framework. In its nondemocratic variant, high policing is devoted to
the preservation of a particular political regime that may consist of the hege-
mony of an oligarchy, the rule of a dictator, or the domination of a tribal clan.
Distinguishing these variants of national security is necessary to avoid falling
into the leftist fallacy that intelligence services are by nature unpalatable to a
democracy. As a matter of fact, all current democracies harbor high policing
agencies. It must, however, be understood that the immediate object of high
policing is the protection of the state apparatus (for example, protecting the
head of the state against assassination), although protecting the state does at
times coincide with protecting its citizens (for example, when there is a terrorist threat).

The State as Intended Victim

Shearing and Stenning (1982: 9) argue correctly that victims have no official
status in the criminal justice system. In criminal law digests, the state is the
party that is cited as the offender's opponent (for example, *The Queen v. NN*),
the real victim being then transformed into a witness of his or her own victimization. However, Shearing and Stenning also stress, correctly, that institutional
victims such as private corporations have created "new systems of justice that
are more responsive to their needs as victims." So have states, when they are the
intended victim of the politically motivated offences targeted by high policing.
There is some irony in the fact that states are much more sensitive to their own
needs as institutional victims than to those of the citizens who they have a duty
to protect. In the high policing model, there is a significant danger that the state
will behave as a privately injured party seeking its own separate partisan interest. Despite appearances, there is an affinity between high policing and private
security, both of these forms of policing being oriented toward the interest of
their client. When the state breaks away from its civil society moorings, it is
actually going through a process of self-privatization.

Absorbent Policing

This is one of the main themes of Fontenelle's eulogy quoted above. High policing
agencies collate data, process these into intelligence (analyzed information) and
threat assessments, disseminate their intelligence products on a need-to-know

basis, store them in various formats for a period of time, and finally dispose of them when they have lost their relevance.

There are two fundamental differences between high policing (or security) intelligence and low policing (or criminal) intelligence. The first is a difference in scope. Police forces collect pertinent intelligence for building criminal cases. In contrast, there seems to be no limit to the appetite for information of the security services: the CIA's *World Factbook* posted on the Internet gives basic information on nearly every country of the world, focusing on their crime and security problems. The second contrast between security and criminal intelligence concerns one kind of "actionable intelligence," that is, intelligence that will spur an agency to undertake public proceedings that go beyond overt or covert surveillance, such as performing an arrest and charging a suspect. For the police, intelligence is just a means to an end—making a case. Security intelligence agencies have a much greater tendency to treat intelligence as an end in itself, absorbing intelligence, and translating it into public judicial proceedings only when there are no more justifiable alternatives. For some high policing agencies—such as the CIA, Israel's Shin Bet and Mossad, or the French foreign intelligence service (DGSE)—actionable intelligence also drives special covert operations aimed at neutralizing an opponent.

The Utilization of Criminals

This is also explicitly mentioned by Fontenelle, when he says that persons involved in a pernicious industry can be tolerated insofar as they can be useful in performing tasks that nobody else would assume or carry out so well. The potential exploitation of crime at the right time is one of the strongest motives behind what is called absorbent policing. Known offenders can be used in a variety of ways (as sources of information or of blackmail, as go-betweens, and as active participants in covert operations). Persons involved in sexual delinquency—particularly prostitutes—have systematically been used throughout the history of high policing in various capacities. However, the utilization of common criminals is a feature that spans the whole spectrum of high policing activities and is a feature of its worst abuses of human rights. Criminal offenders have been used as wardens of political prisoners in concentration camps. Criminal gangs have also been instrumental in the perpetration of genocide, from the 1915 genocide of the Armenian community in Turkey to the "ethnic cleansing" directed against various communities in the former Yugoslavia during the last decade of the twentieth century (Tanner, 2009).

The Use of Informants

Turning one's enemy into a covert asset is perhaps the oldest trick of the intelligence business. There is a chapter on double agents in *The Art of War* by Sun Tzu, the oldest treatise on making war to have reached us (sixth century B.C.). The use as informants of persons involved in illegal organizations and fringe groups labeled as security risks is the most generalized utilization of delinquents in high policing. It must be stressed, however, that not all persons acting as police informants are involved in unlawful activities. In police parlance, an informant is called a human source. When the high policing paradigm was developed in continental Europe, human sources were the main instrument of covert surveillance. We now have created a massive arsenal of technological tools for the purposes of surveillance (Marx, 1988: chap. 10; Brodeur and Leman-Langlois, 2006). All of our natural senses—eyesight, hearing, smelling, touching (lie detectors), and even tasting (poison detecting devices)—now have multiple technological surrogates. Despite the fact that we use a comprehensive array of stealthy technical sources, human sources and undercover operatives can still be singled out as the hallmark of high policing. All post-9/11 commissions have criticized the U.S. intelligence community for having relied on technical rather than human sources in its struggle against Islamic terrorism.

As shown by the public release of the East German Staatsicherheit (Stasi: State Security) archives, the extensive infiltration of human sources is the ultimate achievement of high policing. The archives showed that persons linked together by family, love, and friendship—to quote the most intimate relationships—spied on each other. Not only is the use of police informants the most intrusive instrument of surveillance but it is also the most destructive of the social fabric, as it thrives on betrayal and fosters mutual suspicion and demoralization (Funder 2003). Low policing also makes use of covert informers. However, the primary sources of information for low policing are members of the public acting as complainants or witnesses, as we saw in the previous chapter. The contrast between witnesses who can be summoned to testify in open court and undercover operatives whose identity is generally not disclosed will be discussed later in this chapter.

Secrecy

High policing is cloaked in secrecy to a much greater extent than low policing. The difference between the two is not just a matter of degree but also a matter of nature. Although secrecy plays an increasing part in low policing, police visibility is still a cornerstone of this kind of policing. However, the notions of visibility and of spying are contradictory to one another.

For the purposes of this analysis, secrecy takes two forms. The first is radical secrecy: keeping something unknown from all but the few who have "a need to know" in order to operate. In this sense, persons and organizations become targets of high policing without being aware of it, and many never discover that they have been in the sights of a high policing agency. There is, however, another form of secrecy that is of paramount importance for domestic security. The veil of secrecy may be lifted in small part to intimidate and to produce what is called a "chilling effect." This threatening use of secrecy can be illustrated in reference to Bentham's *Panopticon* (see Foucault, 1977). Bentham's Panopticon is a cylinder-shaped penitentiary where every cell gives into a central interior court, from where prisoners can be observed through the bars of their cell. A steel tower pierced only with slits to allow for outside observation springs from the floor of the central court and reaches up to the ceiling of the prison. Guards exercise surveillance from within this tower, hidden from the sight of prisoners. The latter are fully aware that they are under surveillance. In this sense, the fact that inmates are subject to observation is no secret at all. However, the prisoners cannot know when they are being individually observed, because the few guards inside the tower escape their view. Being under the continuous threat of being personally watched, the prisoners have to keep their behavior in check at all times to avoid potential punishment. This panoptic scheme also saves on manpower, as it maximizes, through stealth, the threatening power of every individual guard.

Fouché, the master practitioner of high policing, made good use of the threatening potential of secrecy: "During my second term [as Minister of Police], I operated much more by acting on public perceptions and through intimidation than by imposing restrictions and using physical coercion.... It is clear that I had the ability to make everyone believe that anytime four persons met together, there would be eyes in my pay to observe and ears to listen" (quoted in Madelin, 1930: 227–228). Blending secrecy with disinformation to produce public paranoia is still one of the most widely used methods of high policing. The cardinal rule of high policing is not to be everywhere without being seen, but rather to be felt everywhere, without being seen. In this regard, the contrast between high and low policing is more subtle than the simple opposition between visibility and invisibility. When they want to, high policing agents can make their presence perceptible without showing themselves in a straightforward way. One can put as much spin (indeed more) on mysteries as on revelations.

Deceit

It was argued at the end of chapter 5 that there was a hard core common to the most harmful forms of crime, which embody either violence or deception. Notwithstanding the wider alternative definition proposed in chapter 4, low policing is traditionally characterized as the potential use of coercive means to counter violence or the threat thereof. It was also pointed out that such policing was directed against only one part of the hard core of crime and disorder. The other mainspring of harmful behavior is deception. In the same way that low policing uses force against violence, high policing fights deception with deceit. There is, however, a crucial difference between high and low policing with respect to the use of means. Insofar as the practice of low policing rests on the use of force, it ranges over a wide spectrum that encompasses both the potential and the actual use of force. In democratic countries, force is threatened rather than applied.

Although there are many degrees of deceit, the logic of deceit is not premised on the difference between potential and actual use. Being deeply woven into the fabric of human relationships, deceit is not as strongly condemned as violence, cunning often being positively viewed. This is why the qualifications made to the use of force—potential use of force, minimal force, and force in the last recourse—do not apply to deceit in the field of policing. In other fields of governance, transparency is an ideal, albeit seldom respected. The notion of spying activities that may *potentially* rely on deceit is ludicrous: spying is by definition a deceitful business. In a similar way, there is no obligation for high policing to use minimal deception or to use deceit in the last recourse. The abuses of deception, such as public disinformation, defamation, entrapment, and provocation, have a much lower profile than physical brutality and are the stock in trade of high policing.

Conflation of Separate Powers

We traditionally distinguish between legislative, judicial, and executive power. In democracies, these powers are exercised independently from one another. In Westminster-style democracies, where all cabinet ministers also sit in Parliament, there is less of a distinction between the executive and the legislative branches of government than in the U.S. "checks and balances" model. Notwithstanding these differences of emphasis, all democracies condemn political interference in judicial proceedings and in preventive custody.

The situation is notably different for high policing. As we stressed in the chapter on police history, the police magistrate enjoyed all three fundamental powers in continental European monarchies (some of which lasted until the end of the First World War): he could establish all kinds of regulations and even penal statutes that even carried capital punishment; he would also preside over trials; finally, he exercised, by definition, all forms of executive power and was charged with carrying out specific assignments from the central power. The concept of the political "coup" had an original meaning from the seventeenth to the nineteenth century that directly contradicted its present meaning: a political coup was then a decisive action *of* the state against its enemies and not an action perpetrated *against* the state by its opponents in order to change the regime (a *putsch*), as the concept is presently understood (Gabriel Naudé 1639/1988; see also L'Heuillet 2001: 47). Such "coups" were spurred by situations of urgency and obviously dispensed with the safeguards of due process. This feature of police coups is explicitly mentioned by Minister of Police Lenoir in his briefing to the court of Austria:

> The speed of the most important operations in this regard—where success almost always depend on timing, and also on having no obstacles, nor any difficulty to foresee or to fear—can admit only with the greatest difficulty legal formalities that are in themselves lengthy and cumbersome. These sorts of operations therefore rest on the King's order and the Magistrate in this regard is granted the Sovereign's authority. (Lenoir, 1779: 53)

This quote from Lenoir is a forerunner of the "executive order" that will be much abused in later centuries.

The pressure of time has not received the attention it deserves in the theory of policing and even in legal theory. The need for quick results is one of the most critical determinants of the suspension of legal protection. The abysmal resurgence of torture by the U.S. government after 9/11 has been justified by the so-called "ticking bomb" argument, according to which the most extreme procedure of interrogation must be applied to stop an impending disaster in time. We know of no ticking bombs that were defused on the basis on information obtained under torture, except in TV serials.

Extralegality

The conflation of the three basic forms of power weakens the legislative and judiciary powers and buttresses the power of the executive. In the most extreme cases, the legislative and judiciary powers are incorporated into the executive and vanish altogether. This incorporation has an impact on policing itself and also on civil society. With respect to policing, it cancels out in practice the notion of police deviance, since it is the executive branch of government that applies the standard for measuring its own performance. This point was neatly encapsulated by a member of the French Assemblée Nationale, who tabled a report in 2002 on the accountability of the French security services. He advocated that they be granted a large amount of unfettered discretion according to the principle that in the field of national security "the rights of the state supersede the rule of law" ("Les droits de l'État commandent à l'État de droit"; France, 2003: 3). In post-9/11 times, this maxim seems to prevail everywhere.

However, the most drastic impact of the primacy of the executive is on civil society. The fundamental principle that no behavior shall be punishable unless it is so provided by law—*nullum crimen sine lege*—is neutralized by high policing. In a letter to Napoleon, Fouché wrote:

> The police, as I conceive it, should be established in order to forestall and prevent offences and to check and arrest such as have not been foreseen by the law....If the police may sometimes disembarrass itself from the forms of justice, it is only from those forms which are by their nature slow, and it is only with the purpose of moving more swiftly than the criminals. (Quoted in Radzinowicz, 1956: 566, translated in text)

The imperative to dispense with all obstacles that slow down police action is again seen to be determinant. On the basis of this quote, it would appear that Fouché only wanted to suspend the application of the most cumbersome parts of the legal procedure. However, in an 1808 report to Napoleon on the French prison population, the minister refers to a particular category of prisoners that he describes as "inmates not tried nor brought to trial for fear that they would be acquitted for lack of legal evidence" (quoted in Madelin, 1930: vol. 1: 502, note 3). These are individuals who were incarcerated pursuant to a measure of high policing.

Of all the features discussed above, there is one that is completely unpalatable to democracy. It is the weakening of the legal and judiciary powers and their progressive dissolution into an unbridled executive power—what was described above as the conflation of all powers. Browder (1975: 216) describes how the top Nazi police leaders—Himmler and Heydrich—relied upon a type of policemen, called Gestapoists, who were willing to take on the duties of "judge, jury, and sometimes executioners." When this feature is combined with the extreme form of extralegality that makes it possible to detain persons for crimes they did not commit and where some crimes are not even defined by any law, it makes for the most murderous political regimes. Nazi and Stalinist terror both rested on five principles: (1) the exclusive primacy of executive power and government by decree, (2) the establishment of a parallel penal system managed by high policing organizations—for instance, the SS and the NKVD, (3) the generalized application of preventive custody under the most debilitating conditions, (4) the institutionalization of physical brutality and of torture, and (5) the rigorous application of these policies both on the national territory and in occupied countries.

A number of policies applied by the United States and some of its allies after the terrorist attacks of 9/11 show the complexity of the issues raised by high policing. The first four characteristics listed above are all in various degrees features of the type of governance that was the hallmark of the "war on terrorism" declared by the United States, but not the fifth one. The most objectionable policies were applied outside the U.S. mainland and, with few exceptions, did not target U.S. citizens. In addition, the number of persons who have been the object of these policing practices cannot be compared with the number of casualties made by any totalitarian regime.

The practice of rendition, the use of "black sites" in foreign countries, and torture are obviously incompatible with human rights and democratic values. They may arguably constitute war crimes or crimes against humanity. However, they raise a much broader issue that goes to the heart of policing. The United States is not the first country to be democratic within its territory and to behave like an abusive occupational force on foreign soil. The great colonial powers, such as Great Britain and France, have also behaved in such a way, even as late as the twentieth century. More decisively, the word "police" comes from a word (*politeia*) that refers to the internal government of a political entity. How, then, should we describe a city—a state—that follows two opposing policies in relation to policing: an internal policy that tries to abide by the values of democracy and an external policy that mocks human rights in the name of furthering civilization or democracy? Answering this question is postponed for a later chapter. However, its relatively novel character should be emphasized. In former times, the "modern" police were responsible for internal security and the military for external security. In the current global context, we are now experiencing with external policing— for example, the UN international "policing" missions—and internal militarization the spread of paramilitary policing in emergent countries. We are far from having forged the conceptual tools to think this predicament through.

High and Low Policing: Operational Procedures

For a period of time spanning roughly the years between the fall of the Berlin Wall in 1989 and the 9/11 terrorist attacks on the United States, there were strong initiatives—particularly on the part of the intelligence community seeking a new mandate—to blend high and low policing. Since the end of the Cold War, security intelligence agencies have been entering domains that were the territory of traditional law enforcement, such as organized crime (Brodeur, 2005a; also see Anderson et al., 1995: 173). On the other hand, police forces tried to establish centralized criminal intelligence units and were increasingly implicated in the struggle against organized and transnational crime (Anderson et al., 1995: 168–170). The situation changed drastically at the turn of the twenty-first century with the advent of global mass terrorism, which afflicted not only the United States (September 2001), but Indonesia (October 2002, with many Australian victims), Spain (March 2003), Morocco (May 2003), Saudi Arabia (May 2004), the United Kingdom (July 2005), and Mumbai (November 2008), to refer only to the most widely known incidents. It is premature to assess the impact of the July 2005 bombings in London, but they have already spurred the Terrorism Act 2006, increasing the period of preventive detention without charge from fourteen to twenty-eight days. New British legislation increased this period to forty-two days in 2008. In the United States, the numerous commissions that investigated why the U.S. policing agencies of every stripe failed to prevent the 9/11 attacks came up with findings that emphasised the gap between high and low policing with respect to their operating procedures. In Canada, two reports from a government commission of inquiry emphasized the same point (Canada, 2006a and b). This gap is generated by three basic operational differences: the capacity for analysis, the use of preventive intelligence versus prosecutorial evidence, and the aim of disruption as against circumvention.

The Capacity for Analysis

Of all U.S. government inquiries into the intelligence and law enforcement failures that led to 9/11, none is more provocative than the "Additional Views" of Senator Richard C. Shelby to a report by the U.S. Senate Select Committee on Intelligence (SSCI; cited as United States, 2002). One of the FBI agents involved in the investigation of the 2001 bombing of the USS Cole stated before the SSCI that there was a "wall" separating criminal investigations from security intelligence in order to preserve "against contaminating criminal investigators with intelligence information" (quoted in United States, 2002: 51). Senator Shelby also quoted one former director of the National Security Agency to the effect that "cops" cannot do the work of "spies" (United States, 2002: 74). Senator Shelby concluded that "Intelligence analysts would doubtless make poor policemen, and it has become very clear that policemen make poor intelligence analysts" (United States, 2002: 62).

The recommendations of the 9/11 commission (United States, 2004: 400) countenanced his diagnosis of the FBI's important shortcomings in the field of counterterrorist intelligence. In Canada, the existence of a "wall" between criminal investigation and security intelligence was tellingly confirmed by the remarks of the former commissioner of the RCMP on intelligence-led policing (ILP), which was developed mainly in the United Kingdom (see National Centre for Police Excellence, 2005). In a public talk given in 2005, ex-RCMP Commissioner Zaccardelli remarked that ILP "reeks of secret service, spy agency work—the capital 'I' in "Intelligence" (Zaccardelli, 2005), and that the police should have no truck with it.

Preventive Intelligence versus Prosecutorial Evidence

The most contentious issue between law enforcement agencies and security intelligence services stems from what Senator Shelby called the police "tyranny of the casefile" (United States, 2002: 62). All law enforcement agencies are geared to convicting perpetrators in criminal proceedings. Due to the public nature of these proceedings, intelligence agencies are extremely reluctant to share information with police organizations because of their fear that their sources and methods will be disclosed in criminal proceedings.

In Canada, this friction between high and low policing is a persistent feature. From 1969 until the present day, there is not one government body that examined the relations between the Canadian intelligence community and the RCMP that did not explicitly refer to the divorce between secret intelligence and public court evidence. This divorce was starkly illustrated in the wake of the two 1985 terrorist bombings of an Air India and a CP Air flight which took off from Canadian airports. These bomb attempts, attributed to Sikh terrorists, killed 331 people—the Air India plane exploded over the Atlantic, killing all 329 passengers and crew—making them by far the most costly acts of terrorism in terms of human lives in the history of Canada. In the first stage of the police investigation, members of the CSIS (Canadian Security Intelligence Service) destroyed audiotapes that might have provided crucial evidence to the police, in order to protect the identity of their informants. This enduring conflict between the CSIS and the RCMP was alleged to have been the source of the failure of the Canadian policing agencies to solve these cases. A commission of inquiry into the bungled investigation was established in 2006 (the Commission of Inquiry into the Investigation of the Bombing of Air India Flight 182). The terms of reference of the commission directs it to inquire into "the manner in which the Canadian government should address the challenge...of establishing a reliable and workable relationship between security intelligence and evidence that can be used in a criminal trial." The commission has not yet tabled its report.

Disruption and Circumvention

The conflicting requirements of intelligence production and evidence disclosure are components of a more wide-ranging contrast between the ways in which the police and the security services operate. This contrast can be illustrated through the discussion of a few examples. The first refers to the aftermath of the 1970 October Crisis described at the end of chapter 5. It provides a striking illustration of the professional culture of a security service, whether it is embedded within a police organization or operating on its own. This culture was described by the Quebec Keable and Duchaîne commissions (Québec, 1981a and b; also see Brodeur, 1980). Having failed to prevent the October Crisis, the counterterrorist forces operating in Quebec succeeded shortly thereafter in transforming the Front de libération du Québec (FLQ)—the terrorist organization responsible for the crisis—into a police colony by saturating it with police informants. They limited their action to monitoring lesser crimes perpetrated by the FLQ and making sure they did not succeed—for example, a failed robbery, which was instigated by a police informant, and a fire-bombing perpetrated by that same informant—while using their informants to steer the group along a course predetermined by the police. Despite efforts by the RCMP to keep it going, the FLQ eventually dissolved, some of its members—including the police informants—joining together again to form a Maoist group. This group met the same fate as the FLQ and also dissolved in the late 1980s, after learning how deeply it was penetrated by informants.

In a similar way, U.S. Judge Charles Breitel documented in a special report the extent to which two U.S. Trotskyite leftist political parties had been penetrated by the FBI (Breitel, 1980). The top leadership of these parties was in significant part composed of FBI informants.

The final example again concerns Canada. Canada's security service—CSIS—is overseen by the Security Intelligence Review Committee (SIRC). SIRC investigated the infiltration by CSIS of an extreme-right organization in the early 1990s. At the end of its investigation, SIRC had to acknowledge that the security service culture of circumvention was to a certain extent justified: "We are also cognizant of the danger that in destroying one group, as opposed to watching it, another one which is worse may be created" (SIRC, 1994: section 13.11). In contrast, the police target individual crime bosses or perform mass arrests, albeit much more rarely, in the hope of obliterating a criminal organization by sending its members to jail. Such police action results in disrupting criminal activities. Their interruption is sometimes durable and, in rare cases, final. In most instances, these disruptive effects are only temporary and the criminal organizations quickly resume their activities, after a short interruption.

The line between the strategy of circumvention and the practice of entrapment is quite thin. In 2006, the RCMP and CSIS arrested eighteen people in Toronto—among them were five minors—suspected of planning to carry out several acts of terrorism. It was publicly disclosed that the group was infiltrated by at least two "moles" and had been under surveillance by CSIS since 2004. A third person not identified as a police informant played an ambiguous role and incited the younger members of the "Toronto eighteen" to participate with him in a training camp, at which he never showed up. It was also revealed by the media that one of the informants—in the pay of the RCMP—had arranged a purchase of phony ammonium nitrate by the terrorist suspects for making explosives. Neither the RCMP nor CSIS offered a denial of this media report. Four of the five arrested youths were released without charge and the remaining one was convicted of a terrorist offence and sentenced to prison. By October 2009, five of the Toronto eighteen had either admitted guilt or had been found guilty of a terrorist offence and had been sentenced to long jail terms. The judge ruling in these cases explicitly rejected the claim that the accused were the victims of entrapment. The intelligence service culture of circumvention fosters conspiracy theories and gross mythologies. The widely screened video entitled "Loose Change," which tries to demonstrate that the World Trade tragedy was engineered by the U.S. intelligence community, is a telling example of this paranoid culture.

Informants

In English law, the existence of a "police-informer" privilege not to have his or her identity publicly disclosed goes back at least to 1794 in the landmark trial for high treason of Thomas Hardy (24 State Trials 199, see Wilson, 1976), where Mr. Justice Grosse decided against disclosure on the basis "that is the law stated; that is the law agreed and argued upon by the counsel on both sides, at p. 820." It was subsequently confirmed that the "police-informer" privilege not to have his identity publicly disclosed was not a matter of judicial discretion but was enshrined in law (*Marks v. Beyfus*, 1890). The absolute character of the police-informer privilege was challenged in Canada in 1980 by a commission of inquiry. This commission, chaired by Mr. Justice Horace Krever, was investigating 368 incidents in which medical information about patients was improperly elicited by the police and disclosed by medical doctors. It was claimed by the commission that the police medical informants did not benefit from the police-informer privilege, since they had transmitted confidential information about their patients without the latter's consent and in violation of their medical oath. The Supreme Court of Canada ruled against the Krever commission on the basis that the police-informer privilege "is not given to the informer and, therefore, misconduct on his part does not destroy the privilege. The privilege is that of the Crown, which is in receipt of information under an assurance of confidentiality." (*Sol. Gen. Can. et al. v. Roy. Comm. (Health Records)*, [1981] 2 S.C.R.).

This ruling meant that the state provided a legal shield to the police and their informers when they engaged in improper behavior. It complicated enormously all judicial proceedings where police informants were involved. For instance, the criminal proceedings against Santokh Khela and Kashmir Dhillon, two members of an extremist Sikh organization accused in Canada of plotting to bomb an Air India plane in New York, lasted from 1986 to 1998. They were initially convicted in 1986 on the basis of the testimony of an FBI informer. Because of the prosecution's refusal to have the informer testify, this case dragged on for twelve years and generated three trials and four appeals, including an appeal in the Supreme Court of Canada. The conviction was finally overturned in 1998.

The legal tradition of protecting police informers implies more than protecting the identity of police sources. The whole field of police informants is in practice off limits for empirical research and it has remained a terra incognita where few have ventured, with the notable exception of Gary Marx, who developed a pioneering body of work on police undercover work and surveillance (Marx, 1974, 1988, and 2003; see also see Settle, 1995, and Billingsley, Nemitz, and Bean, 2001). It nevertheless remains a key topic for the study of high policing. Most of the general features of high policing specifically apply to police informers and agents working undercover.

Police informers have been an object of contempt throughout history. The repulsive pattern of betrayal for money (or some other prize) set by Judas in the New Testament is generally applied to all police informers. In German, however, the original word for a police informer is *Vertrauensleute* or *V-Leute* (reliable persons). The name was apparently coined in 1932 by Reinhardt Heydrich, the notorious head of the Nazi security service (Sicherheitdienst—SD). According to Stokes (1975: 242–243), the German SD was patterned on Heydrich's vague notion of the English Secret Service. V-Leute were not to be hired spies in the high policing tradition of Fouché, but persons of integrity whose judgment would command public respect. Stalin also exploited the dedication of USSR communists to denounce enemies of the state. A single person—Polia Nikolaenko, hailed by Stalin as the "heroic denunciatrix" of Kiev—helped destroy 8,000 people during the Great Terror (Amis, 2002: 145; Montefiore, 2003: 193).

There is strong irony in the fact that informants motivated by lofty ideals have acted on behalf the most barbaric regimes that the world has ever known. Informing the police, or their surrogates, on the misdeeds of others is an activity fraught with ambiguities too deep to be dispelled. It now seems obvious to us that Nazi V-Leute and Stalinist denunciators are not examples of civic virtue that should be followed. Yet we now have a new name—"whistle blowers"—for persons who denounce wrongdoings of various kinds, and we are even enacting legislation to encourage them to come forward and to protect them from retaliation. Three such whistle blowers were actually named persons of the year by *Time Magazine* in December 2002. Clearly, all informants do not fit into the same mold.

Types of Informants

Marx (1988) does not provide a typology of police informants. He uses the word "undercover" to refer to a variety of covert police actions that involve deception (Marx, 1988: 12). These activities are performed by very different operatives, such as members of a public police organization working undercover and police informers that have no official status. Settle (1995) provides a somewhat idiosyncratic categorization of police informants—indemnified dogs (protected witnesses), chocolate frogs (prison informants), and gigs (criminal informers)—that does not take undercover police into account. Here are some basic distinctions.

Anonymous denunciators. This is a very wide category. It ranges from idealistic whistle blowers protecting their identity, to people seeking revenge, blackmailers, and psychopaths writing anonymous letters. Although anonymous denunciators may have collectively an important role—for instance, in identifying persons who engage in tax evasion—anonymous informants do not by definition develop a relationship with a police handler, and they play a marginal role in high policing.

Statutory informants. Many persons are required by various statutes, such as various motor vehicle acts, to report a great deal of information to the police. It was generally thought to be inappropriate to refer to them as police informants (Wood, 1986). However, the number of statutes requiring that information about various transactions be transmitted to the police on a regular basis—for example, in legislation against money laundering and against terrorism—is growing, and the information requested is increasingly intrusive. They are indicative of a trend toward the institutionalization of denunciation.

Police sources. This category is also wide-ranging. It comprises all those who, in various capacities, knowingly provide information to the police. The majority of individuals belonging to this category are people reporting a crime or assisting the police in the context of a criminal investigation, as well as all types of witnesses and people responding to a public call for information (for instance, giving information that may lead to the arrest of a wanted person). Settle (1995: 38) includes civilians engaged in security programs such as "neighborhood watch" among persons practicing what he calls "respectable grassing." Notwithstanding the fact that "respectable grassing" may be a deliberate oxymoron, this inclusion raises a considerable issue. The notion underpinning all police reforms since the early 1980s is that of a partnership between the police, the public, and various institutions having a stake in security. Since all partners of the police trade information with them in various ways, should they all be viewed as police informants? This is an issue that is much too broad to be resolved in the narrow context of this classification of police sources. However, it would seem on first thought reasonable to exclude from the category of police informants people giving information to the police that does not by its nature mention any individual names—for instance, people exchanging statistical information with the police or identifying the problems of their neighborhood in community meetings with the police. Still, this is only a preliminary observation that does not answer the question of whether we are moving toward what Gary Marx and others call a maximum security society.

Delinquent informants. There is a type of police informant that deserves a specific mention. These are persons who give personal information to the police despite having sworn to respect the confidential nature of this information through a formal professional oath or otherwise. A government commission of inquiry was created in the Canadian province of Ontario to investigate breaches of confidentiality of medical doctors—particularly psychiatrists—who gave information about their patients to the RCMP (Ontario, 1980). Doctors are not the only ones who breach their obligation to respect confidentiality. Through my work in various commissions of inquiry, I came across cases where clerics, probation officers, and other criminal justice professionals gave information to the police. In the context of plea negotiations, lawyers may occasionally give confidential information to the police. With the exception of lawyers who are seeking court considerations, delinquent informants are usually not driven by self-interest and want to assist the police in situations of crisis out of their sense of civic duty.

Police undercover officers. The distinction between undercover police officers and police informers is of crucial importance. They differ in at least three respects: undercover police operatives are sworn members of a police organization with the corresponding powers and obligations (informers have no official status except a contract, when they have one); they are not granted benefits over and above their salary (informers are granted various kinds of advantages on a contractual or discretionary basis); they generally act within the context of a specific operation, and they move from one operation to the other (informers are either infiltrated for an extended period of time or definitively blow their cover by testifying in court).

Police informers. They can be defined as any person who provides information and various services to the police without being obliged by law, in exchange for court and/or financial considerations for them or persons close to them.

Informers not only provide information. They may, for instance, provide a cover for a police undercover operative. They are generally first recruited on the basis of a prosecutorial discount of criminal charges that may be brought against them rather than a financial reward, which may be later attributed on the basis of usefulness. It must be stressed that an informer is not always the direct or sole beneficiary of these advantages, the threat of harming closely related persons playing a significant role in the recruitment and handling of an informer. Some police forces, such as the RCMP, make a distinction between two kinds of informers. First, the *police agent* is an informant acting under explicit instructions from his or her handler; in most cases, it is understood that this agent will have to testify in open court. Second, the *police source* is an active and unsupervised criminal providing information on an ad hoc basis to the police, although noncriminals may also be in a position to act in this capacity.

Protected witnesses. These individuals are as much recruited for the information they can provide as for the evidence they can give in court as witnesses for the prosecution. They are referred to under various names such as *delatores* (public denunciators in ancient Rome), *délateurs* (in French-speaking countries), *pentiti* (repenting witnesses in Italy), grasses and super-grasses (in English slang), and under the technical designation of protected witnesses. Police informers and protected witnesses are often confused, although they belong to two distinct categories of police sources. The key difference between them is that police informers are not compelled to testify in court unless there is a special understanding to that effect. With respect to political high policing, a security service will go to great lengths—for instance, violating the law—to keep their informers from blowing their cover through court testimony. There are other differences, as well. The relationship between protected witnesses and the prosecution is much more formalized than that between the police and their informers. Protected witnesses agree to sign a contract that stipulates their obligations and their reward. These rewards can be very high: in one 2009 police operation against organized crime in Quebec (operation "SharQc"), an informer was promised $6 million (Canadian) for testifying against his former accomplices. Rewards have run up as high as $7 million (Canadian) in other provinces. The understanding between the police and their informers is much less explicit, both parties generally trying to take advantage of the other. Finally, protected witnesses testify in open court proceedings and under their own name. The police may try to protect the identity of an informer compelled to testify by limiting the public character of the testimony, using screens, masks, and other identity protecting devices, usually to no avail.

Whistle blowers. They belong in all respects but one—the denunciatory character of their behavior—in a different category from the informants characterized above. They do not hide their identity, and publicly act in their own name. Whistle blowers generally do not inform the police as such, but rather their superiors in the organization to which they belong or the public itself—generally through the press; only if they happen to belong to a police organization, like Serpico (NYPD) or Coleen Rowley (FBI), do they make their denunciation directly to the police hierarchy. Not only are they inspired by the common good rather than by self-interest, but they put themselves in harm's way by blowing the whistle and do not profit from their action. Despite the fact that they are hailed as public heroes—for instance, the FBI agent Coleen Rowley who denounced the blindness of her superior to clues that might have led to the prevention of 9/11—they bear the stigma of having informed on persons close to them and are generally compelled to put an end to their career (Mrs. Rowley is no longer part of the FBI). However praiseworthy their behavior may be, whistle blowers are in the end overwhelmed by the moral ambiguity of informing on their own colleagues.

The types of informants that we have been discussing can be brought together under four broader categories generated by the combination of two dichotomies. The first dichotomy is whether an informant is driven by self-interest or by altruistic values. Altruistic values are here understood in the broadest sense and include such things as compliance with the law in the case of statutory informants. The other dichotomy is whether an informant actually receives external compensation, such as money, or experiences internal (psychological or moral) compensation. The notions of self-interest and external compensation do not coincide, although they are germane: an informant, for instance, might seek internal psychological gratification in the feeling of revenge, and yet not wish for any tangible form of external compensation such as financial or court considerations. It should be stressed that informants acting out of self-interest and being granted external compensation are in most cases also submitted to various forms of coercion.

Figure 7.1 summarizes what has been discussed above, the most important part of the table being for our purposes the bottom right-hand square. Undercover police officers perform their professional duty and to this extent are not guided by self-interest; their external compensation is simply their police salary.

There are items that fit in more than one category or are neutral in respect to them. These have been put in the area bounded by dotted lines at the center of the figure. As previously noted, anonymous informants may be guided by altruistic values rather than by self-interest and hide their identity for the sole purpose of protecting themselves from retaliation. Statutory informants are not motivated by interest or values: they just perform their professional duties.

	Self-Interest			Altruistic Values	
Internal compensation	POLICE SOURCES	*ANONYMOUS DENUNCIATORS*	*STATUTORY INFORMANTS*	WHISTLE BLOWERS	
External compensation	POLICE INFORMERS	*PROTECTED WITNESSES*	*DELINQUENT INFORMANTS*	UNDERCOVER POLICE	

Figure 7.1 Classification of Informants

Some delinquent informants may breach their commitment to confidentiality in order to help the police without expecting anything in return, and others may seek external compensation. Also, there are witnesses willing to testify solely to serve justice and who need protection because their lives are actually in danger. Finally, there are cases where an informant is not originally looking for some external compensation and eventually receives a financial reward because the nature of his relationship with the police changes with time.

Consequences

The use of informants is perceived, with good reason, to be at the core of high policing operations against ideologically motivated crime, such as political or religious terrorism. It is also a vital tool for law enforcement in the fields of consensual and transactional crime, corporate crime, and political corruption. However, the use of informants has also problematic consequences. The case study presented above will serve as a partial illustration of these consequences. Police informants are one of the best illustrations of the theoretical perspective that we outlined in chapter 1, under the heading of "Antinomies."

Compartmentalization. In a Canadian terrorist case, individuals who were deeply implicated in terrorism (in the FLQ) were at the same time acting as informers for the narcotic squad of a large Quebec police force. Their handler from the narcotic squad told them that they were targeted by the counterterrorism unit and managed for a time to keep them one step ahead of his colleagues. The secrecy that shrouds the use of informants fosters a high degree of compartmentalization in high policing: individual case officers are reluctant to share all the information that they get from an informer with their colleagues and with their organization, despite vigorous efforts to implement a policy which stresses that informers belong to the organization rather than to individual case officers. The reluctance to share information is embodied in the "need to know" principle of operation, which builds walls between the various units of the same force, hinders the sharing of information between different forces, and creates a gap between security intelligence agencies and their so-called political masters.

Unreliability. Members of security intelligence agencies are the policing agents to whom the description of "knowledge workers" should fit the best. Yet all the government-sponsored inquiries into these agencies have stressed the problems related to the unreliability of intelligence produced by these agencies—what might be termed the "slam dunk syndrome" in reference to the CIA director's unwarranted conviction that there were unconventional (nuclear) weapons in Saddam Hussein's Iraq. When I was part of the Keable inquiry (Québec, 1981a), I was tasked to review all the debriefing reports of informers reporting to counterterrorist units in Quebec. The greater part of these reports read like a gossip column on "people" suspected of being involved in terrorism (whom they met, which parties they attended, their love affairs, and so forth). In this regard, it must be remembered that at the height of the October Crisis (October16, 1970), close to five hundred persons were arrested and put in preventive custody on the basis of police files that identified them as either members or sympathizers of the FLQ. All were released after a few days, and none of them was ever charged in relation to terrorism. Yet two people who were personally involved in the abduction of James Richard Cross, the British diplomat, completely escaped police notice at the time of the crisis and for more than ten years. One of them was finally prosecuted and convicted in the early 1980s. Although known to the police, the other person was neither arrested nor prosecuted. Thus security intelligence led to the arrest of some five hundred persons having no connection with terrorism, while two individuals criminally involved in the events that triggered the crisis enjoyed impunity, the first one for more than ten years, and the other one until this day.

The highly confidential nature of the intelligence supplied by informers drastically limits the possibility of an independent verification of its truth. This intelligence is often highly defective and cannot qualify as knowledge under any rigorous understanding of the word. Not only is it untrue but in a large number of instances it also provides no basis for action, as knowledge usually can. A significant part of it fits the description of being unreliable and nonactionable gossip.

Licensing criminals. No consequence of undercover operations has generated as much discussion as licensing informers to commit crimes. This consequence of undercover operations was particularly emphasized by Reuter

(1983a). He argues that the value of an informer depends on the depth of his involvement in the delinquent milieu. In order to have their good informers maintain their position, police handlers have no other choice than to license them to commit crimes. This consequence is clearly illustrated in the police compartmentalization case study presented above. Police officers operating undercover are granted a similar licence. This license was enshrined in Canadian law in 2001. Subsection 25.1 (9) b) (ii) of the Canadian Criminal Code states that a public officer and other persons acting at their direction are justified in committing an act or omission that would otherwise constitute an offence if they believe on justifiable grounds that the act or omission is necessary to "Prevent the compromise of the identity of a public officer acting in an under-cover capacity, of a confidential informant or of a person acting covertly under the direction and control of a public officer." This vague legal wording provides a blanket justification for all kinds of criminal behavior.

Corruption. There is no significant divide between the good guys enforcing the law and the bad guys who are violating it. Undercover operatives and informers provide a middle ground through which one moves in fine grada-tions from law enforcement to law breaking. This interface between policing and offending facilitates the perpetration of crimes and provides a springboard for police corruption. Sting operations, which are growing in frequency in the field of counterterrorism, are based upon the facilitation of crime under con-trolled conditions by covert operatives. The line between entrapment and building a legitimate case against a known offender is often difficult to draw. Conversely, police handlers are at risk of being corrupted by the individuals that they supervise. In my experience as a member for several years of a police oversight committee, police operatives spending considerable sums of money and also found in highly compromising situations involving prostitutes often try to justify themselves by hiding behind the (generally unquestioned) shield of conducting an undercover operation. Police informers and their handlers develop at times the fierce loyalty that binds people who live through danger-ous situations together. This loyalty may lead them to share the profits gener-ated by perpetrating offences under a legal license. These profits can be huge, as in the case of drug trafficking or prize money for neutralizing a whole criminal organization. One Quebec police informer was offered $1.3 million (Canadian) for informing on the Hells Angels and eventually testifying against them (he committed suicide before the completion of this police operation).

Of all the consequences of using informants that were discussed above, compartmentalization applies more to security intelligence agencies than to other policing agencies. The facilitation of police corruption affects mostly—but not exclusively—policing agencies combatting transactional crime, particularly drug trafficking. The other consequences—the undermining of the quality of intelligence and the licensing of criminals—can equally be found in security intelligence and in law enforcement agencies. The types of informants that were focused on are confidential informers and undercover operatives. As was stressed, this type of information provider rarely testifies in open court.

The informants who testify in open court are the protected witnesses. Although they were not a focus of the preceding analyses, one development that occurred in Canada should be stressed. Because the criminal justice authorities allegedly did not respect the contracts signed between the prosecution attorneys and their protected witnesses, these (un)protected witnesses created what was to all practical purposes a labor union—L'Association des témoins repentis du Québec (the Association of Special Witnesses of Quebec)—which was active from 2000 to 2007. This attempt at the unionization of police informers is a telling clue to the current institutionalization of informing for the police.

Beyond the New Surveillance

The use of informants is not the only tool of high policing. In research on intelligence, distinctions are made between human intelligence (HUMINT) and signal intelligence (SIGINT). HUMINT is provided by informants and SIGINT by various technological means, most notably by computers used for data mining. HUMINT was the focus of the preceding discussion, but SIGINT also plays an important part in high policing. Before 9/11, SIGINT had the more prominent role, due to the difficulties of infiltrating delinquent organizations. The need for more HUMINT is now widely recognized, after the failure to prevent 9/11.

Reflecting upon the new intrusive technologies, Gary Marx articulated the theoretical model of the "new surveillance" in his seminal book (1988: 217–221) and later writings. The new surveillance is more extensive and intensive; it transcends time and space limitations through technology; its visibility is very low, bordering on the invisible, and its targets are not aware of being under surveillance; targeting specific suspects has shifted to putting whole categories of persons under suspicion; the general aim of surveillance is preventive. The new surveillance fosters the "maximum-security society," which is composed of five interrelated subsocieties: a dossier society, an actuarial or predictive society, an engineered society, a transparent society in which the boundaries that traditionally protected privacy are weakened, and a self-monitored society where auto-surveillance plays a prominent role. This description still applies very widely and was in some respects prophetic. For instance, the new surveillance involves "decentralized self-policing" through hotline reporting, and when the watched become witting or unwitting partners in their own monitoring (Marx, 1988: 218).

The theoretical model of the new surveillance is based on four general considerations:

Privacy is a shared value. Marx writes, for instance, that "important American values are increasingly threatened by the permanence and accessibility of computerized records" (1988: 223). The context of this quote makes it abundantly clear that the value most threatened is "privacy" ("The new surveillance goes beyond merely invading privacy…."—Marx, 1988: 223).

Surveillance is one-sided. This is a crucial tenet, which implies two things. The first is explicitly stated by Marx (1988: 224): the new surveillance is likely to increase the power of large organizations, but not that of smaller ones or individuals. The second is not as fully spelled out. This model of surveillance is unidirectional: surveillance flows from a few points (the state or large corporations) toward sundry targets. However, this direction is in theory not reversible.

Surveillance generates written records. This observation is encapsulated in the title of Kenneth Laudon's book *The Dossier Society* (1986), which is quoted by Marx in several of his papers. Although Marx emphasizes the multisensorial nature of the new surveillance (sounds, sights, smells, body reactions, saliva), he also shares the traditional assumption of the primacy of the written word. However it is conducted, surveillance results in a file that consists in written signs, as opposed, for instance, to visual images.

Surveillance produces actionable intelligence. This consideration is reflected in the belief that surveillance is an actuarial tool for generating predictions that will guide decision makers in their production of an engineered society, which is characterized by the the making of collected intelligence into reality. In theory, this belief is correct, but it rests on the assumption that surveillants can separate intelligence from noise and can also identify what is actionable in the wealth of intelligence that was made free of noise.

By and large, these observations remain true. However, there are countertrends that might undermine their truth in the future.

The cult of visibility and the current exhibitionism. New developments in the technologies of communication have shown to what extent people were ready to shed their privacy. Celebrity has become an ideal among the young and people who want to perpetuate their youth. People have intimate portable phone conversations in public places and make a point of being heard by as many people as possible. There are now a growing number of Web sites, such as Facebook and other "social media," where individuals put information on line that reaches deep into their intimacy and falls into the permanent legal possession of the corporation that owns the site. So-called Internet encyclopaedias embody a new form of "dossier society," where the constitution of a file is the collective work of competing authors. A researcher at the California Institute of Technology (Pasadena) has traced back to the CIA a minimum of 310 Wikipedia edits since June 2004 (Harper's Magazine, 2007). Brodeur (1983: 510–511) had pointed out earlier that there were cases indicating that targets of surveillance had struck a partnership with the agencies spying on them. This logic is pushed to its ultimate conclusions by the current exhibitionism. In a widely circulated paper under the title of "Privacy Is Dead, and Social Media Hold Smoking Gun" (Cashmore, 2010), the author concluded:

> We're living at a time when attention is the new currency: With hundreds of TV channels, billions of Web sites, podcasts, radio shows, music downloads and social networking, our attention is more fragmented than ever before. Those who insert themselves into as many channels as possible look set to capture the most value. They'll be the richest, the most successful, the most connected, capable and influential among us. We're all publishers now, and the more we publish, the more valuable connections we will make. Twitter, Facebook, Flickr, Foursquare, Fitbit and the SenseCam give us a simple choice: participate or fade into a lonely obscurity.

The panoptic logic expounded by Foucault rested on the premise that one person could put the many under observation; this logic has now been inverted: it is now the one who seeks to be seen by all (Mathiesen, 1997).

Disoriented surveillance. In his *Leviathan*, Hobbes described the "natural condition" of mankind as the "war of every man against every man." The foremost result of the covenant was to introduce directionality into this violent chaos: all men transferred their might to the sovereign in exchange for security. Following this transfer, coercion was exercised in only one direction, that is, from the sovereign toward his subjects. The reverse is now happening in the field of surveillance. Surveillance was first exercised in one direction: from the state toward its subjects. We have now witnessed a gradual erosion of the prerogatives of the state in this regard, as large corporations also developed programs of surveillance of their work force. Still, surveillance was one-sided and flowed from the whole to its parts or from the molecules to the atoms. With the development of multifunctional technologies such as the portable phone, in which video camera and other things are integrated, it would seem that we are regressing into a renewed natural condition characterized by the multifocused surveillance of everyone by everyone else. The defining feature of this surveillance war is its lack of any central base from which surveillance is exercised. The state is increasingly the loser in this regression to an unregulated condition. It has not only lost its monopoly on surveillance but it is itself a target of surveillance. Large-scale scandals are now generated by videos made from a cellphone and showing, for instance, police officers grossly abusing their legal powers.

Words and images. High policing generated a "dossier society," which was based on the written word. Interceptions of verbal conversations were generally transcribed or summarized, when perceived to provide significant information (key audiotapes are kept for evidentiary purposes). For many reasons—the power of imaging technologies, the obstacle of illiteracy in the global context— the image is now competing with the written word and may supersede it. It must be stressed that what was called "disoriented surveillance" morphs into a potentially total visualization, which is at the same time beneath and beyond surveillance. It is beneath surveillance: the unfathomable impulse of torturers and executioners to take pictures of themselves perpetrating atrocities does not seem to obey any reasonable purpose transcending a collective pathology. It is also beyond surveillance: when they are made public, these images are used as damning evidence against their authors, such as the pictures taken in the prison of Abu Ghraib, or they are disseminated for the purposes of propaganda, such as the videotapes of the beheading of hostages taken by terrorist groups.

Prediction and engineering. There may have been a time when separating the wheat from the chaff was a feasible task in intelligence. With the present information glut, we are wandering in data smog, to borrow the title of David Shenk's prescient book (1997). An issue of the *Economist* titled "The data deluge" estimated that 1,200 exabytes of digital data will be generated in 2010 (an exabyte is equivalent to 10 billion copies of the *Economist*). The yearly growth rate of information is 60 percent, bringing us closer to a "yottabyte" ("a number currently too big to imagine"; *Economist*, 2010: 5; special report on managing information). Notions of both prediction and engineering rest on the assumption of intelligence as a basis for engineering: one predicts, and engineers act on the basis of adduced knowledge. As U.S. commissions that investigated the failure to prevent 9/11 concluded, the problem was not the dearth of intelligence but the incapacity of discerning what was meaningful in the mass of available information for the purpose of taking action.

Difficulties with predicting and acting on the basis of intelligence are leading us into the era of the accidental society. But accidents should not be exclusively conceived after the pattern of traffic accidents, which are sudden and are not generally caused by a long chain of preceding events in time. Needless to say, 9/11 and the numerous bombings that followed it in places like Madrid, Bali, and London were fully intended by their perpetrators and did not happen by chance. Moreover, they were long in the planning and the making. In the case of 9/11, two of the terrorists who boarded the aircraft later to be used as missiles lived in the United States in the months preceding the attacks under their own name—Khalid Al-Midhar and Nawaf Al-Hazmi—with the knowledge of the CIA, who did not act to stop them until it was too late. There were other warnings of an impending attack, such as the Phoenix memo by FBI officers, who were later dismissed from the organization.

Terrorist attempts are often the outcomes of a lengthy process going back in time. In the accidental society, intended catastrophes such as 9/11 happen in part because of a string of unintentional failures to prevent them. In the current high policing predicament, the mass and the complexity of the intelligence data (collected in several languages, when there are not enough translators) is such that the intelligence community is overwhelmed by the amount of what is collected. Needless to say, this glut of information also affects the sum of video images publicly accessible. Young men who committed grievous school shootings have at times publicly advertised their impending killing spree by posting a video on a Web site like YouTube. No one was in a position to act on this information.

High and Low Policing: An Integrated Model

As was said in the introduction to this chapter, the distinction between high and low policing is not exclusively a distinction between different kinds of policing agencies but also a distinction between types of policing practices. For instance, the consequences of the use of informers apply to both traditional high policing agencies and to law enforcement organizations. We can now suggest a tentative model that attempts to integrate high and low policing in reference to their differences and to the interfaces between them. The model presented is for now incomplete (see Figure 7.2). It is composed of two components, low and high policing. There is yet one component to be integrated, that is, private policing, which also divides into low and high policing. This will be dealt with in the next chapter.

This model rests on key distinctions. As can be seen, the highest nodes of the graph are not low and high policing, but the criminal justice system and two basic kinds of delinquency. Policing theory tends to overlook the fact that policing is embedded within the larger system of criminal justice. The strength of the relationship between various kinds of policing and the criminal justice system is indicated in the diagram, a line in bold print indicating an institutional relationship and a line in ordinary print referring to a weaker link. Low policing is both formally and practically a constituent part of the criminal justice system. High policing is formally part of this system, but is relatively independent

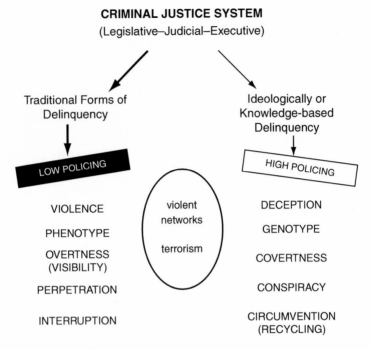

Figure 7.2 Features of Low and High Policing

of it on the practical level. "Private justice" will be addressed in the next chapter; the dotted line in figure 8.1 stresses the weakness of this relationship between private high policing and the criminal justice system.

The second distinction on which the model builds was introduced at the end of chapter 5 on the police in uniform: it is the contrast between crimes of violence and crimes of deception. This contrast initially served as the starting point for the formulation of a more comprehensive distinction, which was consistent with the analyses conducted so far. The wider notion of delinquency was substituted for the legal notion of crime, delinquency encompassing problem situations and forms of disorder that are not necessarily criminalized. The widening of the initial distinction takes into account the fact that only a variable portion of policing activity is devoted to the prevention and the repression of crime. Nonetheless, this portion is far from being negligible when crime investigation is taken into consideration. As was suggested—with all due reservations—at the end of chapter 5, the word "violence" can be used as shorthand for the visible forms of predatory behavior and destructive collective deportment, in the context of a general theory of policing. Although violence and deception are the main categories of delinquency, the crucial theoretical distinction proposed in the above model draws a tentative line between forms of delinquency according to the degree in which they either display violence or deception (often both). Cybercrime and sophisticated white-collar crime are based on deception and should fall under the heading of "high policing," although they are still investigated by low policing detectives, with dubious efficiency. High policing expertise and tactics should be used against these relatively new forms of crime.

The best way to express the gist of this distinction between violence and deception is to use the concepts of phenotype and of genotype, which were first used in genetics and later adopted by linguistics and other social sciences. The genotype refers to the whole pattern of genetic information in the cells of an individual being and the phenotype to its observable traits. The latter are in various degrees the joint product of heredity (the genotype) and of environmental influence. This kind of distinction between what is apparent and what sustains appearances is not specific to genetics. The anthropologist and linguist Benjamin Lee Whorf also used the distinction between a "cryptotype" and a phenotype to designate grammatical categories that are, respectively, covert (cryptic) and overt (Whorf, 1964: 92–93). The gist of this distinction—the difference between surface and deep structures—is present all through the social sciences, particularly linguistics. For our purposes, the distinction between delinquent phenotypes and genotypes encapsulates three pairs of opposed notions: (1) overt deviant behavior and its visible traces, on the one hand, and covert action and its underground ramifications, on the other; (2) incidents occurring separately as opposed to their structural and organizational underpinnings; and (3) short-term events as opposed to long-term projects. The rest of the diagram refers to distinctions and concepts that were previously introduced.

The distinction between phenotype and genotype and their respective implications is useful at the theoretical level of model building. At the practical level, phenotype and genotype overlap with respect to several forms of delinquency and the best way to counter them. There are two main areas of overlap.

The first is network crime in its main forms: politically or religiously motivated crimes, such as terrorism, and traditional organized crime. Terrorism is perhaps the prototypical delinquent activity that blends elements from both sides of the divide. When they are carried out successfully, terrorist attacks are not only visible but also spectacularly violent, and they cause an enduring trauma on the collective psyche of the society in which they were perpetrated. The terrorist phenotype is generally grounded into a deep-seated genotype that may consist of a tightly structured military organization like the former Irish Republican Army (IRA) or of a sprawling amorphous assemblage of groupings like Al-Qaida. Many sorts of traditional organized crime, such as drug-trafficking, also have a phenotype component—street-level drug dealers, crack houses, and other observable phenomena—and a genotype dimension—its supply system and its import-export business. Whether it is motivated by greed or lofty ideals, network crime shares many features with terrorism (Schmid, 2004), and it is a major concern for both high and low policing. There is, however, a huge problem of coordinating high and low policing operations that is still far from being resolved.

The second area where high policing is interfacing with low policing is actually very large and can be called on first approximation smart crime. Smart crime not only implies cunning—which is often displayed by common criminals in perpetrating a robbery—but also the mastery of a relatively high level of technical knowledge. Smart crime is often perpetrated by offenders who have received a formal education in a specialized field of activity. Economic crime is the paradigmatic example of smart crime. It was found in January 2008, for example, that Jérome Kerviel, a trader employed by a French bank—the Société Générale—had risked $50 billion (U.S.), nearly all the bank's capital, on stock market futures, allegedly unbeknownst to any of his bank supervisors. To be perpetrated on such a scale, economic crime requires computer knowledge and a mastery of stockmarkets. Needless to say, computer crime is a hotbed of delinquent activity. One of the most stinging paradoxes of policing is that even though it is increasingly defined as knowledge-based, public policing of all sorts is minimally effective against smart crime. Forensic accountability, a key tool to uncover economic crime, is almost exclusively practiced by private investigative companies. Smart crime is an area where all varieties of policing interface—high and low, public and private. The issue of private high policing will be examined in the next chapter, where the integrated model of policing is further elaborated.

Private Security

Private security is term that encompasses a large variety of components performing diverse functions. One of the aims of this chapter is to assess the scope and diversity of private security. It will be argued that the research on private security has not paid sufficient attention to some of the fastest growing segments of the industry, particularly the production of security equipment and technology and the development of a private apparatus of high policing. It will also be contended that there is a structural homology between public policing and private security, the key distinction between personnel in uniform and plain-clothes investigators being drawn in both sectors.

This chapter is divided into five parts: issues of definition, research, and history; empirical data on the nature and scope of private security; one empirical case study; private high policing; and various theoretical issues such as the powers of private security personnel, the relationship between the public and the private security spheres, and the governance of policing. To conclude, an attempt will be made to articulate the model presented in the previous chapter to its full extent. It is impossible in a single chapter to address in any detail all the issues raised by private security, so a scan of the field will be made and the most pressing issues will be singled out.

Issues of Definition, Research, and History

The issues of the definition of private security and of the various meanings of the notion of privatization will first be addressed, and then some of the main characteristics of the research on private security will be discussed. Finally, a point will be made with respect to the history of private security.

The Definition of Private Security

There is currently no shared definition of private security. In their pioneering work, Stenning and Shearing provided a summary characterization of what distinguished private security personnel from public police: the former are "(a) *privately* employed and (b) employed in jobs whose principal component is some *security* function" (emphasis added; Stenning and Shearing, 1979: 7; also see Stenning and Shearing, 1980: 223; Shearing and Stenning, 1981: 196). This characterization is minimal, as it consists of little else than a repetition of the clause that needs to be defined—private and security. In a report on contract security in Ontario, Shearing, Farnell, and Stenning (1980: 15) added two more differences: private security personnel are privately accountable and have no special powers to maintain the peace. As several authors have noted, this characterization is restricted to private security personnel and does not take into account the "fastest growing segment of private security [which is] the manufacturing, distribution and installation of security equipment and technological systems" (Cunningham, Strauchs, and Van Meter, 1990: 124; also see Jones and Newburn, 1998: 254). The growth of hardware and software technology manufacturing that was evident in the 1990s is now increasing exponentially.

For the sake of a common understanding of the words, we will use a modified version of the definition of private security provided by the U.S. Private Security Task Force (1977):

> Private security includes those self-employed individuals and privately funded business entities and organizations providing security-related *and quality-of-life* services, *physical equipments and technological products* to specific clientele for a fee, for the individual or entity that retains or employs them, or for themselves, in order to protect their persons, private properties, or interest from various hazards. (Quoted in Cunningham et al., 1990: 124; emphasis added)

This formulation is inadequate as a comprehensive definition of private security, since it fails to cover the expanding diversification of private security. However, it at least attempts to remedy the main flaw of traditional definitions, which is their failure to take into account security technology and the implication of the private policing workforce in tasks only distantly related to security, if at all. It is doubtful that the complexity of private security can be successfully encapsulated in a one-sentence definition. The best way to proceed is to provide a set of specifications (such as interest served, aim, mode of response, targeted behaviors, and respect for human rights), as Nalla and Newman (1990:

37–43) did, or to identify several categories of activities (Jones and Newburn, 1998: 254).

There is one crucial limitation to these definitional efforts, which mirrors a corresponding difficulty with defining the public police. It is unduly limiting to define the public police through the traditional notion of law enforcement, because enforcing the law is only one part of what they do. Likewise, equating private policing with the provision of security, as the definition quoted above originally did, is also too narrow. This difficulty stems from the multiplicity of tasks performed by the private police. Furthermore, it does not readily admit of the type of solution provided by Bittner in defining the public police, which also performs a great variety of tasks. This solution consists of defining an agency by its specific means—the use of force—rather than by its multiple goals. As there is no obvious definitional substitute for the actual or potential force in the case of private policing agents, there is therefore no common denominator allowing us to bring theoretical unity to what they do, unless one accepts the alternative definition proposed in chapter 4.

Private security is not only a static notion; it is first and foremost a dynamic concept that refers to a process—the process of privatization. When the first reports on private security were published in the early 1970s (Kakalik and Wildhorn, 1972), privatization meant only one thing: the taking over by the private sector of duties that were previously carried out by public agencies, whether in the field of policing, courts, or corrections. Police privatization now has several meanings, which are not necessarily convergent.

The private penetration of the public sphere. This is the original meaning of the word, which refers to the devolvement to private security agencies of policing functions that until then were performed by public forces. In this sense, the private sector encroaches upon the public one: policing activities are outsourced to private agencies. Despite the fact that the contracting-out originates from public government, the "invasion" was initiated by private agencies and is oriented toward the territory of the public police.

The public penetration of the private market. Public policing agencies are now officially competing against private security agencies in the market. As they do so, they are privatizing themselves. Reiss (1988) documented public police moonlighting in a pioneering report. The trend has now grown and no longer occurs just at the margins of public policing. The marketing of public police services was a long-standing practice in continental Europe (Malochet, 2007).

Private funding of public police organizations. Wealthy residential communities within a city and private corporations channel resources into public policing systems (Bryett, 1996). These resources may comprise physical resources (fitting police cruisers patrolling a designated area with health equipment), space (office space), time (volunteers, computer time), and knowledge (expertise). It was announced in Canada, in February 2008, that an association of bankers was proposing to subsidize an economic crime unit staffed by investigators from the Montreal Police Department. This unit would have its office located within a building owned by a member of this banking association.

Administrative models borrowed from the private sector. The integration of the teachings of business schools into the management of public policing is another facet of privatization. Peter Manning discussed in this respect the importation of Total Quality Management in public policing (Forst and Manning, 1999: 85 and ff.). There are numerous other examples, since many high-ranking police officers have been to business school.

The privatization of security knowledge. This process may be less conspicuous, but is no less pervasive than the preceding ones and has greater potential consequences. The first reports on private security were issued in the early 1970s by private research corporations, such as Rand. This trend has not only continued, but has grown. One of the best sources of data on private security in Europe is an atlas that has been published for seventeen years (Haas, 2007) and sold at a high price. The privatization of the knowledge on security is not limited to knowledge on private security. A great deal of what is known on subject matters ranging from economic crime to terrorism, not to mention police technology, is published by private research firms such as the Rand Corporation, Pinkerton, and Jane's Information Group. The current U.S. government data bank on terrorist incidents is the result of the merger of the Rand Corporation and Pinkerton data banks (Lafree and Dugan, 2009). Data mining is an activity that is predominantly carried out by private companies. What they publish is increasingly intended for a business readership and is sold at very high prices—for instance, over $1,000 (U.S.) for a single report—putting them out of the reach of academic researchers. This limitation on the accessibility of private knowledge will have a growing impact on academic research.

Research on Private Security

Although there is a growing body of research on private security, its volume is much smaller than the research on public policing. For Jones and Newburn (1995: 221), private policing is a subject "which remains significantly underresearched." The limitations on such research mirror on a larger scale the restrictions hindering research on public policing. The principal obstacle to research on public policing is the secrecy that shrouds many of its aspects. This obstacle is magnified in the field of private security. Private companies providing security on a contractual basis are competing against each other and are therefore unwilling to disclose their operational practices. Corporations that have their own proprietary security ("in house") want to avoid the negative publicity that would result from a disclosure of misbehavior or criminal conduct on the part of their employees. When these corporations hire an outside firm to perform special tasks such as forensic accounting, they require by contract that the findings remain confidential, "secrecy [being] placed at a premium" in the forensic accounting industry (Williams, 2005: 195).

There is one more obstacle to research on private security. There are private companies, such as Pinkerton or Garda, that are almost exclusively devoted to security. They are relatively easy to identify and some are well known. Other agencies, however, are part of giant corporations offering a wide array of services. According to its Web site, Dyncorp International is providing the following kinds of services: aviation, contingency, infrastructure, intelligence and training, international development, law enforcement and security, logistics, program management and "projects." Its law enforcement and security component was awarded a $6 billion contract by the U.S. State Department to train the police in Afghanistan. Many other multiservice corporations are also involved in providing private security. Being part of a parent company not exclusively recognized as a security agency, these private security units are difficult to identify and are largely ignored by researchers.

Thus there is little fieldwork on private security, although there are reports replete with data on the size of the market, its profit margins, and economic projections. George Rigakos declared in the introduction to his field study of the Canadian agency Intelligarde: "After an extensive literature review, I could not locate a single published study of private police that examined the *doing* of security from the perspective of line officers" (Rigakos, 2002: 3). In fact, Walsh and Donovan (1989) had previously conducted a study similar to that of Rigakos, but it was pursued on a more limited scale as they studied the tasks performed by a private security agency serving a Brooklyn high-rise apartment complex. Rigakos (2002: 43) finally concludes that "there are strong grounds to question the sense of distinguishing public from private police." This division is viewed by him as becoming less and less meaningful, as both are similarly involved in coercive law enforcement. Jones and Newburn (1998: chaps. 5–6) studied the enormous diversity of public, private, and hybrid policing organizations that were operating in the London borough of Wandsworth, with a focus on their relationships. There are a few other field studies, such as Hobbs et al. (2003) on bouncers, this work ultimately going back to a previous study of formal and informal control strategies in the context of urban culture (Hobbs, 1988: 1). Mopas and Stenning (2000) and Wakefield (2003) are also notable exceptions in having conducted empirical studies on aspects of the private policing of mass private property.

A great deal of research uses survey methodology and the analysis of quantitative data on the number of persons employed in the private security sector as well as the turnover of the companies involved in this kind of work (for instance, the studies published in Jones and Newburn, 2006a). The figures usually do not go back far in time and, despite exceptions (South, 1987 and 1988; Nalla and Newman, 1990), research on private security is essentially ahistorical. Also, these figures are generally found in census data and in information collected by state institutions pursuant to various permit and licence applications by private agencies. Since the private applicants for such permits basically provide the services of security personnel on a contract basis (guards or investigators), the research is therefore focused on manned *contract* security, little being said about in-house security and almost nothing about security technology and its impact. Exceptionally, Shearing et al. (1980: 166, 188) used a survey method and were able to present an overview covering both manned security and equipment.

Furthermore, these statistics on manned security are available only in a limited number of countries, and they generally do not measure the same thing across these countries, thus making comparisons between them problematic. Because of the sparseness and the relative heterogeneity of the available data, generalizations on international trends in private security are based on extrapolations from a narrow empirical basis. These extrapolations do not always succeed in avoiding the pitfall of ethnocentricity, when findings that originally describe private security in North America are said to apply to "most developed countries" (for instance, in Mopas and Stenning, 2001: 67). The significance claimed for research on private security is often in reverse proportion to its empirical basis.

In this regard, two features of the research on private security deserve particular consideration.

The Watershed Syndrome
The recurrent theme of many studies of private security is that its advent is of epochal significance and implies no less than a paradigm shift in the theory of policing. This theme is not only typical of private security but also permeates writings on the privatization of the military forces (Jäger and Kümmel, 2007: 457–462; Andrew, Baker, and Caparini, 2008). In a prescient paper, Shearing (1992: 421) anticipated future developments in policing pluralism (which he greatly helped to bring about). This paradigm shift has been variously described as imbedded control (Shearing and Stenning, 1985), the pluralizing of policing (Bayley and Shearing, 1996: 593; Jones and Newburn, 2006a), and multilateralization (Bayley and Shearing, 2001: 9). Claiming a paradigm shift has now

reached the stage where it is deemed preferable to avoid altogether the state-centered bias apparently ingrained in the meaning of the word "policing" and to talk instead about the (nodal) governance of security (Johnston and Shearing, 2003; Shearing, 2004). Although the rapid growth of private security is an indisputable fact, whether or not it is ushering us into a new age of policing is open to question, particularly in view of the fact that policing is retrogressing toward its past brutality in some of its aspects (for instance, the recourse to the infliction of pain during interrogation and in the course of arrest and crowd control). Prejudging the issue by imposing the idea of a paradigm shift begs the question of whether we are witnessing a momentous change in policing. As will be argued, it is also a manifestation of what could be called the "watershed syndrome."

The watershed syndrome combines two elements. The first one is a tendency to overstate the facts and their significance. In an article on the growth of private security in the European Union (EU), van Steden and Sarre (2007: 224; also see van Steden, 2007) present the following argument. According to estimates made by Morré (2004), the number of private security employees in the EU was over one million in 2003, as compared to some 600,000 in 1996 (De Waard, 1999). This growth leads them to conclude that it "amounts to an increase of some 500,000 employees across EU-Member states in less than a decade." Thus, the "quiet revolution" in policing has become "a noisy 21st century juggernaut" (van Steden and Sarre, 2007: 223). However, this juggernaut may not be as roadworthy as it appears. When De Waard made his meticulous assessment of the number of private security employees in the EU, it was composed of fifteen countries; when Morré (2004) published her own assessment, she estimated the number of such employees in twenty-five European countries, anticipating that the EU would grow from fifteen to twenty-five members in May 2004 (in fact, it now numbers twenty-seven countries). Limiting the account to the fifteen EU countries originally surveyed by De Waard, the number of private security employees grew from 592,050 to 733,010, an increase of 140,960 employees. This is admittedly a significant increase, but it is far from the figure of 500,000 quoted by van Steden and Sarre (2007). The "juggernaut increase" invoked by van Steden and Sarre is partly artificial and reflects the fact that twelve new countries recently joined the EU. When you add new crates of apples, you obviously have more apples to count.

Here is a second example of the tendency to overstate the significance of one's findings. As noted above, van Steden and Sarre's estimates are drawn from a 2003 overview of twenty-five countries that were shortly to join the EU in 2004 (Morré, 2004). At the end of her report, Morré concludes; "Today, *the private security workforce more or less matches the public police workforce in most*

EU Member States and in some Member States they even outnumber the public police" (emphasis added). This misleading conclusion is only partly supported by Morré's own findings. She is correct in asserting that in some countries, the public police are outnumbered by the private: this is, in fact, true in only six of the countries she surveyed, three of them being ex-Eastern Bloc countries (Estonia, Hungary, and Poland). Among the remaining nineteen countries, however, there are only eight countries where the ratio of private to public police exceeds 0.50, and eleven where it is noticeably below 0.50. If one raises this threshold to 0.62, there are altogether sixteen EU countries that fall under it. Thus, sixteen EU countries have nearly twice as many public police as private, and there are only three where the private security workforce "more or less" matches the public workforce.

The second element of the watershed syndrome is the formal primacy of numbers over what they are in fact referring to. Putting aside anecdotal evidence and personal narratives, there is only one argument that supports the claim that we have entered a new epoch of policing, if not a postpolicing era: "a shift (*measured in terms of spending and employment*) in the primary responsibility for protection from public law enforcement to private security has occurred" (Cunningham et al., 1990: 319, emphasis added). Since private police and other private security agents already outnumber public police in some G7 countries, it is claimed that "most developed countries" will inevitably follow the trend. This increase in numbers is allegedly dissolving the state monopoly on policing and is further generating a cascade of transformations, or will shortly. There is considerable skepticism in Europe about the withering away of the state with respect to security. However, even allowing this point for the sake of discussion, there is still a list of basic questions that remain completely unanswered. These include, for instance:

1. Is the alleged plural policing more or less violent than state-centered public policing?
2. Is the alleged plural policing more or less discretionary than public state-centered public policing?
3. Is the alleged plural policing more or less accountable than state-centered public policing?
4. Is the alleged plural policing delivering better security more cost-effectively than state-centered public policing?
5. Is the alleged plural policing more or less equitable than state-centered public policing?
6. Is the alleged plural policing more or less respectful of human and legal rights than state-centered public policing?

These issues have been raised repeatedly in relation to public policing, and we have accumulated knowledge on many of them. We can also raise these questions with respect to private policing, where our knowledge is, however, much more limited. Despite these limitations, we know for instance that private policing is in many respects less accountable than public policing. However, we have no idea how to answer the questions listed above in relation to *plural* policing. Indeed, we have little idea as to how to proceed in answering them. In their study of the relationships between the many policing agencies deployed in Wandsworth (United Kingdom), Jones and Newburn (1998: 199) concluded that their findings did not fit any of the macrosociological models proposed so far. They mention three models: the benign integration of civil society and the state, resulting into a unified system of policing (Johnston, 1992), the tightly coordinated policing complex that threatens civil liberties (Flavel, 1973), and the fortress communities where the affluent are segregating themselves (Davis, 1990). How then can we know whether or not we have entered a new era in policing? All we really have are numbers that indicate a considerable growth in the private sector in terms of spending and employment, with the attendant conviction that these increases are bound to generate transformational effects on policing. One can agree with the numbers while questioning the meaning attributed to them.

Advocacy

There is, finally, another feature of some of the research into private security that deserves more reflection, its character of advocacy. In their influential paper, Bayley and Shearing (1996: 593) write:

> There is a closer connection between the end—safety—and the means—policing—with private police, both commercial and volunteer, than with public police. Governments protect communities by providing police and then limiting their authority; private institutions and informal communities protect themselves by determining what circumstances produce crime and then finding people who know how to change them....Private police are more responsive than public police to the "bottom line" of safety. If safety is not increased, private police can be fired. For public police the bottom line is not safety but clearance rates. But even here failure has few negative consequences. Police are not fired for not achieving this objective.

The striking feature of this paragraph, and of much of the influential work on private security, is its one-sided character: it downplays the problems related to the use of private security and overplays the weaknesses of the public police.

Needless to say, this work shows concern for equity, human rights, and democracy in private security. However, compared to the trenchant criticism of the public police, the critique of private policing has a blunted edge. Interestingly, Forst and Manning (1999) appear at times as if they were putting private security on trial, Manning arguing the case for the prosecution and Forst for the defense. Such adversarial debates are relatively rare. Why is this?

The seminal work of Shearing and Stenning on private security was developed at a time when the criminal justice system was the focus of much criticism for being exclusively oriented toward punishment, and particularly for its overuse of incarceration. I know from personal experience that many academic researchers shared this militant perspective during the 1970s and 1980s. At that time, "abolitionism" did not refer to the abolition of the death penalty (mistakenly taken for granted), but to the abolition of incarceration. In their initial attempts to define the nature of private security, Shearing, Stenning, and their colleagues repeatedly emphasized that private security was part of a wider system of private justice (Stenning and Shearing, 1979: 4; Stenning and Shearing, 1980: 231; Shearing, Farnell, and Stenning, 1980: 249–55; Shearing and Stenning, 1983: 3). They never gave a detailed explanation of what they meant by private justice, other than it implied a shift from punishment to noncoercive models of problem-solving, such as restorative justice (Johnston and Shearing, 2003: 66 and 129; Wood and Shearing, 2007: 41 and 47). As the prospects for the abolition of imprisonment dimmed, the critique of public policing and justice became louder. In the course of their argument against punishment and coercion, Johnston and Shearing (2003: 50) present a rather gruesome narrative of the castrating of a colt, as witnessed by one of the authors near the South African city of Cape Town. The point of their story is then presented:

> During this procedure, the colt also received its first serious lesson in the ruling mentality of humans....This attitude towards governance is reflected in the criminal justice system. For example, one finds it in police programmes for the graduated escalation of force....What we are suggesting is that the state police are comparable to the team of castrators described in our story. (Johnston and Shearing, 2003: 53)

Johnston and Shearing do not tell us whether this comparison with horse castrators applies to all public police (for instance to state police in Western-style democratic countries). Notwithstanding its rhetorical excess, the real problem with this paragraph and the perspective it illustrates is that it uncritically assumes that private nonstate justice will remedy what is wrong with public penal justice merely by virtue of being different from it. Cunnigham et al.

(1990: 302) had already remarked, on the basis of their examination of the work of Shearing and Stenning on private justice, that little was known about the structure and dynamics of private justice systems. However, the picture of private justice drawn by several other researchers offers no evidence that privatization is per se the password that opens the gate to a better world (Lipson, 1975; South, 1987; Henry, 1987). More recently, Williams (2005: 195) referred to private forensic accountants as the purveyors of "a unique form of customized justice" that primarily serves the interest of their clients. In a more somber vein, Zimring (2003: 89) has argued that the U.S. propensity to inflict the death penalty was a direct legacy of the popular justice practice of lynching, which was current until recently in many states of the federation, notably in the South. There are no doubt progressive experiences in private justice that occur in Africa and elsewhere, such as the Zwelethemba model described by Johnston and Shearing (2003: 151–53; see Shearing and Berg, 2006: 205 on popular policing). Nevertheless, the great foreign correspondent Ryszard Kapuscinski reported that in many African countries the task of the police is not so much catching thieves as protecting them from crowds wanting to execute them when they are caught red-handed (Kapuscinski, 2001: 214).

The largely uncritical perspective on private security and private justice that was first articulated by the pioneering research of the late 1970s is now greeted with increased reluctance, both in the United States (Manning, 1999: 86 and 115) and in the United Kingdom (Jones and Newburn, 2002; Loader and Walker, 2006). This favorable bias for privatized practices is in stark contrast with the research on public policing, which is essentially oriented toward diagnosing its weaknesses and proposing remedies for them. Despite paying lip service to the need for reform, particularly with respect to increased accountability, there is no methodical research attempting to sort out "what works" in private security, to use the paradigmatic question asked of public policing. This can be taken to be an indication that we know so little about private security that we do not yet dare to propose concrete reforms of the kind that proliferate in the research on public policing.

History

As previously noted, research on private security shows little concern for history. Instead of history, we have attempts to articulate economic or sociological explanations for the growth of private security. The most frequently cited of these explanations is that the increase in private security is in part the outcome of the emergence and rapid expansion of "mass private property," that is, privately owned space that invites public visitation to ensure its economic survival (for example, a shopping mall). This explanation was proposed by Shearing and Stenning (1981: 228) and discussed in subsequent writings. Jones and Newburn (1998: 106 and ff.) showed, however, that the respective growth of the private police and of mass private property occurred in a reverse order in Britain: the proliferation of mass private property took place after the largest expansion of the private police, and hence cannot explain what preceded it. These two authors (2002: 139) argued that informal ("secondary") social control activities were formalized during the second half of the twentieth century, and that this formalization propelled a massive increase in the number of people employed in both public and private policing in the United Kingdom. Although their argument is based on an examination of the statistical evolution of occupational estimates provided by the Census of Population (Great Britain) from 1951 to 1991, as it was then called, Jones and Newburn do not rely on additional historical analysis. In their answer to Jones and Newburn's criticism, Kempa, Stenning, and Wood (2004: 569) stated that "there [were] insufficient data available to finally settle the question."

Other explanations have been given for the growth of private security, which are essentially based on economic considerations (Cunningham et al., 1990: 236). To all practical purposes, what is to be found in research on private security is, with few exceptions (South, 1987; Nalla and Newman, 1990), intuitive factor analysis without any historical background. There are, however, works on the history of private security, and they were briefly referred to in the chapter on history, particularly in relation to the history of large private corporations in the United States.

Heavy industry in the United States was concentrated in Pennsylvania for close to a century (1860–1960). J. P. Shalloo (1933) from the University of Pennsylvania wrote a monograph on the private police under the sponsorship of Thorsten Sellin. He provides an interesting background on some lesser-known aspects of private policing, which are also discussed in part by Nalla and Newman (1990).

Hybrid power. The railroads and the coal and iron industry were policed by private armies that were empowered by the states of Pennsylvania, Kentucky, West Virginia, and Colorado for the benefit of private corporations (Shalloo, 1933: 59–62). These powers included the use of lethal force, which was grievously abused in Colorado by the Baldwin-Felts private security agency in an incident that resulted in the death of twelve children and two women during a raid on a workers' encampment (Nalla and Newman, 1990: 24). There were many instances of employees working for contract agencies (Pinkerton) and "in-house" security (Ford) firing into a crowd and killing people (Nalla and Newman, 1990: 22 and 26). The crucial point made by Shalloo is that the state can empower special police for the exclusive benefit of private corporations, thus highlighting the fact that there are many power configurations, some of them blending the public and the private sectors together.

Private high policing. Even though loss prevention is mentioned during the nineteenth century in legislation enabling private police, private security agencies were essentially involved in practicing a brand of high policing, where protecting the profitability of large private corporations became the equivalent of political policing protecting national security (Shalloo, 1933: 62). Immigrant labor quickly became the preferred target of the private police (Shalloo, 1933: 59). The private security companies operated in disregard of the law, according to the cardinal principle of high policing that the end justifies the means (Shalloo, 1933: 188). They also systematically resorted to informants, infiltration, and undercover operations, the labor spy being regarded "as one of the lowest forms of human life, from the moral standpoint" (Shalloo, 1933: 177). The connection between such agencies as Pinkerton or Burns and high policing in its technical sense is reflected in the fact that both Burns and Pinkerton were former members of the U.S. Secret Service, Pinkerton even claiming that he founded the secret service (Nalla and Newman, 1990: 20). In their fight against violent secret organizations such as the Molly Maguires, private security agencies were practicing an early form of counterterrorism.

The recruitment of criminals. The use of known criminals in various capacities is one of the hallmarks of high policing. The most violent private security agencies, such as Berghoffs, specialized in strike breaking. Strike breakers were hated so much that the public police were assigned to guard them—"although the public police refused to dine with them, calling them swine" (Nalla and Newman, 1990: 25).

Private investigators. Shalloo (1933: 138) reviews the types of services provided at the beginning of the twentieth century by the Pinkerton National Detective agency. It largely coincides with a contemporary list provided by Gill and Hart (1997b: 549), the only additional service mentioned in the latter text being asset tracing. In some important respects, private policing has not much evolved in the North America since its formal beginnings in the nineteenth century.

The important issue of private high policing will be revisited in a later section of this chapter. Although brief, this foray into the history of private policing in the United States shows that it has been far from being reduced to the status of junior partner to the public police. It took over from the failing public police in the policing of large sections of the economy, where organized labor was perceived as a threat by the business elite. When it did so, it did not provide a less coercive alternative to the public police, but a more violent and repressive one.

Empirical Data

Warfare changed a great deal throughout history. Its transformation is owed not to the evolution of leadership and soldiering (the governance of war) but rather to the development of new weapons and protective devices. In activities involving violence and danger (for example, warfare, fire fighting, policing), the creation of new physical tools has as much importance as the management of people, if not more. Accordingly, this chapter will not only review some of the available empirical data on manned security but also try to provide an account of the security products sold by the manufacturing industry, however limited it might be. First, numerical figures on private security services and products are discussed, followed by an examination of the kinds of services and products available.

The Growth of Private Security Personnel

Students of high policing and security intelligence often refer to the field as "a wilderness of mirrors" (T. S. Eliot, *Gerontion*). In a similar way, the study of private security takes place in a wilderness of numbers. There is great disparity and regional contrasts in the assessments provided by different authors and, indeed, by the same author(s). Table 8.1 lists a series of estimates of the number of private security personnel in the United Kingdom from the early 1970s up until 2002. The estimates range from a low of 25,000 to a high of 333,631 with many intermediate numbers. The highest figure (333,631) applies to the whole private security workforce and not only to uniformed guards.

The remarkable feature of this series is that it does not show a continuous growth over time. The whole spectrum in the estimated numbers of uniformed guards was determined at the earliest stage of research—between 25,000 (Randall and Hamilton, 1972) and 250,000 (McClintock and Wiles, 1972)—and all further estimates fitted between these two figures. The variance is largely explained by two factors. First, these researchers use different sources, such as census data, official statistics from diverse provenance, and data extracted from private business databases (such as British Telecom). Second, they do not measure the same thing: although most of the figures refer to uniformed personnel, some of them include the personnel of the whole private security industry. Figures referring to other countries (such as France and former Eastern Bloc countries) also display a great deal of variation, although there are more quantitative estimates of private security in the United Kingdom than in any other country, including the United States.

There is one source of great variation, which concerns the former Eastern Bloc countries, that needs to be explained. These countries had large public

Table 8.1 Estimates of Private Security in the United Kingdom

1971 Home Office Green Paper (quoted, Williams et al., 1984)	80,000 persons (in-house and contract; data for early 1970s)
McClintock and Wiles (1972)	250,000 (uniformed men; early 1970s)
Randall and Hamilton (1972) (quoted in Jones and Newburn, 1998: 69–70)	40,000 persons (all private security sector; early 1970s), with 25,000 guards
Bunyan (1976)	250,000 (all private industry)
George and Button (1994)	300,000 (all private industry, 1994)
British Security Industry Association (1994) (quoted in Jones and Newburn, 1998: 70)	126,900 (all employment, not including private investigation and in-house security)
Jones and Newburn (1995)	162,303 (all manned security, 1992)
Jones and Newburn (1998: 81, table 3.6)	Low estimate: 47,000 guards (p. 254); highest estimate: 222,457 "manned security." For 1994
Jones and Newburn (1998: 81, table 3.6)	333,631 (all private security industry, including manned security and the manufacture and servicing of equipment)
De Waard (1999)	160,000 (all private industry)
Jones and Newburn (2002: 141)	159,704 (based on 1991 census data)
Button (2002)	217,000 (all private security industry, early 2000s)
Morré (2004)	150,000 (all manned security, 2003)
Van Steden and Sarre (2007)	300,000 (in-house and contract, 1992)
Encyclopedia of Law Enforcement (2005), article by Van Steden and Huberts	220,000 (all private police, 2001; source unspecified)
Encyclopedia of Law Enforcement (2005), article by Van Stenden and Huberts	315,000 persons (all private industry sector, 2001; source unspecified)
Jones and Newburn (2006)	217,000 (all private security industry, early 2000s); source: Button (2002)

militia involved in policing. When they broke from Soviet rule after 1989 and progressively gained full independence, many of these countries first transformed their militia into publicly owned companies that provided security guards, and subsequently privatized them. Such was the case in Estonia and several other countries, such as Poland (European Commission, 2006). When privatization occurs, it instantly generates a large increase in the estimate of private security personnel. Such increases are relatively artificial, since they mostly imply a change in legal status, a public militia becoming a privatized security force. In a converse way, Nalla and Newman (1990: 45–46) have shown that we tend to narrow down the public policing sector to state and local police—most of them in uniform—at the expense of many other policing units embedded in various government departments. They list at least ten U.S. public policing organizations that are excluded from the count. In order to enhance the contrast between the public and the private sectors, it would seem that we count as many people as we can when we assess the number of private agents and as few as possible when we measure the public policing domain.

There are three fairly recent international surveys comparing the number of public police with estimates of private security personnel: De Waard (1999) presents 1996 data on fifteen EU and twelve non-EU countries; Morré (2004) updated the data on the EU and covers twenty-five countries of the EU, as we said; Van Steden and Huberts (2005) give 2001 data on twenty-one countries now part of the EU, five European countries not included in the EU, and six other developed countries (Australia, Canada, Japan, New Zealand, South Africa, and the United States; the time reference for the non-EU and the six other countries is not given). There is also data given on an individual basis for many of these countries (such as Cunningham et al., 1990 for the United States). The most reliable of the international surveys is De Waard (1999); the figures given by De Waard are still quoted without change in later surveys, such as Morré (2004), although they refer to 1996 figures.

Table 8.2 contrasts the estimates of Van Steden and Huberts (2005) for public and private police with those of De Waard (1996) for the five countries that they both covered. The figures given for the public police are generally convergent, Van Steden and Huberts merely replicating the estimates of De Waard for New Zealand and the United States. De Waard's estimate of the number of U.S. public police in 1996 matches Manning's estimate (800,000) in a paper published ten years later (Manning, 2006c: 103). The largest discrepancy concerns South Africa. De Waard's figure, although much higher than Van Steden and Huberts's, is lower than the most recent estimate (144,150 officers and civilians) given by Shearing and Berg (2006: 199). The discrepancy between the estimates of private security personnel is greater than for the public police. De

Table 8.2 Public Police and Private Security Personnel in Non-EU Countries

Country	Public Police Encyclopedia (no date of data given)	Public Police De Waard (1996 data)	Private Police Encyclopedia (no date of data given)	Private Police De Waard (1996 data)
Australia [Prenzler and Sarre (2006), 2001 data]	43,048 [40,492]	51,486	31,752	92,583 [49,408]
Canada	59,090	75,364	82,010	125,025
New Zealand	6,967	6,967	5,478	5,478
South Africa [Shearing and Berg (2006)]	90,000 [144,150]	126,300	350,000	363,928
United States [Manning (2003)]	828,435	828,435	[260,000 (approximate)]	1.5 million
[Manning (2006c)]	421,074 (police officers) 546,920 (all employees)] [660,000–800,000]		1.14–1.5 million	[1.5–2.0 million]

Sources: Jaap De Waard. 1999. "The Private Security Industry in International Perspective." *European Journal on Criminal Policy and Research* 7:143–177.

Encyclopedia: Ronald Van Steden and L.W.J.C. Huberts. 2005. "Private Security Industry Growth in Western Countries." In *Encyclopedia of Law Enforcement*. Vol. 3, *The Private Security Industry*, edited by L. E. Sullivan and M. R. Haberfeld, 1261–1268. Thousands Oaks, Cal.: Sage.

Waard's figures for 1996 are much higher than the later figures of Van Steden and Huberts in the cases of Australia and Canada. Shearing and Berg (2006: 204) assess the number of registered private security officers as 260,000, a figure lower than that given by either De Waard or Van Steden and Huberts. De Waard's estimate of the size of the private security personnel is consistent with the figures given by Cunningham et al. (1990: 176) and by Manning (2006: 103). Cunningham et al. give a projection of 1.8 million private agents for the year 2000, whereas Manning (2006) gives a figure between 1.5 and 2.0 million.

The undisputable finding for most of the countries listed in table 8.2 is that the size of the private security personnel is twice as big as that of the public police. Public police still outnumber private agents in New Zealand, the least populated of these countries. The figures for Australia in table 8.2 are too inconsistent to warrant any strong conclusion—Prenzler and Sarre (2006: 176) estimated that the number of public and private policing personnel was, respectively, 40,492 and 49,408, the rate of growth of the private sector being higher.

Systematic attempts to assess of the number of public and private police were made much earlier in English-speaking countries—particularly in North America—than elsewhere. These efforts generated more consistency, although there is still significant disagreement between the various estimates for these countries, as we have just seen. The situation is more confused, however, for the countries of Europe. Table 8.3 present estimates of the number of public and private police for the twenty-seven countries now comprising the EU. Since there are significant differences between the private security figures provided by Morré for 2003 and by De Waard for 1996, the estimates of Van Steden and Huberts for EU countries are also included for comparative purposes.

As noted previously, there is a tendency by Morré to underestimate the number of public police and to overestimate the size of the private sector. The three countries where the underestimation of the number of public police was greatest are underlined with a thin line. In the case of France, Morré only included the members of the urban Police Nationale in her estimate and did not account for the other French public police force—the Gendarmerie Nationale. The Gendarmerie numbered 105,389 persons (including 1,908 civilians) in 2008; it polices the whole of rural France and small towns. The exclusion of this force from an estimate of the number of public police in France is a serious oversight.

On the right-hand side of the table, the figures showing a potential overestimation of the private police by De Waard are double underlined. They concern three countries—Belgium, Denmark, and Sweden. Underlined with a thick line are the more numerous instances where Morré quotes much higher figures than De Waard, the most extreme cases being Poland and Greece. After checking

Table 8.3 Public Police and Private Security Personnel in the EU

EU Country	Public Police (Morré, 2004)	Public Police (De Waard, 1996)	Private Security (Morré, 2004)	Private Security (De Waard, 1996)	Private Security (Encyclopedia) (2005) 2001
Austria	30,000	29,000	6,790	6,000	5,500
Belgium	39,000	34,712	8,320	11,200	15,000
Bulgaria				40,000	
Cyprus	3,000		1,500		
Czech Rep.	47,400		28,100		50,000
Denmark	14,000	12,230	5,250	2,500	
Estonia	3,600		4,900		5,250
Finland	7,500	11,816	6,000	10,000	
France	145,000	227,008	117,000	3,500	6,000
Germany	250,000	260,132	170,000	70,000	107,400
Greece	49,900	39,335	25,000	176,000	168,000
Hungary	40,000		80,000	2,000	18,769
Ireland	12,000	10,829	20,000		54,981
Italia	280,000	278,640	55,000	5,150	5,150
Latvia	10,600		5,000	43,200	25,000
Lithuania	20,000	24,722	10,000		4,500
Luxembourg	1,573	1,100	2,200	4,500	
Malta	1,800		700	800	1,200
Netherlands	49,000	39,216	30,000	20,200	30,717
Poland	103,309		200,000	10,000	150–250,000
Portugal	46,000	43,459	28,000	15,000	15,000
Romania					20,000

(continued)

Table 8.3 (Continued)

EU Country	Public Police (Morré, 2004)	Public Police (De Waard, 1996)	Private Security (Morré, 2004)	Private Security (De Waard, 1996)	Private Security (Encyclopedia) (2005) 2001
Slovakia	21,500		20,840		
Slovenia	7,500		4,500		4,000
Spain	193,450	186,547	89,450	53,000	90,247
Sweden	18,000	27,000	10,000	16,000	16,000
United Kingdom	141,389	185,156	150,000	160,000	220,000
TOTAL	1,535,530	1,386,180	1,088,550 (733,010)	592,050	

Sources: Jaap De Waard. 1999. "The Private Security Industry in International Perspective." *European Journal on Criminal Policy and Research* 7:143–177.

Encyclopedia: Ronald Van Steden and L.W.J.C. Huberts. 2005. "Private Security Industry Growth in Western Countries." In *Encyclopedia of Law Enforcement. Vol. 3, The Private Security Industry*, edited by L. E. Sullivan and M. R. Haberfeld, 1261–1268. Thousands Oaks, Cal.: Sage.

Lilany Morré. 2004. "Panoramic Overview of Private Security Industry. In the 25 Member State of the European Union, coESS and UNI-Europa."

with other sources in addition to Van Steden and Huberts (2005), it would seem that Morré is right in the case of France (125,210 guards—Haas, 2007: 146) and Greece (30,378 private security workforce—Papanicolaou, 2006: 86). For Ireland, Luxembourg, and Portugal, Van Steden and Huberts have relied on De Waard's estimates. For reasons quoted above, the estimates relating to former Soviet satellites tend to be inflated, the figures quoted by Morré being generally higher than those of both De Waard and Van Steden and Huberts.

However brief it is, this comparative review of the public and private workforce leads to several conclusions. First, there is strong evidence that the number of private security operatives is much higher than the number of public police in only three developed countries (Canada, South Africa, and the United States). According to the latest estimates released in 2009 by Statistics Canada (based on 2006 census data), the number of private police is 102,000 and public police 68,000, which shows a lower ratio of private to public police than is usually given. Second, there is too much variation in the numbers and too many measurement problems to assert that the private policing sector is generally larger than the public sector in the EU countries. In fact, in the majority of EU countries the size of the public police workforce is greater than that of private security agents. Third, in every country that we reviewed, the growth rate of private security is clearly greater than the rate of increase of public police forces. For instance, it is obvious that there will soon be more private security agents than public police in the United Kingdom, if this is not already the prevailing situation. Although it is unlikely that the trend favoring the private sector will be reversed, its strength may decrease in the face of calls for "real police" in the high-anxiety mood of the post-911 era. Fourth, there are large discrepancies between the various developed countries with respect to the ratio of private to public police. Finally, the relative weakness of the numerical data should caution us against any dogmatic theoretical assertions.

The Growth of the Security Manufacturing Industry

The scope of the security manufacturing industry is even more difficult to assess than the size of manned security. Many sources of information are trade publications, which are often unaffordable and inaccessible. Furthermore, the security equipment industry is at the same time highly diversified in its products and tightly integrated within large multiservice corporations. It is almost impossible to determine what part of their turnover comes from military defense contracts, fire security products, and criminal loss prevention instruments, to mention some of the main components.

There is a general agreement among researchers on private security that its revenues were for some time evenly split between manned security and the manufacturing, leasing, selling, and servicing of a very wide array of products ranging from steel fences to the most sophisticated technology (Cunningham et al., 1990: 190). Jones and Newburn (1998: 73) quote similar figures for the state of the United Kingdom's private security industry in 1990. The balance is now tipping in favor of the manufacturing segment. According to Jones and Newburn (1998: 60), the largest sector of private security in terms of total market size is accounted for by electronic and mechanical security equipment. Cunningham et al. (1990: 177 and 205) projected that the highest rate of annual revenue growth in the United States would be for electronic article surveillance, access control, and computer security; also, on the basis of rates of annual growth of *new* companies, the alarm and manufacturing components would experience the highest rate of growth. These projections actually underestimated the growth of the manufacturing segment, which got an additional boost from the resurgence of high-profile terrorism in 2001. In France, the manufacturing of security equipment shares 57 percent of the market, the service sector accounting for the remaining 43 per cent (Haas, 2007: 20; security guard companies form only one among twelve components of the service sector surveyed by Haas).

As said before, Patrick Haas is the editor of a survey on the state of the private security industry that has been published for the last seventeen years (Haas, 2007, which presents data for 2006). It reports on all twenty-five segments of the industry in France, the United States, and worldwide, to the extent that this is possible. It is a fairly reliable source, its previous and present estimates being in line with other research findings. As a trade publication, Haas (2007) gives special attention to private security corporations, which are identified by name. In France, the largest increase in corporate turnover for 2006 was in the field of counterterrorism and homeland security (the marketing of all kinds of security equipment, including border security systems). The manned security component experienced little increase, except for bodyguards and crowd control (Haas, 2007: 18).

In the United Kingdom, the Department of Trade and Industry (now the Department for Business, Enterprise and Regulatory Reform) publishes an annual guide to the British capability in security equipment (Department of Trade and Industry [hereafter, DTI], 2006). In 1995, the total industry turnover was assessed at 2,700 million (DTI, 2006: 3; Jones and Newburn, 1998: 60, quote a similar figure of £2,600 million for 1993). Following the 9/11 attacks, the security industry turnover climbed to £4,861 million in 2003—Jones and Newburn (2006c: 41), quote a figure of £5,415 million for the same period. According to DTI (2006: 3), this growth was "due largely to the effectiveness of solutions developed by UK companies, ranging from CCTV and access control equipment to physical security and crowd management systems." The CCTV market alone was worth £509 million at the end of 2003 (DTI, 2006: 4).

Cunningham et al. (1990: 175), projected that the U.S. security market would be worth $103,150 million (U.S.) in the year 2000, not being able at the time to foresee the major impact of the 9/11 attacks in developing the market. Haas (2007: 246) estimated that the homeland security and counterterrorism segment alone accounted for 20 percent of the U.S. market. He provides estimates of the 2006 turnover of the ten leading corporations in each of the four principal markets of U.S. private security (basing his estimates on the turnover of specialized private security corporations). Haas (2007) could not assess the proprietary security segment. His estimates are as follows: homeland security—$12,291 million (U.S.); electronic surveillance—$16,879 million; guard companies—$11,534 million; fire security—$11,384 million (Haas, 2007: 246–247). Even if we add to the security guard companies' turnover an equal sum for proprietary security, the manufacturing of security equipment and products still has the largest market share.

Two other facts deserve to be mentioned. Many of the leading companies in electronic surveillance and in fire security are the same: Tyco Fire and Security, UTC, Honeywell, GE Security, and Cooper Industries. This is indicative of the high level of integration within the industry. Fire security was mentioned early on in private security research (for example, Shearing et al., 1980: 188), but the practical and theoretical consequences of the integration of criminal loss prevention and fire security were never explicitly considered. In addition, the homeland security sector is dominated by military defense corporations: Dyncorp, Boeing Homeland Security, Northrop Grumman, Lockheed Martin, and General Dynamics being among the ten leading companies. Finally, Haas (2007: 260–264) provides a list of the hundred biggest private security companies worldwide in terms of their turnover. Taking into account the twenty largest corporations, we find that sixteen of them are security equipment manufacturing companies (with a total turnover of $42,370 million), and that four of them provide security guard services on a contract basis, among their many other activities (for a total turnover of $16,621 million).

However sketchy it is, this outline tends to confirm that the development and marketing of security products and technology is the largest component of the private security industry, and that its share of the market is bound to increase because of its superior growth rate. Taking seriously into account the manufacturing sector leads to additional conclusions. The security field shows a considerable diversification and is not limited to the narrow field of policing. Among the twenty top-earning companies, one finds giant corporations such as Tyco Fire and Security, Armor Holdings, and Dyncorp. Armor Holdings is part of BAE Systems, which describes itself as the premier global defense and aerospace company. Dyncorp comprises aviation, contingencies, logistics, security, infrastructure, and maritime divisions. Such diversification has portentous implications for trying to articulate a conception of the governance of security. Some of the provinces of the security domain may form a relatively homogeneous territory, such as fire security and loss prevention, and allow for an integrated theory or paradigm. However, in key sectors, such as homeland security, where military defense, infrastructure protection systems, security technology, and plural policing may all interface, conceptual heterogeneity may defy any rigorous theoretical ordering. In other words, trading policing for security governance may be a self-defeating move for the purposes of knowledge building.

Finally, it was argued above that sudden increases in numbers could be variously interpreted. This reservation also applies to technology. Much has been made of the exponential growth of CCTV in the United Kingdom, McCahill and Norris (2003) estimating that there are 4.2 million CCTV cameras in Britain, that is, one for every fourteen people. Yet, New Scotland Yard issued a warning in May 2008 to the effect that CCTV cameras did not have the intended deterrent effects, since many people do not believe that they are actually in operation, and that only 3 percent of street robberies were solved using CCTV images (Bowcott, 2008). As impressive as they are, like all numbers, the CCTV numbers are not in themselves indicative of a transformation of policing.

The Kinds of Services Provided

Many researchers have proposed categorizations of the main fields of private security (for instance, Shearing et al., 1980: 188; Cunningham et al., 1990: 127; Jones and Newburn, 1995: 227; Forst and Manning, 1999: 29; Manning 1999: 103–107; Wakefield, 2003: 166; Haas, 2007: 6). Most of these categorizations blend the manned security sector and the equipment and technology sectors together. They also reflect in part the framework used to study the public police, which is based on a distinction between uniformed and plainclothes personnel. The basic classification was articulated by the Task Force on Private Security (United States, 1977) and further developed by Cunningham et al. (1990: 127). It comprised the following categories: proprietary (in-house) security, guards and patrol dervices (manned contract security), private investigations, consultants, alarm services, armored car services, locksmiths, and security equipment manufacturing and distributing. The largest category is the last one (security equipment), which is coupled with servicing. There are twenty-six additional service segments included in the service and manufacturing sector, which are separate from the first eight major categories listed above (Cunningham et al., 1990: 190). The classification developed by Cunningham and his colleagues is relatively outdated, the service and equipment sector having grown and further diversified since 1990. However, the basic categories of this classification still provide the framework for legislation aimed at regulating the industry, such as Law 88 enacted in 2006 in the Canadian province of Quebec.

Focusing on manned private security, I have compared various listings of activities and also relied on my own empirical research to produce the following classification.

1. Guarding and surveillance (all kinds of property, physical and intellectual)
2. Investigation (all kinds, including criminal investigations for defense counsels—Gill and Hart, 1997a and 1997b)
3. Expertise (research, consulting, engineering, and so forth)
4. Servicing (a very large category including alarm response, telesurveillance, and the manning of various technological security and fire systems)
5. Transporting valuables
6. Parapolicing (public policing activities, such as criminal law enforcement, performed under special legal authorization; see Forst and Manning, 1999: 29; Rigakos, 2002)
7. Nonsecurity-related activities (quality of life, regulatory, and administrative)
8. Paramilitary activities (providing bodyguards and other kinds of protection in risky situations)

The thread running through these activities is the prevention of loss as opposed to the protection of persons against physical harm and the investigation of violent crime (with the important exception of paramilitary activities mentioned earlier). The latter are for most of their part still carried out by the public police, despite the unfocussed activities of private investigators. However, there are no public police duties that private operatives cannot be deputized to perform. Kinsey (2006: 5–6) enumerates a sample of no fewer than sixty companies that provide private military and security services, particularly with respect to the protection of public officials, corporate executives, and other kinds of VIPs. Media reporting on the Blackwater Corporation and its activities in Iraq has shown that it was empowered by the U.S. Department of Justice to use the most lethal kind of violence (Scahill, 2007; also see Singer, 2003). The classification of the activities is not as important as drawing three key distinctions—in the areas of space, formalization, and license—that provide the context in which these activities are performed and which shape their nature, both in terms of what private agents are allowed to do and what they are actually doing.

Space

There are three kinds of space: public, private, and intermediate. The best example of intermediate space is mass private property, but it is not the only one. There is a private property halo effect, which means that private space encroaches upon public space. Downtown public space that is immediately adjacent to drinking establishments and other night-life spots becomes a de facto annex of these businesses, where queues of waiting patrons are policed by bouncers (Hobbs et al., 2003). The streets bordering the buildings of a large corporation also become part of its territory, particularly in business suburbs.

It is actually very difficult to know what proprietary and contract security personnel are doing within the confines of private corporate space. It is generally believed that their actual power there is greater than the legal powers exercised by the public police in the public space. When they operate in intermediate or public space (for instance, public parks), the scope of what private security personnel can do is more limited, and becomes narrower as we move from intermediate to fully public space. According to my own research, what private security personnel are allowed to do in public space is the subject of intense negotiations between the public police labor unions and the public authorities, the public police being keen to preserve their alleged monopoly over security in the public space.

Formalization

Private security agents perform their duties formally or informally. Formal control is exercised, for instance, by private security personnel working in uniform. Plainclothes security personnel can engage in more informal and less visible controlling activities. Being more visible, formal types of control are easier to regulate, whereas informal control is more discretionary and potentially coercive. The distinction between formal and informal control has immediate relevance for the study of the use of force by private security agents. The public police apply two criteria to safeguard the core of their monopoly on policing: whatever requires the use of coercion and is related to the enforcement of criminal law falls exclusively within the public police domain. Being more covert, informal controls can trespass unnoticed on public police territory. For instance, Hobbs et al. (2003: 2) showed the extent to which bouncers resort to intimidation backed up by violence. Within private corporations,

covert decisions to drop criminal charges against employees who seriously violate the law are routinely taken (Ocqueteau and Pottier, 1995: 190).

License

Informal coercion can be covertly applied, but it lacks legitimacy. The state
retains the ultimate prerogative of licensing private activities, which initially
proliferate outside of its control, with the aim of submitting them to minimum
standards and thus reclaiming a degree of control. Issuing official state permits
not only legitimizes private security, but it potentially extends its scope to a
point where it matches the reach of public policing. The rebirth of private
policing may thus lead to a reinstitutionalization of "special constables" on a
more permanent basis.

The Kinds of Security Equipment

A great wealth of security equipment is offered by the private security manufacturing industry. Not only is there a great diversity of products on the market
but their number is also growing exponentially, particularly in post-9/11 times.
Consequently, it is relatively futile to attempt to draw up even a tentative list of
all products and to classify them, as their nature is constantly evolving. A useful
framework for categorizing security products and technology used to be the
five senses: hearing (all kinds of interception of verbal communications); vision
(video technology and x-ray booths in airports); touch (from crude devices
such as razor wire to sophisticated body sensors); smell (the use of trained animals); taste (breath analyzers). However, identification technology and information and communication technology (ICT) currently go far beyond our
immediate sensory capacity. Hence, instead of proposing a provisional classification, I will proceed as I did for manned security and emphasize key points,
which are closely related.

Complexity. We live in hi-tech times and are constantly assaulted by new
technological developments, some ICT devices being highly complex to use. In
consequence, we tend to lose sight of the fact that a lot of security equipment
was not initially of a hi-tech nature. Such equipment ranges from the physical
(obstacles, bullet-proof material), to the mechanical (armored vehicles), and
the electronic. Even the most basic equipment is now greatly enhanced by the
addition of hi-tech. For instance, the wall built by Israel around Palestinian
lands is riddled with hi-tech sensors that make it a much more formidable
obstacle than was the Berlin wall.

Servicing. It follows from the preceding distinctions that equipment varies
in kind with respect to its servicing needs. Physical equipment generally only

needs to be installed and requires a minimum of maintenance. Other kinds of security equipment are expressly designed to be manned, such as some forms of telesurveillance, where a surveillance device and an operator jointly provide a service to which a customer subscribes. CCTV may be operated in this preventative way. Video cameras can also be used as unmanned recording instruments for the purpose of identifying a potential perpetrator after a crime has been committed.

Training. Using and servicing complex pieces of equipment requires training. Furthermore, technology varies significantly in terms of user-friendliness. If policing personnel—whether public or private—are not properly trained in how to use a particular technology and therefore cannot see how it can improve their performance, they will either abstain from using it or use it improperly. Manning (1992: 390) argued many years ago that "the computer revolution in policing…[had] yet to take place." To a large extent, this assessment still applies today. Furthermore, since Goldstein (1979: 238–242; 1990: 3) called attention to the police syndrome of the priority of means over ends, we have learned that technology may radically change how policing is carried out without significantly changing its external efficiency (Manning, 1992: 389). The key point is to not overlook that the degree to which an organization is affected by technological change does not guarantee that it will be achieving its external goals in a corresponding degree. There is no question that car patrol changed policing, although it is uncertain whether this change brought it closer to achieving its mission.

Aggression. Although the police have been criticized for reacting to incidents rather than preventing them, there is a sense in which all policing must be reactive in order to preserve its democratic character. Internal security is a collective state of being that is achieved by taking defensive measures against predatory behavior. Within the democratic legal tradition there is no contradiction between prevention and actual defense. The police may search a suspect in order to prevent an offence, but they must act under the legal requirement of "probable cause." This requirement means that the police provide a response rather than undertaking preemptive attacks, and it constrains the whole field of low policing. In contrast with armed bands, the military, and high policing organizations, the police are prohibited from engaging in blatant aggressive actions that serve no defensive purpose (for instance, random crackdowns and roundups of citizens). The principle that offence is the best defense cannot be applied by the police regardless of circumstances. However, the line between offence and defense is much more difficult to draw with respect to equipment, and particularly in relation to weaponry. There are some kinds of security equipment that are indisputably defensive such as, for instance, alarm systems or computer firewalls. However, weapons can be used both for offence and defense. In the case of large increases of fire power spurred by the use of auto-matic firearms or in the case of pain-inducing intermediate weapons, it is prob-lematic to argue that these devices only serve defensive purposes.

As stressed before, the potential of new security equipment and technology to transform policing is arguably greater than changes in the policing work-force and its governance. This impact of surveillance technology has attracted much attention in recent years. To complete the picture, a case study examining the potential impact of intermediate weapons, such as stun guns (Tasers), rub-ber bullets, and pepper spray on democratic policing will raise the question of whether intermediate weapons are fostering police tactics of attack rather than defensive measures.

A Case Study of Pain-Inducing Technology

There is currently an impressive and growing body of literature on techno-surveillance (Lyon, 2006). This case study examines another kind of technology—the intermediate weapon—with a particular focus on Conducted Energy Weapons (CEW), better known as Tasers, which is the name of the pri-vate company that is very aggressively marketing these weapons. On October 14, 2007, Robert Dziekanski, a Polish construction worker in the process of immigrating to live with his mother in British Columbia (Canada), died shortly after having been shot at least twice with a CEW—witnesses say he was shot four times—by RCMP officers at Vancouver International airport. Dziekanski spoke only Polish and had been waiting for his mother to pick him up for some twelve hours. He was unarmed, not under the influence of alcohol, and attempt-ing to communicate with RCMP officers sent to the airport when they shot him. A witness (who had to obtain a court order to retrieve his video from the RCMP) filmed the whole episode. When the video film was later shown repeat-edly on TV throughout Canada and the world, it caused a furor, which was intensified when, three days after Dziekanski's death, another man stopped for a traffic violation in Montreal, while apparently intoxicated, was shot with a CEW, and also died. A public inquiry into the death of Robert Dziekanski and the use of CEWs, headed by retired British Columbia Appeal Court Justice Thomas Braidwood, is now being conducted. The Braidwood inquiry released its first phase report in June 2009 (Braidwood, 2009). While contested in its conclusions after its release, the Braidwood first phase report represents the most thorough analysis to date of the Tasers, their use, effects, and risks. No fewer than eight other official investigations have been launched in relation to this affair in Canada. The provinces of Manitoba and Nova Scotia are also reviewing the use of CEWs. One of the bodies investigating the death of Robert Dziekanski has released an interim report (Commission for Public Complaints against the RCMP, 2007, hereafter cited as CPC/RMCP, 2007).

CEWs (stun guns) were invented in 1969 and marketed in the early 1980s by the Jaycor Corporation. Taser International was founded in 1993, and now produces and markets most CEWs. This market is estimated to be in excess of $100 million (U.S.). The NYPD was an early taker. In July 1986, two former NYPD police officers were sentenced to two to six years in prison for torturing a teenage drug suspect with an electric stun gun at a Queens station house in 1985 (Fried, 2008). This incident explains in part the subsequent reluctance of the NYPD to deploy as many Tasers as other U.S. police departments do (Baker, 2008). According to an investigation by the Canadian Broadcasting Corporation in June 2008, the Taser is still used at times to torture suspects in Canada, one of whom was submitted to twenty-three electrical discharges. This investigation also claims that is customary for the RCMP to use the Taser repeatedly on a subject. On April 8, 2009, David McKie from the CBC reported that the RCMP had shocked sixteen people five times or more in 2008 (McKie, 2009).

The CEWs now used by most police departments are the old Taser M26 and the new Taser X26. Both devices can be used in *touch* stun or *probe* modes. In touch stun, the activated Taser is pressed against designated areas of a subject's body in order to produce pain. In probe mode, the Taser fires wired darts over a distance of some 10.6 meters; on impact, electrical current pulses through the darts and produces muscular incapacitation in addition to physical pain. CEWs are as much offensive as defensive weapons. As previously seen, they can be used to torture a suspect. They have also been used illegally as a threatening weapon to perpetrate a residential robbery.

Taser guns are used in at least twenty-eight countries (Amnesty International, 2004: section 4.3, Appendix 3) and possibly as many as forty-four (figures released by Taser Intl.). Taser Intl. claims that more than 12,800 law enforcement, correctional, and military organizations use its CEWs in forty-four countries (CBC News, 2008). In Canada, seventy-three police departments use CEWs. Amnesty International released a report examining the deaths of seventy-four people (mostly in the United States), which occurred after they had been "tasered" (Amnesty International, 2004). Overall, Amnesty International estimates that 290 people have died in North America since 2001, after having been tasered (or "tased"). In Canada, seventeen people have died in the course of stun gun–related incidents. In October 2009, it was revealed that Tasers were used to subdue mental patients in private Quebec clinics, when the police were called in to intervene.

Taser guns are only one of several electrical devices in use. This technology includes Remote Electronically Activated Control Technology (REACT belts worn by prisoners), sticky bullets (nonlethal projectiles delivering an electric shock on impact), electrical water cannon, and xReps (Extended Range Electro-Muscular Projectiles) that can be fired by a shotgun over a distance of 100 meters.

CEWs and other so-called intermediate weapons, such as rubber bullets and pepper spray, raise issues that go beyond the basic facts about their use.

Spread. The RCMP adopted Tasers at the end of 2001 and subsequently bought 549 M26s in 2002. The following year, this number had nearly multiplied by three, with the RCMP possessing 1,427 M26 Tasers. In 2003, the RCMP started to buy the more advanced X26: it had 5 in 2003, and some 1,131 by 2007. By the end of 2007, 9,132 members of the RCMP—out of some 15,000 regular officers—had been trained to use CEWs. (All figures are taken from CPC/RCMP, 2007: 2 and 13). In theory, RCMP members have to file a report each time they use a CEW. These reports grew from 84 in 2002 to 4,025 in 2007 (end of November; CPC/RCMP, 2007: 38, fig. 8). The Braidwood inquiry into the death of Robert Djiekanski opened in February 2009. Coinciding with the opening of this inquiry, the Canadian Association of Chiefs of Police and the Canadian police unions issued a call for all Canadian police to be trained in the use of CEWs and eventually armed with them. These bodies denied any proven link between the use of a CEW and the death of any person having been tasered.

Differential use. CEWs are also in operation in the province of Quebec, where all uses of CEWs also have to be reported. According to the annual reports of the Montreal Police Department, CEWs were used 32 times in 2006 and 28 times in 2007. There are some 15,000 police officers in Quebec. Reviewing the annual reports of all Quebec police departments using CEWs, their use is slightly over 50 times a year. According to Ontario police sources, the Toronto Police Service Emergency Unit uses CEWs some 80 times a year. As we have just seen, there were 4,025 RCMP reports on the use of CEWs, including 804 indicating that a CEW was unholstered but not fired. Subtracting this figure, we obtain a number of 3,271 actual uses of CEWs over a six-year period, with a yearly average of more than 500 uses. Although this is quite high—ten times more than for all police in Quebec—the CPC/RCMP (2007: 18) estimated that "the use of this weapon has been underreported." This difference between the RCMP and the Quebec forces—in fact, all other Canadian police forces—is explained by policy: Tasers are issued only to special shock units in other Canadian police forces, whereas they are much more widespread in the RCMP.

Uncontrolled multiplication. In its interim report on CEW use in the RCMP, the CPC/RCMP (2007: 2) stated that despite there being more than 3,000 deployments, "not one annual report has been produced and the information captured on the Conducted Energy Weapon Usage Form has not been thoroughly examined nor utilized in the development of current CEW policy."

Widening of the range. All the publicity of Taser Intl. revolves around one basic message: Taser Protects Life (Web logo) by reducing officers' and suspects' injuries and deaths. According to the 2007 CPC/RCMP report, CEWs are claimed to present "an option in cases where lethal force would otherwise have been considered" (p.1). This claim is demonstrably mendacious. The recorded use of CEWs far exceeds the infrequent recourse to lethal force. According to a use-of-force breakdown for the Orange County Sheriff Office in Florida, the police use of firearms went down from 5 to 4 between 1999 and 2001. For the same period, the use of Tasers went from 0 to 228 (quoted in Amnesty International, 2004: section 1.9). According to the RCMP reports of the use of its CEWs, they are used more frequently on touch stun than probe mode (1,698 vs. 1,167 deployments; CPC/RCMP, 2007: 38). Since the touch stun mode requires physical contact between the Taser and a body part of the subject, it must be concluded that "CEW use has expanded to include subduing resistant subjects who do not pose a threat of grievous bodily harm or death and on whom the use of lethal force would not be an option" (CPC/RCMP, 2007: 1). Other studies have been conducted to show that the use of less-lethal weapons (CEWs and oleoresin capsicum) reduced the incidence of police and suspect injuries (MacDonald et al., 2009).These studies are fraught with methodological difficulties: not only do they fail to specify was is meant by "injury," but the use of electricity to induce pain leaves few bodily marks. This latter feature explains why electricity—called the "clean torture"—has been systematically used to torture subjects from the 1960s until today. Extensively reviewing these studies, the first phase Braidwood report concluded that "the results are to date inconclusive—it is notoriously difficult to isolate a particular weapon's impact on injuries and deaths, when so many variables are at play" (Braidwood, 2009: 15–16).

A convenient illness. Taser Intl. and other advocates of CEWs have claimed that when death follows being stunned by a Taser, it is not the result of the electric discharge(s) but caused by an illness called "excited delirium." One of the only studies conducted in Canada on "excited delirium" was a review of literature conducted by Sgt. Darren Laur of the Victoria Police Department, who has no professional medical qualifications. According to Laur (2004: 18), the first "body autonomics" (symptoms) of excited delirium are "unbelievable strength." being "impervious to pain," and a capacity "to offer effective resistance against multiple officers over an extended period of time." However striking, these symptoms are misleading. What the subject is really suffering from is "physio-logical exhaustion" (Laur, 2004: 19). This latter condition explains the coinci-dental death of a subject after having been tasered. The person dies from an undetected precondition of exertion, which is independent of the electric impulse(s) that were received. To sum up: excited delirium justifies the police use of a CEW and exonerates them from its potential lethal consequences. The first phase Braidwood report unsurprisingly concluded that it was "not helpful" to blame resulting death on "excited delirium" (Braidwood, 2009: 15). The report also claims that CEWs can cause heart arythmia, which can lead to tachycardia or defibrillation and cause death (Braidwood, 2009: 16).

The consequences of a potential generalization of the use of CEWs and other theoretically nonlethal impact technology on policing are no less severe than the spread of surveillance, because they may undermine such cornerstones of democratic policing as the dual notions of minimum coercion and necessary force. As noted before, CEWs are only one among many products being devel-oped in relation to intermediate-level weapons. There is another kind of con-trol device that was initially marketed by Compound Security Systems in the United Kingdom and which is spreading. It is the so-called "Mosquito," a small device emitting a piercing shriek that can only be heard by younger people (up to twenty-five years of age). The inventor of this device—the engineer Howard Stapleton—has been awarded an IG Nobel in 2006 for developing and market-ing this product.

An IG Nobel is awarded to people who pursue research that "first makes you laugh, and then make you think." Here is the thinking part: Mosquitos are part of a series of products that are referred to as "repellents." In France, a chemical company (Firchim) specializing in cleaning products has developed an evil-smelling liquid substance that can be vaporized near a site (such as fire escapes) to keep homeless people from congregating nearby. Repellents are defined by the various companies marketing them as substances or devices aimed at keeping away certain animals and humans, such as youths and homeless people (explicitly mentioned on French Wikipedia). There are very evil historical precedents to the notion of grouping humans and animals in the same class of noxious beings. Arike (2010: 39) describes a frightening arsenal of "less-lethal" crowd-control devices that include "puke rays" induc-ing nausea, silent audio microwaves that produce uncomfortable auditory sensations (MEDUSA), and "pulsed energy projectiles" that overwhelm the nervous system.

At the theoretical level, the market-fueled expansion of CEWs and other kinds of pain compliance devices may lead us to question the possibility of establishing an efficient governance of security in a market economy. As we shall argue, the spread of security technology may escape the control of the proper authorities, as seems to be the case with the spread of the Taser in Canada, which is in great part driven by the aggressive action of private corporations marketing intermediate weapons. Despite all the caveats and reservations that came out of the reports on the death of Robert Dziekanski and others, the Canadian Association of Chiefs of Police has called in 2009 for a massive investment in acquiring Tasers and ignored commissioner Braidwood's warning that his "support for their use [was] conditional on significant changes made in when, and the way in which the weapon is deployed" (Braidwood, 2009: 16).

Private High Policing

It has already been seen in chapter 7 that high policing and private security were related notions, particularly in light of the fact that they were both instances of a brand of "justice" that was oriented toward institutional victims. Another feature that is shared both by high policing and private security is the cult of secrecy, which is derived from the interests they are trying to protect. States and corporations, respectively, make great use of propaganda and publicity, yet they are averse to sharing core information with other parties. It must also be stressed that the privatization of high policing is as much a two-way street as the privatization of low policing. Research and development undertaken by private corporations involved in national defense are jointly protected by private and public high policing networks. The implication of the private sector in high policing has a solid foundation in the history of policing. It was previously shown in this chapter that high policing, understood as the policing of labor and violent conflict in labor relations, was largely performed by private security agencies.

In chapter 7, high policing was seen to be characterized by nine core features. We have already argued that two of these features—secrecy and institutional victim orientation—immediately applied to private high policing. The other features of high policing will now be reviewed according to their relevance to private high policing. The gist of my argument is that most of the characteristics of high policing do not apply just to private high policing as such, but also to private security when considered as a whole.

Protection of the Political Regime
This is the defining function of high policing. O'Reilly and Ellison (2006: 647) argue that "while public high policing protects against the subversion of the State, private high policing protects against the subversion of the client." This

argument is largely correct. Private security protects corporate clients both from internal subversion—for instance, violence in labor relations or the leaking of information—and external aggression, such as industrial espionage. As is becoming clear, private high security is now increasingly called upon to protect the interests of nation states, supranational and nongovernmental organizations in the transnational context (O'Reilly and Ellison, 2006: 647; see Singer, 2003; Kinsey, 2006; and Jäger and Kümmel, 2007). Like private corporations, states can become private high policing customers. Nevertheless, there are important differences between states and private corporations, which suggest that the notion of clientship cannot be univocally applied to both entities.

The concepts of statehood and of clientship are not used in the same way. When a speaker is talking about "the state," using the singular, it is generally understood that the object being referred to is the government (or the public institutions) of the country where the speaker happens to be. However, if we are speaking about "the client" in the singular, chances are that we will be asked which client we are talking about. There is a logical presumption that the concept of "state" refers to a singular integrated entity (although there are 192 countries, "states," recognized by the United Nations), whereas the notion of a "client" entails a plurality of clients (although a particular provider can refer to one specific client). Consequently, a private high policing agency can openly have several different clients, as long as these are private corporations and are not direct competitors. However, it is doubtful whether the same private high policing agency could overtly be engaged in the protection of the national security of different states, since this would be tantamount to officially sanctioned espionage. In other words, the only kind of high policing that states can allow is of the proprietary kind, where the security provider is exclusively devoted to the protection of the interests of one state client. It may be that the same high policing private agency would be under contract with different potentially conflicting national states, but these practices would have to be covert.

There is another significant difference between states and private corporations. In theory, the notions of statehood and common good are coterminous. As was pointed out in the previous chapter, a conflict of interest between the political regime and the citizenry is a political pathology leading to a self-privatization of the state. However, there is no requirement, whether in theory or in practice, for the interests of the owners of a private corporation (and their managers) to coincide with the interests of its workforce. Labor unions were actually created because these interests were in conflict. Private high policing was originally used by corporate management as a countermove against the action of workers' unions, and this is still the case.

Absorbent Policing

This feature of high policing refers to the hoarding of intelligence and to the deferment of action taken on the basis of the intelligence collected. High policing agencies seem to be waiting for the ideal circumstances in which to use the intelligence they have accumulated. Private high policing is heavily involved in the gathering of intelligence. This involvement is difficult to assess with any degree of precision, because private intelligence units are often embedded within large corporations involved in all aspects of security, from the manufacturing of weapon systems to the management of intelligence systems (such as Raytheon), and thus have a low profile. Intelligence units are also embedded in large accounting and legal firms that provide consultancy services (such as Deloitte, Kroll).

The intelligence thus collected and processed can be roughly classified by using two pairs of opposite categories. First, it can be specific to business (financial and economic intelligence) or tailored to other needs of the client (government or nongovernment clients). Second, the collected intelligence can serve an offensive purpose (for instance, industrial espionage) or a defensive one. In the latter case, one is speaking less of intelligence per se than of defensive technological systems. Finally, there is one kind of all-encompassing intelligence that straddles these two categories: this is risk assessment, which has generated an enormous market for private high policing. The U.S. Total Information Awareness (TIA) project, which the government claimed to have canceled, showed that a high policing initiative in counterterrorism could be largely outsourced, the private sector being the main contributor to its realization (Brodeur and Leman-Langlois, 2006: 180). Rather than having been dissolved, the TIA has now been parcelled out to different public and private high policing agencies.

Private security is in itself absorbent, this general feature naturally extending to private high policing. Private policing, it is currently argued, is just one component of an entire private justice system. Although theoretically correct, this perspective is largely wishful thinking. As was early noted by the U.S. Task Force on private security (1977), a large part of private arrests are not reported to the public police, and it is debatable whether they should be, since "complete reporting and prisoner turnover would hopelessly inundate the nation's criminal justice system." (United States, 1977: viii) Studying private security in France, Ocqueteau and Pottier (1995: 190) also reported that 71 percent of thefts processed by private security agents in shopping malls were cleared without charges ("buried"), sometimes at the instigation of the police themselves. In most of these cases, the stolen article was either given back or paid for (often by the parents of a young shoplifter), the offender acknowledging the offence in writing. In the remaining cases (29 percent), the file was transferred to the police. It would thus seem that private justice consists either of absorbing the case without further processing in exchange for some compensation or transferring it to the police for further criminal justice processing. Jones and Newburn (1998: 185–186) report a similar unwillingness to call upon the police in public markets and shopping malls in the London area.

The Use of Informants and Common Criminals

Infiltration of labor organizations was the original calling of private high policing in the United States (for similar practices in France, see Ocqueteau, 1997: 54). Private agencies specializing in strike breaking, such as Berghoffs, employed common criminal thugs. Those practices have endured. Schlosser (2008) reported in the New York Times that large corporations such as Hewlett-Packard, Wal-Mart, and Burger King used private investigation companies to spy on journalists, activists (Greenpeace), and on organizations defending the interest of underpaid immigrant workers. The case of Burger King is particularly troubling. It hired the services of Diplomatic Tactical Services, a shady private security agency that claims expertise in "criminal/economic crime" and speciales, according to its Web site, in "labor relations" (covert surveillance and undercover operations). The owner of the firm tried to infiltrate the Student/Farmworker Alliance for the benefit of Burger King (Bennett Williams, 2008). She was denied a private investigator's licence in Florida in 2007. One of her former subcontractors, armed security guard Guillermo Zarabozo, has been charged with seizing control of a ship by force, kidnapping, and murdering four people in September 2007 (Schlosser, 2008, and SourceWatch, 2008).

This case is far from being an isolated one. Gimenez-Salinas (2001) has shown that in Spain and other EU countries, legislation regulating private security was enacted at the request of large private security companies to remedy the bad press generated by small private investigation agencies involved in illegal activities. In Canada, it was revealed in May 2008 that a private security agency, with ties to organized crime, had been awarded a contract for the surveillance of prisoners when they needed transportation to a hospital (Chouinard and Noël, 2008).

Deceit and Extralegality

Unlike public policing, private security does not have a blanket mandate to use force in all cases that require it, although it is empowered to use force in specific circumstances. Hence, resorting to deceit is a general trait of private policing as such, and not only of private high policing. The scope of deceit is very wide, as deceitful practices range from "honesty shoppers," posturing as customers to check whether cashiers are involved in stealing, to covert surveillance, undercover operations, and infiltration. As was just seen, the use of informants and the employment of violent operatives implies that private high policing engages in extralegal activities as much as their public counterparts.

Private operatives are also involved in subcontracting practices intended to shield the more accountable public police from potential accusations of abuse. For instance, I have encountered cases in my research on police investigation where the police used private investigators to perform wiretapping on their behalf when they could not make a case for judicial authorization. Individual operators were also used by political dirty tricksters, the most notorious case being the Watergate plumbers. More recently, two private security corporations—CACI Int. and Titan—performed interrogations at Abu Ghraib and in sites in Iraq "under the direct command and supervision of the U.S. Army" (www.caci.com/iraq_faqs.shtml). CACI acknowledged that sixty of its employees acted in this capacity in Iraq, and remained "disheartened that three individuals" working for the company were mentioned by U.S. Army investigators for having possibly abused prisoners in Iraq. "These men left the company in 2004."

Among the nine characteristics of high policing, two are prominent: the protection of the political regime and the conflation of policing, judiciary, and correctional powers. The first of these traits has already been discussed. The second one points to a major difference between public and private high policing. On the one hand, there would appear to be a conflation of different powers typical of high policing in the private sector, in that private police act as prosecutorial authorities in deciding to drop criminal charges in a majority of cases, and they impose corporate sanctions to a certain extent, thus behaving also as sentencing judges. On the other hand, there is no equivalent in the private sector of the totalitarian aggregation of all coercive powers and practices against delinquency and dissidence. Such equivalents are to be found only in extreme cases of local economic colonization (such as United Fruits in Central America).

The previous discussion refers almost exclusively to manned private high security. As elsewhere in private security, the manufacturing of equipment and technology is at the forefront. The situation in this respect is evolving so fast that any detailed description is bound to be obsolete after a few years. Two general remarks should, however, be made. First, data-mining technology is changing the nature of information processing, as it is generating findings that no previous means of analysis, however systematic, could achieve. Second, technology is driving a trend toward signal intelligence (SIGINT and its sundry variants) that is ultimately detrimental to traditional high policing human intelligence (HUMINT). The consequences of this trend toward recording technology have previously been alluded to: it is generating retrogression from the asymmetrical "surveillance society" where the state is the main watchman toward a new natural state where everyone is watching everyone else through various lenses.

Theoretical Issues

In this final section, theoretical issues such as the powers of private security personnel, the relationship between the public and the private security spheres, and the impact of private security on policing will be briefly discussed.

The Powers of the Private Police

The notion of private security is an abstract construct that only provides an unwieldy basis for a discussion of power. The question, "What are the powers of N?" is better asked in relation to people and the type of organization they belong to. Raising the issue of the allocation of power with respect to private police has the additional advantage of being conducive to a comparison of the powers of private and public police (Stenning, 2000: 326; Gans, 2000). This is a very complex issue, and its treatment in the literature is virtually schizophrenic. On the one hand, it is routinely asserted by almost everyone who has studied private policing that its growth brings into question the state's monopoly on coercion (for an early and substantial discussion, see Johnston, 1992: 188 and ff.). On the other hand, any detailed discussion of the legal powers of the private police finds them little different from the minimal powers of arrest granted to ordinary citizens (Stenning and Shearing, 1979). In order to develop a less dichotomous treatment of this issue, we have to make a distinction between the formal/legal authority of the private police and their informal/effective powers, as they are exercised in practice.

Egon Bittner, the authority most frequently quoted in support of a definition of the public police by their use of force, almost never uses the Weberian notion of a monopoly on the use of force. For instance, in most countries, the right of parents to use coercion against their children is explicitly acknowledged. More important, neither Bittner nor the other researchers who focused on the use of violence by the police (Westley, 1970; Muir, 1977; Klockars, 1985) speak from a legal standpoint. What, then, is the main difference between private and public police with respect to the power to use force? This difference does not reside in the use of force itself. Stenning (2000: 328) stresses correctly that it is almost impossible to identify any function of the public police that is not performed under some circumstances by the private police. When duties performed by the private police require the use of force, it is granted to them by the state (for instance, the guards manning armored vehicles that carry money are generally armed). Like prison guards (Bittner's favorite example), private police are allowed to use force, but the circumstances under which they are licensed to have recourse to violence are always limited. Setting aside technical considerations of jurisdiction, the public police are "universally" empowered to use force in all situations that justify coercion in a given territory, whether it be public or private. This enabling rule does not apply to private police, who cannot operate outside private space under a general authorization. Hence, this difference between the private and the public police lies neither in the nature of their mandate nor in the means allowed to enforce it, but rather in the scope of its application. In the case of the public police, the scope of the mandate is potentially all-encompassing, whereas it is strictly bound by a specifically defined context for the private police.

Having established this basic contrast, we can now review the powers of the private police in greater detail, focusing on the Canadian context. Stenning and Shearing (1979) still provide the most extensive discussion of these powers. This initial review of the powers of the private police was updated by Stenning (2000). Needless to say, these powers may vary from country to country, although there are substantial similarities between democratic countries.

Formal Powers

Private police and security personnel may be formally "deputized" or be granted the status of special constables. In these cases, their powers are—for a time—the same as those of the public police. For instance, the employees of Blackwater who look after the security of State Department officials in Iraq can use lethal force. With the exception of these specific cases, the legal powers granted to the private police are at first sight much narrower than those of the public police.

According to Canadian criminal law, the private police have two basic powers. First, they can perform a citizen's arrest when they witness the perpetration of an indictable offence or when they are justified in believing that a person who has just committed an offence is trying to escape from officials who have the lawful authority to make an arrest. Second, they may act as authorized agents of owners of property and arrest without warrant a person found committing a criminal offence on or in relation to that property. The private police derive substantial authority from their status as agents of the owners of property and, in the case of corporate ownership, as representatives of management. Their authority as agents of the owners of property is further bolstered by various local laws such as "trespass of property" acts in force in Canadian provinces and U.S. states. In addition to general property law, there are also a number of other pieces of legislation, such as contract law, employment and labor relations laws, landlord and tenant laws, and laws governing educational institutions, from which the private police can derive substantial powers of coercion and intrusion. Finally, Canadian municipalities have the authority to issue municipal regulations with respect to security. The violation of these regulations, which range from traffic rules to municipal bylaws covering various aspects of the quality of life, is usually punishable by fines. In a growing number of municipalities, private police are tasked with enforcing these municipal regulations and are thereby granted the authority to issue fines and to secure the compliance of potential violators by threatening to issue fines.

When taken together, all these laws make for a significant arsenal. However, it is less the possession of these legal powers that really matters than their amplification through the organizational ethos and willingness of private security agencies to "push the envelope" with the powers that they do have (Rigakos, 2002: 49). Rigakos (2002: 75) describes a training session of Intelligarde recruits, which is given by an instructor "wearing a black Intelligarde uniform with utility belt, handcuff pouch, holster, and 9 mm semiautomatic handgun." The instructor ("D") goes through all the usual tricks of masculine indoctrination. At one point, he declares: "We take the [Ontario] Trespass to Property Act as seriously as the police take the Criminal Code. The Trespass to Property Act is your best friend—treat it with respect." Rigakos, who was taking part in the Intelligarde training, made the following comment: "we all begin to understand the extraordinary powers of arrest enjoyed by security officers. Under s.2 (1) (a) (ii) [of the Trespass to Property Act] anybody can be arrested for any prohibited activity. D lists all the possibilities under federal, provincial and municipal laws" (Rigakos, 2002: 77). The sum of these powers and the aggressive subculture that is promoting their use may now a pose greater threat to privacy and liberty than the state does (Stenning, 2000: 332).

Informal Powers

The informal powers of the private police are in part derived from their formal legal powers, but are not limited to them. For instance, drug testing, lie detector tests, and various kinds of searches have a shaky foundation, if any at all, in the legal police powers formally granted to the private police under specific circumstances. These de facto powers are exercised in a context that expands the reach of the private police. This context is first characterized by low visibility, which at times borders on secrecy: we actually know very little about what goes on within the confines of corporate proprietary (in-house) security. However, we do know that secrecy fosters abuse and impunity. More specifically, low visibility weakens controls and accountability and to that extent increases power. The second kind of contextual power amplification is the relative lack of legal constraints on the powers of the private police. In an April 25, 2008 judgement, the Supreme Court of Canada ruled that random searches for drugs performed inside a school by public police using sniffer dogs were illegal because they did not respect the probable cause requirement for conducting individual searches of schoolchildren (*Q. v. A.M.*, 2008 SCC 19). The police had been called in by the school management acting under a broad "intuition" that drug trafficking was taking place on the premises. After this ruling had been delivered, legal experts argued that if such searches had been conducted on a contractual basis by private police acting under the authority of the school management, their legality would not have been challenged.

The greatest informal means to secure compliance consists of the leverage enjoyed by the private police when they are acting as agents of property owners or representatives of management. One of the most powerful levers is the ability to deny access to a site or to desired goods and services if one does not submit to a search and other policing measures (Stenning, 2000: 334). Another equally powerful lever can be pulled against the employees of a private company: they have to consent to being submitted to surveillance and other security procedures as a condition of their recruitment, continued employment, and potential promotion.

The Power of Appearances

Mopas and Stenning (2001) conducted research concluding that the symbolic power of the private police was not as significant as it was thought to be. Symbolic power is the ability to secure compliance without engaging in overt behavior that forces obedience. Such ability depends largely on physical appearances. In the course of the previously mentioned research on the relationship between the public and the private police, I found, in fact, that one of the most frequent complaints of the public police against the private precisely concerned appearances: the public police complain that private police working in uniform are impersonating them and reaping the compliance benefits of this physical impersonation. This complaint is not unfounded. Photographs depicting the guards employed by Intelligarde (see Rigakos, 2002 and the Web site of this private agency) show that their working clothes are a patchwork of various public police uniforms. For instance, they wear a chequered black-and-white hatband on their police cap, which is in blatant imitation of the British police. The agency has also a small unit of horse guards that could be taken for the iconic RCMP horsemen. Given the importance of the uniform in policing (see chapter 5), the private security regulatory body created in 2006 by the Quebec government is to write guidelines on how the uniformed private police should look in order not to be mistaken for the public police.

The different kinds of powers vested in the private police are exercised differently depending on where they are deployed. There are altogether five types of space where the police are deployed: public space, restricted public space (such as military bases), private space, hybrid space (privately owned grounds generally accessed by the public), and urban no man's lands (such as ghettoes and red-light districts). The more private the territory, then the more the private police can exercise unchallenged powers over it. Inversely, when private police are deployed in public space, their use of policing powers is much more open to contention. Yet, even minimal levels of private policing are no exception to the definition that we have proposed of policing as being the exercise of powers denied to other citizens. It would be illegal for citizens to issue parking tickets or, in certain circumstances, to tow away cars. Furthermore, whether they are private or public, the agents engaged in enforcing parking regulations show a general disrespect for parking regulations as they park in prohibited zones or double-park in order to perform their duties.

The Relationship between Public and Private Police

Much has been said on the topic of the relationship between public and private police (Shearing and Stenning, 1981; Shearing, 1992). The question of whether the private police are junior partners of the public police or whether their relationship is on an equal footing has received close attention since the seminal report of Kakalik and Wildhorn (1972). Relationships can be examined from two standpoints. The first is the strength of the relationship. The question asked then is whether there is a working partnership. The second is its orientation. The issue is then whether all partners are equal, or whether power flows mainly from one source—that may vary according to context—in the direction of the other partners.

The word "network" has a wide meaning. It can refer to a patchwork of agencies loosely in contact to perform an ill-defined task, or it can refer to an integrated partnership working toward a common goal. The fact that one can draw lines between small circles where names are written is not in itself indicative of the existence of a network. As was shown in two case studies of the security arrangements at the 2002 Salt Lake City Winter Olympics and at the 2004 Boston National Democratic Convention, coordinating the many public policing agencies that were involved—the private sector played no part in either of these events—provided a difficult challenge (Manning, 2006b). Manning concludes that "the idea of a coherent field or network of security is not helpful in understanding inter-organizational relationships at the Olympic Games" (Manning, 2006b: 79). If the coordination of public policing agencies is such a daunting task, getting agencies from the public, the private, and the community sectors to work as a team will require much more know-how than we currently have. The field studies that have been conducted so far in this respect are few in number, and they focus on the day-to-day business of policing rather than on special events requiring a high level of security.

The findings of the task force on private policing that I chaired have already been summarized. I will review them briefly, focusing on the issue of the relationship between the public and the private police. The findings of Quebec (2008) concerning sixty-two communities were similar to those of Wakelfield (2002): the relationship between the private and the public police varied greatly from one community to another. More particularly, our findings replicated those of Jones and Newburn (1998: 179–181) in Wandsworth: public and private police operate largely in different spheres and coexist side by side with little contact and no organized coordination. These relationships were at their best in wealthy urban communities that had created their own permanent private security force. These parapolice local units are traditionally headed by a well-connected exofficer from the public force that is policing the city of which these affluent boroughs are a part. This fact accounts in part for the productive working relationship between the public force and the tailor-made private unit. In the majority of communities examined, the relations were either tense, the public police perceiving the activities of private guards on the public territory as an intrusion (Quebec, 2008; Noaks, 2000), or the private and the public police largely ignored each other and were seldom in contact.

The partial reliance of Quebec communities on private security is a process that has been quietly going on for more than thirty years and that will continue to develop. The problems are not triggered by the long-standing reliance on the private police but by a periodic awareness of their intrusive presence, when, for instance, the labor contract between a public police department and the municipal authorities is being renegotiated. The public police apply pressure on their private colleagues in order to get a better deal from the city. Another important factor shaping their relationship is the occupational culture of the public police. Being still militaristic, the public police have an acute sense of hierarchy. When several public agencies are called to provide security, they generally end up competing with each other to determine who is going to be the first among equals. It would be even more difficult for them to bow to the authority of a private partner. Thus, despite the increasing role of private security and other forms of policing in the London borough that they examined, Jones and Newburn (1998: 181) concluded that their activities were "partially underwritten by the Metropolitan police."

The police culture is also structured by a dichotomy between the in-group and the out-group. A survey of police chiefs quoted by Cunningham et al. (1990: 119), shows that the highest response priority was for them "police officer in trouble," whereas "security guard in trouble" only ranked in fifth place, among twelve. Interestingly, what came to be one of the specific tasks of private security—curbing shoplifting and employee theft—had the lowest response priority (also, responding to a burglar alarm had a low ranking, in seventh place). In summary, although the relationship between the public and the private police ranged from productive to conflictual, depending on specific contextual variables, the most common feature was their weakness. Public and private agencies generally went about their respective business in relative ignorance of each other.

There is yet another aspect of the professional culture of the public police that accounts for the weakness of their relationship with private security agents. Whether or not we agree with the concept of the "knowledge worker," Ericson and Haggerty (1997) were correct in stressing the growing role of information in policing. It is one thing to rely on information and another to be motivated and competent in performing information or knowledge work as such. Police culture is action-oriented: recruits join the police for many reasons, but seeking a career in knowledge work is not one of them. We saw in the chapters on criminal investigation and on high policing that knowledge work, particularly the analysis of intelligence, was neither prized nor rewarded. Most intelligence analysts in policing organizations are civilians who have a lower status than police officers. There is, in consequence, a tendency in public policing organizations to outsource knowledge work that requires expertise, such as forensic accounting, data mining, and researching in the cyberspace. Outsourcing is not synonymous with networking. The police have a traditional respect for expertise, but they view it as ancillary to real police work. Private experts are considered as assistants rather than as partners.

The preceding remarks on expertise may help us in proposing an alternative explanation for the growth in private policing. This explanation builds on Jones and Newburn's argument on the formalization of social control. As we briefly saw, Jones and Newburn (2002: 141) argued that a decline in low-level indirect sources of social control coincided with a public outcry for more formalized and visible kinds of control. The vacuum left by the drying out of informal "secondary" sources of control was filled by the private police. The privatization of firefighting also provides support to this perspective. Although much more limited, the privatization of fire protection in the United States sheds some interesting light on the increasing formalization of social control. In 1989, 43.5 percent of the U.S. population was protected by 1,799 "all career" fire departments, whereas

42 percent was protected by some 27,000 "mostly volunteer" or "all volunteer" fire departments. To the limited extent that fire protection was privatized, it essentially affected the rural or small town fire departments staffed by volunteers (Guardiano, Haarmeyer, and Poole, 1992). For fire protection, privatization also coincided with formalization. The private sector stepped in at both ends of the social control spectrum. At the lower end, it formally took over low policing or fire-fighting duties that nonprofessionals did not perform adequately and public agents were wary of carrying out: stationary surveillance, giving information, controlling shoplifting and employee theft, fare dodging on public transport, responding to alarms, and rural fire protection. At the higher end, it is increasingly providing formal expertise in knowledge-intensive fields where the public police performed poorly or could not perform at all. A great deal of development is expected to take place at this higher end of social control.

Governance

The question of the orientation of the relationship between the public and private police raises the issue of governance: when several parties are involved in providing security in the public space, who is in charge? According to the first case study conducted above, the answers are rather simple. The joint private and public ventures are yet very few and, when they are undertaken, the public police are leading the partnership. Quebec (2008) recommended to the provincial government that the public police be officially given the ultimate responsibility in joint security projects. In view of the situation now prevailing in Canada, alternative solutions that would imply a downsizing of the authority of the public police are still of an exploratory nature.

There have been proposals to replace the concept of policing, perceived to be too redolent of the primacy of the state, with the notion of the shared governance of security (Johnston and Shearing, 2003). It is not clear, however, whether we are moving further from the state in switching from policing to governance. As seen in our chapter on police history, Samuel Johnson defined "police" in his 1806 *Dictionary of the English Language* as "the regulation and government of a city or country, so far as regards the inhabitants." Are we then simply progressing toward the past and reinventing the synonymy between policing and governance?

There is a second problem with substituting "the governance of security" for "policing." This problem is essentially empirical. The word "governance" comes from a word referring to the helmsman of a boat and generally means decision making at the upper level. It can thus be applied fittingly to the work of high-ranking administrators. It seems counterintuitive, however, to use this word to describe the activities of the police rank and file, whether public or private, working in uniform or in plainclothes. In what sense do patrolling, guarding, giving information to citizens, watching suspicious individuals, processing intelligence, and performing an arrest qualify as acts of security governance? Substituting "governance of security" to "policing" would leave out more than 90 percent of what the police are actually doing. Still, the governance of security is an emergent field of study that may generate growing interest. The use of this notion raises several difficulties that will be better resolved if they are identified at an early stage.

Semantics. Crawford (1997) and Johnston and Shearing (2003) wrote books addressing a similar topic: the prevention of crime through local community partnerships, albeit with different emphases. Yet the first of these books is entitled *The Local Governance of Crime* and the other one *Governing Security* (emphasis added). Crawford (1997: 3) defines governance as a change in the meaning of government, governance involving local partnership with communities, whereas government is centralized and owned by professionals. For Wood and Shearing (2007: 6) governance is first defined as intentional activities designed to shape the "flow of events," in accordance with Parker and Braithwaite (2003). However, they go on to define governance as "the business of managing our world," having specified that our world includes, "but is certainly not limited to people" (2007: 6). In his influential work on private government, Macaulay (1986: 446) defines private government as "a formally defined organization which makes rules, interprets them in the context of specific cases, and imposes sanctions for their violations." According to this definition, which obviously refers to the governance of people, there is no great structural difference between private and public governments. In addition to private governments, Macaulay (1986: 454) uses the notions of network and social fields. The fluctuating character of definitions impacts on factual assertions: Wood and Shearing (2007: 2) refer to the "widespread and rapid growth" of private governments, whereas Macaulay states that the concept of private government goes back to at least 1913 and that his own analyses are "not new observations" (Macaulay, 1986: 446). Indeed, churches are one of many historical illustrations of private government that are provided by Macaulay (1986: 471). Recent events have shown, however, that for some churches their governance of the security of children under their care was at times dismal.

Information. There is no possible governance without shared information and rules. Public policing organizations are notably reluctant to share information. The same comment applies to the relationships between private security agencies. When all these are brought together, information sharing may become highly problematic. There is an additional difficulty that should not be underestimated. With respect to certain policing operations, such as coun-terterrorism, levels of security clearance play an important role and legally impede the sharing of information between public partners that do not have the same level of security clearance. Being weakly trained outsiders, it is unlikely that private police will have the same level of security clearance as their public colleagues.

Obfuscation. The preceding difficulties are relatively technical. A more substan-tial objection is the following. As we tried to demonstrate in chapter 5, the uni-formed police only spend a part of their time providing security and enforcing the law. If there is one recurrent finding of empirical research on what the police are doing, it is that they are performing a large variety of disparate duties. Furthermore, law enforcement and the provision of security are not duties that neatly coincide. For instance, gambling was outlawed for a long time, and the police cracked down on various gaming houses. States have now found a new source of revenue in legalized gambling, and they are (rather obnoxiously) promoting it as a pleasur-able activity that may make your dreams come true. Like other operations of police "vice squads," cracking down on illegal gambling has almost no relation to secu-rity. It should be noted in this regard that the security agency investigated by Rigakos (2002) is often acting as the private surrogate of a vice squad.

The problem with substituting the governance of security for policing has the structure of a dilemma. Either it will be postulated that the two notions coincide, or it will not. If they are assumed to coincide, the notion of security could become a blanket to legitimize police activities that are arbitrary and potentially harmful, as it often did in the past. In they do not overlap, the noto-rious difficulty of building an integrated body of knowledge on policing will needlessly be made more acute.

The Police-Industrial Complex

There is one more substantial difficulty relating to the governance of security. Whatever the meaning given to governance, it refers to the governance of per-sons (and living beings) rather than to the governance of things. The same remark applies to the concept of privatization. The military have been depen-dent on weapons provided by the private sector for more than a century, yet there was no explicit reference to the privatization of the military until the recent surge in the number of private mercenaries. Yet, as was argued in the preceding parts of this chapter, the manufacturing of security equipment and technology has a greater share of the market than manned security, and the technology sec-tor is growing at a faster pace than manned security. It was also suggested that the impact of technology on policing was greater than changes in the composition of the security workforce and in the ratio between the private and the public police. It might then be inferred that studying security from the standpoint of governance is bound to miss its crucial technological component.

Although manned security and the manufacturing sector are distinct, there is no justification for dichotomizing them. Staffed policing services and the manufacturing of security equipment intersect at key points. Security equipment is often used as a substitute for manned security. For instance, surveillance cameras have replaced watchmen in public transportation, particularly in subways; ticket control is also performed by machines rather than by people. One of the fastest growing markets is privately manned technology, such as systems of telesurveillance. Rather than buying and installing a surveillance device, individuals and companies subscribe to a surveillance system, which comprises CCTV cameras, operators who are constantly watching screens, and intervention teams dispatched to check on potential breaches of security.

There is also an important feed-back effect of security technology on privately manned security. One of the earliest kinds of security equipment is the alarm system. The turnover of corporations manufacturing alarm systems is still one of the largest in the security industry. The universal spread of alarm systems, largely sustained by insurance companies, has generated an increasing problem for the public police. More than 90 percent of triggered alarms are false alarms, on which the public police are spending time that could be used for more productive duties. There are increasing pressures—for instance, by the auditor general of Canada—to devolve the response to alarm systems to the private police. In marketing terms, this is a perfect circle: first, one begins by making a profit by selling privately manufactured security equipment; second, the use of this equipment generates a problem that overtaxes the limited resources of the public police; and third, private manned security is then called upon to resolve the problem and reap in further benefits. There are other examples of such self-sustaining loops. Insecurity in public transportation is feeding a public call for the return of employees to perform menial tasks such as punching tickets, employees who were replaced by machines without anyone realizing that they were playing an important reassurance role. Private police are then hired to answer the public's call, while the machines that were supposed to replace people are kept in service.

Notwithstanding these combinations of private equipment with private manpower, security technology has by itself the potential for transforming policing. The spread of intermediate weapons and of CCTV should be singled out in this respect. The widespread distribution of intermediate weapons has an immediate effect on the police use of force and on low policing itself, since coercion is a core feature of low policing. The exponential growth of CCTV is transforming surveillance and, in consequence, high policing, which is predicated on the exercise of surveillance. One could also make the case that the use of helicopters will, in the long run, have an impact that may rival the advent of the automobile. Considered in all their ramifications, new technologies and equipments manufactured by the private sector may be the driving force in the transformation of policing, if such a thing is actually occurring.

Can there be a governance of the industrial market for security? There is no doubt that the manufacturing sector can be given strong directions by other influential corporate actors or even by the state. In periods of armed conflict, the economy is put on a war footing and can be directed to undertake research and development for needed products. A large corporation may also ask subcontractors to develop specific products. There is, however, an influential tradition in economics going back to Adam Smith's Invisible Hand, which claims that in capitalist economies markets are unpredictable and behave principally according to a mixture of self-governance and external circumstances. In a famous address, U.S. President Eisenhower coined the expression "the military-industrial complex" to refer to this mutuality of internal and external interest. Some of the technology developed for the military has been adopted with great effect by the police (such as armoured vehicles and helicopters).

As was seen previously, a British Columbia police officer wrote a report justifying the use of Taser guns and denying that it was instrumental in causing death (Laur, 2004: 26). He even speculated that a rare gene found in a specific Canadian-Amerindian family by a local "medical geneticist" made the members of this family "more susceptible to the negative effects of Excited Delirium." Needless to say, Canadian-Amerindians are often "tasered." It was also revealed in 2008 that a police officer, who was an active member of a Quebec police force, was promoting the Taser gun in Caribbean countries, where he also acted as an instructor for the company manufacturing them. These examples illustrate the mutual support that the policing and the corporate establishment may provide to each other.

The Laur report cannot de disregarded as mere anecdotal evidence. It was sponsored by the Canadian Police Research Centre, widely circulated, and is influential in deflecting criticism that might lead to a moratorium of the use of CEWs, which was called for in Canada after the death of Robert Dziekanski. Laur (2004) was effectively quoted in the report of the Commission of Public Complaints against the RCMP (2007: 19). It provided grounds to exonerate the police and deny any relation between CEWs and sudden death: "Frequently in sudden unexplained deaths in which the police have been involved, there appears to be a connection to excited delirium, extreme exhaustion, often while resisting arrest during which time a CEW may be used, and subsequent restraint." As we already said, police chiefs and unions were clamoring in 2009 for each police officer to be trained in the use of CEWs and potentially to carry a Taser gun. Although commissioner Braidwood said in his first phase report that "on balance, [he] concluded that our society is better off with these weapons" if significant changes were made in their use (Braidwood, 2009: 16), Taser Intl. is already contesting his conclusions. It would seem that nothing except society's unconditional surrender to its products will satisfy the manufacturer of Taser guns.

The hypothesis that there is a police-industrial complex, which builds on the military-industrial complex and which is pushing its roots deeper and faster, deserves consideration. This hypothesis would provide a more encompassing framework to conceptualize the complexity of the relationships between the public and the private police on the one hand, and the private development and marketing of security products, on the other. The governance of security perspective is more relevant for an understanding of certain aspects of manned security than for explaining the proliferation of security equipment and its impact on policing. However, notions such as plural policing, which were in part developed within the governance of security perspective, are key instruments for reflecting on the future of policing.

To Conclude

Figure 8.1 completes the diagram provided in the previous chapter on high policing and integrates the private sector. The police-industrial complex is deliberately not included in this diagram. This notion is still too hypothetical and is meant above all to stimulate further research. It could eventually be viewed as providing the base on which the diamond-shaped figure is resting. More important, figure 8.1 is an attempt to synthesize the analyses undertaken in the previous chapters. These analyses are based on my own empirical research and also on previous academic work on policing. With the exception of pioneering work on information technology and on surveillance (Manning, 1992 and 2003; Marx, 1985, 2001a and b), the issue of technology is a fairly recent one in police studies (Savona, 2004; Haggerty and Ericson, 2006; Lyon 2006). Research on technology is in part inspired by the rise of CCTV in the United Kingdom (McCahill, 2002; Gill, 2003). Furthermore, police studies are methodologically grounded in sociology, ethnography, and political science. The study of the police-industrial complex needs to play closer attention to economics and to its methods. In the main, the systematic study of police and security technology is only beginning, and it would be premature to try to assess its impact on current conceptions of policing.

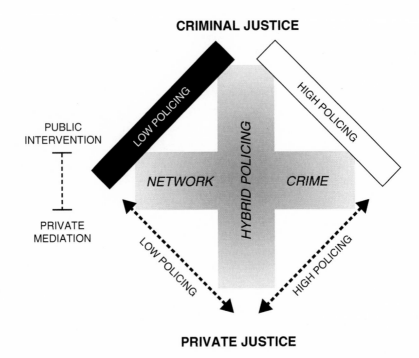

Figure 8.1 An Integrated Model of Policing

The most basic difference between public and private policing is in their relationship to justice. The court's prerogative to exclude evidence has a controlling effect on law enforcement, although it is limited by plea negotiations. As was already suggested in figure 7.2, the varying strength of the relationship between high and low policing on the one hand and the criminal justice system on the other hand is now indicated in the upper part of diagram 8.1, the black rectangle indicating a strong institutional relationship, and the white rectangle referring to a weaker linkage. The relationship between private policing and private justice is depicted by a dotted line to show that it is still weaker than the relationship between public policing and the criminal justice system. Except for pilot projects, which are few in number, private justice is largely justice by default: either charges are dropped for reasons of expediency or justice becomes corporatized (customized) and is driven by the preservation of a company's image and financial interest. The residual character of private justice is the reason why it appears at the bottom of the diagram. The dotted lines should be viewed as having a double direction toward the top and the bottom of the diagram. When a decision to prosecute an offender is made within the private sector, the case is transferred to the public police (upper part of figure 8.1). The dichotomous character of private justice, which is divided between a decreasing reliance on informal sanctions and a growing formalization of justice, was also noted by Jones and Newburn (1998: 193).

The prevention of loss, which is strongly associated with private security (Bottom and Kostanoski, 1990), is mainly achieved by security equipment and technological means. Focusing on manned security, the difference in what the public and the private police are actually doing is not sharp enough to be pinned down by using polar terminology such as the opposition between repression and prevention. One of the few empirical studies of a private security agency concludes that the role of the modern private police "mirrors the aspirations and functions of the contemporary public police" (Rigakos, 2002: 148).

Figure 8.1 uses the words "intervention" and "mediation" to characterize, respectively, public and private policing. These words should not be interpreted in their normative sense, mediation being viewed as the better way to solve problems. There is actually little difference in meaning between these words, which share the feature of referring to a practice that occurs at some intermediate level. The *Oxford English Dictionary* even defines mediation through the notion of intervention. However, intervention is itself defined as "interference." This emphasis on potentially disruptive action captures what still separates public from private policing. Because of their legal and symbolic powers, public police can openly practice various forms of social interventionism. Although private police are actually vested with significant powers, their action is usually underpinned by a "wait and see" attitude rather than by social activism. This difference is one of degree rather than nature. Nevertheless, it can be used as a matrix to generate further contrasts. The contrast between mobility and stasis is of particular significance. For reasons of cost efficiency, there are few static guards left in public police organizations. Providing stationary guards who perform various functions such as access control is still an important market for private security.

Within the diamond-shaped diagram in figure 8.1, there is an area in the form of a cross, which is shaded in grey. These cross-lines are intended as a reminder that there are interfaces between high and low policing and between public and private policing. There is a significant degree of overlap with respect to all kinds of network deviance (organized crime, street gangs, and terrorism). Figure 8.1 does not repeat the differences between high and low policing, which are listed in figure 7.2. Although the differences between high and low policing do not fully coincide as we move from the public to the private sector, they are to some extent analogous. Listing the differences between private high and low policing would have burdened the diagram needlessly. These differences are the subject of a detailed discussion in a previous section of this chapter. However, there is one basic difference that cannot be overemphasized. Whether it is established in the context of high or of low policing, the connection between policing and justice is much more formalized in the public domain. There is no private equivalent of the parallel high policing justice system that was developed by the United States following the terrorist attacks of September 2001 and for which there are several historical precedents in other countries. Macaulay (1986: 447) admits that private governments typically "mimic only part of the public legal system." Another significant difference, although it is not so much reflected at the institutional level, is the following: the top priority of the public police is violent crime, whether perpetrated by individuals, organizations, or large crowds of demonstrators. Private police focus on economic crime, although the protection of VIPs by bodyguards is a growing business.

It has been argued in this chapter that our matrix for defining the police by their capacity to overtly engage in behavior forbidden to the rest of the community also applies to the private police. Although the powers needed to carry on coercive interventions and to mediate through negotiations between conflicting parties are different, these differences are a matter of degree rather than a matter of nature in respect to practice. On the one hand, most of public police time is spent in noncoercive mediation. On the other hand, the private police often forcefully impose their own solution to a conflict, particularly in situations where they have a significant amount of leverage. With respect to an acknowledged statutory role, bouncers and similar actors in the nightlife economy can be said to be "police" in at least a minimal sense. Yet even this minimalist kind of policing is based on a potential recourse to physical coercion, which is effectively countenanced by the public authorities. Whether it is made official in writing or sanctioned by practice, legalization or implicit licensing to operate outside the law is the source of all policing.

Although this may eventually change, there is still a significant difference between the public and the private police in terms of their respective symbolic power and their capacity to stage high-profile social drama. This contrast in symbolic power is reflected in a rule: the higher the stakes in the provision of security then the stronger the call to entrust the public police with the mission to provide it. This rule led to a deprivatization of airport security in Canada after 9/11 and kept privatization at bay in certain fields of security, such as the investigation of violent crime and of organized deviance.

Edges of Policing

The preceding chapters have covered various aspects of both public policing—uniformed police, criminal investigators, high and low policing—and private policing, including private high policing. Nevertheless, the number of policing agencies is much greater than the organizations that have been reviewed so far. Many government departments and services, such as customs, immigration, internal revenue, the postal service, and the public parks, to name just a few, have their own police (Nalla and Newman, 1990: 45–46; Nalla and Newman, 1991; Jones and Newburn, 1998: 122). Public detectives are envious of the wide investigative powers exercised by internal revenue investigators. In most Western countries, the borders are protected by specialized agencies such as coast guard and border patrol organizations. There is also a large cluster of hybrid policing organizations that blend features of public and private policing agencies (Johnston, 1992: 114). In Canada, for instance, searching air passengers and their hand luggage before boarding a plane is a service traditionally provided by private security agencies; after the 9/11 tragedy, the Canadian government decided that they should be trained and accredited by a government agency, the Canadian Air Transport Security Agency (CATSA). To these formal activities should be added a number of practices varying both across countries and in their degree of formalization, which are referred to as self-help (Black and Baumgartner, 1987).

Needless to say, it is beyond the reach of any book to review the characteristics of the whole spectrum of police agencies and self-help practices. It may, however, be possible to provide an account of both ends of the policing spectrum, which constitute the outer edges of policing: military policing at one end and extralegal policing at the other. All other policing undertakings would fall between these two ends of the spectrum and share, in various degrees, some of their features.

In common-law Anglo-Saxon countries, the military do not perform policing duties in normal circumstances; they are called upon only in the context of exceptional crises. Legislation such as the U.S. Posse Comitatus Act greatly limits the use of the military for policing purposes, with the exception of the Coast Guard. It is also argued that the military culture is not germane to policing requirements of minimal use of force (Dunlap, 2001: 35). As was said in chapter 1, formal policing duties were first performed by the military in continental Europe. Illegal control—extralegal policing—is to be found at the other end of the police spectrum. Thus, this chapter is divided into two parts. The first part deals with varieties of military policing, and the second part discusses Gambetta's hypothesis that criminal organizations, such as the Italian mafia, the Russian mafiya, and the Japanese yakuzas, to name just a few, are devoted at least in part to providing protection to clients (Gambetta, 1993), these protection services approximating forms of policing.

Military Policing

The designation "military policing" has two primary meanings. In its narrow sense, it means the policing of the military—by other military. In its wider sense, it means the policing of society *by* military or militarized personnel. In the first sense, we generally talk of the military police (the MPs); in the second sense, we use the word militarized or paramilitary policing (Waddington, 1991: 123–124). In this first part of the chapter, the focus is on militarized policing with just a few words on the military police.

There are at least two models of militarized policing organizations, although almost all police agencies are to some degree militarized. The first model of militarized police is to be found in continental Europe and other countries such as Canada. It refers to an organization that is structured like a military entity and that may answer to the department of national defense rather than the ministry responsible for homeland security. In France, the Gendarmerie nationale, for the greater part of its history, has reported to the minister of defense, whereas in Canada, the RCMP answers to the minister of homeland security. What the two agencies have in common is that they are basically police organizations staffed with militarized personnel. They are part of the criminal justice system, and their use of coercion is guided by the police ethos of minimal force, rather than by military rules of engagement. The second model of militarized police is to be found in many South American countries, such as Brazil. This model refers to soldiers engaged in policing and operating like an army campaigning against internal enemies. The word "paramilitary" is more properly used to refer to this kind of policing apparatus.

After a very brief discussion of military police in its narrow sense, the two models of militarized policing just referred to will be examined, focusing on France for the first one and on Brazil for the second. The focus on these two countries is intended to provide a framework for discussion and inevitably precludes reference to other countries. The discussion of the military police in its narrow sense is based upon a 1993 Canadian case of military dereliction of duty.

The Military Police

In almost all respects, the military form a separate society from civilian society, which is subject to its own mode of governance, although the military are ultimately accountable to civilian authorities in the context of democracy. The separateness of the military is also expressed in military justice, which follows its own legal code, applied by a self-contained system of military police, courts, and corrections. For instance, the death penalty was still part of Canadian military justice long after it had been abolished in Canada in terms of criminal justice.

From January to June 1993, the Canadian Airborne Regiment was deployed to Somalia as a member of an international coalition led by the United States. This ill-fated mission, christened Operation Deliverance, was a failure and generated the biggest scandal in Canadian military history. The Canadian troops grievously mistreated detainees, beating up and torturing to death Shidane Arone, a Somali teenager aged sixteen, who had attempted to steal supplies from the Canadian encampment in Belet Huen. Two of the privates who tortured Arone had photographs taken of them, which showed them with a broad grin as they were beating the youth to death. They were not the only soldiers to have behaved in this way. Belgian soldiers also took pictures of themselves torturing detainees and urinating on them.

When these pictures surfaced in the Canadian press, they created a great shock. In 1995, the Commission of Inquiry into the Deployment of Canadian Forces to Somalia was appointed under the chairmanship of Judge Gilles Létourneau (Canada, 1997). The commission was prematurely terminated by the government in 1997, after having completed just one-third of its mandate. I prepared a study on racial prejudice in the military for the commission (Brodeur, 1997a). Although the commission was not able to fulfil its terms of reference, its proceedings and report were revealing about military police and military justice.

Lack of independence. After the death of Shidane Arone, the military police undertook an investigation and interrogated the military staff involved in this incident. This military police investigation was seen as incomplete. Consequently, the Canadian Forces appointed an internal Board of Inquiry headed by Major-General T. F. de Faye to investigate the affair. General Jean Boyle, the chief of the Defence Staff, testified at the Létourneau inquiry that there were significant discrepancies between the military police reports and the report of the De Faye internal board of inquiry (Brodeur, 1997a: 212). To all practical purposes, the military police reports were all but discarded in the official version of the death of Shidane Arone that was presented by the internal board appointed by the Canadian Forces. It was also claimed that the military police investigators could not pursue their inquiry as far as they should have. One of the two privates directly involved in the death of Arone—Corporal Matchee—tried to hang himself in his cell after having been taken into custody by the military police. He suffered such serious brain damage that he could not be interrogated and was found unfit to stand trial. The general issue that is raised by the early stages of this investigation is whether the military police is independent in its inquiry and in the use made of its findings. Based on the research that I carried out for the Létourneau commission, my answer is that the military police are subject to the military chain of command like everything else in the armed forces, and do not enjoy the independence necessary to pursue an impartial investigation.

Policing the rank and file. Following the military police investigation, several persons were court martialed. The commanding officer of the regiment was tried twice for neglect of duty, and was acquitted both times. The major who had issued an order to "abuse the prisoners" (Brodeur, 1997a: 184) was found guilty of neglect of duty and given a "severe reprimand." The sergeant supervising the men directly responsible for the death of Shidane Arone was convicted of negligence in the performance of his duties. He was jailed for ninety days and demoted. Of the two men that appeared in the pictures depicting Shidane Arone's ordeal, only one could stand trial. He was convicted and sentenced to imprisonment for five years; the severity of punishment thus increased for the lowest ranks in the chain of command. Finally, the colonel heading the entire Canadian Battle Group in Somalia was not formally held to account and was promoted to brigadier general in 2008 (retroactive to year 2000). The military police, it would seem, was originally set up to control the rank and file, its reach not extending to commissioned officers. In its report, the Létourneau inquiry took the diametrically opposite position on military justice, harshly blaming the commanding officers of the Somalia mission and recommending that the rank and file be awarded the customary medal for having served in a peacekeeping mission.

However brief, this analysis suggests that organizations that are structured in accordance with highly differentiated formal hierarchies are not successful in policing themselves. This observation applies as much to the police as to the military. In view of later events in the so-called war against terror, the incidents that marred the Somalia peacekeeping mission cannot be considered as an exceptional episode devoid of general significance.

Militarized Policing

The number of police forces operating in the countries of continental Europe is much smaller than in North America and even than in the United Kingdom. For instance, Sweden has only one police force (the Rikspolis). The basic structure of public policing in continental Europe is generally dual: there are two main national policing forces, one of them being a police force in the usual sense of the word and the other one a militarized organization. The two types of policing forces operate on a national or a relatively independent regional basis. In France, these two forces are the Police nationale, under the authority of the minister of the interior (home secretary), and the Gendarmerie nationale (GN), a military organization that is part of the country's armed forces and, for now, under the authority of the French Department of National Defense. Although the French government enacted new legislation bringing the GN under the authority of the Department of the Interior with effect from January 2009, the force will nevertheless retain its military character.

Whether a police force is under the authority of the police or the armed force minister is not the main factor in determining whether or not this force is militarized (or paramilitary). In France, the Compagnies républicaines de sécurité (CRS) are part of the national police and under the authority of the Ministry of the Interior. They were created in 1944 as a mobile force to control riots and potential political uprisings. They also epitomize militarized policing in all respects, except for the fact that they are answerable to the police minister. Spain, Italy, and the Netherlands have a similar structure of policing, which comprises a police agency and a militarized policing force. Belgium also had such a dual structure until the police and the gendarmerie merged in 2001. The French Gendarmerie was officially created during the Revolution in 1791. It replaced the Maréchaussée, whose history goes back to the thirteenth century. The French model spread into continental Europe in the wake of the Napoleonic conquests.

There are also militarized policing agencies outside Europe, most notably in Canada. The RCMP was founded in 1873 under the name of North West Mounted Rifles and was explicitly patterned after the Royal Irish Constabulary (Macleod,

1976: 8). Today, the RCMP is the largest Canadian police force, with more than 26,000 employees, including regular police members and civilian staff.

France provided the template for the dual structure of policing in Europe (Emsley, 1999, 2002: 477; Luc, 2002; Merriman, 2006.) The 1903 government decree that defined the GN's mission declares that "the Gendarmerie is a force created to look after public safety, to maintain order, and to enforce laws" (quoted in Dieu, 1993: 51). Section 148 of the decree specifies that the GN is charged with policing the military and with judicial and administrative policing. The military police was discussed above. France is one of few countries where the same organization polices both the armed forces and the national territory. What is called "judicial police" (*police judiciaire*) corresponds to criminal investigation departments in other countries.

The meaning of administrative policing is less straightforward. It refers to a wide spectrum of duties, ranging from traffic policing across the entire French territory to crisis intervention in emergency situations. Haenel et al. (1996: 16) enumerate no fewer than ten kinds of duty, not including special demands by various ministries, such as the protection of nuclear power plants. Among all these tasks, there are two general assignments that are the hallmark of all militarized police in continental Europe. First, they perform all the customary duties performed by uniformed police, including law enforcement, in the context of rural communities. This is also the main assignment of the Canadian RCMP. This feature is both distinctive and relatively unaccounted for in mainstream police theory, which focuses almost exclusively on urban policing. Second, militarized police are specialized in the maintenance of public order, understood as the policing of all mass events and, more specifically, riot control (Dieu, 1993: 155; Fillieule and Della Porta, 2006). In metropolitan France, the CRS are also specialized in riot policing and join forces with the GN. However, in the French overseas territories, the GN is exclusively responsible for the maintenance of public order. Whether or not they have a militarized police force as such, all countries of continental Europe have militarized police units that are specialized in crowd control. It is not so much the greater licence of the military to use physical force (Waddington, 1991) that accounts for the use of militarized or paramilitary policing as their capacity for disciplined maneuver, which is the key requirement for professional crowd control that avoids wanton brutality (Dieu, 1993: 162).

These two general features of militarized policing do not completely account for its specificity. Some of its more important characteristics are briefly discussed below.

The military as archetype. All policing organizations comprising a large body of uniformed personnel have borrowed from the military and are still militarized to various degrees, since military forces were historically the first agencies charged with upholding public order. The maintenance of an army was for a long time the defining feature of statehood, and the military consequently provided the original prototype of all subsequent public organizations. The dominance of the military model extends to the private security sector, which still mimics some of the residual military features of public police forces.

Pluralism. As seen in the previous chapter, plural policing seems to be the order of the day. In France, the dual public ordering structure that integrated a police and a military component was perceived as an expression of police pluralism and a safeguard of democracy (Dieu, 1993: 26). This perspective underlines a key theoretical point: policing pluralism is not determined by the number of police forces within a country but rather by the diversity of the types of organizations to which these forces belong. Policing pluralism may be more authentic in a country with only three policing organizations, each representing a different type of policing, than in a country with thousands of police organizations, each embodying the same policing model.

Visibility. Uniforms play an important role for the military. In 1872, one year before the creation of the RCMP, Judge Alexander Morris, the chief federal representative in the Canadian North-West, wrote to Prime Minister Macdonald that the police force to be created "should also be under military discipline and if possible be *red coated*—as 50 men in red coats are better here than 100 in other colours" (quoted in Macleod, 1976: 14). However, the significance of uniforms for militarized policing goes well beyond the deterrent effects of police visibility. Section 96 of the 1903 decree that instituted the French GN in its modern form made wearing the uniform compulsory in the performance of all of its duties (including criminal investigation) in order to preserve the corps from falling into disrepute as a result of carrying out "occult missions." In the original conception of militarized policing, wearing the uniform is a police signature that guarantees organizational accountability, every operation being signed for, as it were. According to this model, the militarized police are limited to the performance of low policing duties.

Intelligence. The requirement for being clearly identifiable at all time implies that militarized police cannot in theory engage in covert policing. Being deployed in rural communities, the French GN depends on citizens rather than on informers to gather intelligence. François Dieu (1993: 389) has noted that the ethos of visibility eventually conflicted with the GN's increasing investigative functions and that special legal exemptions had to be made to allow gendarmes to act as plainclothes investigators. The gradual blurring of the line between rural and urban communities has resulted in an increase in the similarity between gendarmes and police. This development was perceived as a dilution of the high legal standards of the GN.

Insulation. The difference between the in-group and the out-group was never stronger than in the military. Militarized policing shares this character of segregation, according to which traits such as unconditional loyalty to the organization, esprit de corps, and masculine values are ingrained into the professional culture. The endogenous character of militarized police organizations was strikingly shown by the recruiting practices of the Spanish Guardia Civil, even after General Franco had left office in 1975. From 1979 to 1989, more than 40 percent of all new recruits into this force were either sons of its members (*Hijos del Cuerpo*) or had close family ties with its members (or former members). In 1983, 1,000 new recruits were selected out of 12,008 applicants; 75% of the new recruits were Hijos del Cuerpo. This percentage decreased to 21% in 1992 and continues to decrease. Still, the percentage of all recruits admitted from 1979 to 1992 who had close family ties to members of the force was a high 37.5% (Morales Villanueva, 1994: 276).

There is another factor cutting across all militarized police forces, which also accounts for their insulation. They are not unionized, this prohibition often being stated by the law. Although it has been criticized for its corporatism, police unionization has contributed significantly to the opening up of police organizations. In Europe, police unions are often part of larger labor organizations that join together practitioners of different trades. More extensively, police unions bring many of their grievances to an open forum, whether they are organizational demands or complaints by individual members. In doing so, they trigger—at times, unwittingly—a process that enhances the openness of the debate on public security and makes policing organizations more susceptible to external influence.

The chain of command. There is a fundamental organizational feature of the armed forces, which was transmitted to all police forces of Europe, with the exception of the British police. The difference between enlisted men and commissioned officers provides the backbone of the structure of the armed forces. This difference between the rank and file and their military officers was largely transmitted to European police forces, where officers are in part directly recruited through lateral entry, as in the army, and in part selected through the promotion of the rank-and-file members who succeed in examinations. In the Anglo-Saxon policing tradition, all officers are promoted from the rank and file, and the difference between officers and the persons under their command is less stringent. However, this difference is perceptible in militarized police forces, even within the Anglo-Saxon tradition. The RCMP is a militarized police organization that always resisted any form of unionization, despite several attempts by its members. Its decision-making processes were investigated by a Task Force on Governance and Cultural Change in the RCMP, which released a report topically entitled "Rebuilding the Trust." "We have observed," say the members of the Task Force, "a number of attitudes and values in the RCMP that affect the way in which decisions are made. For example, we heard more than once that the culture is one of fear and intimidation and that some who are in a position of command use their authority to intimidate others" (Canada, 2007: 41).

The features discussed above apply with variable emphasis to all militarized police forces. None of them contradicts as such democratic policing and some of them actually foster more transparency and visibility (Fontaine, 2007). The highly centralized nature of militarized policing may result in organizational rigidity, and indeed it often does. However, it is not in all respects incompatible with change. Once an authoritarian organization decides to change, the new policies are quickly and forcefully implemented, precisely because this type of organization is highly disciplined. For example, the French GN decided some twenty years ago to open itself up to research and external input. As a result, the GN has become a policing organization that is more open to innovation than the French Police nationale, which is still averse to research. However, there is a second model of militarized policing, which is, as we shall immediately see, incompatible with democratic values.

Paramilitary Policing

The second kind of militarized policing to be examined is found in many countries of Africa, Asia, and Latin America. It is referred to here as paramilitary policing to stress the fact that the military element supersedes the police element. Unsurprisingly, paramilitary policing dominates all other forms of policing in military dictatorships. Some of its worst excesses in brutality took place during the "dirty wars" that were waged in several South American countries against political opponents between 1960 and 1970. The paradigmatic example of Brazil, where paramilitary policing still prevails, will be used to present the features of this kind of policing.

As was shown by Pinheiro (1991) and Holloway (1993), paramilitary policing has a long history in Brazil and was simultaneously developed in different cities and states. At the present time, the Brazilian states are policed by two different organizations, a civilian police (*Policia Civil*) and a paramilitary police (*Policia Militar*). The paramilitary police go back a long way in Brazilian history, having been created in 1831 in Rio de Janeiro with the name of Corpo de Guardas Municipais Permanentes. From the outset, this corps was involved in military operations against political insurgents (Holloway, 1993: 97). It became the Corpo Militar de Policia da Corte in 1866 and adopted its present name of

Policia Militar in 1920. In 1906, a French military mission was called upon to train the state police (*Força Publica*) in Sao Paulo. This policing organization was then linked to the armed forces, and its members were referred to as soldiers. According to Pinheiro (1991: 168), the Brazilian government was then criticized for its intention to militarize all the Brazilian police forces. The militarization of all Brazilian police forces was finally achieved in July 1969 with the enactment of Decree-Law No. 667, which centralized the state police under the army; the paramilitary forces were under the supervision of an army brigadier general on active duty. The situation evolved after 1974, when the urban guerrillas were crushed by the military.

Holloway (1993: 280) stresses the fact that the paramilitary police first created in Rio de Janeiro provided the model for similar organizations throughout the country. He also provides early arrest statistics (May 30–June 17, 1831) drawn from the national archives of Rio (Holloway, 1993: 78). These statistics show that fewer than 20 percent of arrests were triggered by criminal offences, with 80 percent of all 224 arrests being directed against breaches of public order (disorder and public insult, possession of weapons, curfew violation, and vagrancy). Interestingly, these figures also show that slaves and sailors formed 50 percent of the persons arrested for public order violations. The paramilitary performed a disciplinary function with respect to slaves and indentured persons, such as sailors, meting out the punishment that they felt was deserved by the person they had arrested. Thus, they behaved as the surrogates of the slaves' owners and acted at the same time as police, judges, and punishers. Holloway (1993: 283) notes that the early role of the police as a disciplinary agent directed against slaves and have-nots left a persistent legacy in police techniques and in the mutually hostile attitudes between the police and those segments of society that felt the brunt of their action. In his extensive review of paramilitary policing and police vigilantism in Brazil, Pinheiro also emphasizes that workers, protesters, and the dispossessed were the main, if not the exclusive, targets of the paramilitary. The two authors agree that the similarities between the Brazilian paramilitary police and its nineteenth-century European counterparts (the French gendarmes, Italian carabinieri, and Spanish civil guards) were coincidental, and that the Brazilian paramilitary model is an original response to problems defined locally (Holloway, 1993: 280).

In the terminology of this book, it can be said that paramilitary policing possesses the most basic feature of high policing: it combines the policing, judicial, and punitive functions, which are kept apart in the European model of militarized policing. To explore the extent to which paramilitary policing fits into the high policing paradigm, we will use the authoritative work of Paulo Sergio Pinheiro (1991) as a guide.

In 1965, the military seized power in Brazil. In December 1968, the military government suspended indefinitely all civilian legislative bodies and ruled by executive decree, the country being placed under martial law. As was said, all Brazilian state police were centralized under military command in July 1969, in order to fight politically motivated armed dissent. As a result of the 1969 decree, the paramilitary police were licensed to use as much physical force as an army in campaign, thus being granted de facto impunity in waging war against terrorists. Mobile police shock units were created in various cities, such as the Rondas Ostensivas Tobias de Aguiar—the fearsome ROTA—in Sao Paulo. The "dirty war" lasted from 1968 to 1974, and the government succeeded in decimating the urban guerrillas. The legacy of the dirty war still pervades the Brazilian police.

Despite the fact that the war against the "internal enemy" had been won, the paramilitary shock troops were not dismantled, and they were instead turned against conventional crime. The de facto impunity that they enjoyed during the dirty war was even given a legal status by a 1977 amendment to the 1969 Military Constitution, which brought the paramilitary police under the separate authority of military justice and enshrined in law their right to make their own rules. In the words of Pinheiro (1991: 172), "the military police role combined into one functional entity what Brazil's republican regime (1889—present) sought to keep separate—political repression (the maintenance of political order) and the control of common crime." The traditional line separating criminal law enforcement from political policing was thus erased. Not only was this line erased but the paramilitary shock policing also contaminated civil policing. The civil police were accused of being incompetent, and their reputation dwindled by comparison to the ruthless efficiency of the paramilitary. The civil police strove to regain their lost prestige by adopting the methods of the paramilitary and began to physically eliminate criminals through the use of death squads, which have become a permanent feature of Brazilian policing. According to Pinheiro, a ROTA 720-man unit killed 129 people in Sao Paulo in the course of the first nine months of 1981; by comparison, the death squads operating in Rio de Janeiro killed an average of 200 people per year between 1969 and 1972 (Pinheiro, 1991: 176).

There are nonetheless differences between paramilitary policing and death squads. First, despite the high number of fatalities for which they are responsible, the Policia Militar manage to maintain an appearance of respectability, pretending that its victims were killed in police self-defence. The death squads are stealthy vigilantes who make no claim to respectability, although they enjoy the support of large elements of the propertied classes. Second, the paramilitary operate with complete impunity outside civilian justice. By contrast, "there has been some investigation into death squad activity" (Pinheiro, 1991: 177). Third, there is a difference in the scale of police operations. Since they operate openly, the paramilitary round up large numbers of suspects through extensive dragnets, and they focus as much on groups as on individuals. The death squads are a clandestine operation targeting individuals. The most dramatic contamination of civil policing by the paramilitary in Brazil was studied by Huggins et al. (2002). This is the recourse to kidnappings, torture, and the "disappearing" of persons. In their study of Brazilian police "violence workers," Huggins and her colleagues interviewed approximately as many members from the civil police as from the military police. They could not say whether the perpetration of atrocities was more prevalent in the civil or the paramilitary police.

Although Brazil reestablished a civilian government in 1985 and enacted a new constitution in 1988, the violence of the paramilitary police did not decrease. Between 1983 and 1992, the paramilitary police killed 6,053 civilians in the state of Sao Paulo, with a yearly average of 605 civilians (Chevigny, 1995: 148). The casualties reached a peak in 1991 (1,074, with 898 civilians killed in the metropolitan area) and in 1992 (1,470).

The most accurate figures were provided by Nancy Cardia (2005: 293), who meticulously went through the statistics provided by the Secretariat of Public Security of the state of Sao Paulo. Cardia compared the casualties resulting from the actions of the civil and of the paramilitary police. Between 1996 and 2002, 1,911 people were killed in conflict with military police officers, the number of casualties increasing from 128 in 1996 to 435 in 2002. For the same period, 143 military police officers were killed in action. The number of people killed by civil police officers was 226, growing from 22 in 1996 to 43 in 2002. There were 82 civil police officers killed in action. Not only is the number of civilians killed by the Policia Militar close to nine times greater than the number of the civil police victims, but the ratio of civilians casualties to police killed in action is much higher in the case of the paramilitary (13.3: 1) than for the civil police (2.7: 1). Interestingly, the number of paramilitary police injured in action is eight times higher than that of the civilian police (2,134 vs. 265), which may be the result of a narrower definition of injury in the civil police.

The magnitude of these figures on Brazilian paramilitary police killings was emphasized by Pinheiro in an enlightening comparison (Pinheiro, 1991: 182). In 1978, says Pinheiro, the 132 formal death sentences carried out in South Africa were denounced as being enormous by the international community. In comparison, 129 civilians were killed by a *single* ROTA unit in one Brazilian city (Sao Paulo) over a period of nine months, in 1981. Pinheiro (1991: 179) also provided figures on arbitrary arrests and preventive detention. In 1977, the Policia Militar arrested 160,000 people in Rio de Janeiro, only 20,795 of these arrests leading to court proceedings. From January to September 1981, 5,327 people were detained "for investigation" by the paramilitary in the city Sao Paulo: of this number, only 71 were convicted of a crime. For the first half of 1981, 62,220 persons were in preventive custody for further investigation. These figures are admittedly old, statistics on preventive custody being hard to come by in Brazil. Nevertheless, all the recent statistics on police killings given above show that the level of repression was constantly rising after the military relinquished power in 1985.

To conclude, it might be asked what the relationship between paramilitary policing and high policing is. The characteristics of high policing that were previously discussed can be divided in two broad categories: substance and means. The means of high policing—secrecy, absorption of intelligence, infiltration, the use of informants and common criminals, and extra-legality—do not apply as much to paramilitary policing in itself, as to its extreme by-products, deaths squads and the use of torture (Huggins et al., 2002: 7). However, the core features of high policing can easily be found in paramilitary policing. In accordance with high policing, the basic aim of paramilitary policing in Brazil and elsewhere is the preservation of the political regime and of the power relationships defining the social and economic ordering. The conflation of legislative, judicial, and executive powers is the specific hallmark of high policing: it was an entrenched feature of paramilitary policing from its historical beginnings in Brazil, and still is today. Paramilitary policing is governed by arbitrary rules spun by the military themselves. Military self-governance voids the distinction between legality and extralegality of any significance. All escalation in violence, which may seriously breach the rule of law, can be legalized by the very organization that is breaking the rules. Being a law unto themselves, the paramilitary can act as police, judges, jailers, and executioners in broad daylight. These features of high policing first characterized the initial focus of the paramilitary on terrorism and politically motivated deviance. After the 1974 recycling of the paramilitary policing into the repression of conventional crime, they applied to nearly all Brazilian policing.

The picture that emerges from the statistics discussed above is that of an asymmetrical conflict that pits the paramilitary against the violent elements of civil society. In view of the high number of casualties—both among civilians and the police—resulting from the action of the paramilitary, it could be asked whether such action qualifies at all as policing. To provide a tentative answer to this question, we have to draw basic distinctions between the police and the military in the usual sense of the word. They mainly differ with respect to firepower and ethos. The firepower of an army is immeasurably greater than that of a police organization, as it relies on artillery, tanks, and naval and air power.

Police use handguns, intermediate weapons such as Tasers and pepper spray and, for special SWAT teams, precision rifles and submachine guns. The military and the police use of firepower and physical force are, respectively, based on different principles. As was stressed previously, the police ethos is based on the minimal use of force needed to resolve a threatening situation. The military have no such commitment to limit the use of force. Indeed, maximum conceivable force may be used to compel the unconditional surrender of a defeated enemy, as was used against Japan at the end of World War II. With regard to these distinctions, paramilitary policing is a hybrid model: it combines a military ethos of unbridled use of force with (enhanced) police firepower. Being first and foremost soldiers, the paramilitary are not limited to using the traditional police arsenal, although their firepower is much less destructive than the devastation exerted by a full-fledged military armament.

The militarized policing forces operating in the context of democracies are not significantly different from conventional police forces: they follow an ethos of minimum force and have no greatly enhanced firepower. However, they are basically different from the hybrid paramilitary model just described. In this regard, Pinheiro (1991: 182) offered a brief comparison of some Brazilian ROTA paramilitary units with the Italian carabinieri. (The statistics for Italy were provided by the Ministry of the Interior.) During the troubled period between 1974 and 1980, when the Italian police were struggling against the terrorist Red Brigades, 17 terrorists were killed during confrontations with either the civilian or the militarized police. However, 56 Italian civilian police and carabinieri died in shoot-outs with terrorists or were assassinated between 1975 and 1981. To repeat previously given figures: one Brazilian ROTA unit operating in the city of Sao Paulo killed 129 civilians in the first nine months of 1981, without losing any of their men. Clearly, then, militarized policing as practiced in continental Europe and other countries such as Canada follows a different model from the type of policing that is exemplified by the paramilitary in Brazil and similar countries. Only the latter is incompatible with democratic values.

Extralegal Protection

The type of military policing that is occurring in Latin America can serve as an introduction to the other boundary or edge of policing, extralegal policing. In a challenging work, Diego Gambetta (1993) has argued that delinquent organizations such as the Sicilian Mafia were composed of a set of "firms" operating outside the law and using violence to provide protection services to a wide array of clients. Viewed together, these firms constitute what Gambetta calls the industry or business of private protection. Gambetta's model of organized crime was applied by his disciples to the Russian mafiya (Varese, 2001) and to the Japanese yakusa (Hill, 2003). Gambetta's perspective was criticized by Paoli (2003: 19), who stressed that the Italian mafia performed functions that varied greatly in the pursuit of different ends and that one could not single out one particular function as providing the key to mafia activity.

Since the topic of this book is policing rather than organized crime as such, it will not take sides as to whether mafia-like organizations are performing a single protective function or whether they are multifunctional businesses. Neither will the time-honored issue of the level of organization that can be attributed to criminal enterprises be addressed (Reuter, 1983b). However, it cannot be doubted that criminal organizations are involved, to a significant extent, in the business of private protection. Whether or not Gambetta and his followers are providing a complete picture of mafia-like criminal organizations, they raise questions that are at the core of any comprehensive theory of policing.

Two lines of questioning deserve to be pursued. First, Gambetta and his followers offer a detailed exploration of the business of private *protection*, although they do not address the issue of *security*—the word "security" does even not appear in the subject index of Gambetta (1993), Varese (2001), or Hill, (2003), nor does it occur in Paoli (2003). Does this imply that the two notions can be used interchangeably, or do they really have a different meaning and different implications? Second, core notions, such as the use of force and the management of trust (or the lack thereof), which are used in the definition of (public) policing also apply quite straightforwardly to the business of private protection as it is practiced by mafia-like organizations. This conceptual transferability raises an issue that is generally not addressed within the research on policing: what is it that distinguishes legal/legalized policing from extralegal protection, apart from the obvious and institutional fact that one takes place legally and the other outside of the law? Both of these lines of questioning will be addressed.

Protection

The notions of security and protection are closely intertwined, although they initially belong to different semantic fields, the subjective and the objective. Etymologically, security is a word that refers to a particular emotion, which is peace of mind (*se-curitas*: the absence of worry). This is how the concept has been used from Stoic to modern Cartesian philosophy. The word took on an objective meaning with the work of Jeremy Bentham and now refers at the same time to the external condition of not being at risk and to the feeling corresponding to being in such a condition. However, recent empirical research on security has shown that there is not an automatic match between a secure condition and the feeling of security (Skogan, 1990a). For example, local variations in crime rates do not automatically translate into corresponding variations in feelings of security within a community. Policing strategies aiming to reduce crime are not the same as strategies aiming to increase feelings of security, as was repeatedly shown by assessments of the effect of community policing programs. To sum up, security is a dual notion that refers to two realms of phenomena—mental and external—that evolve independently of each other.

Protection is a more straightforward one-dimensional notion. It comes from a Latin word meaning shelter and refers to various activities aiming to preserve someone or a corporate entity from property loss or personal harm. In this respect, its meaning is similar to the objective meaning of security. There are several kinds of protection. At the basic level, protection is afforded to persons and to their property, as the meaning of the word indicates. However, Gambetta and his colleagues have developed a deeper understanding of protection by distinguishing among five questions: (1) Processes: what kind of protection is provided? (2) Providers: who provides the protection? (3) Customers: who is afforded protection? (4) Objects: what is being protected? (5) Threats: from whom are the consumers being protected? The detailed answers that are provided to these important questions cannot be fully discussed within the confines of this chapter. Nonetheless, each of them will be examined with a view to extracting a point that is relevant to a theory of policing.

Processes. Protection is either internal or external. Internal protection is provided by an organization for its own activities. External protection is provided to customers whether they have requested it or not. Varese (1996: 133–134) makes a distinction between the three kinds of external "protection" that is provided by mafia-like organizations: predatory protection that is so overpriced that it usually leads to the bankruptcy of the client; extortionary protection where a premium is extracted for bogus protection; true ("protective") protection that provides a genuine service to the client in return for a reasonable fee. Critics of Gambetta claimed that he and his disciples underestimated the part of extortion in the "protection" provided by criminal organizations (Lupo, 1996). Actually, Gambetta (1993: 2) refers to Charles Tilly's remarks on the ambiguity of protection (Tilly, 1985: 170). Protection is expressed in two contrasting tones, one being comforting (security) and the other ominous (dependency). In his lectures, Gambetta acknowledged that mafia protection tended to drift toward extortion.

Providers. The providers of private protection, according to this perspective, are mafia-like organizations. There is also a crucial point that emerges from what Gambetta and his followers such as Hill (2003) do not say. In a book sub-titled "the business of private protection," Gambetta has nothing to say about legal private security agencies. Tellingly, he writes that within his perspective, comparisons of the Sicilian Mafia "with ordinary businesses—such as the auto-mobile, insurance, and advertising industries—become possible" (Gambetta, 1993: 10). The glaring omission in this quick enumeration of potential terms of comparison is that of the private security industry in the conventional sense of the words. Although Varese (2001: 8) mentions that legal private protection firms are significant players in the Russian private protection market, he also argues that legal security firms are ready to offer services that go beyond those legally provided by their Western counterparts, and that some of these firms are "closely connected to established criminal groups" (2001: 64–65).

Gambetta's neglect of the legal private security sector may be explained by its relatively small importance in Italy and other Mediterranean countries. There could, however, be a deeper explanation. On the one hand, the public/private protection dichotomy appears to be coextensive with the distinction between legal and extralegal protection, all private protection being submitted to the unchecked imperative of profitability. On the other hand, although he occasionally refers to illegal transactions (Gambetta, 1993: 42), Gambetta wrote in the introduction to his book that "common distinctions such as between legal and illegal markets lose analytical significance" in the model he develops (1993: 10). It would then seem that the distinction between legal and extralegal protection does not apply within the business of private protection. Although we might disagree with Gambetta, his position is a strong indication of the dif-ficulty in differentiating between private legal and extralegal policing without falling back upon formal legalistic criteria.

Consumers. If the distinction between legal and illegal markets has little ana-lytical significance for private protection, we can surmise that the range of its customers is very wide and spans both sides of the legal divide. In the light of previous analyses of private high policing, the important question is not whether customers looking for protection belong to legitimate or illegal enter-prises, but whether they are asking for legal or extralegal services. For instance, legal businesses seeking protection from labor unions and, at times, workers on strike are likely to contract the services of criminals masquerading as a legal security agency or to resort directly to mafia-like organizations.

Objects. What can be protected falls into two categories: entities and rela-tions between entities. Persons and property are entities. However, transactions are processes that connect people and things and put them in contact. In the model provided by Gambetta and his followers, a mafia becomes a protection industry when three factors converge: a significant increase in the number of transactions; a failure of the state to protect these transactions; the availability of a private workforce (the mafiosi) to protect the increasing number of transactions. In what circumstances do transactions need to be protected? The answer is simple. Transactions basically rest on trust between the contracting parties; extra protective guarantees are thus needed when trust is lacking. Although it also protects persons and their properties from violence and theft, a mafia organization truly becomes involved in the private protection industry by providing guarantees for transactions between distrustful parties (Gambetta, 1993: 24 and 234–244; Lupo, 1996: 29).

Threats. Mafias protect their customers from three kinds of threats: criminal predation, law enforcement, and competitors. The first kind of threat is the raison d'être of all protection, whether legal or extralegal. The two other kinds of threats are more specific to extralegal protection. There is no need to elaborate on the protection given against law enforcement, since the public police have a mandate to stop illegal transactions. However, the protection against competition requires further examination. In legal markets, a business may need protection from competitors in the narrow sense of being protected against economic espionage and similar threats. However, the legal way of besting competitors and eventually driving them out of business is to provide a better product or a better service than they. It is not to eliminate the competition through murder and violent intimidation. The situation is different with respect to illegal markets where questions of territory and of cornering a market are of more importance than the quality of the products and services offered. Consequently, the physical elimination of competitors is an option that is kept open by murderous protectors. Not only is the option always open, but it is also an option favored by criminal protectors even if it is not chosen by their customers. In engaging in predatory murder, mafia-like organizations generate insecurity and feed the need for their protective services. The more insecurity there is, the greater the demand for protection. The more violent and predatory the afforded protection, the greater the insecurity.

This brief review of the dimensions of protection leads to a general conclusion: extralegal protection results in divorcing protection from security. This conclusion is obvious, when the protection afforded is either of the predatory or of the extortionary kinds, as was seen above. Ovid's famous interrogation on who shall protect us from our protectors applies principally to these perversions of protection. Even in the case when true protection is provided, it can hardly be said to bring peace of mind to the parties being protected. As we just saw, extralegal protection has to be more violent than necessary to sustain the market for illegal protection services. It is thus the same organization that generates the problem and its solution, which feed back into each other in an upward spiral of profit for the criminal organization. This predicament uniquely characterizes extralegal protection. Furthermore, the sanctions taken in the case of nonpayment for the protection afforded are drastic and foster a climate of intimidation that has no parallel in the market of legal private protection.

Policing

The preceding section was devoted to unpacking the various dimensions of protection. Without undertaking a systematic comparison between legal and extralegal protection, differences between the kinds of protection provided by mafia-like organizations and by legal agencies were emphasized. Although the concept of policing is wider than the provision of protection, protective activities lie so much at the core of policing that an organization that provides protection could be referred to as a policing agency. Mafia-like organizations will now be examined from the angle of policing and the issue of the difference between legal and extralegal policing will be raised in the conclusion to this chapter. The examination of mafia-like organizations as if they were policing agencies will essentially build on specific analogies that were drawn by researchers on various types of mafias. These researchers had no intention of articulating a comprehensive parallel between the various kinds of rule enforcement organizations.

Reversibility

We have seen that the distinction between public and private protection superseded the divide between legal and extralegal protection, which was also said by Gambetta to be of little analytical relevance. In this respect, there is an old Italian legal tradition, which is discussed by Gambetta (1993: 6–7). According to the legal scholar Santi Romano, associations such as the Sicilian Mafia "create their own order, like the state and its legal institutions" (Romano, 1918, quoted in Gambetta, 1993: 5). This conception of the mafia as a sui generis juridical order was adopted by Italian high court magistrates such as Guiseppe Guido Lo Schiavo (Lupo, 1996: 46) and the notorious Corrado Carnevale. It led them to rule systematically in favor of mafiosi who appealed their conviction. These magistrates viewed mafia-like associations as independent private governments operating benevolently on a smaller scale than the state and for which, what may appear as murder should be regarded as capital punishment (Gambetta, 1993: 7). Consequently external intervention by the Italian state was deemed to be an intrusion into the self-contained legal order in which murder could be reverted to capital punishment. According to this reversibility, predatory behavior would translate into acts of governance: theft of property became a seizure of goods, personal violence amounted to punishment, and extortion was just a form of income tax.

Most researchers on large-scale criminal organizations have been influenced to various degrees by this reversibility in putting a label on violent behavior. Gambetta (1993: 7) justifiably disputes this representation of the Mafia as a private government. Still, this reversibility between concepts seems prima facie to apply when we debate the nature of policing. Bittner's definition of the police as a mechanism for the distribution of coercive force according to perceived needs applies as fittingly to extralegal as to legal policing. Peter Manning (2003: 3) argued that "policing [was] a formally organized control agency with the potential for intervention in situations in which trust and mutual dependency have gone awry." This is the very argument that is used to explain the birth and growth of mafia-like organizations.

There is one last kind of reversibility that applies to policing personnel rather than to policing practices. Both the public police and private security agencies use common criminals in different capacities, particularly as informants and infiltrators. This is particularly true in the fields of high and paramilitary policing. This relationship between legal and extralegal policing personnel is also reversible. Varese (2001: 4 and 59) has shown that in the last days of the Soviet regime and in the years immediately following its demise, a great number of state security employees were demobilized and recycled themselves in the Russian mafiya.

Analogies

The reversibility of murder to capital punishment and vice versa is logically underpinned by a notion of equivalence according to which all forms of taking lives are equivalent, independently of who is doing the killing. The various self-contained "juridical orders" should be further explored in order to identify analogous practices, such as the use of violence or the exchange of guarantees to substitute for a lack of trust, when they occur. Such an exercise may produce debunking effects, particularly when carried across the public and the private policing sectors. If the industry of private protection should come into focus in the course of this exercise, Gambetta's assumption that all private protection is basically the same would be tested. For now, only tentative observations can be offered. There are four points at which all private security intersects.

Private security is nonstate protection. Although it appears to be a tautology, this assertion actually refers to a complex situation and calls for several reservations. As we have seen, there is a hybrid sector that straddles the public and the private domains. The state has also begun to involve itself in private security through regulations. Although there is now a great deal of diversity in the degree of control exercised by the state, it is foreseeable that state control will increase in all democratic countries. Finally, state control cannot by definition extend to the extralegal private protection industry as such. However, just as there is a form of toleration that is unofficially granted to certain trades, such as prostitution, extralegal private protection may also be tolerated by the state, if it suits its purposes.

Private security agents provide services to customers in exchange for remuneration. This proposition applies to all private protection firms, whether they are operating legally or not. The kind of remuneration and its extent may vary considerably from one private agency to the other, the tariff for extralegal protection being disproportionately higher.

Private security has an ambiguous relationship with the law. The dichotomy between legal and extralegal protection is too simplistic. One of the greatest differences between public and private policing is that the former takes place in a strongly textured legal environment, whereas the latter occurs in a weakly textured legal setting. Many of the powers of the public police are explicitly regulated by warrant requirements, admissibility of evidence constraints, and jurisprudential rulings. By contrast, private security operates in a legal limbo where outdated legislation not meant to regulate private policing—citizen's arrest, trespassing law—provides the legal benchmarks. In this environment, private security enjoys a policing free ride and exercises covertly, de facto, and unaccountably the powers legally granted to the public police.

Private high policing and extralegal protection often coincide. It is overwhelmingly difficult to discriminate between legal and extralegal policing in fields such as labor relations, economic intelligence, general surveillance, and close personal protection (bodyguards).

In the field of private security, private policing has been referred to as private governance and even presented as the embodiment of private government. When conceived as the industry of private protection, the mafia is the crucible in which the notion of private government is undergoing its most severe test. Not only are the criteria to separate maleficent from beneficent private governments not agreed upon, but it is questionable whether the idea of a private government is revealed to be more than a metaphor when subjected to detailed scrutiny.

To Conclude

In the first part of this chapter we drew a contrast between two kinds of military police: militarized police, who are legitimately operating in western continental

Europe and in countries such as Canada and other countries of the British Commonwealth; and paramilitary police, who are deployed in Latin America and elsewhere, where they operate both within and outside the law. We tried to show that the first model of military policing was as much compatible with democratic values as nonmilitary policing, whereas the second was destructive of democracy.

The second part of the chapter was devoted to extralegal policing and mainly discussed the work of Diego Gambetta and other researchers who have studied the Italian mafia and mafia-like organizations in other countries such as Russia and Japan. It was found that these organizations were at least in part engaged in providing protection, just as the public police and private security agencies were. Our discussion focused on the difference between protection and security, stressing the fact that mafia-like organizations deliberately generated insecurity to increase the demand for the kind of protection that they could provide. It was also found that organizations providing protection shared several features and were even mirror images of each other with respect to certain aspects of their activities, regardless of whether they operated legally or not. It was argued that the line between legal and extralegal policing has become so blurred that it needs to be redrawn.

Public Policing

It must be acknowledged from the beginning that the assertion that there is no difference between legal public policing and extralegal protection is in itself contradictory and, needless to say, counterintuitive (if not shocking). There is, indeed, a vast normative difference between what is labeled as legal and as extralegal. However, the issue that we raise is whether there remains a difference after peeling off the legal label that is attached by the state. After all, there are notorious historical examples—the Cheka, the Gestapo, the Securitate, and the Stasi, just to mention a few—where differences vanished once the legal varnish was dissolved.

The issue of difference can be addressed in two ways. We can search for an essential difference that can separate legitimate from illegitimate policing in all circumstances. We can also look for as many criteria as we can find, arguing that it is their addition that provides the difference that is sought for. The second way will be followed. High policing is extremely difficult to characterize in relation to the issue of legitimacy and illegitimacy. The criteria used to develop a contrast between high and low policing will not be reviewed again. The following discussion concerns mainly low public policing.

Ends. Legitimate public policing aims at providing protection and other services equally to all members of society. There is not even such pretence in the case of illegitimate protection. Two remarks should be made with respect to policing ends. First, Bittner and his followers never saw any need to mention in their definition of policing that the police are using force for legitimate ends. The medical profession (particularly surgery) provided a key reference for Bittner. In the same way that it was for him unnecessary to mention that surgeons operated on people for their own good, it went without saying that the police used violence for the common good. It can be objected that Bittner was misled by the medical analogy and actually begged the question of specifying the legitimate end(s) of policing. Putting aside the explosive issue of legal abortion, researchers such as Robert Jay Lifton (1986) have provided ample proof that the medical establishment can be diverted into pursuing criminal ends as much as the police. Second, the end criterion illustrates the need for a nonessentialist approach. It clearly differentiates between legitimate and perverted forms of public policing, but it cannot be exclusively relied on as a benchmark to assess the legitimacy of private policing. The fact that private security is a service offered only to customers who can afford it is not sufficient grounds for declaring it illegitimate.

Means. The criterion of means is clear-cut: legitimate policing is constrained by the rule of the minimal use of force to resolve a crisis situation. Illegitimate policing is not bound by such a rule, as we saw in the case of paramilitary policing.

Operations. This criterion is closely related to the previous one. As was seen, the hallmark of public policing is its visibility. Visibility is both an instrument of legitimate policing and a partial guarantee of its legitimacy. This guarantee is only partial: in nondemocratic states, abuses may occur in broad daylight to maximize intimidation. However, even in the latter case, the worst abuses, such as extralegal executions and torture, remain shrouded in secrecy. The consequences of violating secrecy are much more drastic in relation to illegitimate policing than to legitimate policing. All public police officers have to respect the confidential nature of some of the intelligence on which they operate. However, a breach of confidentiality is punished by a variety of sanctions ranging from a reprimand to dismissal and, in extreme cases, court proceedings. In the case of organizations that use extreme illegitimate violence, breaches of secrecy are punishable by death.

Organization. Although this criterion has no normative associations, it is a powerful one to distinguish public policing agencies from mafia-like organizations and paramilitary policing. The level of organizational structure is much higher in public police forces than it is in criminal organizations. As yet, no criminal organization has been examined closely enough to separate myth from reality with respect to the tightness of its organization. All accounts that we have tend to suggest that the organizational fabric of criminal gangs is much more loosely textured than the pseudomilitary language used by Joseph Valachi (Maas, 1968) would lead us to believe. The organizational criterion is applied in the opposite sense in relation to paramilitary policing forces. The formal structure of these forces is much more developed and authoritarian than that of the conventional police forces. Authoritarian structures are more conducive to large-scale abuses than flexible ones.

Ethos. If there is a criterion that comes close to providing an essential demarcation between legitimate and illegitimate policing, it might be this one. The official motto of many police forces is "to protect and serve." Although the police often fall short of this ideal, it encapsulates a fundamental insight. The verb "to serve" comes from a Latin word that first referred to the work of slaves and evolved to refer to devotion (as in "devoted to God"). Protection can be seen as a favor that is arbitrarily granted by dominating protectors to persons of lower status and greater vulnerability. The fact that these persons are asking for protection is viewed as evidence of their one-sided dependency. Military protectors, warlords, and mafia capos provide such protection to their charges. Protection can also be conceived as the right of free persons living in a society ruled by law. According to this conception, protection is one service among others that is afforded within a community of equals who provide for each other in diverse ways. The kind of reception that is made to a call for assistance is the most visible sign of the public service ethos.

Private Security

The criteria for distinguishing legitimate private security firms from illegitimate ones are similar to the preceding ones, although they are applied with a different emphasis.

Ends. Public policing aims at the common good, whereas the industry of private protection, whether legitimate or not, provides its services to customers on a contractual basis. This difference between public policing and private protection of any kind cannot be denied. However, there is more to this issue than meets the uncritical eye. First, legitimate private security companies are often hired by public government to serve the public, which they do—competently so. This does not happen with illegitimate protection firms, unless there is a perversion of public governance. Second, there is a public aspect of private enterprise that is uniquely found in democracies. Only people with limited knowledge of authoritarian regimes believe that private enterprise products and services are offered to anyone who can afford them under such oppressive regimes. Actually, the access of ordinary citizens to the private market is, most of the time, drastically constrained under dictatorships. There are products and services privately available that are made accessible only to a chosen few (such as a "nomenklatura"). In other words, publicly open private markets are a belated democratic invention. For instance, denizens of a free community may hire whichever private security firm best fulfils their needs. It would be a serious mistake to believe that Sicilian villagers can give their business to the mafia organization that offers them the best conditions for their protection.

Means. Private security may have chipped away at the alleged public police monopoly on the use of physical coercion. However, legitimate private security differs significantly from public policing and also from illegitimate private protection in this respect. Like the public police, they must abide by the requirement of keeping the use of coercion to a minimum. In contrast with them, private uniformed personnel are generally not entitled to carry firearms, unless they are involved in specialized tasks such as the transportation of money and other valuables. In most countries, private investigators must apply for a permit to carry a firearm, although they generally stand a greater chance of obtaining it than ordinary citizens. Needless to say, the constraints on the use of violence by legitimate private agencies are immeasurably greater than the limits set in this regard to illegitimate protection "firms," which solely follow the dictates of expediency (for example, avoiding "too much heat"). There is another key difference that separates private security from both the public police and the criminal protectors. As was repeatedly argued in chapter 8, private security is deeply involved in the manufacturing and marketing of security technology and uses it for its own purposes to a significant extent.

Operations. The largest part of legitimate private security consists of uniformed guards. In this regard, private security operates in the same way as the public police and relies to a great extent on strategies of visibility. Despite media stereotypes, the delinquent industry of private protection operates in a covert way. The distinction between legitimacy and illegitimacy agencies is much less clear-cut with respect to plainclothes ("detective") agencies. When the state enacts legislation to regulate private security, it is generally impelled to act in order to curb the abuses of private investigation agencies, which are often staffed by persons that were previously convicted of criminal offences.

Organization. As was seen, there is a great difference between the level of organization of the public police forces and of criminal groups. This difference is also significant with respect to private security agencies, and it increases as we move from small businesses to large companies. As Paoli (2003: 225) stresses, "it is clear that mafia families cannot be considered firms."

Ethos. It was emphasized above that the contrast between the public service ethos and the predatory culture of mafia-like organizations was a decisive factor. Although it may not be as vivid, there is also a stark contrast between the commitments of private legitimate business to providing a service to the public and the extortionary practices of mafia-like organizations, particularly with respect to its more vulnerable clients.

The differences that we just discussed are patterned after those between the public police and delinquent policing. There is one further difference that is specific to legitimate businesses: in normal circumstances, they do not dispose of their competitors through the use of violence. The opposite is true of criminal organizations, notwithstanding their alleged efforts to resolve their conflicts through negotiated agreements.

I will repeat what was said at the beginning: it is the resulting addition of these various differences that builds into an undeniable contrast. This being said, it could be argued that the key differences between public and private legitimate policing, on the one hand, and illegitimate protection, on the other, are to be found with respect to ethos and to the readiness to have recourse to violence. Both paramilitary policing and the protection provided by organizations operating outside the law have no respect for the public and use unfettered violence.

A thorough discussion of the differences between legitimate and illegitimate policing ultimately merges into an attempt to identify what is specific to democratic policing. This is a discussion that goes much beyond the relatively narrow focus of this chapter and must be pursued for its own sake, as it is in Manning (2010).

Conclusion

This book has covered a broad range of topics. It did not present a single argument progressively developed in each of the chapters, which can be summarized at the end of the work. Although two diagrams integrating low and high policing and the public and the private sectors into a final model were presented (see figures 7.2 and 8.1), each of the nine chapters was also a self-contained whole, in which specific conclusions relevant to the topic under discussion were formulated. Reviewing all of these specific conclusions would make this general conclusion tediously long. Instead, the main points that were made in the various chapters will be emphasized to the extent that they contribute to the development of a general theory of policing.

There are several broad distinctions that cut across the whole field of policing, such as uniformed and plainclothes policing, high and low policing, and public and private policing. All these distinctions were articulated in detail in the various chapters of this book. However, there is one important distinction that is quickly drawn in chapter 1, which deserves reconsideration. It is the distinction between general or all-purpose police forces, whether public or private, and policing organizations with a specific and, generally, narrow mandate. How narrow this mandate in fact is may vary greatly. The FBI is a police force specialized in enforcing federal criminal law in the United States. Since federal criminal law encompasses a great diversity of crimes, the FBI's mandate is fairly wide, although narrower than that of all-purpose urban police departments. The policing units with the most specific mandate are those that are charged with administrative policing on behalf of a particular government department (such as income tax).

So far, the theory of policing has essentially focused on general and all-purpose police forces and has singled out among them uniformed police, who are the policing personnel dealing with the greatest variety of situations. This focus has significant theoretical implications. Following a line of reasoning that is also valid in the field of policing, Max Weber argued that the state could only be defined by its means—coercion—since defining it by its ends would be a self-defeating task. According to Weber, the state can pursue any goals it wants and can also add indefinitely to them according to new circumstances. Police scholars such as Herman Goldstein and Egon Bittner have also argued that the number of situations that the police were called upon to solve was so great that the only way to introduce conceptual unity into a theory of policing was to describe the police through their means—force—rather than through their ends. As long as we consider multipurpose police agencies or, indeed, the whole of policing, it would seem that the argument in favor of defining policing by its means has to prevail, even if the means identified are not limited to the use of force. However, if we focus on policing agencies with narrower terms of reference, and particularly on administrative policing units, the notion of law enforcement takes on an increasing prominence. In this narrower sense, policing is an activity aimed at detecting rule-breakers and at deterring potential offenders.

A similar point can be made with respect to the history of policing. As was seen in chapter 2, one of the earlier texts on policing is to be found in Montesquieu's *The Spirit of the Laws*. "Thus," writes Montesquieu, "one must not confuse great violations of the laws with the simple violations of the police." The great violations of the laws were serious crimes for which the offender was prosecuted in front of a local parliament, acting as a criminal court. The violations of "the police" were breaches of the various sets of regulations governing behavior in all walks of life under the French monarchy. Violations of the police regulations were quickly dealt with by police officers, who acted both as constables and investigators detecting violations of the rules and as judges imposing penalties (the head of the police also had legislative powers). This model, which concentrated all powers in the hands of the police, was later replaced by the reform of policing that occurred in England at the beginning of the nineteenth century. The British reform introduced two key changes in the notion of policing. First, policing was no longer considered as synonymous with the internal governance of all things, but was defined in relation to the prevention and repression of crime and disorder. Second, the distinction between the executive, judiciary, and legislative powers was vigorously upheld, the police being limited to the exercise of executive powers.

Although these changes were heralded as a revolution in policing, they are not reflected in reality as much as might have been expected. As was shown in chapter 5, it is now widely acknowledged that in practice all-purpose police organizations continue to perform many other functions than just crime prevention and repression. The separation of executive from judicial power is not as clear cut as the British police reformers intended it to be. The blurring of the divide has not attracted much attention because it mainly involves personnel that are defined as assisting the police rather than the police officers themselves. For a variety of reasons, among which economic considerations are paramount, there has been a multiplication of policing assistant personnel who are often designated as "wardens." Some of these wardens, such as game wardens, have been operating for a long time. Others, such as traffic wardens, police community support officers, and environmental protection wardens, have been deployed in more recent times. All of them have the power to issue "Fixed Penalty Notices," as they are called in England. Needless to say, public police officers could impose penalties for traffic violations a long time ago and still can, but they have been partly relieved of these duties by the creation of traffic wardens. The quasi-judicial power of these wardens to impose penalties—which can be challenged in court—should not be exaggerated as signifying a return to a police concentration of powers. Yet, the institution of wardens and similar personnel has a significant theoretical meaning. It shows that the separation of the powers of the state has always been fragile and that policing as a way of resolving problems is more constrained by time and circumstantial imperatives than it is by the due process of law. It also shows that rule enforcement plays an important role in policing and that some policing agencies are not engaged in a such a variety of duties that they can only be defined by their means, as Max Weber's criticism of any attempt to define the state by its aims would have it. Although fines are a form of imposition, they do not intuitively qualify as an exercise in the use of physical coercion. Finally, police wardens certainly qualify as agents of policing as much as private security guards do. However, they are almost never taken into account in comparing the number of public and private police. This is yet another example of the tendency to underestimate the number of the public personnel involved in policing duties.

The notion of an "intensive quantity" was introduced in chapter 1. It was subsequently used in chapter 3, which focused on representations of police work in crime fiction and in the press. Intensive quantities are single events with a very high potential of being replicated in one media format or another—the written press, the electronic press, the Internet. The overwhelming sum of these media replications results in the establishment of a low-definition environment. This hybrid environment is composed of the actual world in which we live and act and an over-dramatized pseudo-reality over which we have no control. Both components compete and merge together to create perceptual uncertainty where our sense of reality is undermined. A few examples will highlight the nature of this process.

Reports by the U.S. justice and education departments estimated that some 740,000 violent crimes are committed annually in schools, and that they involve a population of approximately 7.7 million students (reported in the *Encyclopedia Britannica Blog* discussing "Violence in U.S. Schools"). Despite these impressive figures, all the data presented in *Indicators of School Crime and Safety* (2007; http://nces.ed.gov), a joint publication of several U.S. government departments, show that violent crime has been decreasing in U.S. schools from 1993 to 2005, with the minor exception of bullying. Yet the public remains convinced that violence in schools—not only in the United States—has been inexorably rising since the 1990s. The impact on public opinion of school shootings that occurred, for instance, in Columbine and Virginia Tech, but also in other countries such as Germany and Finland, accounts in no small part for the strong conviction that is held by the public. There are thirty-nine Internet pages listing various videos that were made in connection with the shootings at Virginia Tech, which are posted on the Web site YouTube. The number of times that a particular video was viewed is indicated under its title. In adding up the number of times that the videos listed on the first fifteen pages were viewed, I came up with the figure of some five million viewings and further estimated that the material corresponding to the full thirty-nine pages was viewed more than twelve million times.

As was recounted in chapter 5, Robert Dziekanski, a Polish citizen who wanted to immigrate to Canada, died at Vancouver airport after being shot four times with Taser guns by police officers. His ordeal was filmed by a witness using a cellphone. Other cellphone videos were made in relation to this event and were posted on YouTube. When I checked (2009), there were some 888 YouTube videos relating to the death of Robert Dziekanski, the first of these having been viewed by 85,000 people. Setting a very conservative average of 1,000 viewings for each of the 888 videos gives the figure of 900,000 viewings.

So far, the defining criminal event of the twenty-first century is 9/11. There are innumerable postings on the Web showing images of this tragedy. I selected at random nine films that were at the beginning of the list of videos that could be viewed on an Internet site; this tiny selection was viewed five and a half million times.

All the previous examples focus on visual representations, which are progressively superseding the written world in media such as the Internet. The key lesson that emerges from these examples is the following. The world of images that is generated by the electronic press and the Internet is not fictitious in the sense of having no correspondence with facts in reality. On the contrary, it consists of images truly depicting the factual event that was recorded on camera. Their fictitious character stems from the disproportionate ratio between the limited occurrences of violent events in reality and their unlimited replications in images that are viewed by millions of people. The surrogate world of representations is saturated by violence, whereas violence is a relatively rare occurrence in advanced democracies. The noxious and at the same time awesome power of intensive quantities is that they neutralize the impact of carefully collected and analyzed statistics on public opinion and policy making. In the face of the uncontrolled proliferation of images depicting school shootings, it is almost pointless to argue that violence in U.S. schools is in fact steadily decreasing. The most overwhelming demonstration of the power of images is the 9/11 attacks. In the seven years following 9/11, the whole government of the United States was geared to the war against terrorism, despite the fact that not one single terrorist attack of the kind that was feared was perpetrated on U.S. territory.

Although they did not exclusively focus on the means used by the police, the chapters on the history of policing and on police representations provide elements that serve as a background to the definition of the police proposed in chapter 4. The history of policing shows that the pressure of time is constantly spurring the police to solve the problems they are confronting by dispensing with the formal requirements of the due process of law. Montesquieu believed that "scarcely any formalities are needed" in policing and that the police have "regulations rather than laws," these regulations being of the nature of self-regulations that are internally developed. This conception of the police as self-regulated lawlessness is pushed to its ultimate conclusions in high policing. It has also a strong echo in crime fiction, which was discussed in chapter 3. Leaving aside virtuous torturers and justice-seeking serial killers who are featured in crass TV serials, rogue cops and hard-boiled private eyes who enforce their own brand of justice are prized characters of police fiction, and they are to a certain extent ideal types, in the sense used by Max Weber, who embody universal features of policing.

In chapter 4, agents of policing were defined by their authority to use means that all other citizens were prohibited from using under normal circumstances. Summarizing the discussions that addressed various aspects of this definition throughout the book, it can be concluded that the basis for this police authority blends elements derived from the law, custom, and practice. It comprises the following elements: the first five elements to be discussed are derived from the law and its interpretation by the courts; the last four stem from custom and practice.

Legal clauses that protect the police in the performance of their duty. The best-known of these protective clauses concerns the use of the "necessary force" for the purposes of administering and enforcing the law. There is a cluster of legal concepts, such as "reasonable grounds," "probable cause," and several others, surrounding these legal protections.

Legislation that defines circumstances under which the police are justified in committing an act or omission that would otherwise constitute an offence. These circumstances generally comprise the investigation of criminal activity. The Canadian Criminal Code also allows a police officer to direct the commission of an act or omission constituting a potential offence by a person—for instance, a police informant—under his authority [CCC 25.1 (8)].

Legislation that allows the police to commit acts that would otherwise constitute an offence pursuant to the obtaining of various kinds of judicial authorizations (warrants). It must be stressed that the judiciary exercise a very weak supervision of the police, who experience very few refusals when they apply for a warrant, particularly in the field of electronic surveillance.

Various other pieces of legislation, which are to be found in civil, state, and provincial law, and in other local regulations, play an enabling role for private security agencies. It was emphasized in chapter 8 how much the private police relied on Ontario's provincial trespassing law to exercise coercive powers in the housing developments that they policed.

Legal jurisprudence, particularly when emanating from a country's Supreme Court, is also a source of empowerment for the police. However, jurisprudence is as much a source of limitation of the powers of the police as it is a source of empowerment. Nevertheless, jurisprudence limiting the powers of the police can be superseded by the enactment of new legislation that runs counter to a judgment. When the Canadian Supreme Court expressed doubt as to the legality of police counter-sting operations in the field of narcotics, the government reacted by passing a law that officially authorized them.

Traditional deference of people for figures of authority ranks first among the practical sources of the police prerogative to disregard the law in certain circumstances, the public police being the archetypical figures of authority. A large part of the public police's charisma trickles down to the lower echelons of the police assemblage. The drivers of almost any vehicle bearing a resemblance to a police car, for example, can disrespect the traffic regulations with relative impunity.

People's ignorance of their rights is another amplificatory source of police power, along with their bowing to police intimidation and their explicit consent to renounce their rights. The latter kind of behavior is common in the private corporate environment and enhances the power of private in-house security to the point where it surpasses the power of the public police.

Delegation of coercive policing powers— an unofficial, albeit quite real, practice—constitutes a third source of practical empowerment. Bouncers and such security providers in the nighttime economy are often de facto police deputies. There are historical cases where organized criminals were also unofficial police deputies, as when the Luciano Mafia family agreed to police the docks of New York in order to protect the United States against enemy infiltration during the Second World War.

Reluctance of people to challenge the police bolsters their defiant attitude toward the law. There is almost no prosecution of people involved in policing for abusing their power. Even the judiciary are reluctant to confront the police, and they grow cynical from having to withstand police perjury in court without being able to do anything about it.

There are a few clarifications on the proposed definition of policing that ought to be given in conclusion.

First, does the definition abolish any notion of police deviance? Since the police possess the authority to use prohibited means, it could be claimed that anything they might do would be ipso facto legal. However, in the same way that defining the police by their use of force does not entitle them to use indiscriminate violence, defining them by their authority to use otherwise prohibited means does not imply that they have been granted a licence to break the law at will. Four points should be made in this regard. (1) Despite being impressive, the scope of their authority to use prohibited means is constricted with regard to the mass of prohibited behavior. For example, a constable on the beat cannot just walk into a store and leave with a stack of goods. This person would be prosecuted for theft. (2) The notion of the abuse of power by the police is as vital in the definition given in this book as it is in Bittner's, and the mechanisms for keeping it in check would still operate. (3) Police may act in two capacities. They may act, on the one hand, as sworn police officers or accredited policing agents of various kinds; on the other hand, they may also act as private persons. When they abuse their power in a misguided attempt to fulfil the aims of the organization to which they belong, they are guilty of police organizational deviance. Police organizational deviance is generally treated with leniency by police disciplinary bodies and by the courts, who tend to view it as overzealous police behavior. When some police usurp their powers for personal private gain—for instance, in perpetrating "shakedowns," stealing from court exhibits, and extorting favors from sex workers—they are acting like common criminals and usually receive stiffer sentences when they are prosecuted. (4) Despite all that has just been said, there is no denying that the proposed definition calls attention to the very thin line separating the legitimate use of prohibited means from their abusive use. Indeed, the proposed definition is intended to raise this very issue. As was argued in chapter 7, high policing comes very close in some of its aspects to dispensing altogether with the notion of police deviance. In some so-called failed or failing countries and in undemocratic regimes, it is the police who are the most nefarious public enemy of the people.

The second question to be raised is, does the requirement of a minimal use of the coercive means of policing apply as much when the notion of policing means is extended to cover all prohibitions that are in effect authorized by law, custom, and practice, as described above? The answer is a qualified "yes." The restrictions on the use of "necessary force" are the same as in the Bittner model. However, this requirement of minimum use might be spurious in relation to such practices as the control of identity and the use of search warrants in particular circumstances such as a terrorist threat.

Third, if the police are endowed with so much power in their authority to use prohibited means, what is keeping them from establishing a police state? There are at least two answers to this question. The first is provided by the traditional checks and balances inherent in a democracy. Defining the police by their use of force does not imply that they will be driven to create a violent state. The same restraining forces that hinder the establishment of a violent state also impede the establishment of a general police state, when types of behavior that are otherwise illegal are permissible under special circumstances for agents of the state. On a deeper level, the police form an institution that is almost completely ancillary to the state. It is they who are molded by the state and not the state that is molded by them. This situation is in stark contrast with that of the military. There have been very few police putsches throughout history, if any at all. On the other hand, there is a significant number of military coups d'état, such coups even being the rule in many unstable countries. The risk of a state being overtaken by institutions presumably under its command is serious with respect to the military and almost negligible with respect to the police. High policing may be an exception, as is shown by present-day Russia, where all power rests with Mr. Putin, an ex-KGB agent who surrounded himself with cronies from the former Soviet intelligence services.

Finally, what is it that is gained both in knowledge and in practice by the proposed definition? The answer is that there are at least two concrete gains. First, the proposed definition breaks the spell that police violence holds on us, which is largely the product of media hype. There are many important issues confronting us with regards to policing—for instance, issues of surveillance, intelligence, high policing, and technology—which are distantly related to the use of force. Second, the proposed model raises the following radical issue: is it possible to bring policing entirely under the ambit of the law, even when the law is understood in its opportunistic meaning of legalization? This book is an argument to the effect that the answer to this question should be in the negative.

Chapters 5 through 9 of the book are devoted to an examination of the most important pieces of the police assemblage. Since these chapters were intended to be as exhaustive as the limitations of one chapter would allow, they cannot be further summarized without avoiding repetition. Some of the main arguments developed in these chapters will, however, be briefly revisited.

Chapter 5 dealt with the police in uniform. The feminization of the police, which now affects mostly the uniformed police, is one of the most important new developments in policing. However, in view of its recent occurrence, we are not yet in a position to assess its consequences for policing. An issue that should be closely followed is whether or not the recruitment of women will accelerate the present move toward intermediate nonlethal weapons that spare the police from having to engage in physical contact with suspects in order to subdue them. It is presently premature to try answering this question.

As it was stressed in chapter 4, Bittner formulated his definition of the police through the use of force by observing the work of uniformed police, to whom this definition most readily applies. The general capacity to use force in all circumstances that justified it was assumed to single out what is specific in police work. The analyses performed in chapter 5, in fact, lead to the conclusion that uniformed police work is characterized by a dual specificity. On the one hand, the police use means that are otherwise prohibited, the most conspicuous of these being the use of force. From a descriptive point of view, violence is an exploding concentration of physical energy. As such, it might be considered as the quintessence of action, that is, the kind of external behavior with the most perceptible impact. When the police are thus engaging in the kind of action for which they have a specific authority, they can be said to be behaving in the most "active" sense of the word. There is a general agreement, however, shared by the police themselves, that they seldom use force and their other powers in the course of their daily occupations.

A significant part of chapter 5 was devoted to examining the research findings on what the uniformed police actually did. These findings contrasted (1) time spent fighting crime with time spent doing something else, (2) time spent being proactive with time spent waiting to react to occurring events and incoming calls, (3) time spent in the field with time spent in the police station, (4) time spent in engaging in specific activities and time spent on random patrol and maximizing their visibility for the purpose of reassuring the community, and, finally, (5) time spent in contact with citizens and time spent in isolation. With respect to these five opposite pairings, it was generally found that the uniformed police spent less time on activities related to the first item of all pairings and more time in engaging in action related to the second item. The only likely exception concerned the time spent in the field as compared to the time spent in the police station. Although there were locations where the time spent out-of-station was greater than that in-station, the latter was always significantly higher than expected. The character of such activities—doing miscellaneous things unrelated to a core function, waiting for calls and reacting to them, spending time in police stations, doing random patrol and maximizing their visibility, and not being in contact with people—is that they barely qualify as being action at all. Such activities differ greatly from those characterized by the use of force, and they would appear at the opposite end of a spectrum of intensity. Yet, they may be a specific feature of policing activity as much as is the use of force.

In addition to what they do, the uniformed police also exist on a symbolic plane. Since they are physical icons of order, their mere deployment into an area makes it seem more secure and eventually becomes a self-fulfilling prophecy—the area becomes, in fact, more secure. As was repeatedly emphasized in chapter 4, the police use of force is more potential than actual. They provide the tangible "or else," and most people do not dare to experience what the alternative to complying with the police may be. In other words, the presence of police is perceived as a sign of an impending action, which they do not always have to perform in order to produce a deterrent effect.

Finally, the existence of a police force is a symbol of normalcy, as opposed to the deployment of a military force, which symbolizes a state of emergency and of exception. In the case of low-intensity conflicts, police become prime targets of guerrillas and terrorists who want to destabilize a country. What is suggested here is that the police do not always have to act in order to produce an impact. Furthermore, it may be possible that the police are, in fact, having more effect by being a threat than in carrying out this threat, the threat leaving more to imagination than its (potentially unimpressive) fulfillment. Needless to say, the threat has to be forcefully realized when necessary in order to maintain its credibility. *It is this pairing of forcefulness—at times, pushed to the extreme—and underacting that is the specific feature of police action.* It would be interesting to find out whether any other profession shares this characteristic. The military are a problematic example, because their behavior is dichotomized depending on whether they are acting in the context of peace or in the state of war. They are relatively inactive in peacetime and overactive in war.

Criminal investigation is the least researched part of low policing. It should be a testing ground for the hypothesis that police work is information processing and knowledge work. The results of testing the knowledge work hypothesis are mixed. In policing research, the word "knowledge" is used without a precise definition and encompasses both true statements and uncertain beliefs whose truth value is not taken into account. Epistemologists distinguish between three kinds of knowledge, according to their respective source and scientific value: hearsay, inductive-empirical knowledge, and theoretical-deductive knowledge. Hearsay or second-hand knowledge is rated as the lowest form of knowledge (many epistemologists do not recognize hearsay as knowledge at all). Although hearsay is the lowest kind of knowledge, we saw in chapter 6 that is was the most potent factor in solving a criminal case. Criminal investigation is traditionally understood as the identification and location (arrest) of criminal perpetrators. Identifying and locating a suspect is almost always the result of the testimony of a witness or an informant, which is technically hearsay and second-hand knowledge from the standpoint of the police investigator. Witnesses being often wrong, the police try very hard to get a confession from a suspect, a process that has much more to do with psychological acumen than with information processing. With cleared cases being solved in a matter of hours, detectives are not given the occasion to trigger the information process. The investigations that are the most information-intensive are unsolved inquiries that adduce vast amounts of inconclusive information.

There is a third segment of investigation, however, which has attracted even less attention than the first two (identification and location). It is what might be called the "conviction investigation," where the detectives bring together all the elements of proof that will secure a court conviction or a plea of guilty. Getting a suspect to plead guilty is a negotiation rather than an information-gathering process. However, putting together a winning case for the prosecution is a painstaking process in high-profile trials (homicide, organized crime, terrorism). In today's highly technical courtroom environment, this process can assume great complexity and requires experience and skill in processing information. It is thus during criminal trials that the knowledge work hypothesis best fits the facts. This statement must, however, be qualified. As noted by many jurists, the kind of logic that prevails in judicial proceedings is quite different from the logic of science.

Private investigation is a topic that is even less researched than the work of public detectives. Nevertheless, two conclusions can be drawn at this stage. With one exception, it does seem that cooperation between public and private investigators is very limited. There was no trace of it in my own research on homicide investigation. The research literature on investigation is almost silent on this subject. The exception that was just referred to is, however, quite notable and concerns economic crime. The public police readily admit that their competence in forensic accounting is almost nonexistent. Private firms such as Deloitte and Touche, Kroll, and others are called in the fill the gap. There does not yet seem to be a great deal of active cooperation; private and public investigators seldom conduct a joint investigation into suspicious accounting.

Private investigators proceed to examine the books of an individual or a firm suspected of wrongdoing, and the result of the examination is then passed on to the public police for the purposes of a potential prosecution.

Although there is little actual cooperation between public and private investigators, there is a great deal of contact between uniformed police and detectives. The rule that governs their contacts is the following: the quicker that a case is resolved, the greater the role of the uniformed patrol. This rule even applies, as was seen, in the case of homicide inquiries, where detectives often limit their role to taking delivery of suspects already arrested in quasi-flagrante delicto by the patrolmen called to the scene of the crime. In chapter 5, we repeatedly confronted the difficulty of determining with some degree of precision what it was that the uniformed police did. When this question is asked of the joint operation of uniformed police and investigators, a partial answer can at least be given: they feed the criminal courts and indirectly fill the prisons. With respect to countries such as the United States, which has less than 5 percent of the world's population and 25 percent of its prisoners, this is no small undertaking. The linkages between the police and the other components of the criminal justice system are very much understudied.

A great deal of effort was devoted to establishing the connections of high policing with other kinds of policing such as low criminal policing and private security. High policing does not only refer to a type of organization but also to a way of doing policing, which is practiced in various degrees by all large policing organizations, whether public and private. There are organizations such as the security and intelligence services that are entirely devoted to high policing. There are also traditional urban police departments, such as the NYPD, which has developed a large intelligence unit, posting officers in various other countries following the 9/11 attacks. Such a municipal unit may be as efficient as the FBI special section that is devoted to protecting U.S. national security.

Among the nine features of high policing listed in the book there are two deserving of further comment. The use of infiltration and police informants on a regular basis is one of the oldest tactics of high policing. All policing organizations use informants and to this extent are practicing high policing. However, the practice of using informants may spread well beyond policing organizations. Following high-profile cases of whistle-blowing, government agencies and private corporations are putting into operation several mechanisms through which denunciators will be able to report illegal or reprehensible practices within an organization. It is too soon to assess whether this social institutionalization of informing will have more beneficial effects than it has had under undemocratic political regimes that encouraged the denunciation of unorthodox behavior. In view of past experience that took a turn for the worse in these countries, this extension of high policing practices to civil society in democratic countries needs to be closely monitored.

The second feature of high policing that should be further considered is what was previously called the conflation of executive, judicial, and legislative powers. This conflation of powers generally takes the form of a concentration of all powers into the hands of the executive. Far from being an academic construct that has significance only for historical studies of repressive and totalitarian political regimes, the concentration of power in the hands of the executive heralds a passage to the dark side, such as was experienced during the George W. Bush administration. Places such as Guantanamo, Abu Ghraib, and the black sites where suspects disappeared after "rendition" were all created and administered by high policing officials (such as the CIA, with the support of a few serviceable legal advisers), who acted under a veil of secrecy as police, jail-keepers, tormentors, judges, and covert legislators running an executive decree factory.

The broader issue raised by high policing is that developing an adequate theory of policing cannot avoid tapping the resources of political science. The measures that are currently taken against network crime such as terrorism and organized crime cannot be reduced to a set of toolkits and best practices, as provided, for example, by situational prevention. With a certain amount of doggedness, it may still be possible to argue that the wall being built in Israel, allegedly to fend off suicide bombers, is just another situational prevention device, albeit developed on a massive scale. It is more heuristic to view it as a political measure that is taking us back years to former apartheid times and walls dividing countries.

Our extensive review of the research literature and field work on private security leads to the following conclusion. The present state of empirical research does not warrant the kind of vast conclusions that have been derived from it. To a large extent, empirical research is still focused on a discussion of the significance of the basic figures, such as an estimation of the number of people employed by the private security industry, the kind of products and services offered, and the turnover of the industry, often presented in relation to the various sectors of production. The estimation of private security personnel is inconsistent and displays a marked tendency to overestimate the size of the private security personnel and to underestimate the number of public police. Furthermore, little critical judgment is used on what is being counted. For instance, the large state militia of the former Eastern-bloc countries that were privatized over a very short period of time, and that operate no differently under their new private regime than they did when they were state militia, are counted among the private security staff just as if they were members of the

Pinkerton, Wells Fargo, and Burns agencies. The research on the industry's turnover is at best speculative, since it relies on the figures released by the industry.

The very few empirical studies that focus on what private uniformed security personnel actually did concluded that there was no marked difference between their ways of operating and those of the public police. This conclusion should be taken with caution because of the small number of studies. According to an argument propounded in chapter 8 (figure 8.1), the biggest difference between public policing and private security is that the former has an incomparably stronger link to a system of criminal justice. Although there are private justice initiatives sprinkled here and there in diverse countries, there is presently nothing that is remotely equivalent to the public criminal justice system and that can compensate in any significant way for the current wave of mass incarceration. As a whole, private justice essentially functions by default, in dropping charges against a high number of persons who could be prosecuted for petty offences, thus further clogging the public courts, which are already overwhelmed by the number of cases they have to process.

To the extent that policing is not an activity that is performed independently of the other components of the criminal justice system, the increase of private security personnel has had little impact on penal justice. As has just been said, mass incarceration keeps growing, the penal system being fed by the public police with little assistance from private security in either feeding the system or diverting people from it. The developments in security technology are much more portentous than the increases in private security personnel. The integration of all risk management in one encompassing system geared to the prevention of fire, natural disasters, and crime is progressing at a fast pace. For instance, 9-1-1 calling systems process all kinds of emergency. This technological integration is not paralleled by an attendant coordination of the various personnel involved in risk management. With few exceptions, generally occurring in small communities, firemen, police, and ambulance all constitute separate personnel.

The hypothesis of the existence of a police-industrial complex proposed in this book requires, needless to say, a great deal of empirical confirmation. Chapter 8 could have focused on surveillance technology rather than on intermediate weapons, such as the Taser gun. Being a developing market that is much smaller than surveillance technology, the marketing of Taser guns exhibits in a more conspicuous way the workings of a police-industrial complex. In addition to the illustrations given in chapter 8, the unabashed lobbying of Taser International toward police chiefs and police union leaders, including financial contributions to their annual conventions, shows all the signs of an alliance between public practitioners and private providers of technology. The final reason for focusing on security technology is that it displays one of the most basic features of policing, which has always evolved in uncontrolled—"ungoverned"—ways with unforeseen side effects.

David Matza coined the expression "the evil causes evil fallacy" to lambaste the belief that all causes of delinquency had to be as evil as the criminal effects that they generated. In a similar way, the expression "the goodness causes goodness fallacy" might also be coined to rebuke the belief that beneficial effects can only accrue to the actions of virtuous people. However critical we may be of the work of Gambetta and his disciples, it must be admitted that criminal organizations are actually involved in the business of private protection, and that not all the kinds of protection that they are providing are tantamount to criminal extortion. In other words, their protection can be genuine. This is one of the points that were made in the last chapter of this book. There is another issue that was raised, which is closer to the heart of policing and which should be highlighted. It is the controversial issue of "policing by consent."

Military policing, as discussed in chapter 9, sheds some light on this issue. Two kinds of military (or militarized) policing were contrasted. First, military policing as practiced by big policing organizations operating in continental Europe, which contributes significantly to the life of democracy in these countries, was discussed. Second, paramilitary policing as it is practiced in many emergent countries and particularly in Latin America was also considered. Not only does the latter make little contribution to democracy, it is most often the offspring of the abolition of democracy. There are numerous differences between military and paramilitary policing besides whether or not they are compatible with democracy. The most conspicuous one is the very high number of casualties that result from paramilitary policing and attendant death squads. No less important, and more significant for our purposes, is the quite substantial number of casualties taken by the paramilitary forces themselves. It is the comparatively high number of casualties suffered by paramilitary policing forces that takes us to the heart of the problem of policing by consent.

There are two different notions of policing by consent. The first one is embedded in a mythical history of British policing, rightly criticized by Robert Reiner, Clive Emsley, and many other British scholars. The main elements of this notion of policing by consent are the limited powers of the police (for instance, they did not carry firearms), the fact that their defining status is as citizens rather than as professional police and, above all, the consistently high rates of approval that they enjoyed in the 1950s and the following decade. British bobbies were as much part of the British national identity as the RCMP still are in Canada. All this is claimed to be gone to a large extent in the United

Kingdom. At least one thing is indisputable: the rates of approval for the police have fallen dramatically in Britain, particularly among the disenfranchised youths and the ethnic minorities.

The second notion of policing by consent goes much deeper. Its foundation is the general consent of the citizenry not to violently resist policing. The police can operate only in a territory that has been previously pacified, generally by the military. They are not an instrument of pacification, but of peacekeeping. This is the reason why the paramilitary policing model that we described has slipped into a war as opposed to a policing paradigm. The most ominous sign of the failure of a policing apparatus is when, first, it encounters systematic armed resistance, and second, the police are attacked and ambushed in the context of an offensive against them, rather than as a defensive move by criminals wanting to avoid being arrested. In this second sense of the expression, the consent of a community to be policed is the sine qua non condition of policing.

Another question remains, among many others. What is the degree of coordination prevailing among the components of the policing apparatus that were the focus of this book? Different kinds of vocabularies can be used to refer to this apparatus. The first, which comprises words such as "assemblage," "mosaic," or "quilt," does not prejudge the issue of coordination. The other kind of vocabulary is premised on words such as "network" (the master word), "system," or "linkages." It cannot be disputed that some of the various parts of the police assemblage act at times as locally integrated networks, where the public police almost always perform the coordinating functions. The key objection to using the vocabulary of integration instead of the more neutral vocabulary of aggregation to talk about policing, however, is that the former wording presumes that the problem of policing coordination has been resolved and that we have entered into an era of police fusion. This is a grievous mistake. There is not one study of the joint performance of some of the components of the police assemblage that have not concluded that the sharing of information and the coordination of action were severely lacking. In all fairness, it must be said that these studies focused on crises that spun out of control. There may have been successful police large-scale interventions—in the case of natural disasters or the undisclosed success in preventing a terrorist attack—that were not sufficiently documented or that were not made public. In any case, the establishment of working policing networks is a task that is standing before us rather than behind us.

Appendix
A Sample of Policy Implications

The purpose of this book is to increase the body of knowledge on policing rather than to develop policy recommendations. To use a well-known distinction initially drawn by Banton (1964), it is more of a work *on* the police than *for* the police. As was emphasized in the introduction and in chapter 5, one of the motivations behind the writing of the book in its present form was the realization that most of the research on policing focused on the police working in uniform. Another concern also played a significant role. The desire to reform the police, which spurred the drive toward community policing and like-minded initiatives, also generated a considerable imbalance between policy-oriented studies and research that was pursued for the sake of knowledge. Policy-oriented studies increasingly outnumbered theoretical publications. By simply knowing what works without knowing why, however, evaluative research on policing ended up in its quest for successful experiments being able only to provide an expansive set of ambiguous proposals that increased the fragmentation of police action. Many of the proposed reforms were implemented top down and built on a narrow basis of knowledge. For instance, whether police culture, which favors action over communication, would be welcoming to policies that aim to promote a dialogue between the police and the citizens was not examined in any methodical way. After some twenty years of community policing, Zhao and Thurman (1997) have shown that the type of duties which the policing rank and file considered as having priority were far from reflecting the priorities embedded in community-oriented and problem-solving policing, the fascination with crime-fighting and law enforcement being as strong as ever for the police. This book was written with a view to making a contribution to redressing the imbalance between practice and theory, which has so far largely favored more practical concerns.

It must be stressed that there is no conflict between research on and for the police and between theory and practice. Not only are they fully compatible, they complement each other. I did not believe that it was necessary either to add one more policy-oriented study to the large body of literature or to review this literature that keeps reviewing itself more than competently. I am, however, convinced that there are numerous policy implications that flow from this book. In order to support this claim, I will briefly outline some practical recommendations that can be derived from each of the chapters of the book.

Chapter 1 draws a tentative map of policing in its current diversity. This map is a theoretical one in the sense that it tries to account for the full scope of policing in all Western-like countries taken as a whole. Needless to say, no single country exhibits the full range of the policing repertory. Countries differ widely in the knowledge that they have of the police organizations operating in their territory. The U.S. Bureau of Justice statistics has collected national statistics and gives a precise estimate of the number of public state and local police forces: their number in 2004 was 17,876. Canada has no national estimate of its number of public police forces, but by combining various sources, we can estimate that there are approximately 220 Canadian police forces; the data on private security are too sketchy to be used. With the growing number of agencies of all kinds involved in policing, *there is an urgent need for states to have a clear picture of who is engaged in policing activities in their respective territory; government measures should be taken to fill this need.* This is the baseline from which the "governance of security" should proceed. Certain areas—for instance, in-house private security—are terrae incognitae, which should be explored in depth. Until this is done, large corporations are, to all practical purposes, policing themselves.

Chapter 2 presents an outline of the history of policing. For the purposes of policy making, the history of public policing can be divided into two periods. The first extended roughly from the creation of the French police in 1667 to the 1829 reinvention of the police in England. For France—and, soon, throughout continental Europe—the police was to embody, in a perceptible and constant manner, the abstract notion of public governance, considered in its full breadth. The conception of policemen as the prime agents of internal governance was narrowed by the British in 1829 to the provision of security, defined as the prevention of crime and disorder and as law enforcement. This curtailment of the police mandate was later adopted by nearly all Western countries, including France, and it generated a paradoxical situation. In law and in public representations, the police was considered as a law enforcement and crime-fighting organization. In fact, the police officers deployed in the field were still called upon to act as general agents of governance, confronted with a huge diversity of situations.

Contemporary reforms of policing, such as problem-oriented policing, have sought to bridge the gap between the single-focused legal definition of the police mandate and the multi focused policing activities actually taking place in society. Little consideration was given to police history by the reformers. Yet, the evolving historical context of policing has molded the collective expectations and attitudes toward policing and thus has an effect in determining how wide "the window of opportunity" to reform the police really is. Despite repeated efforts, contemporary reformers never succeeded in convincing either the police rank and file or the public that crime fighting should not be the only priority of policing organizations. The practical implication of this discussion is that *policy making with respect to policing should be based on a more comprehensive appreciation of the whole context of policing.* Such context-driven policy making should assess the various factors that constrain the possibility of introducing enduring change into policing organizations. The weight of the historical context and of traditions is not the only constraining factor, but it certainly is one of them. Most of the problems that affect policing today originated very early in its history.

Chapter 3 focused on the content of the images and representations of policing and on the overwhelming influence that they have on public opinion. The nature of these representations should certainly be taken into account, along with historical factors in developing context-sensitive policies. It should be noted that the fixation of policing legislation and of police literature on criminal matters developed concurrently after the refocusing of the police mandate on crime in nineteenth-century England. There are two pressing issues that stem from giving representations of policing overdue importance.

The first concerns police organizations as such. Although the bigger policing agencies have developed guidelines for dealing with the media, these efforts are still in their infancy. The majority of policing organizations have no explicit policies in this respect and no specialized personnel to handle communications with the press and the general public. Even when they have trained personnel to apply media guidelines, the relationships with the press seem to be guided by improvization in the course of critical incidents and confused with manipulative public relations operations when there is time to stage them (for instance, media shots of police surrounded by a careful display of seized weapons and drugs). *Policing agencies should refrain from treating the management of police images in all their aspects as a sideshow and develop guidelines that are both explicit and focused on providing valid knowledge rather than self-serving (dis)information.*

The second issue is broader and relates to the making of crime legislation. The scourge of policy making is to enact legislation on the basis of the single overdramatized case—such cases make up what were called intensive quantities in chapter 1. However tragic were the murders of James Bulger in 1993 and of Holly Wells and Jessica Chapman in 2002, they were the catalysts of disproportionate measures that are bringing the United Kingdom closer to a much-feared Orwellian "surveillance society." After the abduction and murder of James Bulger by two ten-year-old boys, the state lost control over the multiplication of surveillance cameras in public space, which now number some 14 million units. The murder of two schoolgirls—Wells and Chapman—by Ian Kevin Huntley, who had been hired as a caretaker in the local school, triggered legislation that may result in developing a security file on all persons involved in one form or another of child caretaking. Their number has been estimated to be in excess of 11 million individuals. Needless to say, *intensive quantities should be balanced against robust statistical data in drawing criminal law policies.*

Chapter 4 defined the police by its power to use means that are prohibited as being legal violations for other members of society. The immediate policy recommendation implied by this definition is that policing organizations and their staff should be made accountable for their use of these powers. Such a recommendation may appear trivial with regard to public constabularies, which have been submitted to several accountability requirements since their creation. For instance, most public police officers in Western-like democracies must account for every shot that they fire through their service weapon. One of the key points made in this book, however, is that the scope of policing extends far beyond public constabularies and encompasses a growing number of agencies. When this is realized, the issue of accountability becomes much more problematic. For instance, we have very little idea of the extent to which high policing organizations are accountable when they engage in the protection of national security and in counterterrorism. The explanation for our present ignorance is quite simple: almost everything that concerns high policing agencies—including how they account for themselves and what they disclose to the persons who have the legal authority to oversee their activities—is protected by state secrecy. Private security provides an even broader example of weak and questionable accountability. Although private security personnel exercise de facto wide policing powers, they operate in a near vacuum with respect to accountability. A few states have moved to supervising in minimal way contract security agencies by creating official boards on which the majority of members come from the private security industry itself. *There is a pressing need to adapt the structure of policing accountability to the present proliferation of policing agencies.*

Chapter 5 is in part devoted to showing that uniformed patrolpersons are operating within a circle of visible appearances. They increase security and feelings of reassurance through their own visibility; when they are being proactive, they are spurred to action by perceiving visual signs—such as people running on the street—which indicate that a dangerous incident may be in the making. This suggests a number of recommendations.

First, after extensive review of the literature on what the police are actually doing, it was concluded that uniformed police devoted between one-third and one-half on their time to crime control and law enforcement. One question that is almost never raised, however, is whether or not these figures reflect what can be actually seen by the police and by the citizens who called them. Is the low involvement of patrols in crime control due to the fact they neglect to respond to criminal incidents occurring in plain view, or is it due to the fact that crime hides itself from the eyes of the police? Most incidents that are openly perceptible in the course of patrolling the streets represent instances of disorder and breaches of the peace rather than crime events. A review of what kinds of incidents are perceptible to the police on patrol should be made and the priorities of patrol work should be reassessed in relation to what types of threatening incidents can be identified by the police on the basis of their reliance on visual scans of the environment.

Second, reacting to visible clues is basically to pick up on things that stand out from the habitually perceived environment (for instance, a lone child crying in a shopping mall). Radars reflect only what stands out from the ordinary on their screen. Hence, groups standing in visual contrast with the dress and demeanor of the majority are more vulnerable to being profiled by the police— ethnoracial minorities are actually called "visible minorities" in Canada. As Reiner (2000a) argued, racial discrimination takes many forms, which, brought together, permeate all policing. Similarly, this book argues that profiling people on the basis of their visible appearance is a built-in feature of the job of policing the streets—scanning the environment in search of suspicious things. *It follows that the policies directed against racial profiling should rely on a much deeper understanding of how the police actually perform their duties and should not be limited to drawing an abstract line between (good) criminal profiling and (bad) racial profiling without addressing how this demarcation can in fact be made in policing practice.*

Third, criminals who are resisting arrest when caught in the process of perpetrating a violent crime are in fact reacting against a police threat to them. If a policing team had not interfered with the perpetration of a crime, there would have been no open conflict between the police and the criminals they happened to have caught red-handed. This is why resisting arrest and other reactive violent behavior against the police do not provide as such the indication of a breakdown in the social consent to be policed (unless they multiply and become the general rule, as it seems the case in countries like Brazil and Mexico). However, *attacks against the police which are initiated by individuals or groups acting as if they were at war with the forces of order do indicate (the beginning of) a breakdown in the acceptance of policing. The occurrence of such incidents should be closely monitored.* As statistics recording assaults against the police are notably unreliable, the monitoring that we are proposing should be a joint endeavor by the police and civilian authorities.

Finally, the research on the feminization of the police has focused on the capacity of women to be recognized as equals in a culture that prizes masculine values. Police administrators have been sensitized to this problem. There are, however, a significant number of more concrete issues—intermarriage between police persons, parental leave, sexual harassment, handling situations that involve the use of violence, pressures for being armed with intermediate weapons—that urgently require policy answers. *Few police organizations have developed the full range of necessary policies in this respect; they should conduct a thorough study of the implications of recruiting a large number of women as peace officers in order to articulate adequate policies on this matter.*

Chapter 6 presents a typology of criminal inquiries; it emphasizes the role of investigators in putting together the evidence to be presented in court; and it presents data showing that most homicide cases are cleared in a very short time by intervening patrol persons who make an arrest and deliver the suspect(s) to the criminal investigators dispatched to the scene. The work of criminal investigators was critically assessed by Greenwood et al. (1975 and 1977) and subsequent researchers, who made a large number of policy recommendations. The recommendations formulated here follow the analyses pursued in chapter 6. Before making these recommendations, it should be stressed that in a great number of police forces, all recruits begin their career by working in uniform; a proportion of them are later promoted to detective with minimal training in investigation.

The first recommentation recognizes that despite the role of patrol persons in clearing up crime, the channels of communications between the police staff working in uniform and the criminal investigation department (CID) could be much more productive. The policing reforms inspired by community policing have actually increased the gap between patrol persons and criminal investigators. *Police forces should develop flexible mechanisms to feed the various detective squads with the relevant information from the patrols working the streets. CID commanders should also make their information needs known throughout the force.*

Second, a basic distinction was made between whodunit and what-is-it investigations. The purpose of a whodunit investigation is to find the perpetrator(s) of a reported crime. In contrast, a what-is-it investigation starts with an identified suspect whose behavior in specific circumstances is questionable, and aims to determine whether that person should be criminally prosecuted. Most investigations are viewed by the public and policy makers as whodunit investigations. However, recent developments such as cyber-deviance, corporate practices detrimental to the environment, and high-profile economic crime will lead to an increase of what-is-it inquiries, particularly in the field of white-collar crime. This type of investigation is often conducted in continental Europe by magistrates—*juges d'instruction*—who have the expertise to pursue them successfully (this judicial function will apparently be abolished in the years to come). *Everything indicates that the implication of the police in what-is-it investigations will grow. They need to be properly trained and to be teamed up with private experts—for instance, forensic accountants.* At the present time, the new types of crime are well beyond the knowledge of most detectives. This lack of expertise leads them to ask constantly for new legislative "tools" to enable them to perform their duties, when the real cause of their difficulties is their inability to use the legal instruments already available to them.

Finally, there is another field where detectives are in need of more training. According to our findings, homicide detectives could be described as criminal evidence managers for the purpose of securing a legal conviction. This description also applies to detectives in charge of wide-ranging investigations into organized crime. The complexity of managing courtroom evidence has grown exponentially. In some cases involving several defendants, the evidence is stored on CDs containing millions of pages. If one takes seriously the role of detectives as criminal evidence managers, they need to be trained in the use of all the new instruments to collate and present information.

Chapter 7 is devoted to high policing. Its content is difficult to summarize, as it tries to break new ground in introducing and discussing the concept of high policing. A recommendation to extend to the whole police web the accountability requirements to which low public policing is already submitted was already made with respect to the content of chapter 4. High (political) policing was defined through its specific features in chapter 7.

Among these features, there is one which is of paramount importance. It is what we called the conflation of executive, judicial, and legislative powers for the benefit of the high policing apparatus in its struggle against particular kinds of threats, such as terrorism and political dissidence. Such a conflation of powers was at times achieved on a massive scale—for instance, in Nazi Germany and Soviet Russia—and resulted in the enduring establishment of a police state with murderous results. On a much narrower but still significant scale, some counterterrorist policies articulated by the George W. Bush administration after 9/11 seemed to rest on a conflation of different powers: arrested persons were given a fabricated legal status—"illegal enemy combatant"—that deprived them of their rights and justified extraterritorial rendition and other excessive repressive measures; executive orders sentenced arrested suspects to indefinite terms of incarceration without trial; an occult quasi legislation on the definition and the use of torture drawn by the president's legal advisers authorized the covert reinstitutionalization of torture. All supporters of democratic policing should be on the watch for attempts to bring together executive, judicial, and legislative powers (government by executive decree). *If the checks and balances mechanisms already embedded in government fail to prevent such a concentration of power, a special watchdog body should be created to signal and, if necessary, to refer actions threatening democratic values to the courts.*

Second, the concrete hallmark of high policing is the resort to preventive detention. Proposals are regularly made in various democratic countries for the passage of a preventive detention statute against terrorists (for a recent example in the United States, see Farmer, 2009). These proposals make the point that such statutes already exist for indefinitely incarcerating sexual predators with a demonstrated proclivity toward violent behavior. The passage of such statutes in the field of high policing has almost nothing in common with the enactment of these statutes when they are to be applied to common criminals. Demonstrating a proclivity toward violent sexual behavior on the basis of repeated offences is completely different from demonstrating a proclivity toward terrorism in the case of individuals without any criminal record and who were prevented by the police from perpetrating their first attack. Consequently, *the conditions to be met for institutionalizing preventive detention should be kept separate from the justifications needed for the extended preventive custody of common criminals.*

Finally, as the police keep reminding us, the key to the prevention of terrorism is the infiltration of terrorist cells by informants and police undercover operatives. A review of past cases where terrorist acts were allegedly prevented reveals that police infiltrators often played an active role in the preparation of an attack, at times recruiting the potential terrorists, spurring them to action, and even providing them with fake explosives. In such cases, *the line between entrapment and prevention is very thin, and guidelines for police informants and undercover operatives should be developed to prevent them from crossing this line.*

Chapter 8 attempts to cover the broad field of private security. With very few exceptions, most studies on private security are conducted from the outside and basically try to assess the growth and the scope of private security, and to provide explanations for its increase. Such an external standpoint makes it difficult to formulate proposals for reform.

Recommendations on private security have already been made in relation to previous chapters. It was proposed that the state of government knowledge on how many and what kind of private security agencies were operating in a country should be greatly improved, particularly in respect to in-house agencies. It was also claimed that *there is a pressing need to adapt the structure of policing accountability to the present proliferation of policing agencies.* This recommendation applies especially to private security agencies, which are one of the fastest developing components of the policing web. Among private security agencies, small agencies and, particularly, small investigative agencies should be submitted to much more accountability.

In the same way that we should acknowledge the fact of plural policing in all its implications, however, we should also question the assumption that accountability is essentially an exercise in the supervision of police behavior. Consistent with the assertion that technology has the greatest potential to transform policing, all policing organizations should account publicly for their policies in acquiring technology. *The potential of policing and surveillance technology to change the nature of policing is so great that special government boards should be created to grant or to refuse the authorization to acquire such technology.* This requirement should be made stringent in the case of the acquisition of so-called "intermediate weapons" and pain-inducing technology. The private corporations selling these harmful contraptions use an extremely aggressive marketing strategy. If the police are excepted from the obligation to account in a public forum for their decisions to fit their staff with such devices, pain-inducing technologies will creep in, as unchecked as the exponential proliferation of surveillance cameras was.

Finally, there is one proposal that would be applied internally by private security agencies that needs to be be made, despite the acknowledged difficulty of implementing it. Private security agencies are not ordinary businesses, because they exercise powers that may violate the basic rights of citizens. *In the same way that members of some professions are sworn to confidentiality or to other obligations, all members of private security agencies should take an oath to respect the constitutional rights of citizens, as expressed in the country where they are conducting their business*—such as the Constitution, a Charter or Bill of Rights, and so forth. One of the practical obstacles to such a proposal is the high turnover in the personnel recruited to fill guard and patrol duties. It might indeed be argued that an agency will have to keep on swearing in new incoming personnel. This obstacle can be circumvented if the staff turnover is not too high. If it proved to be too high, this very finding would justify by itself having attempted to implement a swearing-in procedure.

Chapter 9 explores the edges of policing such as military and paramilitary policing and delinquent social control. Violent military and paramilitary policing of the kind that is practiced in Brazil and other emergent countries often stems from police corruption, to which it is considered an alternative. *One of the ways to avoid resorting to such drastic answers is to develop policies against police corruption, which blend a repressive approach with systemic measures, such as affording the police a decent salary.*

Delinquent social control fills the vacuum left by the failure of the state to provide security and order in areas that have been deserted by the police. *The antidote to delinquent social control is to reclaim the abandoned territories.* In the present context of the reinvention on a massive scale of ethnic ghettoes filled with legal and illegal immigrants, reclaiming these increasingly forbidden territories is a complex enterprise that involves much more that the occasional exercise in saturation policing, and should comprise actions taken on the social and economic levels.

This appendix has presented some of the policy implications of the analyses conducted throughout this book. They are meant to be an answer to criticism claiming that the preceding chapters are devoid of policy implications. It is important to stress that the proposals made above are only a sample of what can concretely be done with this book, and that they also suggest that this sample could easily be expanded.

Bibliography

An Act for Improving the Police in and near the Metropolis. 1829. 10 Geo. 4. c. 44. *The Statutes.* Revised, third edition, Vol. 3. www.statutelaw.gov.uk.

Ainsworth, Peter B. 2001. *Offender Profiling and Crime Analysis.* Cullompton, Devon: Willan.

Alex, Nicholas. 1969. *Black in Blue: A Study of the Negro Policeman.* New York: Appleton-Century-Crofts.

Alexander, James I. 1978. *Blue Coats: Black Skin: The Black Experience in the New York City Police Department since 1891.* Hickville, N.Y.: Exposition Press.

Allen, Mary Sophia. 1925. *The Pioneer Police Women.* London: Chatto and Windus.

Altheide, David L. 2002. *Creating Fear: News and the Construction of Crisis.* New York: Aldine de Gruyter.

Amis, Martin. 2002. *Koba the Dread: Laughter and the Twenty Million.* Toronto: Alfred A. Knopf.

Amnesty International. 2004. "USA: Excessive and Lethal Force? Amnesty International's Concerns about Deaths and Ill-Treatment Involving Police Use of Tasers." www.amnesty.org/en/library/info/AMR51/139/2004.

Anderson, Malcolm. 1989. *Policing the World: Interpol and the Politics of International Police Cooperation.* Oxford: Clarendon.

Anderson, Malcom, Monica den Boer, Peter Cullen, William C. Gilmore, Charles D. Raab, and Neil Walker. 1995. *Policing the European Union.* Oxford: Clarendon.

Andrew, Alexandra, Deane-Peter Baker, and Marina Caparini, eds. 2008. *Private Military and Security Companies: Ethics, Policies and Civil-Military Relations.* London: Routledge.

Andrieux, Louis. 1885. *Souvenir d'un préfet de police.* 2 vols. Paris: Jules Rouff.

Antunes, George, and Eric J. Scott. 1981. "Calling the Cops: Police Telephone Operators and Citizens Calls for Service." *Journal of Criminal Justice* 9 (2):165–180.

Argenson (d'), René. 1866. *Notes intéressantes pour l'histoire des mœurs et de la police à Paris à la fin du règne de Louis XIV*, published by Lorédan Larchey and E. Mabille. Paris: Frédéric Henry.

Arike, Ando. 2010. "The Soft-Kill Solution. New Frontiers in Pain Compliance." *Harper's* 38–47, March.

Ascoli, David. 1979. *The Queen's Peace: The Origins and Development of the Metropolitan Police, 1829–1979*. London: Hamish Hamilton.

Bahn, Charles. 1974. "The Reassurance Factor in Police Patrol." *Criminology* 12(3): 338–345.

Baker, Al. 2008. "Tasers Get a More Prominent Role in Crime Fighting in New York." *New York Times*, June 15, 24.

Bamford, James. 1982. *The Puzzle Palace: A Report on NSA, America's Most Secret Agency*. New York: Houghton Mifflin.

———. 2001. *Body of Secrets*. New York: Doubleday.

Banks, Anna, and Stephen B. Banks, eds. 1998. *Fiction and Social Research: By Ice or Fire*. Walnut Creek, Cal.: Altamira.

Banton, Michael. 1964. *The Policeman in the Community*. London: Tavistock.

Bauer, Alain, ed. 2007. *La criminalité en France: rapport de l'Observatoire national de la délinquance 2007*. Paris: CNRS Éditions.

Bayley, David. 1983a. *Encyclopedia of Crime and Justice*. Edited by Stanford H. Kadish. New York: Free Press.

———1983b. "The Police and Political Order in India." *Asian Survey* 23(4): 484–496.

———. 1985. *Patterns of Policing*. New Brunswick: Rutgers University Press.

———. 1991. *Forces of Order: Policing Modern Japan*. Berkeley: University of California Press.

———. 1994. *Police for the Future*. New York: Oxford University Press.

———, ed. 1998. *What Works in Policing*. New York: Oxford University Press.

Bayley, David, and James Garofalo. 1989. "The Management of Violence by Police Patrol Officers." *Criminology* 27(1):1–25.

Bayley, David, and Clifford Shearing. 1996. "The Future of Policing." *Law and Society Review* 30(3):585–606.

———. 2001. *The New Structure of Policing: Description, Conceptualization and Research Agenda*. Washington, D.C.: U.S. Department of Justice. Office of Justice Programs, National Institute of Justice.

Bayley, David, and David Weisburd. 2009. "Cops and Spooks: The Role of Police in Counterterrorism." In *To Protect and To Serve: Policing in an Age of Terrorism*, edited by D. Weisburd, Th. E. Feucht, I. Hakimi, L. F. Mock, and S. Perry, 81–99. New York: Springer Verlag.

Beattie, John M. 1986. *Crime and the Courts in England, 1660–1800*. Princeton: Princeton University Press.

———. 2001. *Policing and Punishment in London, 1660–1750: Urban Crime and the Limits of Terror*. Oxford: Clarendon Press.

Bell, Ian. 2003. "Eighteenth-Century Crime Writing." In *The Cambridge Companion to Crime Fiction*, edited by M. Priestman, 7–17. Cambridge: Cambridge University Press.

Benjamin, Walter. 1972. "Kriminalromane auf Reisen." In *Schriften*, 381–383. Frankfurt am Main: Suhrkampf.

Bennett, Trevor, and Ruth Lupton. 1992. "A National Activity Survey of Police Work." *Howard Journal* 31(3):200–23.

Bennett, Wayne, and Karen M. Hess. 2001. *Criminal Investigation*. Sixth edition. Belmont, Cal.: Wadsworth, Thomson Learning.

Bennett Williams, Amy. 2008. "Tomato Pickers Feeling Spied On." www.news-press .com.

Bentham, Jeremy. 1821. "Constitutional Code." In *The Works of Jeremy Bentham*, edited by J. B. Bowring, vol. 9. Edinburgh, 1843.

———. 1996. *The Collected Works of Jeremy Bentham: An Introduction to the Principles of Morals and Legislation*, edited by J. H. Burns and H.L.A. Hart. Oxford: Clarendon.

Bercal, Thomas. 1970. "Calls for Police Assistance: Consumer Demands for Government Service." In *Police in Urban Society*, edited by H. Hahn, 267–277. Beverley Hills, Cal.: Sage.

Bigo, Didier. 1996. *Polices en réseaux: l'expérience européenne*. Paris: Presses de Sciences Po.

———. 2000. *Border Regimes and Security in an Enlarged European Community Police. Cooperation with CECCs: Between Trust and Obligation*. San Domenico, Italy: European University Institute.

Billingsley, Roger, Teresa Nemitz, and Philip Bean, eds. 2001. *Informers: Policing, Policy, Practice*. Cullompton, Devon: Willan.

Bittner, Egon. 1970. *The Functions of Police in Modern Society*. Washington, D.C.: National Institute of Mental Health.

———. 1974. "Florence Nightingale in Pursuit of Willie Sutton: A Theory of the Police." In *The Potential for Reform of Criminal Justice*, edited by H. Jacob, 17–44. Beverly Hills, Cal.: Sage.

———. 1983. "Urban Police." In *Encyclopedia of Crime and Justice*. Vol. 3, edited by S. H. Kadish, 1135–1139. New York: Free Press.

———. 1990. *Aspects of Police Work*. Boston: Northeastern University Press.

———. 1991. "De la faculté d'user de la force comme fondement du rôle de la police." *Cahiers de la Sécurité Intérieure* 3:224–235.

———. 2007. *See* Brodeur 2007.

Black, Donald. 1968. "Police Encounters and Social Organizations: An Observation Study." PhD dissertation, Sociology, University of Michigan.

———. 1970. "The Social Organization of Arrest." *Stanford Law Review* 23:1087–1111.

———. 1976. *The Behavior of Law*. New York: Academic Press.

———. 1983. "Crime as Social Control." *American Sociological Review* 48:34–45.

———. 2004. "The Geometry of Terrorism." *Sociological Theory* 22(1):14–25.

Black, Donald, and Mary Pat Baumgartner. 1987. "On Self-Help in Modern Society." *Dialectical Anthropology* 2(1):33–44.

Bloch, Ernst. 1962. "Philosophische Ansicht des Detektivromans." In *Schriften*, 37–63. Frankfurt am Main: Suhrkampf.

Bondois, Paul-Martin. 1936. *Le Commissaire Nicolas Delamare et le "Traité de la Police."* Paris: Félix Alcan.

Bottom, Norman, and John Kostanoski. 1990. *Introduction to Security and Loss Control.* Englewood Cliffs, N.J.: Prentice Hall.

Boucher d'Argis. 1765. "Police." In Denis Diderot and Jean d'Alembert, *Encyclopédie ou dictionnaire raisonné des sciences, des arts et des métiers*, 12: 905. Neufchastel: Samuel Faulche.

Bourdier, Jean. 1996. *Histoire du roman policier.* Paris: Éditions de Fallois.

Bowcott, Owen. 2008. "CCTV Boom Has Failed to Slash Crime Say Police." *Guardian*, May 6.

Bowling, Ben, and J. Foster. 2002. "Policing and the Police." In *The Oxford Handbook of Criminal Justice*, edited by M. Maguire, R. Morgan, and R. Reiner, 980–1033. Oxford: Clarendon.

Bowling, Ben, and Coretta Philips. 2003. "Policing Ethnic Minority Communities." In *Handbook of Policing*, edited by T. Newburn, 128–155. Cullompton, Devon: Willan.

Box, Steven, Chris Hale, and Glen Andrews. 1988. "Explaining Fear of Crime." *British Journal of Criminology* 28(3):340–356.

Boydstun, John E., Michael Sherry, and Nicholas P. Moelter. 1977. *Patrol Staffing in San Diego: One- or Two-Officer Units.* Washington, D.C.: Police Foundation.

Braidwood, Thomas R. 2009. *Restoring Public Confidence: Restricting the Use of Conducted Energy Weapons in British Colombia.* Vancouver, B.C.: Braidwood Commission on Conducted Energy Weapons Use.

Bratton, William, and Peter Knobler. 1998. *Turnaround: How America's Top Cop Reversed the Crime Epidemic.* New York: Random House.

Breitel, Charles D. 1980. *Final Report of Special Master.* New York: Political Rights Defence Fund.

Brisson, Luc, and Jean-François Pradeau. 2006. "Introduction." In *Platon, Les Lois, Livres I à VI*, 7–57. Paris: GF Flammarion.

Brodeur, Jean-Paul. 1980. "La crise d'octobre et les commissions d'enquête." *Criminologie* 13:79–98.

———. 1983. "High and Low Policing: Remarks about the Policing of Political Activities." *Social Problems.* Thematic Issue on Justice (June), 30(5):507–520.

———. 1984a. *La délinquance de l'ordre: recherches sur les commissions d'enquête I.* Montréal: Hurtubise HMH.

———. 1984b. "La police: mythes et réalités." *Criminologie* 17:9–42.

———. 1994a. "Police et coercition." *Revue Française de Criminologie* 35:457–485.

———. 1994b. "Policing Appearances." *Journal of Human Justice* 5(2):58–83.

———. 1997a. *Violence and Racial Prejudice in the Context of Peacekeeping: A Study Prepared for the Commission of Inquiry into the Deployment of Canadian Forces in Somalia.* Ottawa: Minister of Public Works and Government Services Canada.

———. 1997b. "Parliamentary Oversight v. Independent Review." *Retfaerd* 78(3):13–42.

———. 2003. "Violence and the Police." In *International Handbook of Violence Research,* edited by Wilhem Heitmeyer and John Hagan, 207–226. London: Kluwer Academic Publishers.

———. 2004. "Expertise Not Wanted: The Case of the Criminal Law." In *Experts in Science and Society,* edited by E. Kurz-Milcke and G. Gigenrenzer, 123–158. New York: Plenum.

———. 2005a. "Cops and Spooks: The Uneasy Partnership." In *Policing: Key Readings,* edited by T. Newburn, 797–812. Portland, Ore.: Willan. Originally published in *Police Practice and Research. An International Journal* 1(3):299–321.

———. 2005b. *L'enquête policière.* Montréal: Presses de l'Université de Montréal.

———. 2007. "An Encounter with Egon Bittner." *Crime Law and Social Change* 48:105–132.

———. 2008. "The Royal Canadian Mounted Police and the Canadian Security Intelligence Service: A Comparison between Occupational and Organizational Cultures." Paper presented to the Commission of Inquiry into the Investigation of the Bombing of Air India Flight 182. Ottawa: Commission of Inquiry into the Investigation of the Bombing of Air India Flight 182. (The commission's report, with the commissioned studies, are forthcoming).

Brodeur, Jean-Paul, and Benoît Dupont. 2008. "Introductory Essay: The Role of Knowledge and Networks in Policing." In *The Handbbok of Knowledge-Based Policing: Current Conceptions and Future Directions,* edited by T. Williamson, 9–33. Chichester, West Sussex: John Wiley and Sons.

Brodeur, Jean-Paul, and Stéphane Leman-Langlois. 2006. "Surveillance Fiction or Higher Policing." In *The New Politics of Surveillance and Visibility,* edited by K. D. Haggerty and R. V. Ericson, 171–198. Toronto: University of Toronto Press.

Brodeur, Jean-Paul, and Dominique Monjardet, eds. 2003. *Connaître la police: grands textes de la recherche anglo-saxonne.* Cahiers de la sécurité intérieure. Paris: La Documentation Française.

Brooks, Tim, and Earle Marsh. 1995. *The Complete Directory to Prime Time Network and Cable T.V. Shows.* New York: Ballantine.

Browder, George C. 1975. "The SD: The Significance of Organization and Image." In *Police Forces in History,* edited by G. L. Mosse, 206–229. London: Sage.

Brown, David, and Susan Iles. 1985. "Community Constables: A Study of a Police Initiative." In *Policing Today,* edited by K. Heal, R. Tarling, and J. Burrows, 43–59. London: HMSO.

Brown, Jennifer, and Frances Heidensohn. 1996. "The Nature of Police Work and Women's Entry into Law Enforcement." In *Doing Justice, Doing Gender*, edited by S. E. Martin and N. C. Jurik, 51–76. Thousand Oaks, Cal.: Sage.

———. 2000. *Gender and Policing: Comparative Perspectives*. New York: Palgrave Macmillan.

Brundage, Anthony. 1988. *England's "Prussian Minister": Edwin Chadwick and the Politics of Government Growth, 1832–1854*. University Park: Pennsylvania University Press.

Bryett, Keith. 1996. "Privatization—Variation on a Theme." *Policing and Society* 6(1):23–37.

Buisson, Henry. 1950. *La police: son histoire*. Third edition. Preface by M. Juillard. Périgueux: Imprimerie Moderne.

Bunyan, Tony. 1976. *The History and Practice of the Political Police in Britain*. London: Julian Friedmann.

Burrows, John, and Roger Tarling. 1987. "The Investigation of Crime in England." *British Journal of Criminology* 27(3):229–251.

Button, Mark. 2002. *Private Policing*. Cullompton, Devon: Willan.

Cain, Maureen. 1973. *Society and the Policeman's Role*. Boston: Routledge and Kegan Paul.

———. 1979. "Trends in the Sociology of Police Work." *International Journal of the Sociology of Law* 7:143–67.

Camps, Francis E. 1966. *The Investigation of Murder*. London: Michael Joseph.

Canada. 1981a. *Commission of Inquiry Concerning Certain Activities of the Royal Canadian Mounted Police* (M. Justice D. C. McDonald, Chairman). Second Report. "Freedom and Security under the Law." Vols. 1 and 2. Ottawa: Minister of Supply and Services Canada.

———. 1981b. *Commission of Inquiry Concerning Certain Activities of the Royal Canadian Mounted Police* (M. Justice D. C. McDonald, Chairman). Third Report. "Certain R.C.M.P. Activities and the Question of Governmental Knowledge." Ottawa: Minister of Supply and Services Canada.

———. 1997. *Dishonoured Legacy: The Lessons of the Somalia Affair*. Report of the Commission of Inquiry into the Deployment of Canadian Forces to Somalia (Judge Gilles Létourneau Sherman, Chairman). 5 vols. Ottawa: Minister of Public Works and Government Services Canada.

———. 2006a. *Report on the Events Relating to Maher Arar*. First report. 3 vols. Ottawa: Minister of Supplies and Services Canada.

———. 2006b. *A New Mechanism for the RCMP's National Security Activities*. Second report. Ottawa: Minister of Supply and Services.

———. 2007. *Rebuilding the Trust. Report of the Task Force on Governance and Cultural Change in the RCMP* (Brown Report). Ottawa: Minister of Public Safety.

Canadian Centre for Justice Statistics. 2005. *Adult Correctional Services in Canada*. Catalogue no. 85–211-XIE. Ottawa: Statistics Canada.

Canadian Police College. 1997. *Women in Canadian Policing, Challenge 2000*. Ottawa: Canadian Police College. www.cpc.gc.ca/rdc/womwrk_e.pdf.

Cardia, Nancy. 2005. "Violence in Sao Paulo: Its Profile and the Responses from the State, the Private Sector and Civil Society." In *Public Problems—Private Solutions? Globalizing Cities in the South*, edited by K. Segbers, S. Raiser, and K. Volkmann, 279–305. Aldershot, Hants.: Ashgate.

Cashmore, Pete. 2010. "Privacy Is Dead, and Social Media Hold Smoking Gun." *CNN.com*. http://edition.cnn.com/2009/OPINION/10/28/cashmore.online .privacy/index.html.

CBC News. 2008. *Taser FAQs. What Are Tasers?* www.cbc.ca/news/background/ tasers/index.html.

CEPOL, European Police College. 2007. *Perspectives of Police Science in Europe. Project Group on a European Approach to Police Science (PGEAPS)*. Final Report. CEPOL Series No. 2. Bramshill, UK: CEPOL.

Chadwick, Edwin. 1829. "A Preventive Police." *London Review* 1:252–308.

Chassaigne, Marc. [1906] 1975. *La lieutenance générale de la police de Paris*. Geneva: Slatkine-Megoriatis Reprints.

Chatterton, M. 1987. "Assessing Police Effectiveness: Future Prospects." *British Journal of Criminology* 27(1):80–86.

Chen, David W. 2010. "Crime Survey Raises Questions about Data-Driven Policy." *New York Times*, February 9, A10.

Chesnais, Jean-Claude. 1981. *Histoire de violence*. Paris: Editorial Pluriel.

Chevigny, Paul. 1995. *Edge of the Knife: Police Violence in the Americas*. New York: New Press.

Chouinard, Tommy, and André Noël. 2008. "Un loup dans la bergerie." *La Presse*, May 29, A2.

Clarke, R.V.G. and J. M. Hough. 1984. *Crime and Police Effectiveness*. Home Office Research Study No. 79. London: HMSO.

Clément, Pierre. [1866] 1978. *La police sous Louis XIV*. Geneva: Slatkine Megoriatis Reprints.

Cohen, Bernard, and Jan Chaiken. 1987. *Investigators Who Perform Well*. Washington, D.C.: National Institute of Justice, U.S. Department of Justice.

Cohen, Stanley. 2002. *Folk Devils and Moral Panics*. Third edition. London: Routledge.

Colquhoun, Patrick. 1796. *A Treatise on the Police of the Metropolis*. Second edition. London: Joseph Mawman.

———. 1800. *A Treatise on the Commerce and Police on the River Thames*. London: Joseph Mawman.

———. 1802. *A Treatise on the Functions and Duties of a Constable*. London: Mawman and Hatchard.

Commission for Public Complaints against the Royal Canadian Mounted Police. 2007. *RCMP Use of the Conducted Energy Weapon (CEW). Interim Report, Including Recommendations for Immediate Implementation*. Ottawa: CPC/RCMP.

Committee on Identifying the Needs of the Forensic Science Community; Committee on Science, Technology, and Law Policy and Global Affairs; Committee on Applied and Theoretical Statistics, Division on Engineering and Physical Sciences. 2009. *Strengthening Forensic Science in the United States: A Path Forward*. Washington, D.C: National Academies Press.

Comrie, M. D., and E. J. Kings. 1975. "Study of Urban Workloads: Final Report." Unpublished. Home Office Police Research Unit.

Cordner, Gary W. 1979. "Police Patrol Workload Studies: A Review and Critique." *Police Studies* 2(2):50–60.

———. 1989. "The Police on Patrol." In *Police and Policing: Contemporary Issues*, edited by D. J. Kenney, 60–71. New York: Praeger.

Cordner, Gary W., and Kathryn Scarborough, eds. 2007. *Police Administration*. Sixth edition. Cincinnati: Anderson.

Cordner, Gary W., Kathryn Scarborough, and Robert Sheehan, eds. 2004. *Police Administration*. Fifth edition. Cincinnati: Anderson.

Cordner, Gary W., and Robert Sheehan, eds. 1999. *Police Administration*. Fourth edition. Cincinnati: Anderson.

Cordner, Gary W., and Robert Trojanowicz. 1992. "Patrol." In *What Works in Policing? Operations and Administration Examined*, edited by G. W. Cordner and D. C. Hale, 3–18. Highland Heights, Ky.: Academy of Criminal Justice Sciences; Cincinnati: Anderson.

Crawford, Adam. 1997. *The Local Governance of Crime: Appeals to Community and Partnership*. Oxford: Clarendon.

Critcher, Chas. 2003. *Moral Panics and the Media*. Buckingham, UK: Open University Press.

Critchley, Thomas A. [1967] 1978. *A History of Police in England and Wales 900–1966*. Revised edition. London: Constable.

Cumming, Elaine, Ian Cumming, and Laura Edell. 1965. "Policeman as Philosopher, Guide and Friend." *Social Problems* 12(3):276–286.

Cunningham, William C., John J. Strauchs, and Clifford W. Van Meter. 1990. *Private Security Trends 1970–2000. The Hallcrest Report II*. Boston: Butterworth-Heinemann.

Daly, Martin, and Margo Wilson. 1988. *Homicide*. New York: Aldine de Gruyter.

Davis, James R. 2000. *Fortune's Warriors: Private Armies and the New World Order*. Vancouver: Douglas and McIntyre.

Davis, Mike. 1990. *City of Quartz*. London: Vintage.

———. 2006. *Planet of Slums*. London: Verso.

Deflem, Mathieu. 2002. *Policing World Society. Historical Foundations of International Police Cooperation*. New York: Oxford University Press.

Department of Trade and Industry (DTI). 2006. *Security Equipment in the UK: A Guide to UK Capability*. London: DTI.

Dershowitz, Alan M. 2002. *Why Terrorism Works: Understanding the Threat, Responding to the Challenge*. London: Yale University Press.

De Waard, Jaap. 1999. "The Private Security Industry in International Perspective." *European Journal on Criminal Policy and Research* 7:143–177.

Dewerpe, Alain. 1994. *Espion. Une anthropologie historique du secret d'État contemporain.* Paris: Gallimard.

Dienstein, W. 1952. *Technics for the Crime Investigator.* Springfield, Ill.: Charles C. Thomas.

Dieu, François. 1993. *Gendarmerie et modernité.* Paris: Montchrestien.

Ditton, Jason, Jon Bannister, Elizabeth Gilchrist, and Stephen Farrall. 1999. "Afraid or Angry? Recalibrating the 'Fear of Crime.'" *International Review of Criminology* 6:83–99.

Ditton, Jason, and Martin Innes. 2005. "The Role of Perceptual Intervention in the Management of Crime Fear." In *Handbook of Crime Prevention and Community Safety,* edited by N. Tilley, 595–623. Cullompton, Devon: Willan.

Donzelot, Jacques, Catherine Mével, and Anne Wyvekens. 2003. *Faire société.* Paris: Éditions du Seuil.

Dorn, Nicolas, and N. South. 1991. "Mirroring the Market." In *Beyond Law and Order: Criminal Justice Policy and Politics in the 1990s,* edited by R. Reiner and M. Cross, 91–106. London: Macmillan.

———. 1992. *Traffickers: Drug Markets and Law Enforcement.* London: Routledge.

Douglas, John. 1996. *Mindhunter: Inside the FBI's Elite Serial Crime Unit.* New York: Pocket.

Doyle, Aaron. 2004. *Arresting Images: Crime and Policing in Front of the Camera.* Toronto: University of Toronto Press.

Dunlap, Colonel Charles J. 2001. "The Thick Green Line: The Growing Involvement of Military Forces in Domestic Law Enforcement." In *Militarizing the American Criminal Justice System: The Changing Roles of the Armed Forces and the Police,* edited by P. B. Kraska, 29–42. Boston: Northeastern University Press.

Economist. 2010. *The Data Deluge, Special Report on Managing Information.* February 27–March 5.

Ekblom, Paul, and Kevin Heal. 1982. *The Police Response to Calls from the Public.* Research and Planning Unit Paper No. 9. London: Home Office.

Elias, Norbert. 1996. *The Germans: Power Struggles and the Development of Habitus in the Nineteenth and Twentieth Centuries,* edited by M. Schröter. New York: Columbia University Press.

———. 1998. *Norbert Elias on Civilization, Power, and Knowledge: Selected Writings,* edited with an introduction by Stephen Mennel and Johan Goudsblom. Chicago: University of Chicago Press.

Emsley, Clive. 1983. *Policing and Its Context, 1750–1870.* London: Macmillan.

———. 1991. *The English Police: A Political and Social History.* Hemel Hempstead. UK: Harvester Wheatsheaf.

———. 1996. *Crime and Society in England, 1750–1900.* Second edition. Harlow, Essex: Longman.

———. 1999. *Gendarmes and the State in Nineteenth-Century Europe.* New York: Oxford University Press.

———. 2002. "La gendarmerie et l'état." In *Gendarmerie, état et société au XIXe siècle,* edited by Jean-Noël Luc, 465–477. Paris: Publications de la Sorbonne.

———. 2003. "The Birth and Development of the Police." In *Handbook of Policing,* edited by T. Newburn, 66–83. Cullompton, Devon: Willan.

Ericson, Richard V. 1981. *Making Crime: A Study of Detective Work.* Toronto: Butterworth.

———. 1982. *Reproducing Order: A Study of Police Patrol Work.* Toronto: University of Toronto Press.

———. 1993. *Making Crime: A Study of Detective Work.* Second edition. Toronto: Toronto University Press.

Ericson, Richard V., Patricia M. Baranek, and Janet B. L. Chan. 1987. *Visualizing Deviance: A Study of News Organization.* Toronto: University of Toronto Press.

———. 1989. *Negotiating Control: A Study of News Sources.* Toronto: University of Toronto Press.

———. 1991. *Representing Order: Crime, Law, and Justice in the News Media.* Toronto: University of Toronto Press.

Ericson, Richard V., and Kevin D. Haggerty. 1997. *Policing the Risk Society.* Toronto: University of Toronto Press.

European Commission. 2006. *15 Years of Private Security Services in Estonia, with Some Parallels to Latvia and Lithuania.* Riga: Technical Assistance Information Exchange Instrument, Roundtable, Social Dialog in Security Sector in the Baltic States.

Farmer, John, Jr. 2009. "Playing Chicken with Suicide Bombers." *New York Times,* September 27, 13.

Fielding, Nigel. 1996. "Being Used by the Police." In *Policing.* Vol. 1. *Cops, Crime and Control: Analysing the Police Function,* edited by R. Reiner, 243–250. Aldershot, Hants.: Dartmouth.

Fielding, Nigel, and Jane Fielding. 1992. "A Comparative Minority: Female Recruits to a British Constabulary Force." *Policing and Society* 2(4):205–218.

Fielding, Nigel, Martin Innes, and Jane Fielding. 2002. *Reassurance Policing and the Visual Environmental Crime Audit in Surrey Police: A Report.* Guilford: University of Surrey.

Filleule, Olivier, and Donatella Della Porta, eds. 2006. *Police et manifestants: maintien de l'ordre et gestion des conflits.* Paris: Presses de Sciences Po.

Fishman, Mark, and Gray Cavender, eds. 1998. *Entertaining Crime: Television Reality Programs.* New York: Aldine de Gruyter.

Fitzgerald, Marian, Mike Hough, Ian Joseph, and Tarek Qureshi. 2002. *Policing for London. Report of an Independent Study Funded by the Nuffield Foundation, the Esmée Fairban Foundation and the Paul Hamlyn Foundation.* Cullompton, Devon: Willan.

Flavel, W. 1973. "Research into Security Organisations." Unpublished paper presented to the Second Bristol Seminar on the Sociology of the Police.

Fogelson, Robert M. 1977. *Big City Police*. Cambridge: Harvard University Press.

Fontaine, Jean-Yves. 2007. *Socioanthropologie du gendarme: gendarmerie et démocratie*. Paris: l'Harmattan.

Forst, Brian, and Peter K. Manning. 1999. *The Privatization of Policing, Two Views*. Washington, D.C.: Georgetown University Press.

Foucault, Michel. 1977. *Discipline and Punish*. New York: Random House.

———. 1981. "Omnes et Singulatim: Towards a Criticism of 'Political Reason.'" In *The Tanner Lectures on Human Values II*, edited by S. McMurrin, 223–254. Salt Lake City: University of Utah Press.

Fouché, Joseph. [1816] 1968. "Letters to the Duke of Wellington." In Sir Leon Radzinowicz, *A History of English Criminal Law and Its Administration*. 3:555–556. London: Stevens and Sons.

———. 1993. *Mémoires*. Paris: Arléa.

France. 2003. *Rapport à l'Assemblée nationale, renseignement*. Rapporteur spécial: M. Bernard CARAYON, Document #256. www.assemblee-nat.fr/12/budget/plf2003/b0256–36.asp.

Freedman, Jonathan L. 2002. *Media Violence and Its Effect on Aggression: Assessing the Scientific Evidence*. Toronto: University of Toronto Press.

Fried, Joseph P. 2008. "Ex-officers Get 2 to 6 Years in Queens Stun Gun Torture." *New York Times*, May 20, B3.

Friendly, Albert, and Ronald L. Goldfarb. 1967. *Crime and Publicity: The Impact of News on the Administration of Justice*. New York: Twentieth Century Fund.

Funder, Anna. 2003. *Stasiland: True Stories from behind the Berlin Wall*. London: Granta Books.

Fyfe, James. 1981. "Who Shoots? A Look at Officer Race and Police Shootings." *Journal of Police Science and Administration* 9(4):367–382.

———. 1988. "Police Shootings: 'Environment and Licence.'" In *Controversial Issues in Criminal Justice*, edited by J. E. Scott and T. Hirschi, 79–94. Beverly Hills: Sage.

Gagnon, Camille. 1999. *Médiapolis*. Montréal: Québec Amérique.

Galliher, John F., Patrick Donovan, and David L. Adams. 1975. "Small-Town Police: Troubles, Tasks, and Publics." *Journal of Police and Administration* 3:19–28.

Gambetta, Diego. 1993. *The Sicilian Mafia: The Business of Private Protection*. Cambridge: Harvard University Press.

Gans, Jeremy. 2000. "Privately Paid Policing: Law and Practice." *Policing and Society* 10(2):183–207.

Garofalo, Raffaele. 1914. *Criminology*, translated by Robert W. Millar. Boston: Little, Brown.

Gatrell, V.A.C. 1990. "Crime, Authority and the Policeman-state." In *The Cambridge Social History of Britain, 1750–1950*. Vol. 3. *Social Agencies and Institutions*, edited by F.M.L. Thompson, 243–310. Cambridge: Cambridge University Press.

Gatrell, V.A.C., Bruce Lenman, and Geoffrey Parker, eds. 1980. *Crime and the Law. The Social History of Crime in Western Europe since 1500*. London: Europa.

George, Bruce, and Mark Button. 1994. "The Need for Regulation of the Private Security Industry." *A Submission to the House of Commons Home Affairs Select Committee*. November. London.

Gill, Martin, ed. 2003. *CCTV*. Leicester: Perpetuity Press.

Gill, Martin, and Jerry Hart. 1997a. "Exploring Investigative Policing. A Study of Private Detectives in Britain." *British Journal of Criminology* 37(4):549–567.

———. 1997b. "Policing as a Business: The Organisation and Structure of Private Investigation." *Policing and Society* 7(2):117–141.

Gilsinian, James F. 1989. "They Is Clowning Tough: 911 and the Social Construction of Reality." *Criminology* 27(2):329–344.

Gimenez-Salinas, Andrea. 2001. "La Génesis de la Ley 23/1992 de Seguridad Privada." PhD dissertation, Departamento de Ciencia Juridica, Universidad de Castilla.

Goldstein, Herman. 1979. "Improving Policing: A Problem-Oriented Approach." *Crime and Delinquency* 25(2):236–258.

———. 1990. *Problem-Oriented Policing*. New York: McGraw-Hill.

Greenberg, Bernard, Carola Elliot, Lois Craft, and H. Steven Procter. *Felony Investigations: Decision Model*. Washington, D.C.: National Institute of Law Enforcement and Criminal Justice.

Greene, Jack, and Carl B. Klockars. 1991. "What Police Do." In *Thinking about Police*, edited by C. B. Klockars and S. D. Mastrofski, 273–284. New York: McGraw-Hill.

Greenwood, Peter W., Jan M. Chaiken, and Joan R. Petersilia. 1977. *The Criminal Investigation Process*. Lexington, Mass.: D. C. Heath.

Greenwood, Peter W., Jan M. Chaiken, Joan R. Petersilia, and Linda L. Prusoff. 1975. *The Criminal Investigation Process: Observations and Analysis*. Santa Monica, Cal.: Rand Corporation.

Griffiths, Curt T., Brian Whitelaw, and Richard B. Parent. 1999. *Canadian Police Work*. Toronto: International Thompson.

Guardiano, John R., David Haarmeyer, and Robert W. Poole Jr. 1992. *Fire Protection Privatization: A Cost-Effective Approach to Public Safety*. www.reason.org/ps152.html.

Guillauté, M. [1754] 1974. *Mémoire sur la réformation de la police en France*. Paris: Herman.

Haas, Patrick. 2007. *Atlas 2008: le panorama économique du marché de la sécurité*. Seventeenth edition. Paris, En Toute Sécurité.

Haenel, Hubert, Richard Lizurey, and René Pichon. 1996. *La gendarmerie*. Paris: Presses Universitaires de France.

Haggerty, Kevin D., and Richard V. Ericson, eds. 2006. *The New Politics of Surveillance and Visibility*. Toronto: University of Toronto Press.

Hale, C. 1996. "Fear of Crime: A Review of the Literature." *International Review of Victimology* 4:79–150.

Haller, M. H. 1976. "Historical Roots of Police Behaviour: Chicago 1890–1925." *Law and Society Review* 10:303–323.

Harper's Magazine. 2007. "'Harper's Index and Sources." December. Index, 17; sources, 76.

Hart, H. L. A. 1994. *The Concept of Law*. Oxford: Clarendon.

Havard, J. 1960. *The Detection of Secret Homicide*. Basingstoke: Macmillan.

Hawkins, Darnell F., ed. 2003. *Violent Crime: Assessing Race and Ethnic Differences*. Cambridge: Cambridge University Press.

Hay, Douglas, and Francis Snyder. 1989. "Using the Criminal Law, 1750–1850: Policing, Private Prosecution, and the State." In *Policing and Prosecution in Britain 1750–1850*, edited by D. Hay and F. Snyder, 3–51. Oxford: Clarendon.

Hayes, Ben. 2004. *From the Schengen Information System to SIS II and the Visa Information (VIS): The Proposals Explained*. Statewatch Report. www.statewatch.org.

Heidensohn, Frances. 1994. "We Can Handle It Out Here. Women Officers in Britain and the USA and the Policing of Public Order." *Policing and Society* 4(4):293–303.

———. 2003. "Gender and Policing." In *Handbook of Policing*, edited by Tim Newburn, 556–577. Cullompton, Devon: Willan.

———. 2005. "Women in Control?" In *Policing: Key Readings*, edited by Tim Newburn, 751–760. Cullompton, Devon: Willan.

Heinrick, Jeffrey. 2006. "Everyone's an Expert: The CSI Effect's Negative Impact on Juries." *Triple Helix* 3 (Fall):59–61.

Henderson, Lesley, ed. 1991. *Twentieth Century Crime and Mystery Writers*. Chicago: St. James Press.

Henry, Stuart. 1987. "Private Justice and the Policing of Labor: The Dialectics of Industrial Discipline." *Private Policing*, SAGE Criminal Justice System Annuals, 23:45–71.

Herbert, Rosemary, ed. 1999. *The Oxford Companion to Crime and Mystery Writing*. Oxford: Oxford University Press.

Hickman, Matthew J., and Brian A. Reaves. 2003. *Local Police Departments 2000*. Washington, D.C.: U.S. Department of Justice, Office of Justice Programs, Bureau of Justice Statistics.

Hill, Peter B. E. 2003. *The Japanese Mafia: Yakusa, Law, and the State*. New York: Oxford University Press.

Hobbes, Thomas. [1651] 1985. *Leviathan*. Penguin: Harmondsworth.

Hobbs, Dick. 1988. *Doing the Business*. Oxford: Oxford University Press.

Hobbs, Dick, Philip Hadfield, Stuart Lister, and Simon Willow. 2003. *Bouncers: Violence and the Governance in the Night-time Economy*. New York: Oxford University Press.

Holdoway, Simon. 1993. *The Resignation of Black and Asian Officers from the Police Service*. London: Home Office.

———. 1996. *The Racialisation of British Policing*. London: Macmillan.

Holloway, Thomas. 1993. *Policing Rio de Janeiro: Repression and Resistance in a 19th-Century City*. Stanford: Stanford University Press.

Home Office. 1995. *Review of Police Core and Ancillary Tasks: Final Report and Appendices*. London: HMSO.

Hornung, Rick. 1991. *One Nation under the Gun: Inside the Mohawk Civil War*. Toronto: Stoddardt.

Hough, J. M. 1980. *Uniformed Police Work and Management Technology*. Research Unit Paper 1. London: Home Office.

House, C. H. 1993. "Changing Role of Women in Law Enforcement." *Police Chief* 60(10):139–144.

House of Commons. 1828. *Report from the Selected Committee on the Police of the Metropolis*. London, July 11, 1828.

———. 1908. *Report of the Royal Commission upon the Duties of the Metropolitan Police*. London: His Majesty's Stationery Office.

Howe, Adrian, ed. 1998. *Sexed Crime in the News*. Sydney: Federation Press.

Huggins, Martha K., Mika Haritos-Fatouros, and Philip G. Zimbardo. 2002. *Violence Workers: Police Torturers and Murderers Reconstruct Brazilian Atrocities*. Berkeley: University of California Press.

Innes, Martin. 2003. *Investigating Murder: Detective Work and the Police Response to Criminal Homicide*. Oxford: Oxford University Press.

———. 2004a. "Signal Crimes and Signal Disorders: Notes on Deviance and Communicative Action." *British Journal of Sociology* 5(3):335–355.

———. 2004b. "Crime as a Signal, Crime as Memory." *Journal for Crime, Conflict and the Media* 1(2):15–22.

Innes, Martin, and Nigel Fielding. 2002. "From Community to Communicative Policing: 'Signal Crimes' and the Problem of Public Reassurance." *Sociological Research Online* 7(2):1–17.

Institut de Police du Québec. 2000. *Les Actes du Colloque sur la femme policière, s'unir pour grandir ensemble, 21–22 octobre 1999*. Nicolet, Québec: Institut de Police du Québec.

International Association of Chiefs of Police. 1995. *Murder in America: Recommendations from the IACP Murder Summit*. Available by calling 1-800-THE-IACP.

Irvine, Chris. 2008. "Labour Has Created 3,600 New Offences since 1997." *Telegraph* (UK), September 4, 2008.

Jäger, Thomas, and Gerhard Kümmel. 2007. *Private Military and Security Companies: Chances, Problems, Pittfalls and Prospects*. Wiesbaden: VS Verlag für sozialwissenschaften.

Jakubowski, Maxim, ed. 1991. *100 Great Detectives*. London: Xanadu Press.

Jobard, Fabien. 2001. "Comprendre l'habilation à l'usage de la force policière." *Déviance et Société* 25(3):325–345.

———. 2002. *Bavures policières?—La force publique et ses usages*. Paris: La Découverte.

Johnson, David R. 1979. *Policing the Urban Underworld: The Impact of Crime on the Development of the American Police, 1800–1887*. Philadelphia: Temple University Press.

Johnson, Samuel. 1806. *A Dictionary of the English Language*. London.

Johnston, Les. 1992. *The Rebirth of Private Policing*. London: Routledge.

———. 2000. *Policing Britain: Risk, Security and Governance*. Harlow, UK: Longman.

Johnston, Les, and Clifford Shearing. 2003. *Governing Security: Explorations in Policing and Justice*. London: Routledge.

Jones, S. 1983. "Community Policing in Devon and Cornwall." In *The Future of Policing*, edited by T. Bennet, 82–103. Cambridge: Institute of Criminology.

Jones, Trevor, Brian MacLean, and Jock Young. 1986. *The Islington Crime Survey*. Aldershot, Hants.: Gower.

Jones, Trevor, and Tim Newburn. 1995. "How Big Is the Private Security Sector?" *Policing and Society* 5(3):221–232.

———. 1998. *Private Security and Public Policing*. Oxford: Clarendon Press.

———. 2002. "The Transformation of Policing? Understanding Current Trends in Policing Systems." *British Journal of Criminology* 42(1):129–146.

———. 2006a, eds. *Plural Policing: A Comparative Perspective*. New York: Routledge.

———. 2006b, eds. "Understanding Plural Policing." In *Plural Policing: A Comparative Perspective*, edited by Jones and Newburn, 1–11. New York: Routledge.

———. 2006c. "The United Kingdom." In *Plural Policing: A Comparative Perspective*, edited by Jones and Newburn, 34–54. New York: Routledge.

Juristat. 2001. *Sentencing in Adult Criminal Courts, 1999/00*. Catalogue no. 85–002-XIE, 21(10). Ottawa: Statistics Canada.

———. 2005. *Adult Correctional Services in Canada, 2003/04*. Catalogue no. 85–002-XIE, 25(8). Ottawa: Statistics Canada,

———. 2006. *Adult Correctional Services in Canada, 2004/05*. Catalogue no. 85–002-XIE, 26(5). Ottawa: Statistics Canada.

Kakalik, James S., and Sorrel Wildhorn. 1972. *Private Security in the United States*. Washington, D.C.: US Department of Justice, National Institute of Law Enforcement and Criminal Justice, Law Enforcement Assistance Administration.

Kaluszynski, Martine. 2002. *La république à l'épreuve du crime: la construction du crime comme objet politique, 1880–1920*. Paris: Maison des Sciences de l'Homme.

Kapuscinski, Ryszard. 2001. *The Shadow of the Sun*. New York: Alfred A. Knopf.

Keefe, Patrick Radden. 2006. *Chatter: Uncovering the Echelon Surveillance Network and the Secret World of Global Eavesdropping*. New York: Random House.

Keegan, John. 1994. *A History of Warfare*. New York: Vintage.

Kelling, George. 1978. "Police Field Services and Crime: The Presumed Effects of a Capacity." *Crime and Delinquency* 24(2):173–184.

————. 1983. "On the Accomplishments of the Police." In M. Punch, *Control in the Police Organization*, 152–168. Cambridge: MIT Press.

Kelling, George, and Mark H. Moore. 1988. *The Evolving Strategy of Policing.* Perspectives in Policing 4. Cambridge: John F. Kennedy School of Government, Harvard University.

Kelling, George, Tony Pate, Duane Dieckman, and Charles E. Brown. 1974a. *The Kansas City Preventive Patrol Experiment: A Summary Report.* Washington, D.C.: Police Foundation.

————. 1974b. *The Kansas City Preventive Patrol Experiment: Technical Report.* Washington, D.C.: Police Foundation.

Kempa, Michael, Philip Stenning, and Jennifer Wood. 2004. "Policing Communal Spaces: A Reconfiguration of the 'Mass Property' Hypothesis." *British Journal of Criminology* 44(4):562–581.

King, Peter. 2000. *Crime, Justice and Discretion in England 1740–1820.* Oxford: Oxford University Press.

Kinsey, Christopher. 2006. *Corporate Soldiers and International Security.* New York: Routledge.

Kinsey, R. 1985. *Merseyside Crime and Police Surveys: Final Report.* Liverpool: Merseyside County Council.

Klockars, Carl B. 1985. *The Idea of Police.* Law and Criminal Justice Series 3. Beverly Hills: Sage.

Knox, Jim, and Stephen MacDonald. 2001. "Diary of a Police Officer." Police Research Series 149. London: Home Office, Research Development Statistics Publications.

Knox, Sara L. 1998. *Murder: A Tale of Modern American Life.* Durham: Duke University Press.

Kuhn, Thomas S. 1970. *The Structure of Scientific Revolutions.* Second edition, enlarged. Chicago: University of Chicago Press.

Kuykendall, Jack. 1982. "The Criminal Investigation Process: Toward a Conceptual Framework." *Journal of Criminal Justice* 10:131–145.

————. 1986. "The Municipal Police Detective: An Historical Analysis." *Criminology* 24(1):175–202.

Lafree, Gary, and Laura Dugan. 2009. "Research on Terrorism and Countering Terrorism." In *Crime and Justice: A Review of Research*, edited by M. Tonry, 38:413–477.

La Mare, Nicolas de. 1722. *Traité de police.* Expanded edition. Paris: Michel Brunet.

Lane, Roger. 1967. *Policing the City, 1822–1885.* Cambridge: Harvard University Press.

————. 1980. "Urban Police and Crime in Nineteenth Century America." In *Crime and Justice: An Annual Review of Research*, edited by Norval Morris and Michael Tonry, 2:1–43.

————. 1992. "Urban Police and Crime in Nineteenth Century America." In *Modern Policing.* Vol. 15 of *Crime and Justice: An Annual Review of Research*, edited by M. Tonry and N. Norris, 1–50.

———. 1997. *Murder in America: A History*. Columbus: Ohio State University Press.

Laudon, Kenneth. 1986. *The Dossier Society: Value Choices in the Design of National Information Systems*. New York: Columbia University Press.

Laur, Darren. 2004. *Excited Delirium and Its Correlation to Sudden and Unexpected Death Proximal to Restraint*. Ottawa: Canadian Police Research Centre.

Lawrence, Regina G. 2000. *The Politics of Force: Media and the Construction of Police Brutality*. Berkeley: University of California Press.

Lebeuf, Marcel-Eugène. 2000. "L'évolution des femmes dans la police." In Institut de Police du Québec (2000), *Les Actes du Colloque sur la femme policière, s'unir pour grandir ensemble, 21–22 octobre 1999*, 16–21. Nicolet, Québec: Institut de Police du Québec.

Leinen, Stephen. 1984. *Black Police, White Society*. New York: New York University Press.

———. 1993. *Gay Cops*. New Brunswick: Rutgers University Press.

Leishman, Frank, and Paul Mason. 2003. *Policing and Then Media: Facts, Fictions and Factions*. Cullompton, Devon: Willan.

Lenoir, Jean Charles Philippe. 1779. "Mémoire sur la Police en France, et particu-lièrement sur la Police de Paris, présenté à la Reine de Naples (seconde version) et présenté dans sa première version à l'Impératrice d'Autriche." Manuscript, Add. 4651. Cambridge: University Library.

Lenz, Timothy O. 2003. *Changing Images of Law in Film and Television Crime Stories*. New York: Peter Lang.

Lévy, René. 1987. *Du suspect au coupable: le travail de police judiciaire*. Geneva: Éditions Médecine et Hygiène.

Leyton, E. 1995. *Men of Blood: Murder in Modern England*. London: Constable.

L'Heuillet, Hélène. 2001. *Basse politique, haute police: une approche philosophique et historique*. Paris: Librairie Arthème Fayard.

Liang, Hsi-Huey. 1992. *The Rise of Modern Police and the European State System from Metternich to the Second World War*. Cambridge: Cambridge University Press.

Lifton, Robert J. 1986. *The Nazi Doctors: Medical Killing and the Psychology of Genocide*. New York: Basic Books.

Lilly, J. R. 1978. "What Are the Police Now Doing?" *Journal of Police Science and Administration* 6:51–60.

Lipson, M. 1975. *On Guard: The Business of Private Security*. New York: Quadrangle/New York Times.

Loader, Ian, and Aogán Mulcahy. 2003. *Policing and the Condition of England: Memory, Politics and Culture*. Oxford: Oxford University Press.

Loader, Ian, and Neil Walker. 2006. "Necessary Virtues: The Legitimate Place of the State in the Production of Security." In *Democracy, Society and the Governance of Security*, edited by J. Wood and B. Dupont, 165–195. Cambridge: Cambridge University Press.

Lofland, Lyn H. 1973. *A World of Strangers: Order and Action in Urban Public Space.* New York: Basic Books.

Loubet del Bayle, Jean-Louis. 1992. *La police: approche socio-politique.* Paris: Montchrestien.

Luc, Jean-Noël, ed. 2002. *Gendarmerie, état et société au XIXe siècle.* Paris: Publications de la Sorbonne.

Lundman, Richard J. 1980. *Police Behavior A Sociological Perspective.* Oxford: Oxford University Press.

Lupo, Salvatore. 1996. *Storia della mafia, dalle origini ai giorni nostri.* New revised and enlarged edition. Rome: Donzelli Editore.

Lyon, David, ed. 2006. *Theorizing Surveillance: The Panopticon and Beyond.* Portland, Ore.: Willan.

Maas, Peter. 1968. *The Valachi Papers.* Toronto: Bantam.

Macaulay, Stewart. 1986. "Private Government." In *Law and the Social Sciences,* edited by L. Lipson and S. Wheeler, 455–518. New York: Russel Sage Foundation.

MacDonald, John M., Robert J. Kaminski, and Michael R. Smith. 2009. "The Effect of Less-Lethal Weapons on Injuries in Police Use-of-Force Events." *American Journal of Public Health* 99(12):2268–2274.

Macleod, Ross C. 1976. *The NWMP and Law Enforcement, 1873–1905.* Toronto: University of Toronto Press.

Macleod, T. C. 2002. *Parapolice: A Revolution in the Business of Law Enforcement.* Toronto: Boheme Press.

Macpherson, William. 1999. *Report of an Inquiry into the Investigation of the Murder of Stephen Lawrence.* London: HMSO.

Madelin, Louis. 1930. *Fouché, 1759–1820.* 2 vols. Paris: Librairie Plon.

Maguire, Mike. 2003. "Criminal Investigation and Crime Control." In *The Handbook of Policing,* edited by T. Newburn, 363–393. Collumpton, Devon: Willan.

Maguire, Mike, Lesley Noaks, Richard (Dick) Hoobs, and N. Brearly. 1993. *Assessing Investigative Performance.* A Study Commissioned by the Home Office. Cardiff: School of Social and Administrative Studies, University of Wales, College of Cardiff.

Malochet, Virginie. 2007. *Les policiers municipaux.* Paris: Le Monde, Partage du savoir, Presses Universitaires de France.

Mandel, Ernest. 1984. *Delightful Murder: A Social History of the Crime Story.* London: Pluto Press.

Manning, Peter K. 1971. "The Police: Mandate, Strategy and Appearances." In *Crime and Justice in American Society,* edited by J. Douglas, 149–194. Indianapolis: Bobbs-Merrill.

———. 1977. *Police Work: The Social Organization of Policing.* Cambridge: MIT Press. Second edition, Prospect Heights, Ill.: Waveland, 1997.

———. 1980. *The Narcs' Game: Organizational and Informational Limits on Drug Law Enforcement.* Cambridge: MIT Press. *See below,* 2004, for second edition.

———. 1988. *Symbolic Communication: Signing Calls and the Police Response.* Cambridge: MIT Press.

———. 1992. "Information Technologies and the Police." In *Modern Policing.* Vol. 15 of *Crime and Justice: An Annual Review of Research,* edited by M. Tonry and N. Morris, 349–398. Chicago: University of Chicago Press.

———. 1998. "Media Loops." In *Popular Culture, Crime, and Justice,* edited by F. Y. Bailey and D. C. Hale, 25–39. New York: West/Wadsworth.

———. 1999. "A Dramaturgical Perspective." In *The Privatization of Policing,* edited by Peter Manning and Brian Forst, 51–124. Washington, D.C.: Georgetown University Press.

———. 2003. *Policing Contingencies.* Chicago: University of Chicago Press.

———. 2004. *The Narcs' Game: Organizational and Informational Limits on Drug Law Enforcement.* Second edition. Prospect Heights, Ill.: Waveland.

———. 2006a. "Detective Occupational Culture." In *Encyclopedia of Police Science,* edited by J. Greene, 390–397. New York: Routledge.

———. 2006b. "Case Studies of American Anti-terrorism." In *Democracy, Society and the Governance of Security,* edited by J. Wood and B. Dupont, 52–85. New York: Cambridge University Press.

———. 2006c. "The United States of America." In *Plural Policing: A Comparative Perspective,* edited by T. Jones and T. Newburn, 98–125. New York: Routledge.

———. 2010. *Democratic Policing in a Changing World.* Boulder, Colo.: Paradigm.

Manning, Peter K., and John Van Maanen. 1978. *Policing: A View from the Street.* New York: Random House.

Marenin, Otwin. 1982. "Parking Tickets and Class Repression: The Concept of Policing in Critical Theories of Criminal Justice." *Contemporary Crises* 6:241–266.

Martin, John P., and Gail Wilson. 1969. *The Police: A Study in Manpower; The Evolution of the Service in England and Wales 1829–1965.* London: Heinemann.

Martin, Susan Ehrlich, and Nancy C. Jurik. 1996. *Doing Justice, Doing Gender.* Thousand Oaks, Cal.: Sage.

Marx, Gary T. 1974. "Thoughts on Neglected Category of Social Movement Participant: The Agent Provocateur and the Informant." *American Journal of Sociology* 80(2):402–443.

———. 1985. "I'll Be Watching You: Reflections on the New Surveillance." *Dissent* 32 (Winter): 26–34.

———. 1988. *Undercover: Police Surveillance in America.* Berkeley: University of California Press.

———. 2001a. "Technology and Social Control: The Search for the Illusive Silver Bullet." In *International Encyclopedia of the Social and Behavioral Sciences,* edited by P. B. Baltes and N. J. Smelser, 23:15506–15512. Amsterdam/New York: Elsevier.

———. 2001b. "Murky Conceptual Waters: The Public and the Private." *Ethics and Information Technology* 3(3):157–169.

———. 2003. "A Tack in the Shoe: Neutralizing and Resisting the New Surveillance." *Journal of Social Issues* 59(2):369–390.

Mastrofski, Stephan D. 1983. "Police Knowledge of the Patrol Beat: A Performance Measure." In *Police at Work: Policy Issues and Analysis*, edited by R. R. Bennett, 45–64. Beverly Hills: Sage.

Mathiesen, Tomas. 1997. "The Viewer Society: Michel Foucault's 'Panopticon' Revisited." *Theoretical Criminology* 1(2):215–234.

Mawby, Rob. 1991. *Comparative Policing Issues: The British and American Experience in International Perspective*. London: Unwin.

———. 1992. "Comparative Police Systems: Searching for a Continental Model." In *Criminal Justice: Theory and Practice*, edited by K. Bottomley, T. Fowles, and R. Reiner, 108–132. London: BSC/ISTD.

———. 2000. "Core Policing: The Seductive Myth." In *Core Issues in Policing*. Second edition, edited by F. Leishman, B. Loveday, and S. Savage, 107–123. Harlow, UK: Pearson, Longman.

———. 2002. *Policing Images: Policing, Communication and Legitimacy*. Cullompton, Devon: Willan.

———. 2003. "Models of Policing." In *Handbook of Policing*, edited by T. Newburn, 15–40. Cullompton, Devon: Willan.

Maxfield, Michael G. 1989. "Circumstances in Supplementary Homicide Reports." *Criminology* 27(4):671–695.

McCahill, Michael. 2002. *The Surveillance Web*. Cullompton, Devon: Willan.

McCahill, Michael, and Clive Norris. 2003. "Estimating the Extent, Sophistication and Legality of CCTV in London." In *CCTV*, edited by M. Gill, 51–66. Leicester: Perpetuity Press.

McCann, Brigitte, and Mathieu Turbide. 2004. "On ne servira pas de chair à canon." *Le Journal de Montréal*, January 16, 15.

McClintock, F. H., and Paul Wiles, eds. 1972. *The Security Industry in the UK: Papers Presented to the Cropwood Round-Table Conference, July 1971*. Cambridge: Cambridge Institute of Criminology.

McConville, Mike, Andrew Sanders, and R. Leng. 1991. *The Case for the Prosecution*. New York: Routledge.

McCormick, Peter, and Frederick Elliston, eds. 1981. *Expositions and Appraisals*. Notre Dame: Notre Dame University Press.

McKie, David. 2009. "RCMP Shocked 16 People Five Times or More Last Year." *CBCNews*, April 8. http://www.cbc.ca/canada/story/2009/04/08/taser-2008.html?ref=rss.

McShane, Larry. 1999. *Cops under Fire: The Reign of Terror against Hero Cops*. Washington, D.C.: Regnery.

Meloche, Serge. 2000. "L'intégration des policières au SPCUM: innover pour grandir ensemble." In *Les Actes du Colloque sur la femme policière, s'unir pour grandir ensemble, 21–22 octobre 1999*, edited by Institut de Police du Québec, 57–63. Nicolet, Québec: Institut de Police du Québec.

Merriman, John. 2006. *Police Stories: Building the French State, 1815–1851*. New York: Oxford University Press.

Mesplède, Claude. 2003. *Dictionnaire des littératures policières*. 2 vols. Nantes: Éditions Joseph K.

Milgram, Stanley. 1970. "The Experience of Living in Cities." *Science* 167:1461–1468.

Miller, Susan. 1999. *Gender and Community Policing: Walking the Talk*. Boston: Northeastern University Press.

Miller, Wilbur R. 1975. "Police Authority in New York and London City 1830–1870." *Journal of Social History* 8:81–101.

———. 1977. *Cops and Bobbies: Police Authority in New York and London, 1830–1870*. Chicago: University of Chicago Press.

Miyazawa, Setsuo. 1992. *Policing in Japan: A Study on Making Crime*, translated by Frank G. Bennett, Jr., with John O. Haley. Albany: State University of New York Press.

Monjardet, Dominique. 1996. *Ce que fait la police: sociologie de la force publique*. Paris: La Découverte.

Monkonnen, Eric H., ed. 1990. *Crime and Justice in American History*. Westport, Conn.: Meckler.

———. 1992. "History of Urban Police." In *Modern Policing*. Vol. 15 of *Crime and Justice: An Annual Review of Research*, edited by M. Tonry and N. Norris, 547–577.

Montefiore, Simon Sebag. 2003. *Stalin: The Court of the Red Tsar*. London: Weidenfeld and Nicolson.

Montesquieu. [1748] 1989. *The Spirit of the Laws*, translated and edited by Anne M. Cohler, Basia Carolyn Miller, and Harold Samuel Stone. Cambridge: Cambridge University Press.

Moore, Mark, and George Kelling. 1983. "To Serve and Protect: Learning from Police History." *The Public Interest* 70 (Winter):49–65.

Mopas, Michael S., and Philip C. Stenning. 2001. "Tools of the Trade: The Symbolic Power of Private Security—An Exploratory Study." *Policing and Society* 11:67–97.

Morales Villanueva, Antonio. 1994. "España y su Guardia Civil." *Cuadernos de la Guardia Civil* 10:275–284.

Morgan, Rod, and Tim Newburn. 1997. *The Future of Policing*. Oxford: Oxford University Press.

Morn, Frank. 1982. "*The Eye that Never Sleeps*": *A History of the Pinkerton National Detective Agency*. Bloomington: Indiana University Press.

Morré, Lilany. 2004. "Panoramic Overview of Private Security Industry." In the 25 Member State of the European Union, coESS and UNI-Europa. www.coess.org/pdf/panorama1.pdf.

Morris, Nigel. 2006. "Blair's 'Frenzied Law Making': A New Offence for Every Day Spent in Office." *Independent*, August 16.

Morris, Pauline, and Kevin Heal. 1981. *Crime Control and the Police: A Review of Research.* Home Office Research Study 67. London: Home Office.

Mucchielli, Laurent. 2004. "L'enquête de police judiciaire en matière d'homicide." *Questions pénales* 16(1):1–4.

———. 2006. "L'élucidation des homicides: de l'enchantement technologique à l'analyse du travail des enquêteurs de police judiciaire." *Déviance et Société* 30(1):91–119.

Muir, William Ker, Jr. 1977. *Police: Streetcorner Politicians.* Chicago: University of Chicago Press.

Nalla, Mahesh K., and Graeme R. Newman. 1990. *A Primer in Private Security.* New York: Harrows and Heston.

———. 1991. "Public versus Private Control: A Reassessment." *Journal of Criminal Justice* 19:537–547.

Napoli, Paolo. 2003. *Naissance de la police moderne.* Paris: La Découverte.

National Centre for Police Excellence. 2005. *Guidance on the National Intelligence Model.* Produced on behalf of the Association of Chief Police Officers. Wyboston, Bedford: Centrix.

National Research Council. 2003a. *Fairness and Effectiveness in Policing: The Evidence.* Committee to Review Research on Police Policy and Practices, Wesley Skogan and Kathleen Frydl, eds., Committee on Law and Justice, Division of Behavioral and Social Sciences and Education. Washington, D.C.: National Academies Press.

———. 2003b. *The Polygraph and Lie Detection.* Committee to Review the Scientific Evidence on the Polygraph, Board on Behavioral, Cognitive, and Sensory Sciences and Committee on Nationals Statistics, Division of Behavioral and Social Sciences and Education. Washington, D.C.: National Academies Press.

Naudé, Gabriel. [1639] 1988. *Considérations politiques sur les coups d'état.* Paris: Éditions de Paris.

Newburn, Tim, ed. 2003. *Handbook of Policing.* Plymouth, Devon: Willan.

———, ed. 2005. *Policing: Key Readings.* Cullompton, Devon: Willan.

Newburn, Tim, Tom Williamson, and Alan Wright, eds. 2007. *Handbook of Criminal Investigation.* Cullompton, Devon: Willan.

Noaks, Lesley. 2000. "Private Cops on the Block: A Review of the Role of Private Security in Residential Communities." *Policing and Society* 10:143–161.

Nova Scotia. 1989. *Report of the Royal Commission on the Donald Marshall Jr. Prosecution.* Halifax: Royal Commission on the Donald Marshall Jr. Prosecution.

Ocqueteau, Frédéric. 1997. *Les défis de la sécurité privée: protection et surveillance dans la France d'aujourd'hui.* Paris: L'Harmattan.

———. 2006. *Mais qui donc dirige la police?* Paris: Armand Colin.

Ocqueteau, Frédéric, and Marie-Lys Pottier. 1995. *Vigilance et sécurité dans les grandes surfaces.* Paris: L'Harmattan, Institut des Hautes Études de la Sécurité Intérieure.

O'Neill, M., and C. Bloom. 1972. "The Field Officer: Is He Really Fighting Crime?" *Police Chief* 39:30–32.

Ontario. 1980. *Report of the Commission of Inquiry into the Confidentiality of Health Information* (the Krever Report). Toronto: Queens Printer for Ontario.

——. 1998. *The Commission on Proceedings Involving Guy Paul Morin: Report* (the Honourable Fred Kaufman, Chairman). Toronto: Ontario Ministry of the Attorney General, Queen's Printer for Ontario.

Oppel, Richard A. 2004. "Pentagon Opens Criminal Inquiry of Halliburton Pricing." *New York Times*, February 24, 2004.

O'Reilly, Conor, and Graham Ellison. 2006. "Eye Spy Private High: Re-conceptualizing High Policing Theory." *British Journal of Criminology* 46:641–660.

Orwell, George. 1946. "Decline of the English Murder." In *Decline of the English Murder and Other Essays*. Harmondsworth: Penguin.

Osterburg, J. W., and R. H. Ward. 2000. *Criminal Investigation: A Method of Reconstructing the Past*. Third edition. Cincinnati: Anderson.

Pagon, Milan, ed. 1996. *Policing in Central Europe: Comparing Firsthand Knowledge with Experience from the West*. Ljubljana: College of Police and Security Studies.

Palmiotto, Michael J. 1994. *Criminal Investigation*. Chicago: Nelson-Hall.

Paoli, Letizia. 2003. *Mafia Brotherhoods: Organized Crime, Italian Style*. New York: Oxford University Press.

Papanicolaou, Georgios. 2006. "Greece." In *Plural Policing, A Comparative Perspective*, edited by T. Jones and T. Newburn, 77–97. New York: Routledge.

Parker, C., and John Braithwaite. 2003. "Regulation." In *Oxford Handbook of Legal Studies*, edited by P. Cane and M. Tushnet, 119–145. New York: Oxford University Press.

Perelman, Chaïm. and Lucie Olbrechts-Tyteca. 1969. *The New Rethoric: A Treatise on Argumentation*. Notre Dame: University of Notre Dame Press.

Perlmutter, David D. 2000. *Policing the Media: Street Cops and Public Perceptions of Law Enforcement*. Thousand Oaks, Cal.: Sage.

Philips, David. 1980. "A New Engine of Power and Authority: The Institutionalization of Law-Enforcement in England." In *Crime and the Law: The Social History of Crime in Western Europe since 1500*, edited by V. A. C. Gatrell, B. Lenman, and G. Parker, 155–189. London: Europa Publications.

Pillorget, Suzanne. 1978. *Claude-Henri Feydeau de Marville, Lieutenant Général de Police de Paris—1740–1747*. Paris: Pedone.

Pinheiro, Paulo Sergio. 1991. "Police and Political Crisis: The Case of the Military Police." In *Vigilantism and the State in Modern Latin America: Essays on Extra-Legal Violence*, edited by M. K. Huggins, 167–188. New York: Praeger.

Pinkerton, Allan. 1870. *Tests on Passengers Conductors Made by the National Police Agency*. Chicago: G. H. Fergus.

——. 1877. *The Mollie Maguires and the Detectives*. New York: G. W. Carleton.

———. 1878. *Strikers, Communists, Tramps and Detectives*. New York: G. W. Carleton.

Poe, Edgar A. 1986. *The Annotated Tales of Edgar Allan Poe*. Edited with an introduction, notes, and a bibliography by Stephen Peithman. New York: Avenel Books.

Polk, Kenneth. 1994. *When Men Kill*. Cambridge: Cambridge University Press.

Powell, Michael. 2009. "Police Polish Image, but Concerns Persist." *New York Times*, January 3, 1.

Prenzler, Tim, and Rick Sarre. 2006. "Australia." In *Plural Policing: A Comparative Perspective*, edited by T. Jones and T. Newburn, 169–189. London: Routledge.

Press Council. 1983. *Press Conduct in the Sutcliffe Case: A Report by the Press Council*. London: Press Council.

Priestman, Martin. 2003. *The Cambridge Companion to Crime Fiction*. Cambridge: Cambridge University Press.

Proença Junior, Domicio, and Jacqueline Muniz. 2006. "Stop or I'll Call the Police." *British Journal of Criminology* 46:234–257.

Propp, Vladimir. 1975. *Morphology of the Folktale*. Second edition. Austin: University of Texas Press.

Pruvost, Geneviève. 2007. *Profession: policier. Sexe: féminin*. Paris: Éditions de la Maison des Sciences de l'Homme.

———. 2008. *De la "sergote" à la femme flic: une autre histoire de l'institution policière (1935–2005)*. Paris: La Découverte.

Punch, Maurice. 1975. "Research and the Police. In *The Police and the Community*, edited by J. Brown and G. Howes. 83–93. West Mead, Farnborough, UK: Saxon House and Lexington Books.

———. 1979. *Policing the Inner City: A Study of Amsterdam's Warmoestraat*. Hamden, Conn.: Archon Books.

Punch, Maurice, and T. Naylor. 1973. "The Police: A Social Service." *New Society* 24(554):358–361.

Québec. 1981a. *Rapport de la Commission sur des Opérations Policières en Territoire Québécois* (the Keable Report). Québec: Ministère des Communications.

———. 1981b. *Rapport sur les événements d'octobre 1970* (the Report by J.-F. Duchaîne). Quebec: Gouvernement du Québec, Ministère de la Justice.

———. 1993. *Rapport de l'enquête spéciale tenue sur les désordres qui ont fait suite à la conquête de la coupe Stanley par le club Canadien*. Québec: Ministère de la Sécurité Publique.

———. 2008. *Comité de recherche sur la prestation de services de sécurité dans les endroits publics*. Rapport Final (Jean-Paul Brodeur, Benoît Dupont, and Michel Sarrazin). Québec: Ministère de la Justice.

Radzinowicz, Sir Leon. 1956a. *A History of English Criminal Law and Its Administration*. Vol. 2. London: Stevens and Sons.

Radzinowicz, Sir Leon. 1956b. *A History of English Criminal Law and Its Administration*. Vol. 3. London: Stevens and Sons.

———. 1968. *A History of English Criminal Law and Its Administration*. Vol. 4. London: Stevens and Sons.

Randall, P., and P. Hamilton. 1972. "The Security Industry in the United Kingdom." In *The Security Industry in the UK: Papers Presented to the Cropwood Round-Table Conference, July 1971*, edited by F. H. McClintock and P. Wiles, 18–26. Cambridge: Cambridge Institute of Criminology.

Rashbaum, William K. 2010. "Retired New York Police Officials Question Integrity of Crime Data." *New York Times*, February 7, 20.

Reiner, Robert. 1985. *The Politics of the Police*. Brighton: Harvester Wheatsheaf.

———. 1991. *Chief Constables*. Oxford: Oxford University Press.

———. 1992a. "Policing a Postmodern Society." *Modern Law Review* 55(6):761–781.

———. 1992b. "Police Research in the United Kingdom: A Critical Review." In *Modern Policing*. Vol. 15 of *Crime and Justice: An Annual Review of Research*, edited by Michael Tonry and Norval Morris, 435–508. Chicago: University of Chicago Press.

———. 1992c. "Fin de Siècle Blues: The Police Face the Millennium." *Political Quaterly* 63(1):37–49.

———. 1994. "The Dialectics of Dixon: The Changing Image of the TV Cops." In *Police Force, Police Service: Care and Control in Britain*, edited by M. Stephens and S. Becker, 11–32. London: Macmillan.

———. 2000a. *The Politics of the Police*. Third edition. Oxford: Oxford University Press.

———. 2000b. "Romantic Realism: Policing and the Media." In *Core Issues in Policing*, edited by F. Leishman, B. Loveday, and S. Savage, 52–66. London: Longman.

———. 2000c. "Crime and Control in Britain." *Sociology* 34(1):71–94.

———. 2002. "Media Made Criminality: The Representation of Crime in the Mass Media." In *The Oxford Handbook of Criminology*. Third edition, edited by M. Maguire, R. Morgan, and R. Reiner, 376–416. Oxford: Clarendon.

———. 2003. "Policing and the Media." In *Handbook of Policing*, edited by T. Newburn, 259–282. Cullompton, Devon: Willan.

Reiss, Albert J. 1971. *The Police and the Public*. New Haven: Yale University Press.

———. 1988. *Private Employment of Public Police*. Washington, D.C.: US Department of Justice, National Institute of Justice.

Reith, Charles. 1952. *The Blind Eye of History*. London: Faber.

Ressler, Robert K., Ann W. Burgess, and John E. Douglas. 1988. *Sexual Homicide: Patterns and Motives*. Lexington, Mass.: Lexington Books.

Reuter, Peter. 1983a. "Licensing Criminals: Police and Informants." In *ABSCAM Ethics: Moral Issues and Deception in Law Enforcement*, edited by G. M. Caplan, 100–117. Cambridge, Mass.: Ballinger.

———. 1983b. *Disorganized Crime: The Economics of the Visible Hand*. Cambridge: MIT Press.

Richardson, James F. 1970. *The New York Police: Colonial Times to 1901*. New York: Oxford University Press.

———. 1974. *Urban Police in the United States*. Port Washington, N.Y.: Kennikat Press.

Riedel, M., M. A. Zahn, and L. Mock. 1985. *The Nature and Patterns of American Homicide*. Washington, D.C.: U.S. Government Printing Office.

Rigakos, George S. 2002. *The New Parapolice, Risks, Markets and Commodified Social Control*. Toronto: University of Toronto Press.

———. 2005. "Beyond Public-Private: Towards a New Typology of Policing." In *Re-Imagining Policing in Canada*, edited by D. Cooley, 260–319. Toronto: University of Toronto Press.

Romano, Santi, 1918/1951. *L'ordinamento giuridico*. Florence: Sansoni.

Rosenbaum, Dennis P. 2006. "The Limits of Hot Spots Policing." In *Police Innovation: Contrasting Perspectives*, edited by David Weisburd and Anthony A. Braga, 245–266. Cambridge: Cambridge University Press.

Rudé, George. 1964. *The Crowd in History: A Study of Popular Disturbances in France and England, 1730–1848*. New York: John Wiley.

———. 1985. *Criminal and Victim: Crime and Society in Early Nineteenth-Century England*. Oxford: Clarendon.

Ruggiero, Vincenzo. 2003. *Crime in Literature Sociology of Deviance and Fiction*. London: Verso.

Rumbaut, Rubén, and and Egon Bittner. 1979. "Changing Conceptions of the Police Role: A Sociological Review." In *Crime and Justice: An Annual Review of Research*, edited by N. Morris and M. Tonry, 1:239–288. Chicago: University of Chicago Press.

Ryan, Lorna. 1997. *Reading the Prostitute: Appearance, Place and Time in British and Irish Press; Stories of Prostitution*. Aldershot, Hants.: Ashgate.

Saint-Germain, Jacques. 1962. *La reynie et la police au grand siècle*. Paris: Hachette.

Saint-Simon, Louis de Rouvroy, duc de. 1953. *Mémoires*. 7 vols. Paris: Gallimard.

Sanders, Andrew, and Richard Young. 2002. "From Suspect to Trial." In *The Oxford Handbook of Criminology*. Third edition, edited by M. Maguire, R. Morgan, and R. Reiner, 1034–1075. Oxford: Clarendon.

Sanders, William B. 1977. *Detective Work*. New York: Free Press.

Savona, Ernesto U. 2004. *Crime and Technology: New Frontiers for Regulation, Law Enforcement and Research*. Dordrecht: Springer.

Scahill, Jeremy. 2007. *Blackwater*. New York: Nation Books.

Schlosser, Eric. 2008. "Burger with a Side of Spies." *New York Times*, May 7, A27.

Schmid, Alex. 2004. "Links between Terrorist and Organized Crime Networks: Emerging Patterns and Trends." In *Trafficking: Networks and Logistics of Transnational Crime and International Terrorism*. Proceedings of the International Conference on Trafficking: Networks and Logistics of Transnational Crime and International Terrorism. Courmayeur Mont Blanc, Italy, December 6–8, 2002, edited by Dimitri Vlassis, 189–210. Milan: ISPAC.

Schmitt, Carl. 1927. *Der Begriff des Politischen*. Archiv für Sozialwissenschaften und Sozialpolitik 58 (1927) S. 1 bis 33.

Schneider, John C. 1980. *Detroit and the Problem of Order, 1830–1880: A Geography of Crime, Riot and Policing*. Lincoln: University of Nebraska Press.

Schwartz, Richard D., and James C. Miller. 1964. "Legal Evolution and Societal Complexity." *American Journal of Sociology* 70(2):159–169.

Security Intelligence Review Committee (SIRC). 1994. *The Heritage Front Affair: Report to the Solicitor General of Canada*. Ottawa: Security Intelligence Review Committee.

Senior, Hereward. 1997. *Constabulary. The Rise of Police Institutions in Britain, the Commonwealth and the United States*. Oxford: Dundurn Press.

Servan, Antoine J. M. 1767. *Discours sur l'administration de la justice criminelle*. Geneva.

Settle, Rod. 1995. *Police Informers: Negotiation and Power*. Annandale, New South Wales: Federation Press.

Shalloo, Jeremiah P. 1933. *Private Police with Special Reference to Pennsylvania*. Philadelphia: American Academy of Political and Social Science.

Shapland, Joanna, and Dick Hobbs. 1989. "Policing on the Ground." In *Coming to Terms with Policing*, edited by R. Morgan and D. Smith, 11–30. London: Routledge.

Shapland, Joanna, and Jon Vagg. 1987. "Using the Police." *British Journal of Criminology* 27(1):36–39.

———. 1988. *Policing by the Public*. London: Routledge.

Shearing, Clifford D. 1984. *Dial-a-Cop: A Study of Police Mobilisation*. Toronto: Research Report of the Centre of Criminology, University of Toronto.

———. 1992. "The Relation between Public and Private Policing." In *Modern Policing*. Vol. 15 of *Crime and Justice: An Annual Review of Research*, edited by Michael Tonry and Norval Morris, 399–434.

———. 2004. "Thoughts on Sovereignty." *Policing & Society* 14(1):5–12.

Shearing, Clifford D., and Julie Berg. 2006. "South Africa." In *Plural Policing: A Comparative Perspective*, edited by T. Jones and T. Newburn, 190–221. New York: Routledge.

Shearing, Clifford D., Margaret B. Farnell, and Philip C. Stenning. 1980. *Contract Security in Ontario*. University of Toronto, Center of Criminiology.

Shearing, Clifford D., and Jeffrey S. Leon. 1977. "Reconsidering the Police Role: A Challenge to a Challenge of a Popular Conception." *Canadian Journal of Crime and Corrections* 19(4):341–343.

Shearing, Clifford D., and Philip C. Stenning. 1981. "Modern Private Security: Its Growth and Implications." In *Crime and Justice: An Annual Review of Research*, edited by M. Tonry and N. Morris, 3:193–245. Chicago: University of Chicago Press.

———. 1982. *Private Security and Private Justice: The Challenge of the 80s*. Montreal: Institute for Research on Public Policy.

———. 1983. "Private Security: Implications for Social Control." *Social Problems* 30(5):493–506.

———. 1985. "From the Panopticon to Disneyworld: The Development of Discipline." In *Perspectives in Criminal Law: Essays in Honour of John LL. J. Edwards*, edited by A. N. Doobs and E. L. Greenspan, 335–348. Aurora, Ont.: Canadian Law Books.

Shearing, Clifford, Philip Stenning, and Susan Adario. 1985. *Criminal Investigation: An Introduction to Principles and Practice*. Cullomption, Devon: Willan.

Shenk, David. 1997. *Data Smog: Surviving the Information Glut*. San Francisco: HarperEdge.

Sherman, Lawrence. 1986. "Policing Community: What Works?" In *Communities and Crime*. Vol. 8 of *Crime and Justice: A Review of Research*, edited by Albert J. Reiss and Michael Tonry, 343–386. Chicago: University of Chicago Press.

———. 1990. "Police Crackdowns: Initial and Residual Deterrence." In *Crime and Justice: A Review of Research*, edited by Michael Tonry and Norval Morris, 12:1–48. Chicago: University of Chicago Press.

———. 1992. "Attacking Crime: Policing and Crime Control." In *Modern Policing*. Vol. 15 of *Crime and Justice: An Annual Review of Research*, edited by Michael Tonry and Norval Morris. Chicago: University of Chicago Press, 159–230.

———. 1996. "Repeat Calls for Service: Policing in the Hot Spots." In *Police Operations: Analysis and Evaluation*, edited by G. Corner, L. Gaines, and V. Kappeler, 277–292. Cincinnati: Anderson.

Sherman, Lawrence, Denise Gottfredson, Doris MacKenzie, John Eck, Peter Reuter, and Shawn Bushway. 1997. *Preventing Crime: What Works, What Doesn't, What's Promising? A Report to the United States Congress*. College Park: University of Maryland.

Sherman, Lawrence, and Dennis P. Rogan. 1998. "Effects of Gun Seizures on Gun Violence: 'Hot Spots' Patrol in Kansas City." In *What Works in Policing*, edited by David H. Bayley, 177–196. New York: Oxford University Press.

Silver, Allen. 1967. "The Demand for Order in Civil Society: A Review of Some Themes in the History of Urban Crime, Police and Riot." In *The Police: Six Sociological Essays*, edited by D. J. Bordua, 1–24. New York: John Wiley and Sons.

Silverman, Eli B. 1999. *NYPD Battles Crime? Innovative Strategies in Policing*. Boston: Northeastern University Press.

———. 2006. "Compstat's Innovation." In *Police Innovation: Contrasting Perspectives*, edited by David Weisburd and Anthony A. Braga, 267–283. Cambridge: Cambridge University Press.

Simmel, Georg. 1970. *The Sociology of Georg Simmel*, edited by K. H. Wolff. New York: Macmillan.

Simon, David. 1991. *Homicide*. Boston: Little, Brown.

Simpson, Philip L. 2000. *Psycho Paths: Tracking the Serial Killer through Contemporary American Film and Fiction*. Carbondale: Southern University Press.

Singer, Peter. 2003. *Corporate Warriors: The Rise of the Privatized Military Industry*. Ithaca: Cornell University Press.

Skogan, Wesley. 1986. "Fear of Crime and Neighbourhood Change." In *Communities and Crime*. Vol. 8 of *Crime and Justice: A Review of Research*, edited by A. J. Reiss and M. Tonry, 203–229. Chicago: University of Chicago Press.

———. 1990a. *Disorder and Decline*. New York: Free Press.

———. 1990b. *The Police and the Public in England and Wales: A British Crime Survey Report*. Home Office Research Study 117. London: HMSO.

———. 2006. "The Promise of Community Policing." In *Police Innovation: Contrasting Perspectives*, edited by David Weisburd and Anthony A. Braga, 27–43. Cambridge: Cambridge University Press.

Skolnick, Jerome H. 1966. *Justice without Trial: Law Enforcement in Democratic Society*. New York: John Wiley.

Smith, Bruce. 1925. *The State Police*. New York: Macmillan.

Smith, Douglas, and Jeremy Gray. 1985. *Police and People in London: The PSI Report*. Aldershot, Hants.: Gower.

Smith, Douglas A., and Jody R. Klein. 1984. "Police Control of Interpersonal Disputes." *Social Problems* 31(4):108–132.

Smith, N., and C. Flanagan. 2000. *The Effective Detective: Identifying the Skills of an Effective SIO*. Police Research Series 122. London: Home Office.

SourceWatch. 2008. *Guillermo Zarabozo*. www.sourcewatch.org/index.php?title= Diplomatic_Tactical_Services&printable=yes.

South, Nigel. 1987. "Law, Profit and "Private Persons": Private and Public Policing in English History." In *Private Policing*, edited by C. D. Shearing and P. C. Stenning, 72–109. Newbury Park, Cal.: Sage.

———. 1988. *Policing for Profit*. Newbury Park, Cal.: Sage.

Southgate, P., and Paul Ekblom. 1984. *Contacts between Police and Public: Findings from the British Crime Survey*. Home Office Research and Planning Unit Report 77. London: HMSO.

Sparks, Richard. 1992. *Television and the Drama of Crime: Moral Tales and the Place of Crime in Public Life*. Buckingham, UK: Open University Press.

Spehner, Norbert, and Robert Allard. 1990. *Écrits sur le roman policier: bibliographie analytique et critique des études et essais sur le roman policier et le film policier*. Longueil, Qué.: Le Préambule.

Stallion, M., and D. S. Wall. 1999. *The British Police: Force and Chiefs Officers, 1929–2000*. Bramshill, Hook, UK: Police History Society.

Stansfield, Ronald T. 1996. *Issue in Policing: A Canadian Perspective*, Toronto: Thompson Educational Publishing.

Stelfox, Peter. 2009. *Criminal Investigation. An Introduction to Principles and Practice*. Cullompton, Devon: Willan.

Stenning, Philip C. 2000. "Powers and Accountability of Private Police." *European Journal on Criminal Policy and Research* 8:325–352.

Stenning, Philip C., and Clifford D. Shearing. 1979. "Search and Seizure: Powers of Private Security Personnel." A study paper prepared for the Law Reform Commission of Canada. Commission de réforme du droit du Canada, Criminal Law series.

———. 1980. "The Quiet Revolution: The Nature, Development and General Legal Implication of Private Security in Canada." *Criminal Law Quarterly* 22:220–248.

Stokes, Lawrence D. 1975. "Otto Ohlendorf, the Sicherheitdienst and Public Opinion in Nazi Germany." In *Police Forces in History*, edited by G. L. Mosse, 231–261. London: Sage.

Stolleis, Michael. 2000. "Was bedeutet 'Normdurchsetzung' bei Policeyordnungen der frühen Neuzeit?" *Helmholz R.H., Grundlagen des Rechts. Festschriften für Peter Landauzum 65*, 739–757. Paderborn, Schöning.

Storch, Robert. 1975. "The Plague of the Blue Locusts: Police Reform and Popular Resistance in Northern England, 1840–1857." *International Review of Social History* 20:61–90.

———. 1976. "The Policeman as Domestic Missionary: Urban Discipline and Popular Culture in Northern England, 1850–1880." *Journal of Social History* 9(4):481–509.

Styles, John. 1989. "Print and Policing." In *Policing and Prosecution in Britain 1750–1850*, edited by D. Hay and F. Snyder, 55–111. Oxford: Clarendon.

Suskind, Ron. 2006. *The One Percent Doctrine: Deep inside America's Pursuit of Its Enemies since 9/11*. New York: Simon and Schuster.

Tanner, Samuel. 2009. "Dynamiques de participation et processus de cristallisation de bandes armées dans les crimes de masse: Retour sur la violence en ex-Yougoslavie." PhD dissertation, Université de Montréal, École de Criminologie.

Tarling, Roger. 1988. *Police Work and Manpower Allocation*. Research and Planning Unit Paper 47. London: Home Office.

Taylor, David. 1997. *The New Police in Nineteenth-Century England: Crime, Conflict and Control*. Manchester: Manchester University Press.

———. 1998. *Crime, Policing and Punishment in England, 1750–1914*. New York: St. Martin's Press.

Tien, J. M, J. W Simon, and R. C. Larson. 1978. *An Alternative Approach in Police Patrol: The Wilmington Split-Force Experiment*. Washington, D.C.: U.S. Government Printing Office.

Tilly, Charles. 1985. "War Making and State Making as Organized Crime." In *Bringing the State Back In*, edited by P. B. Evans, D. Rueschemeyer, and T. Skocpol, 169–191. Cambridge: Cambridge University Press.

Tompkins, Joyce M. 1932. *The Popular Novel in England, 1770–1800*. London: Methuen.

Treaster, Joseph B. 2005. "Police Quitting: Hundreds of Officers, Feeling Outmatched, Have Left Force." *New York Times*, September 4, 1 and 24.

Trojanowicz, Robert C., and Bonnie Bucqueroux. 1989. *Community Policing: A Contemporary Perspective.* Cincinnati: Anderson.

United Kingdom. 1999. *The Stephen Lawrence Inquiry. Report of an Inquiry by Sir William MacPherson of Cluny advised by Tom Cook, The Right Reverend Dr John Sentamu, Dr Richard Stone.* Presented to Parliament by the Secretary of State for the Home Department by Command of Her Majesty. London: Stationery Office.

United States. 1977. National Advisory Committee on Criminal Justice Standards and Goals. *Private Security: Standards and Goals, From the Official Private Security Task Force Report.* Cincinnati: Anderson.

———. 1997. Congress. *Secrecy: Report of the Commission on Protecting and Reducing Government Secrecy* (Senator Daniel Patrick Moynihan, chairman). Washington, D.C.: U.S. Government Printing Office.

———. 2002. *September 11 and the Imperative of Reform in the U.S Intelligence Community—Additional Views of Senator Richard C. Shelby Vice Chairman, Senate Select Committee on Intelligence.* Washington, D.C. www.iwar.org.uk/ news-archive/tia/Shelby.pdf.

———. 2004. National Commission on Terrorist Attacks upon the United States. *The 9/11 Commission Report: Final Report of the National Commission on Terrorist Attacks upon the United States.* New York: Norton.

Van Steden, Ronald. 2007. *Privatizing Policing. Describing and Explaining the Growth of Private Security.* Amsterdam: Bju Legal Publishers.

Van Steden, Ronald, and L. W. J. C. Huberts. 2005. "Private Security Industry Growth in Western Countries." In *Encyclopedia of Law Enforcement.* Vol. 3, *The Private Security Industry,* edited by L. E. Sullivan and M. R. Haberfeld, 1261–1268. Thousands Oaks, Cal.: Sage.

Van Steden, Ronald, and Rick Sarre. 2007. "The Growth of Private Security: Trends in the European Union." *Security Journal* 20:222–235.

Varese, Federico. 1996. "What Is the Russian Mafia?" *Low Intensity Conflict and Law Enforcement* 5(2):129–138.

———. 2001. *The Russian Mafia: Private Protection in a New Market Economy.* New York: Oxford University Press.

Vergara, Camilo José. 1997. *The New American Ghetto.* New Brunswick: Rutgers University Press.

Volkmann, J. W. 1801. *P. Colquhoun's Polizei von London.* Leipzig: in der Baumgartnerschen Buchhandlung.

Von Hentig, Hans. 1919. *Fouché: Ein Beitrag zur Technik des politischen Polizei in nachrevolutionären Perioden.* Tubingen: Mohr.

Von Justi, J. H. G. [1782] 1969. *Grundsätze des Policey-Wissenschaf.* Gottingen: Verlag des Wittwe Vandenhoek; Frankfurt: Sauer & Auvermann Verlag.

Waddington, P. A. J. 1991. *The Strong Arm of the Law.* Oxford: Clarendon Press.

———. 1993. *Calling the Police.* Aldershot, Hants.: Avebury.

Wade, John. 1829. *A Treatise on the Police and Crimes of the Metropolis.* London: Longman, Rees, Orme, Brown and Green.

Waegel, William B. 1982. "Patterns of Police Investigation of Urban Crimes." *Journal of Police and Administration* 10(4):452–465.

Wakefield, Alison. 2003. *Selling Security: The Private Policing of Public Space.* Cullompton, Devon: Willan.

Walker, Samuel. 1977. *A Critical History of Police Reform.* Lexington, Mass.: D. C. Heath.

———. 1992. *The Police in America: An Introduction.* New York: McGraw-Hill.

Walsh, W. F., and E. J. Donovan 1989. "Private Security and Community Policing: Evaluation and Comment." *Journal of Criminal Justice* 17:187–197.

Webber, Grégoire Charles N. 2005. "Legal Lawlessness and the Rule of Law: A Critique of Section 25.1 of the Criminal Code." *Queens Law Journal* 31:122–147.

Weber, Max. 1946. "Politics as a Vocation." In *From Max Weber: Essays in Sociology,* edited and translated by H. Gerth and C. Wright Mills, 77–128. New York: Oxford University Press.

———. 1978. *Economy and Society.* Berkeley: University California Press.

Webster, John A. 1970. "Police Task and Time Study." *Journal of Criminal Law, Criminology and Police Science* 61:94–100.

Weisburd, David, and Anthony Braga, eds. 2006. *Police Innovation: Contrasting Perspectives.* New York: Cambridge University Press.

Weiss, Robert P. 1986. "Private Detective Agencies and Labour Discipline in the United States." *Historical Journal* 29:565–586.

Wellford, Charles, and James Cronin. 1999. *An Analysis of Variables Affecting the Clearance of Homicides: A Multistate Study.* Washington, D.C.: Justice Research and Statistics Association.

Westley, William. 1970. *Violence and the Police: A Study of Law, Custom and Morality.* Cambridge: MIT Press.

Whitaker, Gordon P. 1982. "What Is Patrol Work?" *Police Studies* 4: 13–22.

White, Captain W., and E. I. C. Service. 1839. *The Police Spy, or the Metropolitan Police: Its Advantages, Abuses and Defects.* Montana: Kessinger.

Whorf, Benjamin Lee. 1964. *Language, Thought and Reality.* Cambridge: MIT Press.

Williams, Alan. 1979. *The Police of Paris—1718–1789.* Baton Rouge: Louisiana State University Press.

Williams, Davis, Bruce George, and Emma MacLennan. 1984. *Guarding against Low Pay: The Case for Regulation in Contract Security.* London: Low Pay Unit.

Williams, James W. 2005. "Governability Matters: The Private Policing of Economic Crime and the Challenge of Democratic Governance." *Policing and Society* 15(2):187–211.

Wilson, Edmund. 1950. "Why Do People Read Detective Stories?" In *Classics and Commercials: A Literary Chronicle of the Forties.* New York: Farrar, Strauss.

Wilson, Geoffrey Philip. 1976. *Cases and Material on Constitutional and Administrative Law.* Second edition. Cambridge: Cambridge University Press.

Wilson, James Q. 1968. *Varieties of Police Behavior*. Cambridge: Harvard University Press.

―――. 1978. *The Investigators*. New York: Basic Books.

Wilson, James Q., and George Kelling. 1982. "Broken Windows: The Police and the Neighborhood Safety." *Atlantic Monthly* 249(3): 29–38.

Wilson, James Q., 1983. *Thinking about Crime*. Basic Books: New York.

Wood, Gerald. 1986. "Police Informants in Canada: The Law and Reality." *Saskatchewan Law Review* 50(2):249–270.

Wood, Jennifer, and Benoît Dupont. 2006. *Democracy, Society and the Governance of Security*. Cambridge: Cambridge University Press.

Wood, Jennifer, and Clifford Shearing. 2007. *Imagining Security*. Cullompton, Devon: Willan.

Wycoff, Mary Ann, and Peter K. Manning. 1983. "The Police and Crime Control." In *Evaluating Performance of Criminal Justice Agencies*, edited by G. P. Whitaker and C. D. Philips, 15–32. Beverly Hills: Sage.

Young, Malcom. 1991. *An Inside Job: Policing and Police Culture in Britain*. Oxford: Oxford University Press.

Zaccardelli, Giuliano. 2005. *Speaking Notes for a Presentation on Intelligence-Led Policing at the Canadian Association of Chiefs of Police Conference*. Ottawa, Ont., August 23. www.rcmp-grc.gc.ca/speeches/sp_cacp_3_e.htm.

Zhao, Jihong, Matthew Scheider, and Quint Thurman. 2002. "The Effect of Police Presence on Public Fear Reduction and Satisfaction: A Review of the Literature." *Justice Professional* 15(3):273–299.

Zhao, Jihong, and Quint C. Thurman. 1997. "Community Policing: Where Are We Now?" *Crime and Delinquency* 43(3):345–357.

Zimring, Frank E. 2003. *The Contradictions of American Capital Punishment*. New York: Oxford University Press.

Zimring, Franklin E., and Gordon Hawkins. 1997. *Crime Is Not the Problem: Lethal Violence in America*. New York: Oxford University Press.

Index

absorbent policing, 227–8, 290–1
Abu Ghraib, 250, 292, 347
administrative policing, 314
agents of policing, 21, 339
Air India plane bombing, 236, 239
Alex, Nicholas, 171
Anglo-American policing, 11
Anglo-Saxon policing, 23, 216, 310, 316
antinomies (discordances), in theory of policing, 7–8
    violence, 38–9
The Art of War (Sun Tzu), 229
Association des témoins repentis du Québec, 247

Baldwin-Felts private security agency, 266
ballistics, 204, 211
Bayley, David, 5, 103, 263
Bentham, Jeremy, 39, 45–6, 62, 230, 323
Bereitschaftspolizei (Bepo), Germany, 23
bibliography of essays, on police fiction, 86–7
Bittner, Egon, 20, 103–26, 293, 336
Blackwater, 14, 274, 279

border patrol, 27
Bounty hunters, 30
Brazilian policing, 317–20
    casualties, from the actions of civil and of paramilitary police, 320–1
    police killings, 320–2
British model of policing, 336
    creation of English police, 62–5
    discretionary imprisonment, 59–60
    police reform of 1829, 60–2
    prevention of crimes, 65–6
    spies and watchmen, 67–8
    targets, 66–7
    from 1660 to 1785, 58–60
British Telecom, 268
Bundeskriminalamt (BKA), Germany, 139
Bureau of Alcohol, Tobacco, Firearms, and Explosives (ATF), United States, 24
Bureau of Investigation's General Intelligence Division, 74

CACI Int., 292
Canadian Aboriginals, 178
Canadian Airborne Regiment, 311
Canadian Air Transport Security Agency (CATSA), 309

Canadian Battle Group in
    Somalia, 312
Canadian Criminal Code (CCC), 6, 32,
    166, 246, 340
Canadian criminal law, 6
Canadian Security Intelligence Service
    (CSIS), 24, 224, 236
Catholic heretics, 54
CCTV, 86, 135, 277–8, 282, 303, 305
CEWs, 283–8, 304–5
Chadwick, Edwin, 60, 62
Chicago Alternative Policing Strategy
    (CAPS), 172
Christie, Agatha, 87
Clément, Pierre, 53
coercive policing powers, 6, 44, 104,
    107, 118, 125, 127, 142, 165, 225,
    231, 259, 264, 267, 280, 292, 308,
    328, 340–1
collective violence. See riots
Colquhoun, Patrick, 18–19
Community Security Establishment
    (CSE), 26
Compagnies républicaines de sécurité
    (CRS), 23, 146
compartmentalization, 244–5
completeness, notion of, 9–10
Cornwell, Patricia, 93
Cosa Nostra, 33
counterterrorism, 26, 187, 200
crime fiction, 87
crime profiling, 211–12
crimes, committed in schools, 338
crime scene analysis, 84, 93, 95, 189,
    204, 209, 211, 213
Crime Scene Investigation, 95, 211
criminal investigation, 344–6, 356–7
    agencies, 23
    amount of time preparing cases for
        the prosecution, 194
    body of research, 186–92
    clearance or clear-up rate of
        criminal cases, 190–2, 205–7

conviction investigation, 345
efficiency of, 193–4
evidence-based classification,
    197–205
homicide, 189–90
identification factors, 207–9
as information processing, 194
investigative powers of
    police, 194–7
location factors, 209–10
orientation of, 188–9
postclearance work, 216–18
on a private basis, 192–3, 345–6
as a reactive process, 187–8
review articles, 185
scientific policing and
    forensics, 210–12
theories of, 212–20
criminal profiling, 93, 204
criminology, 182
Critchley, Thomas A., 58
Cross, James Richard, 245
CSI effect, 95
cybercrime, 253

d'Argenson, Marquis, 53, 56, 225
d'Argis, Boucher, 47
data mining, 93
death penalty, 51, 61–2, 264–5, 311
deceitful practices, 291–2
Decree-Law No. 667, Brazil, 318
de Faye, T. F., 312
Defense Criminal Investigative
    Service, 26
definition of policing, 47–8, 103, 341
    private security, 255–8
de La Mare, Nicolas. See La Mare,
    Nicolas de
de la Reynie, Gabriel Nicolas, 48
delinquency and criminal justice
    system, 251–3, 349, 360
de Mayenne, Turquet, 48
democratic policing, 135–6

demographical variables, of police
  age, 142–3
  blacks, 147
  education, 149–50
  Hispanics, 147
  racial and ethnic minorities, 147–9
  sex, 143–7
  women, 143–6, 148
detective stories, 92–3
DGSE, 228
Dictionary of the English Language
  (Samuel Johnson), 48
DNA fingerprinting, 202, 204, 211, 219
DNA tests, 219
Doyle, Aaron, 80
Doyle, Conan, 93
Draft Riots (1863), 73
Drug Enforcement Administration
  (DEA), 24

ECHELON spying program, 26
87th Precinct series of novels, 94
electronic intelligence (ELINT), 26
electronic surveillance, 132
Elias, Norbert, 107, 121
English Secret Service, 239
epistemic approach, to criminal
  investigation, 212–15
Ericson, Richard, 37, 153, 213
ethnic cleansing, 228
Europol, 27
evidence-based classification, of
  criminal investigations
  case-processing investigation, 204
  differentiation, 203–4
  identification inquiry, 204
  integrated investigations, 203
  location inquiry, 204
  maxi-trial, 204
  murder, 198–9
  proactive and event-centered, 200
  proactive and hybrid, 201
  proactive and suspect-centered, 200

reactive and event-centered, 201–2
reactive and hybrid, 202
reactive and suspect-centered, 201
retrospective and
  event-centered, 202
retrospective and hybrid, 202–3
retrospective and
  suspect-centered, 202
external security services, 26
extralegality, 291–2
extralegal policing, 310
  comparison between legal
  and, 327–9
  notions of security and
  protection, 322–7
  and private security, 328–9
  reversibility factor, 327–8

fatalities, 39
Federal Bureau of Investigation
  (FBI), 23, 35, 74, 237
feminization of the police, 5, 143–7
  consequences for policing, 343, 356
  duties, 145
  history, 143
  numbers, 144–5
  masculinization of female
  officers, 180
  promotion, 145
  quotas, 146
  tutelage, 146
Fixed Penalty Notices, 337
Fontenelle, Bernard le Bovier de, 56,
  225, 227
foreign intelligence services, 26
forensic medicine, 93
forensic science, 93
Foucault, Michel, 48
Fouché, Joseph, 48, 54–6, 230, 233
French Declaration of Human
  Rights, 51
French Direction de la sécurité
  extérieure (DGSE), 26

French Direction de la surveillance du
   territoire (DST), 23, 224
French mercenaries, 29
French model of police, 336
   creation of the French "Lieutenance
      générale de police" and its
      context, 48–50
   crime prevention, 56–7
   fundamental aspects, 44–5
   goals and priorities, 52–4
   issue of police discretion, 45
   lawfulness of police
      operations, 54–6
   low status, 46
   major themes, 45–6
   meaning of the Word "Police," 47–8
   mirror-image relationship between
      the police and targets, 55–6
   prevention, 56–7
   surveillance, 46
   system of policing, 50–2
   targets of policing, 54
Front de libération du Québec
   (FLQ), 237, 244
The Function of the Police in Modern
   Society (Bittner), 104

Gambetta's hypothesis, 310, 322–8
Gestapoists, 233
Goldstein, Herman, 282, 336
governance of security, 9, 261, 300–5,
   352
Governing Security, 301
grey areas, of policing, 8
Guardia di Finanza (GdF), Italy, 24

hard-to-solve-major-inquiries, 201–2
Harris, Thomas, 93–4, 96
Heidensohn, Frances, 12, 143
high policing and low policing, 55,
   346–7, 357–8
   actionable intelligence, 228
   capacity for analysis, 235–6

conflation of separate
   powers, 231–2
deception, 230–1
extralegality, 232–4
features, 252
Fontenelle's eulogy, 225–6
fundamental differences, 228
and kinds of delinquency, 251–3
legitimacy and illegitimacy, 330–4
model, 251–4
operational procedures, 234–8
preventive intelligence vs.
   prosecutorial evidence, 236
protection of political regime, 226,
   288–9
secrecy, 229–30
status of state, 227
strategy of circumvention, 236–8
surveillance, 247–51
use of informants, 229
utilization of criminals, 228
hired police informants, 8
history of policing, 339, 352–3
   British model, 57–68
   definition of word "police," 47–8
   French model, 44–57
   North American model, 68–78
Hobbes, Thomas, 39, 183, 249
Hobbs, Dick, 32, 217
homegrown terrorism, 23
human intelligence (HUMINT), 26,
   247, 292
hybrid agencies, 26
   private, 29–30
hypnosis, 211

image intelligence (IMINT), 26
images of policing, 339, 353–4
   characteristics of media content of
      crime and policing news
      stories, 80–2
   constraints on the production of
      news, 82–6

contrast between police fiction and
crime research , 99–100
crime and police fiction, 86–97
low-definition environment, 94–97
media impact, 100–2
media as police, 85–6
significance of policing
representations, 97–9
information channels, 86
informants, 244
anonymous, 240
classification, 244
consequences of using, 244–7
corruption, 246
delinquent, 241
police, without obliged by
law, 241–2
police sources, 240–1
police undercover agents, 241
protected witnesses, 242
statutory, 240
unreliability of, 245
whistle blowers, 242–3
in-house private security, 32
instigation, 201
integrated model, of policing, 251–4,
306
intelligence-led policing (ILP), 235
intensive policing, 14
intensive quantity, notion of, 39–40,
337
internal policing agencies, 23
internal security, in private sector, 28
International Peacekeeping Forces, 27
international perspective, of
policing, 10–12, 27
Interpol, 27
investigative journalism, 85
Irish Republican Army (IRA), 253

Kafka, Franz, 20
Klockars, Carl B., 104, 214
knowledge industry, of private
security, 28–9
Kuykendall, Jack, 187

La Mare, Nicolas de, 18–19, 47, 53–4
Lenoir, Jean Charles Philippe, 50–5,
58, 232
Latin-American military police
divisions, 12
The Laws of Plato, 18
Le Carré, John, 90
legal lawlessness, 6
Lemay, Corporal Marcel, 177
Létourneau inquiry, 312
Lex Talionis, 5
Liang, Hsi-Huey, 223
The Local Governance of Crime, 301
Louis XIV, 49–50, 53, 57

Mafia, 33–4, 121, 333; see also private
protection, business of
maintaining order, 176–7
Manning, Peter, 94–5, 258
Marks v. Beyfus, 238
Marx, Gary, 239–40, 247–8
McDonald commission, 130–1
means of policing, 164
media reporting, 101
bias, 81
frequency, 80–1
police stories, 81–2
publishing formats, 82
seriousness of crime, 81
time constraints in, 83
violence, 81
Megan laws, 40
Mémoire sur la Police en France,
et particulièrement sur la Police
de Paris, 47
MI5, 24, 75, 224
MI6, 26, 224
microcrises, 109
military "asymmetrical conflict," 179
military forces, 176, 179–80

military intelligence, 315
Military Intelligence. *See* MI5; MI6
military policing, 349, 360
   agencies, 25, 310–11
   vs. conventional police forces, 322
   insulation, 316
   investigation, 312
   militarized policing, 313–17
   military police, 25, 311–13
   paramilitary policing, 317–22
   rank and file, 312–13
minimal forces, 106–12
mirror effect between crime and penal
   justice, 5–6
Mohawk reservations, 178
Mollie Maguires, 73–4
Morris, Alexander, 171
Mossad, 228
Moynihan, Patrick Daniel, 37
Muir, William Ker, Jr., 112
multifunctional contract agency, 28

Napoli, Paolo, 48
Nazi security service, 239
Nazi terror, 233
"need to know" principle of
   operation, 245
New York Metropolitan Police, 73
Night Watch, 50
9/11. *See* September 11, 2001
NKVD, 233
noncontractual policing, 134
North America, police model
   flawed realization, 70–2
   hybrid system, Canada, 75–6
   importation of English model,
     68–70
   public and private policing, 72–5
NYPD, 14, 102, 147–8, 171, 243, 284,
   346

objects of knowledge, 36–8
October Crisis, 1970, 236–7

Oka Crisis of 1990, 177–80
Orwell, George, 20

Pain-inducing technology, 283–8, 359
Panopticon (Bentham), 230
Paoli, Letizia, 33
paramilitary policing, 317–22, 360
parapolice units, 25–6, 37, 298
Paris Guard, 50
patrol functions, 171–2
Patterns of Policing (David Bayley), 5, 104
pepper spray, 322
phenomenology, 38
Pickton, Robert, 203
Pinkerton National Detective
   Agency, 28, 73–4, 258, 267
plainclothes ("detective") agencies, 50,
   64, 88–9, 116, 124, 129–30,
   139–40, 142, 189, 193, 198, 213,
   225, 278, 280, 301, 315, 333
Plato, 12
plural policing, 8, 315
Poe, Edgar Allan, 69, 88, 91–3
"police," meanings of the word
   as an adjective, 19–21
   as a common noun, 18–19
   as verb, 21
Police authority, 339–41
Police aux frontières (PAF), 27
police corruption, 246–7, 360
police coups, 232
police fiction, 100
   clues, processing of, 92–3
   constables and investigators, 88–9
   criminal investigation, 91–4
   genre, 87–8
   insiders and outsiders, 89–90
   murder investigations, 91
   private eyes and public
     investigators, 89
   reactive nature of, 92
   super-sleuths and great
     criminals, 90–1

tools of the trade, 92–4
police force, use of
    Oka Crisis of 1990, 177–80
    vs. military forces, 176, 179–80
police-industrial complex, 302–5,
    348–9
police informants, 85–6
"police-informer" privilege, 238
police integrity, 20
police penetration, 20
police staff, 19
police-use-of-force paradigm, 105–6,
    136–8, 225
    demand-side theory, 123–4, 137–8
    depoliticization, 121–2
    formal oppositions, 127–8
    fragmentation, 122–3, 137
    opposite terms within, 124–5
    police visibility, 122
    progressive orientation, 121
    substantial oppositions, 125–7
    as testing tool, 128–30
    virtual vs. actual force, 122, 137
police visibility, 8
police work, nature of
    book reviews, 160
    calls attendance, 155
    committed and uncommitted
        time, 152–3
    competence vs. performance, 151–2
    frequency of interventions, 161–2
    MIN/MAX classification, 159
    night shift, 159
    observational studies, 158
    police mandate, 161
    reactive and proactive
        mobilization, 153–61
    riots, 175–7
    similar professions, 162–4
    time in Station and out of
        Station, 161
    of uniformed police, 162, 343–4
Policeywissenschaft, 19, 48

policing appearances and its
    significance, 174–5
policing by consent, 349–50
Policing for London Survey (PFLS), 102
political protection, 288–9
politicization, 20
polygraph evidence, 212
Posse Comitatus Act, 12, 310
powers of police, 194–7, 231–2, 340
    private security, 294–6
Pravda, case of, 82
private protection, business of
    consumers, 325
    entities and relations between
        entities, 325–6
    internal and external, 324
    and kinds of threats, 326
    providers, 324–5
private security, 3, 347–8, 358–9
    agencies, 28–30
    case study of pain-inducing
        technology, 283–8
    criterion of means, 333
    definition issues, 255–8
    ethos, 333–4
    in EU, 273–4
    formal powers, 294–5
    governance, issue of, 300–2
    growth of security manufacturing
        industry, 275–8
    growth of security personnel, 268–75
    high policing, 329
    historical issues, 265–8
    impact of technology on
        policing, 302–5
    informal powers, 295–6
    information sharing and
        rules, 301–2
    kinds of security equipment, 281–3
    kinds of services provided, 278–81
    legitimate, 332–3
    in non-EU countries, 271
    in nonstate protection, 328–9

private security (*continued*)
  obfuscation, issue of, 302
  operations, 333
  organizational structure, 333
  power of appearances, 296–7
  private high policing, 267, 288–93
  relationship with public
    police, 297–300
  relationship with the law, 329
  research issues, 258–65
  services and remuneration, 329
  in United Kingdom, 269
  use of informants, 291
  use of known criminals, 267, 291
  use of security equipment, 303–5
Propp, Vladimir, 88
Prosecution of Offences Act, 60
Protestants, 54
Pruvost, Geneviève, 12, 145–8
psychological profiling, 93
public police departments, 23
public policing, 8
  agencies, 22–7
  criterion of means, 331
  ethos, 332
  legitimate, 330–1
  operations, 331
  organizational structure, 331–2

Quebec provincial police force
  (QPF), 85, 177

Rand Corporation, 28
reassurance policing, 172
Reiner, Robert, 80–2, 110, 120
Reiss, Albert, 30, 152, 257
Ressler, Robert, 95–6
restructuring policing, 35
result-oriented theory, of criminal
  investigation, 215–20
reversible processes, 12–13
Rigakos, George, 22, 259, 295

riots, 23, 57, 175–7
Romano, Santi, 33
Rondas Ostensivas Tobias de
  Aguiar, 319
Royal Canadian Mounted Police
  (RCMP), 23, 75–6, 130, 171,
  235–6, 310, 314, 316–17
Royal Irish Constabulary, 313

Schengen Information System, 27
scientific policing, 210–12
Security Intelligence Review
  Committee (SIRC), 237
self-discordant theory, 13–15
self-help initiatives, 8
September 11, 2001, 10, 26, 39, 232–3,
  235, 308, 338
serial killings, 95
Shearing, Clifford, 151, 227, 256,
  263–4, 294–95
Shidane Arone's ordeal, 312
Shin Bet, 228
signal intelligence (SIGINT), 26, 247,
  292
Simenon, Georges, 90, 98
Skogan, Wesley, 172
smart crime, 254
Smith, Adam, 45–6
social control agents
  delinquent enforcement, 33–5
  unregulated control, 31–3
Sol. Gen. Can. et al. v. Roy. Comm.
  (*Health Records*), 238
Somalia peacekeeping mission, 313
specialized administrative policing
  agencies, 24–5
specialized private agencies, 28
specialized agencies, 23–4
The Spirit of the Laws
  (Montesquieu), 44–6, 336
Staatwissenschaften, 48
Stalinist terror, 233

"state of emergency," notion of, 55
Stenning, Phillip, 227, 256, 263–4
Stinchcombe, 217
surveillance model, new, 247–51

Taser guns, 304–5, 322, 338
technological surveillance, 86
Terrorism Act 2006, 235
terrorist bombings, 236
terrorist phenotype and genotype, 253
theory of policing, 3, 335–6
    aboriginal territories, 112
    antinomies, 38–9
    on the basis of consent, 110–11
    Bittner's perspective on the
        police, 104–9, 114–20
    competence, 116–20
    deceptive objects, 36–8
    definition of "police," 103
    demand-side theory, 123–4
    democratic policing, 135–6
    extralegality, 133–4
    legislative hollowness, 115
    minimal state and minimal
        force, 106–12, 136–7
    monopoly of the legitimate use of
        force, 112–15
    need for force, 107–10
    noncontractual policing, 134
    notion of intensive quantities, 39–40
    police-use-of-force
        paradigm, 121–8
    progressive orientation, 136
    public and private policing,
        114–15
    role of police, 113–14
    selective policing, 119
A Theory of the Police (Bittner), 104
thief-takers, 59
Titan, 292
Traité de la Police (Nicolas de
    La Mare), 47

transnational policing, 10
triads, 33
TV crime fiction, 88, 100–1
24, 91

UKUSA treaty, 26
undercover policing, 32
uniformed police, 354–6
    men vs. women, 140, 343–4
    synecdoches of detective and
        constable, 140–1
uniformed public policing, 8
UN international "policing"
    missions, 234
UN peacekeeping operations, 27
U.S. Bureau of Justice Statistics, 11
U.S. Bureau of Labor Statistics, 39
U.S. Central Intelligence Agency
    (CIA), 26, 224, 226
U.S. Department of Homeland
    Security, 23
U.S. Drug Enforcement Agency
    (DEA), 27
U.S. National Security Agency
    (NSA), 26
U.S. Total Information Awareness
    (TIA) project, 290

Vertrauensleute, 239
violent domestic threats, 23
Visa Information System, 27
visibility, concept of
    basic points, 164–5
    constructed, 168–9
    of crime and disorder, 166–70
    Hale's perspective, 170
    investigative, 168
    Kelling's perspective, 170
    military policing, 315
    offender, 169–70
    physical, 168
    police, 170–4

visibility, concept of (*continued*)
  policing appearances and its
    significance, 174–5
  symbolic, 168
V-Leute, 239

Wade, John, 63, 67
weapons of mass destruction (WMD), 28
Weber, Max, 112, 164, 336–7
Whorf, Benjamin Lee, 253
William J. Burns International
    Detective Agency, 73–4, 267

Williams, Alan, 48, 50, 53
Wimsey, Lord Peter, 89
The Wire, 99
Wolff, Christian, 18, 48
Workingmen's Benevolent Association
    (WBA), 73
World Factbook (CIA), 228

yakuzas, 33

zero tolerance policing,
    14

Printed in the USA/Agawam, MA
August 13, 2014

595077.008